Happy Father's Day!

Love,
Amy & Bonnie
2013

A Mustard Seed

Also by Angus Buchan and published by Monarch Books:

Faith Like Potatoes
A Farmer's Year
Come of Age

A Mustard Seed

A DAILY DEVOTIONAL

Angus Buchan

MONARCH
BOOKS
Oxford, UK & Grand Rapids, Michigan, USA

First published in South Africa in 2007 by Shalom Ministries

This edition published by Monarch Books
an imprint of
Lion Hudson plc
Wilkinson House, Jordan Hill Road,
Oxford OX2 8DR, England
Email: monarch@lionhudson.com
www.lionhudson.com/monarch

ISBN 978 0 85721 126 2
e-ISBN 978 0 85721 386 0

Acknowledgments
Unless otherwise stated, Scripture quotations are from The Authorized (King James) Version. Rights in the Authorized Version are vested in the Crown. Reproduced by permission of the Crown's patentee, Cambridge University Press.
Scriptures marked NKJV are taken from the New King James Version. Copyright © 1982 by Thomas Nelson, Inc. Used by permission. All rights reserved.
Scripture quotation marked AMP is taken from the Amplified® Bible, Copyright © 1954, 1958, 1962, 1964, 1987 by The Lockman Foundation. Used by permission. (www.Lockman.org)
Scripture quotation marked NIV is taken from the Holy Bible, New International Version copyright © 1973, 1978, 1984 by the International Bible Society. Used by permission of Zondervan and Hodder & Stoughton Limited. All rights reserved. The "NIV" and "New International Version" trademarks are registered in the United States Patent and Trademark Office by International Bible Society. Use of either trademark requires the permission of International Bible Society. UK trademark number 1448790.

A catalogue record for this book is available from the British Library.

Printed and bound in the UK, January 2013, LH27.

Dedication

I would like to dedicate this book to my grandchildren:

Kyla Rae Buchan
Jaimee Kate Buchan
Kai Reece Praschma
Callum Gregor Hull
Emma Jayne Porée
and
Caleb James Porée

My prayer for my grandchildren is that they will walk by faith and not by sight (2 Corinthians 5:7), and that they will trust the Lord Jesus Christ all of their lives.

I was recently sent a photograph taken at the Mighty Men Conference that was held at Shalom in April 2007, which shows a white light descending upon and spreading out over the tent. I can only describe it as looking like hot butter melting and flowing over the whole roof of the tent.

I've not yet met Bruno, the man who took the photograph; he comes from Phalaborwa, a town in the northern part of South Africa. He wept when he first saw the photograph and he was reluctant to send it to me because he wasn't sure what my reaction would be. I choose to believe that it was the glory of God that descended upon the tent, which was filled to capacity, totalling 7,400 men. We were speaking about the light of God, about the glory of God's presence, at the very time this photo was taken.

His email appears below:

> Good evening Angus
>
> My apologies for not emailing this magnificent photograph to you [before now]. To be honest, I have been hesitant to pass it on, as I do not want people to "think" that this photograph has been fabricated. I am totally convinced this is "the light" that you mentioned in the Conference that some people had witnessed over Shalom MMC.
>
> I was overjoyed of what was revealed to me when I downloaded my photographs from my digital camera on Tuesday afternoon after the MMC 2007. I sat in front of my computer while the photographs downloaded; at first I thought the photograph was overexposed/poor quality. As I marveled at the photograph it became a reality to me that this is possible the Presence of our Lord. I wept, it was with utter amazement what I was looking at … the manifestation of our Lord. We arrived a bit late on Friday night at Shalom Farm. As we approached the food tent I took photographs; this one was the first one. I DID NOT SEE ANY "LIGHT" WHEN TAKING THIS PHOTOGRAPH. The Conference had just started and most of the flock were in the main tent.
>
> When analysing the photograph, the light came way above the natural lights that were on top of the tent. I did a comparison with one of the other photographs that had been taken during the day. Therefore, I have no doubt that this is "the Light" of the Lord.

Is this called a Glory Cloud? Some close friends have seen this photograph and have been skeptical. I have prayed about sending this photograph to you knowing that the Lord will bless you mightily!

For me it is a big AMEN.

God Bless

Just another boy for Jesus

Bruno Bargiacchi
Phalaborwa

Acknowledgments

Thanks to:

Yvonne Ashwell, my faithful and dedicated typist;
Ann Roux, my editor;
Laetitia le Roux for the original cover design and layout.

With our best wishes and special love
from
Angus and Jill Buchan

I am deeply grateful to the many others whose lives and writings have helped to shape this book. Among others they include:

Streams in the Desert by L. B. Cowman, *The Complete Gathered Gold* by John Blanchard, *Glimpses of God Through the Ages* by Esther Carls Dodgen, *The Pursuit of God* by A. W. Tozer and *Prayer* by Philip Yancey.

About Shalom Ministries...

Jill and I found Jesus as our personal Lord and Saviour on 18 February 1979, just two years after settling in Greytown, Kwa-Zulu Natal Midlands, South Africa. Originally from Zambia, we bought a piece of land on which we planned to farm crops and livestock. We had very little to start with, but even as brand new Christians, we were content with our farm, which we later called SHALOM.

In 1980, the Lord gave us a clear vision. Very simply and clearly through His Word, we believed our responsibility to be the following:

1 The Great Commission – Mark 16:15
2 Caring for Orphans and Widows – James 1:27
3 Equipping Saints for the Work of Ministry – Matthew 28:20.

In November 1989 we felt the Lord call us to hire town halls and preach the Gospel, wherever He would lead. In 1990, we held our first campaign in Ladysmith, Kwa-Zulu Natal. I remember the feeling of pure excitement and anxiety as I walked into the municipal office to hire the town hall. Since then, we haven't turned back and our Lord has remained faithful. We have started using the media as a tool to spread the Gospel as well, through books, TV, magazines, radio stations and so on.

Our children's home, Beth-Hatlaim (house of lambs), was opened in 1995 and we have been blessed with children. We have faced many challenges, deaths and much joy since we started, but again, the Lord has never let us down. We thoroughly enjoy each personality that the Lord sends us to care for. Our four eldest have already left home to study in Durban, while our youngest has just started to walk. It is amazing to watch them grow so quickly and to show and teach them our Saviour's love.

The Shalom Fellowship started as local folk met to worship God. We meet on Sundays and during the week. We are involved in various community projects and outreach programmes in our area, to equip the saints.

As we look back over the years, we are so blessed to see how our Lord has and is fulfilling His vision in our lives. We trust you will also be able to seek God for your vision, that He will make it plain and write it on your heart (Habakkuk 2:2–3) and that you will run with it. Never forget the focus, JESUS CHRIST. He is your first priority... then family... then the work of the Lord.

Angus and Jill Buchan

For more information on Angus Buchan and Shalom Ministries please visit http://www.shalomtrust.co.za/.

Preface

As I waited on the Lord before writing another devotional, God laid it on my heart that in these last days, we need to live by faith like never before. The Lord led me to that beautiful Scripture which says that if we have faith the size of a mustard seed we can tell a mountain to be removed into the sea (Matthew 17:20). Then I looked at the Gospel of Mark, where the Lord says to us very clearly, "To what shall we liken the kingdom of God?... It is like a mustard seed" (Mark 4:30–31, NKJV). It is the smallest of seeds but when it is planted in good soil, it germinates and grows into a great tree. The branches are so big that the birds of the air can come and lodge in it and rest in its shadow.

God is showing us that if we walk by faith the kingdom of God will be very near us. We will walk and live in His strength. However, if we are determined to make a plan ("the farmer makes a plan"), we can rest assured that we are going to experience hell on earth.

This book of daily devotions is dedicated to the foot soldiers of the Lord – not necessarily the generals, officers, and super-spiritual – but to those who say, "Lord, if You don't meet me every day I'm just not going to make it." It is dedicated to those Christians who have to get up every morning and walk the talk, go through the daily grind and face the day-to-day challenges. The Lord has laid it upon my heart that each one of us needs a mustard seed of faith to get through every day so that we can walk in the fullness of what God has prepared for us in His kingdom.

May God bless you richly as you read these words every day and may it give you the strength and the stamina, the perseverance and the joy to see your mustard seed of faith moving mountains for you every day.

Angus Buchan

Shalom Ministries PO Box 373 Greytown
South Africa
3250
Email: shalom@futuregtn.co.za
www.shalomtrust.co.za

Foreword

One element contained within the Lord's Prayer is the petition we are to make for "daily bread". Here Jesus, by implication, reminds us of the miracle of provision during the exodus when the daily ration of manna rained upon the Israelites which they were commanded to consume on the day. They were prohibited from retaining any of it for the following day. They were to feed off God's abundant, fresh and daily supernatural supply. Their very survival depended on their obedience in this regard.

Much like Moses, Angus has a deep passion and concern for God's people to embrace both the gravity and glory of this principle – our profound need of God's daily bread; time spent in His presence to hear His voice and sense His heart.

There are times when, after meeting with someone, one could walk away from a potentially inspiring moment feeling somewhat deflated. The whole experience is made worse by the fact that one would approach the encounter with a raised level of expectancy. One of a few people with whom this is never the case is the author of this treasure trove. Angus epitomizes the metaphor of the biblical broken vessel of grace whose intimacy with, and vulnerability before, God renders him an inspirational person in the best sense. He is, in a figurative sense, a well of salvation from which so many thirsty souls have come to draw living water, freely.

Spending time with the streams of life which God graciously causes to flow through him is guaranteed to leave you not only challenged, but changed through the love of the Father, who would draw you near to Himself as you, through these meditations, would draw near to Him.

Fred May
Senior Pastor of Shofar Christian Church, Stellenbosch, South Africa

The just shall live by faith

Romans 1:17

For therein is the righteousness of God revealed from faith to faith: as it is written, The just shall live by faith.

Hopefully we will all have had the chance to sit down and rest during the Christmas season. But when faced with a new year, it is so easy to be filled with anxiety as we contemplate the massive challenges awaiting us over the next twelve months.

The only way to overcome fear and anxiety is with faith. When faith moves in, anxiety and fear move out. How do we get faith? Faith comes with attentive listening, and listening should be rooted in the Word of God (Romans 10:17). John Wesley (1703–91) was a professional theologian who tried to do everything he could to live the life of a holy man. He tried to discipline his body, to fast, to go without the normal comforts of every day living, but he failed miserably every time. He therefore became dejected and completely disillusioned with life. It was only when, just as Martin Luther (1483–1546) had, he discovered that the just shall live by faith that he was liberated and found total freedom.

The outcome of this year does not depend on you but on God, and He promises you an abundant life (John 10:10). Your ability to get through this year is not even dependent on your faith. It is only when you trust in God's faithfulness that He will see you through. Not only will you get through the year, but you will excel while doing so! You will find that if you walk by faith you'll make very few wrong decisions. You will have more time on your hands and even be able to accomplish more.

Towards the end of his life, when he became extremely tired, Charles Haddon Spurgeon (1834–92) said that he was going to try and attempt less and accomplish more. This year God is telling us to strive less and trust Him more. If you do this you will see the difference in your lives.

"Attempt great things from God and expect great things for God," said William Carey, a man who made a decision to walk by faith and not by sight. In 1793, he went to India with his young family, where he expected to be an evangelist. He failed miserably – I don't think he led a single soul to Christ. The man was at the end of his tether having buried most of his children, one next to the other (they had died of tropical diseases), and his wife had gone insane.

Maybe you are there today as you face this new year? I encourage you to do what William Carey did. He remained faithful. He kept his eyes fixed on Jesus, the Author and the Finisher of his faith. God honoured his faithfulness and Carey found his vocation in life. He had an incredible ability with languages and he began translating the Bible from English into Sanskrit, Hindustani, and Burmese. He later started a huge printing press and became the chief interpreter for the British government in the New Delhi High Court. As a result of William Carey's faithfulness, there are countless millions of Indians today who know Jesus Christ as Lord and Saviour, and the Bible is written in all of their languages.

So, as you face this new year, do it with faith in God and get ready for an incredible journey of excitement, of challenge – and most of all, of fulfilment in God.

The mustard seed

Matthew 17:20

If ye have faith as a grain of mustard seed, ye shall say unto this mountain, Remove hence to yonder place and it shall remove; and nothing shall be impossible unto you.

When considering history, especially in a biblical sense, it is amazing how the Lord has a habit of always taking the smallest, weakest, and the most unimportant to glorify Him!

The mustard seed is the smallest of seeds. As a farmer, I'm familiar with seed. When buying seed to plant my crop, I normally pick big, healthy seed with the greatest potential for germination. I would never pick the smallest seed. But Jesus does. He picks the smallest seed – people like you and me whom the world has cast aside, deeming us to be hopeless.

The good news is that the Lord promises that if our faith is but the size of a mustard seed we will be able to tell a mountain to throw itself into the sea. I have experienced this not once but many times in my own life and, as you start this new year and sow that seed of faith, you too can expect a huge return. Why? Because that's God's principle! It's the way He designed life. If you plant a grain of corn (maize) you can expect a 300–400 per cent return, because that is how God created its genetic composition. If you plant a seed in earnest faith – whether it is seeds of money, effort, your lifestyle, or the amount of time you dedicate towards your family, your business and most of all, toward your Christian walk with the Lord – you can expect a 400 per cent return this year.

In other words, what I am implying is that it is impossible to out-bless God. The more you dedicate your time, your prayer, your reading of the Word and, yes indeed, your finances to God, the more He will give back to you. Take heed though: don't give it with the aim of receiving a return. Give it because you love and trust Him. Then you can tell that mountain to be moved into the sea and it will happen.

Remember when the prophet Elijah asked the widow with a young child to feed him, though she only had enough oil and oatmeal to make one last cake? She was planning on lying down with her little son to die together after enjoying their last meal. However, she sowed that seed of faith and made an oatcake for the man of God and fed him. When she returned there were enough ingredients to make food for her and for her son. So the miraculous provision of meals continued until the new season arrived.

God is no respecter of persons. If any man or woman chooses to put their faith in God, even if it be the size of a mustard seed, He will multiply it a hundredfold.

In closing, a little boy took his mustard seed of faith: two small fish and five barley loaves of bread, and gave them to the Master. The Master prayed over the food, handed it to His disciples and 5,000 men (this did not include the women and children) were fed, after which twelve baskets were filled with leftovers! Do you honestly believe that this boy was the only person among 5,000 who brought food with him? I don't believe that for a minute. He was, however, the only one who was willing to put his trust in the Lord Jesus Christ and the Lord blessed him.

This year, start to walk by faith and not by sight (2 Corinthians 5:7) and see what God will do with your mustard seed of faith. If you keep it in the storeroom, it will remain the same size until this time next year. In fact it will go mouldy and probably die, but if you sow it in good soil you are bound to reap an abundant crop.

Lift up mine eyes

Psalm 121

I will lift up mine eyes unto the hills, from whence cometh my help. My help cometh from the Lord, which made heaven and earth. He will not suffer thy foot to be moved: he that keepeth thee will not slumber. Behold, he that keepeth Israel shall neither slumber nor sleep. The Lord is thy keeper; the Lord is thy shade upon thy right hand. The sun shall not smite thee by day, nor the moon by night. The Lord shall preserve thee from all evil: he shall preserve thy soul. The Lord shall preserve thy going out and thy coming in from this time forth, and even for evermore.

It is early morning and I am sitting looking at the Drakensberg Mountains, here in South Africa. I feel that Jesus is saying to me, "Have faith in Me, because I am as solid and as steadfast as these very mountains. I am immovable and yet I am alive."

Mountains fascinate me because although they are immovable, their appearance constantly changes. Early this morning they were lying in shadow. Now, as the bright sun has risen, the shadows have gone and one can see the beautiful green grass of summer covering them like a smooth carpet. There are very few shadows left.

Our heavenly Father is very similar to a mountain. He is solid. He is faithful. He is awesomely massive and yet He is so extremely exciting because He is constantly changing. He never falls behind. He is always up to date. He is very relevant to the circumstances and the situation that you and I are living in at the moment. He has promised us that He will never leave us, nor forsake us (Hebrews 13:5). We may cry out to God this very morning: "Master, please increase our faith so that we can enjoy You, we can trust You, and we can have confidence in You alone.

"My help comes from Jesus Christ alone. Not from the mountains, nor from people, but from God and Him alone. Amen and Hallelujah!"

I AM
(Faith – acknowledging who God is)

Hebrews 11:1

Now faith is the substance of things hoped for, the evidence of things not seen.

God calls Himself "I AM". That means He is everything. He is the past, the present, and the future. There is no person, no creation, nothing greater than Him. He is "I AM". He is life itself.

Tomorrow morning I am going to dedicate a little girl at her mother and father's home. The family requested a private dedication and because they are involved members of a local church, I am more than happy to comply. For various reasons the ceremony will take place on a Saturday morning. I will encourage her mother and father to have a family altar in their home. The Bible says that if you raise your child in fear of the Lord, he or she will not stray from that way when they grow old.

The Bible also says, "So then faith comes by hearing, and hearing by the word of God" (Romans 10:17, NKJV). We must speak God's holy Word just like He did, for as we speak it and hear it, it becomes a reality in our homes. God spoke the Word and the world came into being (John 1:1). We are not just speaking any word – we are speaking God's holy Word from the Bible. For example, the Word of God says, "What things soever ye desire, when ye pray, believe that ye shall receive them, and ye shall have them" (Mark 11:24).

I had that experience when I was losing the battle against a terrible bushfire on our farm. The fire was heading for my neighbour's huge timber plantation. If it had jumped the fence and got into his forest, I would have lost every single thing I owned and would have walked from my farm with only my wife, my children, and the clothes on our backs. I cried out to God that day and He heard my prayer. He literally changed the wind. There was a strong north wind blowing that was fanning the fire, pushing it towards my neighbour's property in the south. The Lord calmed the wind and turned it around. He roused a strong south wind and, as often happens, that south wind was accompanied by a cold front. As the wind died down, the cold front appeared and a gentle drizzle started to put out the fire. God definitely answers prayers!

The multiplier of our every need

Mark 6:41–44

And when he had taken the five loaves and the two fishes, he looked up to heaven, and blessed, and brake the loaves, and gave them to his disciples to set before them; and the two fishes divided he among them all. And they did all eat, and were filled. And they took up twelve baskets full of the fragments, and of the fishes. And they that did eat of the loaves were about five thousand men.

Jesus told the disciples not to send the multitude away but to feed them. Then by raw faith, calling those things that weren't as if they were, He took the little boy's breakfast – two small fish and five small barley loaves of bread. Jesus blessed the meal and multiplied the food! A total of 5,000 men (not counting the women and the children who were there with them) were fed, and twelve baskets were filled with the leftovers that very same day.

We need to ask ourselves a question: Have we ever really gone without food? Why is it then that we continually fret and worry? We are stressed to the extent that we are causing ourselves to be physically sick, suffering from ulcers, high blood pressure, or depression. Yet Jesus has always given us enough food and clothes for every day.

Do you remember the story of the two little birds sitting on the telephone line? The one little finch said to his friend, "Why are the people running to and fro, storing up food and goods in their houses and looking so worried and stressed out?" The other little bird replied, "They probably do not know our Father in heaven who supplies all of your and my needs everyday."

Have faith in God! (Mark 11:22)

Orderliness

Matthew 6:33

But seek ye first the kingdom of God, and his righteousness; and all these things shall be added unto you.

Any good farmer will tell you that in order to produce a healthy, abundant crop the field has to be prepared in an orderly manner.

First, in spite of the fuel prices shooting through the roof, you must plough deeply. Yes, you will use much more fuel but it will benefit you in the end.

Next a level seedbed should be prepared with a disc or cultivator, ensuring that it is nice and smooth. Then the best seed that money can buy should be purchased. Never buy second-grade seed if you're looking for a bumper crop.

Fertilize heavily. Make sure your plant population is planted exactly according to the specific requirements. The depth and the spacing of the seed must be exact. Ensure that your crop is not negatively impacted upon by weeds, grass, insects, or soil deficiencies. Then leave the rest to the great farmer Himself. His capable hands will carry the crop through drought, floods, hail, or fire. He will not fail you. We shall reap utter failure if we choose to live a life of selfishness, greed, stubbornness, turning our backs on the advice of the greatest husbandman who has ever lived. But, if we choose to lead a life of holiness and obedience, we will be blessed a hundredfold; people will come from far and wide to see the goodness brought about in our lives as well as the lives of our families by the love and grace of our Lord Jesus Christ, the supreme farmer.

You must be born again

John 3:3

Jesus answered and said unto him, Verily, verily, I say unto thee, Except a man be born again, he cannot see the kingdom of God.

John 3:7

Marvel not that I said unto thee, Ye must be born again.

It is absolutely vital to be born again. A. W. Tozer said, "Like a man going into the desert without a guide, or a man going to sea without a compass, it's not only vital, it is a matter of life or death."

There's got to be a significant change in our lives. We can't pray that prayer of commitment and remain the same. In the same way that the earth orbits the sun, we must orbit Jesus Christ. He must be everything to us. Not even one of the most important factors in our lives, but the most important one! His friends become our friends, His enemies our enemies, His ways our ways, His rejection our rejection, His life our life, and His future our future.

In a nutshell, it calls for a complete lifestyle change, a 180-degree turnabout. The true Christian has met God and knows from what they have been saved. They have genuinely repented their former sinful lifestyle and started all over again.

I can honestly tell you that the day that I did that (18 February 1979) my life was transformed. I had a new horizon, a new beginning, a new awareness of sin. I didn't want to hurt my Lord any more. I consulted Him on every single issue and He has never let me down since then.

A new beginning awaits you if you bow the knee and pray the sinner's prayer with me today:

Dear Lord Jesus,
I acknowledge You as Lord and Saviour of my life.
I repent of all my sin and I ask You today to take over full control of
every aspect of my life.
Amen.

Is anything too hard for God?

Jeremiah 32:27

Behold, I am the Lord, the God of all flesh: is there any thing too hard for me?

If there is one thing that annoys our God more than anything else, it is unbelief. For example, the children of God constantly disappointed Yahweh by doubting Him in the desert. They built the golden calf because Moses didn't come down from the mountain soon enough. They continually complained because they had no food, no water, no clothing, and yet their clothing never wore out and their food and water lasted for forty years in the desert. Their unbelief resulted in every single one of them dying in the desert.

The only two men who crossed the Jordan to enter into Canaan, the land of milk and honey, were two men of faith – Joshua and Caleb. Why? Because they had a different spirit! In Numbers 14:24 God says, "But my servant Caleb, because he had another spirit with him [faith], and hath followed me fully, him will I bring into the land whereunto he went; and his seed [family] shall possess it." So, due to their unbelief, approximately 2.5 million Israelites perished in the desert without seeing the Promised Land. We have to believe that nothing is too hard for God. All we have to do today is to ask God to increase our faith. "And the apostles said unto the Lord, Increase our faith" (Luke 17:5).

Let that be our prayer today – and nothing will be too hard for God.

Spending time with God

Mark 6:46–47

And when he had sent them away, he departed into a mountain to pray. And when even was come, the ship was in the midst of the sea, and he alone on the land.

Matthew 14:23

And when he had sent the multitudes away, he went up into a mountain apart to pray: and when the evening was come, he was there alone.

Luke 6:12

And it came to pass in those days, that he went out into a mountain to pray, and continued all night in prayer to God.

Jesus withdrew from the crowds on a regular basis to spend time in prayer. It even appears that the busier He became, the more time He spent on His own in the presence of His Father God. If that was necessary for the very Son of God, how much more so for you and me! For it is in the quietness that the still, small voice of God can speak to us. It is then that our strength can be restored to equal that of an eagle (Isaiah 40:31).

That is the time that we can receive clear instruction from God as to what we must do next. It is in solitude "up the mountain" in the presence of God that our faith grows, simply because we gain perspective on our priorities and He can speak to us. Then we realize how huge God is and how small we are; we see how powerful God is and how negligible our problems appear. This fundamental realization becomes quite attainable in God's presence and the so-called obstacles become totally insignificant.

Priorities become obvious and we start putting things in the correct order: God first, then our wives or husbands, the family, the ministry followed by our business and other concerns. Then we find that we actually have more time at hand because we received the blueprint on organizing our lives directly from God. God says, "Be still, and know that I am God" (Psalm 46:10).

A blind preacher named George Matheson (1842–1906) said that in the hour of distress we cannot hear the voice of God but in the stillness of waiting on God His voice sounds loud and clear. Matheson says, "God's voice demands the silence of the soul. Therefore, my soul, in order to hear from God, you must rest to receive your heart's desire." It is only when you allow your heart, palpitating because of personal concerns, to slow down and let the petty problems of this humdrum world pale into insignificance, that you can hear the Almighty God clearly.

The following extract is quoted from *Streams in the Desert*:

Tread in solitude your pathway,
Quiet heart and undismayed.
And you will know things strange, mysterious,
Which to you no voice has said.

While the crowd of petty hustlers
Grasps at vain and meagre things
You will see a great world rising
Where soft sacred music rings.

Leave the dusty road to others,
Spotless keep your soul and bright
As the radiant ocean's surface
When the sun is taking flight.

From the German of V. Schoffel

The power of the Word

John 14:14

If ye shall ask anything in my name, I will do it.

There is so much power in the spoken Word of God that when Jesus Christ was tempted in the desert for forty days and forty nights, He did not tell the devil to leave Him alone. And He could quite easily have done that, because He is God! Instead, every time the devil attacked the Lord with words, He answered with Scripture, "It is written, Man shall not live by bread alone, but by every word of God" (Luke 4:4, NKJV); "It is written, thou shalt not tempt the Lord thy God" (Luke 4:12).

Jesus knows the power of the spoken word. Remember, the battle is in the mind, not in the heart. "For the weapons of our warfare are not carnal but mighty through God to the pulling down of strong holds" (2 Corinthians 10:4). As we speak the Word by faith, God answers it.

Last week I visited a town called Middelburg, situated in the Mpumalanga Province of South Africa. It was absolutely incredible what God did. I spoke to a group of about a thousand people on the Saturday, followed by a meeting in the local Dutch Reformed Mother Church on the Sunday morning. The church is a hundred years old and apparently it was the first time that English was spoken from that pulpit!

God is a miracle-working God. We saw people's lives change for ever. In the evening, at the culmination of the weekend, people were literally hanging from the balconies in a Corpus Christi Church (Afrikaans charismatic church). The place was packed to capacity. There was an excitement, a sense of expectancy. The presence of the Holy Spirit was tangible from the outset of the meeting.

At the end of the meeting we were reminded that the maize farmers in that area were experiencing the plight of a dry spell. They asked us to pray for rain. We prayed together as a group and applied the Word of the Lord, "If you ask anything in My name, I will do it" (John 14:14, NKJV); and "If you love Me, keep My commandments" (verse 15, NKJV). That's very important. Our Lord only responds to holiness; to holy men and women.

The following day the international weather report on the internet forecast that there would be no rain anywhere in South Africa. However, as soon as I arrived home, I received the most beautiful phone call to say that close on 25 mm of rain had fallen on the farms in the Middelburg area!

Your light has come!

Isaiah 60:1

Arise, shine; For your light has come! And the glory of the Lord is risen upon you. (NKJV)

The Lord doesn't say in this Scripture that the light has come; He says that your light has come. If we look at Malachi 4:2, it says, "But unto you that fear my name shall the Sun of righteousness arise with healing in his wings; and ye shall go forth and grow up as calves of the stall."

What a beautiful blessing to start the day with! Light cannot truly be appreciated in light. There has to be darkness. If you take a match and strike it in broad daylight you can hardly see it. But when the match is struck in the pitch blackness of night, you can see it from a vast distance.

Isaiah 60:2 says that darkness shall cover the earth. And so this is our time to shine by faith for Jesus Christ. He says, "My light has come for you," and He tells us that healing has come through Him, and that we shall go forth and grow up as calves of the stall.

I cut my teeth on agriculture while farming in Scotland many, many years ago. We had to put the dairy cows' young calves in stalls for the winter because they were unable to survive out in the open: sometimes the snow was up to a metre deep. When spring came and the sun started to melt the snow, revealing the first shoots of green grass, we would let these calves out of the stalls where they had been boxed in for six months. They would dash from their stalls and go absolutely berserk, charging around the paddock with their tails in the air. It was a most awesome and beautiful sight to see.

I believe that this is what God is saying. We need to get out there and tell people that our light, our Jesus, has come. He's living within us and no matter how dark it might get in this world, we shall shine by faith.

Choices

James 2:23

Abraham believed God, and it was imputed unto him for righteousness: and he was called the Friend of God.

Abraham believed God in a very literal sense. In order to succeed as a Christian in this modern day and age, we have to believe that the Word of God was written by holy men who were directed by God and filled with the Holy Spirit to write the Scriptures.

Dr Billy Graham was confronted with this very issue. Many years ago he and two other evangelists were taking the USA by storm, filling stadiums, sports fields, and huge halls, having amazing responses to God's Word. Billy Graham was very much the junior of the three.

One of the evangelists was a fine, good-looking chap. He was asked to play the main role in the epic movie, *The Robe.* The other man was a greatly anointed speaker. They approached Billy Graham proclaiming that they needed to go back to Bible college and really study the Scriptures because it could not all be interpreted in a literal sense. They maintained that some parts of the Bible should be read as one does folk tales, and that it only gave Christians an idea of what they need to believe in.

One evening Billy Graham felt very perturbed and he went out into a forest. In the forest he opened his Bible and placed it on a tree stump. Then, while kneeling, he prayed and made a pact with God. "Lord, I don't understand everything that's written in the Bible but I make a choice. I choose today to believe Your Word, over and above anybody else's opinions. Please help my unbelief." With that, he got up and returned home. The rest is history. He became the greatest evangelist in recent times, with literally millions of people listening to him speak the Word and many subsequently deciding to serve Christ.

The fate of the other two evangelists who didn't believe God's Word makes for grim reading. The one, who used to be a more successful evangelist than Billy Graham, died penniless. His body had to be shipped back to his hometown where he had a pauper's funeral. The other one is living in a tiny apartment somewhere in Canada, a bitter and disappointed man, an agnostic.

You see, faith is the substance of things hoped for; it's the evidence of things unseen (Hebrews 11:1). You don't always have to understand everything in order to believe. All you have to do is to know the Author of the Book. He will enable you to trust Him.

13 January

Pride

1 Peter 5:5

For God resists the proud but gives grace to the humble.

Martin Luther was asked which virtues he considered to be the most important for a man of God to have. He replied, "The first one is humility, the second one is humility and the third one is humility." There's nothing more distasteful than an arrogant, boastful Christian. When we start to trust God, He always honours His Word because He responds to faith. The more He blesses us, the harder it becomes to remain humble. I'm sharing this reading with you because I myself have been convicted by the Holy Spirit about being very careful to remain humble, lest I fall.

A few years ago I was travelling with our big truck, a yellow Seed Sower, to go and preach the gospel in the heart of Central Africa. It was in the northern part of Mozambique that I had a glimpse of humbleness and humility like I had never seen before in my life. People were getting saved and healed. We were overjoyed by the goodness of God but one can become very arrogant in a situation like that.

That night we camped in a very primitive African village, where there was no water or lights, only grass huts. The minister of the church had a very quiet, reserved wife. She taught me a very important lesson on humility, one I think I will never forget as long as I live.

The village had a 44-gallon (210-litre) open drum filled with water. Although there was a great shortage of water in that area, the minister said that our team – there were about ten or twelve of us – could use as much of the water as we liked. From the way he spoke, we assumed that there had to be a pipe or a borehole close by.

We acted like typical westerners and got stuck in straight away! We washed our clothes, our hair, ourselves, used the water for cooking and by evening there was not a drop of water left in the drum. It was empty. The villagers never said a word.

I settled down that night in my tent that stood pretty close to the minister's hut and the empty 44-gallon drum. Being a farmer I'm a very light sleeper and the slightest noise usually wakes me. I suppose you get used to that over the years. When a cow calls, I need to know that it is not in trouble; when a chicken makes a noise, I need to know that there's not a mongoose in the pen.

At about half past three that morning I heard the gentle patter of delicate feet going past my tent. Half an hour later the footsteps returned and I heard the gushing of water; a lovely sound to me. Then the patter of feet sounded again, and so it continued until about half past five when the sun came up. Then the sounds ceased.

When I got up, I wanted to wash my face and brush my teeth but remembered that we used all the water the night before. I went to see if maybe I could find a cupful of water at the bottom of the drum. To my surprise the drum was almost overflowing with fresh, clean, cool water. I went straight to the pastor's hut and asked him where the water had come from. "Oh no, my brother," he said, "my dear wife brought the water."

By then his wife was busy mowing the fields and was not even in sight. She had walked to and fro with a 20-litre bucket to the stream that was almost half a kilometre away to fill that 210-litre drum with water before the sun came up. She did this for us out of love without expecting so much as a thank you. This touched me very deeply and humbled me tremendously.

Needless to say, we did thank her in more ways than one. We gave her a lovely gift and blessed them. But once again God showed me, "Angus, this is humility: when you do something purely because you love the people and not because you are expecting a reward." Such humility is a true trait of a man or woman of God.

Healing

2 Kings 5

Please read the story in 2 Kings 5 of Naaman, the commander of the Syrian army; the most powerful man in Syria besides the king. Naaman contracted leprosy. He was a man of great valour but nevertheless a leper. His servants loved him dearly and begged him to go to the man of God, the humble Elisha, who lived in a little hut. When the commander and his entourage arrived at the hut, the prophet didn't even come out to greet them. This was the first slap in the face of this affluent man!

Secondly, Elisha sent his servant to tell Naaman to go and immerse himself seven times in the water of the unimposing River Jordan if he wanted to be healed of the leprosy. Immediately, pride filled Naaman's heart, and he was outraged. He said, "Are there not bigger and better rivers in Syria?" Naaman expected the man of God to come out and just proclaim healing over his body.

He was about to return to Syria when his servants begged him to do as he had been told. He reluctantly dipped himself seven times in the River Jordan and the Bible says that when he came out of the river his skin was like that of a little child. He was completely healed from the leprosy. He then presented the servant of God with a gift, but Elisha refused to accept it for he knew it was God who had healed Naaman.

I always like to say that according to God's economy of faith, two and two equals seven. How often do we miss out on the blessing of a physical or mental healing because we refuse to be humble in the sight of God? Many times God will tell you to do something that doesn't make any sense. In order for Him to be able to bless you, you have to faithfully obey.

The first miracle that Jesus ever performed was at the wedding in Cana, where He turned water into wine. When the wine ran out before the conclusion of the celebrations, Jesus told the waiters to fill the vats with water. What a ridiculous instruction! They went to Mary, the mother of Jesus, and said, "The Master told us to fill the vats with water." She replied, "Just do what He tells you to do." They obeyed and of course the finest wine of the whole banquet was then served.

Let us search our hearts and be sure that there is no false pride residing there. Let us put our faith in the Lord and simply do what He tells us to do.

Faith without works is dead

James 2:20

But wilt thou know, O vain man, that faith without works is dead?

Robert H. Schuller, the evangelist, speaker, and author, once spoke of his father who is a farmer in the Midwest of America – a region notorious for often being struck by tornados. Once, the surface of this piece of earth was literally cleared by a twister. It destroyed all the barns and the houses. Cattle and tractors were sucked up into the sky never to be seen again. Schuller's dad has a favourite saying: "Tough times don't last but tough people do." After the tornado's destruction, almost all regional farmers moved away, but his father went back, rebuilt his farm, and started again.

At Shalom we always say that faith has feet. It's a doing word. It is no use sitting down in your armchair, waiting for God to miraculously come and put everything right. God will honour hard work every single time. Faith is actually the substance of things hoped for; it's the evidence of things not yet seen (Hebrews 11:1). God will give you a word as you are waiting on Him but then you should go out and act on it. If Peter hadn't got out of the boat and walked on the water, Jesus could never have helped him. But Peter had to physically get out of the boat and actually walk towards Jesus.

Yes, the troubles of this life can sometimes swamp us as they did Peter. The moment he took his eyes off Jesus and looked at the size of the waves he was overcome with fear and started to sink. But, praise God, the Lord was able to reach out and save him. Many a man of faith felt as if he was sinking at some time in his life, but God always honours faith and He will help those who are walking by faith, time and time again. But, no matter how many natural gifts they may have, the person who stays in the boat, who stays seated in their armchair, will never achieve their full potential unless they get up and start to move.

I remember many years ago my brother and I were sitting talking to a man who was a very good squash player. My brother is a professional sportsman, a golfer. This man was saying how he used to play squash for his agricultural college. "But," he said, "if I had trained harder, I could have gotten national colours in squash." My brother responded, "Yes, but 'if' is a big word. If I'd played more golf, I could have been the British Open golf champion."

When a person said to Gary Player, "You're so lucky, Gary, that you're such a good golfer." He said, "Yes, it's amazing. The more I practise, the luckier I seem to become!"

Faith is a doing word. As we start to exercise our faith and begin to use the natural abilities God has given us, we will literally move mountains for God.

Reality

Hebrews 13:5

I will never leave thee nor forsake thee.

As you are reading your devotional today, I am asking you to remind yourself of one fact: Jesus is not an historical figure. It's not like reading about Alexander the Great or Napoleon Bonaparte because Jesus Christ is not in the grave. He's alive, He's well, and He's listening to your heart conversing with Him as you are reading this book right now.

You need to understand, He wants to spend time with you. He wants to hear about all your expectations, your dreams, your visions. He also wants to hear about your heartache, your suffering, and your pain. He asks you this morning to talk to Him, to love Him and have communion with Him.

He would even rather have you be angry with Him than not talking to Him at all. I would, however, not advise you to assume that attitude seeing that God is Love. Jesus Christ loves you so much that He actually died for you. "Greater love hath no man than this, that a man lay down his life for his friend" (John 15:13). We're not talking about an historical figure; we're talking about someone who is alive, pulsating and ready to walk with you towards everything you have to face today.

John G. Lake, a Canadian-born evangelist who came out to South Africa from America in 1908, said that when you get up in the morning and you have finished dressing, washing your face, brushing your teeth, and combing your hair, you should look into the mirror and say to yourself, "Wherever you go today, Jesus is going with you." Then get out there and get stuck in.

What an opportunity! It puts things into the right perspective, doesn't it? The Bible says, "If God is for you, no man can stand against you" (Romans 8:31). As you go out into the world today, know that God goes with you. You have nothing to fear.

You need to be on your best behaviour though, because you don't want to embarrass your Lord. Most importantly, you don't want to go to a place where Jesus would not be comfortable. That always stands you in good stead. When you go into a bar or an unscrupulous place like one of those adult shops that are censored because of the sexual merchandise, you need to ask yourself, "Would Jesus go in here?" If the answer is no, then be sure that you don't go anywhere near the place. When you pick up a book to read today, ask yourself, "Would Jesus be comfortable reading this book?" If the answer is no, don't read it.

You will suddenly find yourself going to the right places, reading the right material, eating the right food and speaking the right language. The Bible tells us, "The joy of the Lord is your strength" (Nehemiah 8:10). Your life will be revitalized and you will go out into the world with power and joy.

Ambition

Philippians 4:13

I can do all things through Christ Jesus who strengthens me.

Today, by faith, as we consider what the day might hold for us, we need to ask ourselves, "What am I going to do today to allow God to improve my situation?" How big is God? He is as big as you allow Him to be.

Recently, while visiting Sweden, I was approached by a lady who asked me to pray for her people. She explained to me that many Swedish people were keeping Jesus in a matchbox, so to speak. Every day they would open up the matchbox slightly and let Him out for a little bit before putting Him back again. That's how big God is to them. That's why many of those people are in such dire straits. For me, God is so big, so absolutely huge, that nothing is impossible for Him.

We were experiencing a period of drought on our farm recently. As I was driving down the road returning from a campaign in Richards Bay, I realized that the maize smelt like silage. It was dying. The amazing thing was that as we were preaching on the Saturday night in Richards Bay, it started to pour with rain. On the Sunday morning it was still raining. I phoned home and not a drop had fallen on the farm. I was so disappointed.

A week before, we had launched a campaign in Johannesburg for the drought-stricken Mpumalanga area. During the meeting on the Sunday night we prayed for rain and on the Monday an incredible miracle was witnessed when a shower of rain measuring almost an inch (25 mm) fell on our host's farm. Yet, back at my home, there was no rain.

Temperatures rose to 38°C and higher. The maize was literally going silver as it started to die. My young son Fergie, whose farm I'm currently living on, started to look extremely despondent. I called him in and said, "Son, sit down. I want to talk to you." We sat down together and I asked, "Do you know how big God is? We want this farm to grow; we want it to be a blessing to others. Where I've just preached, it's been raining. I've been preaching faith and speaking out faith. Let's do so now!" My son prayed first and then I prayed after him.

Right now as I'm writing this passage, gentle rain is falling on this farm. We've already had an inch, and it looks as if the rain has set in for the next few days. Yes indeed, we can do all things. We can even ask God to send rain and He shall do so. Elijah the prophet asked the Lord to keep it from raining and He did so – for three years! Then the prophet asked the Lord to allow the rain to return and it came. This is why we are so in love with Him.

Go out today, knowing that God is as big as you will allow Him to be.

The sin of unbelief

Romans 14:23

Whatsoever is not of faith is sin.

At Shalom we say that if you have to attempt something, make sure that it is so big that if it is not from God it is doomed to fail. The reason we say that is because God needs to get all the glory. We also say that if your vision doesn't scare you, it's not big enough because we have to learn to lean on God.

The Lord will always honour the work of faith. Always! He simply loves it when we step out of our boats to walk on the water. This is why He called Abraham His friend. To my knowledge God has not called anybody else in the Bible His friend. Yet He says, "Abraham is My friend." Why? Was it because Abraham was such a good man? No.

In Genesis 12 we read how Abraham presented his beloved wife Sarah as his sister in order to save his own skin. Apparently Sarah was a very beautiful woman. When Abraham left his farm in Ur of the Chaldees to go to an unknown destination he was confronted by the pharaoh and his army. Abraham knew what was coming. He knew that Pharaoh would kill him in order to claim his wife. He said to his wife, "Don't tell him that I'm your husband. Tell him that I'm your brother."

What a cowardly thing to do! I don't think any man reading this book would ever do that to his wife in order to save his own skin. Of course, we know the rest of the story. The Lord sent His angel to Pharaoh and said to him, "Do not touch that woman. She is actually Abraham's wife."

Pharaoh got such a fright that he gave Sarah back to Abraham the very next day together with a whole lot of gifts, telling him to get the heck out of there and not to come back!

So why did God call Abraham His friend? Purely because Abraham believed in the promises of God; Abraham was a man of faith. He waited almost a hundred years for his son Isaac – a most beautiful child. When Isaac was about thirteen years old, God said to Abraham, "I want him back." God never tempts, He tests. He tested Abraham. Abraham did not hesitate. He took Isaac up onto the mountain and offered him as a living sacrifice. God was so touched by this man's love for Him and by his faith, that He told him, "Don't kill the boy. There's a young ram caught in the thicket. Use the young ram as a sacrifice." That's why He loved Abraham.

Today, let us pray the prayer that the apostles prayed in Luke 17:5: "Lord, increase our faith."

Putting God first

Isaiah 40:31

Those who wait upon the Lord shall renew their strength; they shall mount up with wings as eagles; they shall run, and not be weary; and they shall walk, and not faint.

We have a funny response at Shalom to remarks such as, "You're so lucky that you've managed to have such a beautiful maize crop"; "You're so lucky that your cattle are so fat"; "You're so lucky that the sun always seems to shine at Shalom." Obviously that's very humbling for us, because it is true. God does love us (in the same way that He loves you) and we always reply, "Well, there was a little bit of divine cheating involved."

Many years ago when I was a new believer, a dear friend of mine, a Methodist minister in Greytown, was busy obtaining his theology degree while he was shepherding the flock. Any pastor or minister will understand the immensity of the task and the challenge, especially if you are committed to a vibrant church that is growing. The bottom line was that he never had much time to study. He would go into the examination room, write his exams, come out and say, "Angus, I don't think I could possibly have passed, because I did no studying whatsoever." When the results came out, his marks would be in the eighties and nineties, and he would say to me, "A little bit of divine cheating. The Lord knew that I was about His work and He devised a plan for me." I think he was also a very humble man.

It reminds me of Eric Liddell, whose story was told in the epic 1981 movie, *Chariots of Fire*. He was picked to compete in France for the British Olympic team, but because he refused to run on Sundays he was unable to take part in the 100 metres, the heats for which were to take place on the Sabbath. The Prince of Wales, the future king of England, rebuked him and tried to put pressure on him by saying that he was partaking for his country. Liddell refused, saying, "I don't run for my King, the King of kings, the Lord Jesus Christ, on the Sabbath. On Sundays I rest." Yet God redeemed him for they allowed him to compete on the Monday and the Tuesday in races for which he wasn't even training. He ran the 400 metres and the 200 metres among others and returned home with a gold medal for the former and a bronze medal for the latter.

The part in the movie that touched me very deeply was when a Scottish Christian man walked along the starting line just before the race started, shaking hands with all of his competitors, saying, "May the best man win!"

His opponents were looking on in a state of amazement. As you know, when you are competing on that level you are brainwashed to beat your opponents at all cost and are usually instructed not to have anything to do with them. And there was this man saying, "May God bless you," and "May the best man win!" Then, of course, when the starter's pistol sounded he won the race hands down, teaching the other athletes a lesson in running!

I really believe that God honours that kind of dedication and that He will honour you today if you put Him first in your life.

A sound mind

2 Timothy 1:7

For God did not give us a spirit of timidity, but a spirit of power, of love and of self-discipline. (NKJV)

As I am writing today's reading I'm sitting in my prayer room looking through the window at a big black and white Friesian dairy cow. This cow doesn't have a care in the world. It's early in the morning, there is dew on the grass, and she is grazing with the utmost delight. She's totally carefree. She's not concerned about where she'll be eating tomorrow morning or even this afternoon. Her tail is swishing backwards and forwards as the odd fly causes a bit of an irritation but, apart from that, this cow is totally unconcerned. She is God's creation, and God is feeding her.

The Lord has impressed upon me many times that when I start to become fearful, faith goes out of the window, so to speak. Faith and fear are direct opposites. If you are fearful today you will not be able to trust God. I would encourage you, as you go out today, to be like that Friesian dairy cow. Just live for today; don't be concerned about tomorrow. Jesus says that tomorrow has enough concerns of its own. Thank Him for today and before you go about your business, praise Him for the family, the health, the work, and the food He's given you today. Don't even worry about tomorrow, because tomorrow might never come. Jesus might come back today and take us home to be with Him in glory.

The good news is that faith is the substance of things hoped for, it's the evidence of things not yet seen (Hebrews 11:1). That cow is not concerned about what's going to happen tomorrow. All she's doing at the moment is filling her rumen (her tummy) with sweet grass, enjoying the sun beating down upon her back, and she is totally at peace.

As you go on your way today, know one thing: if God is for you, there is no one who can stand against you (Romans 8:31). That is how you will get through this day – just by putting your trust in the One who is totally and absolutely trustworthy.

Revenge is Mine

Romans 12:19

Do not take revenge, my friends.

The author Margaret Bottome writes that nothing demands greater strength than doing nothing. How often we try to justify ourselves, we want to make our case heard or try to explain our side of the story to people! It takes tremendous courage and faith to say nothing. Bottome suggests that maintaining composure is often the best evidence of power. By just saying nothing…

On the evening of the Last Supper, just before Jesus was betrayed, the disciples were arguing about who was going to have the best seat in heaven and who was going to be seated nearest to the Master. Amid their quarrelling Jesus stood up, filled a basin with water, took a towel, and started to wash the dirty feet of His disciples. Can you imagine how devastated they must have been when they realized what He was actually saying? In effect, He was saying that if you want to be the greatest in the kingdom of God you have to be the least. If you want to be first, you have to be prepared to be last.

Maintaining composure… When Jesus was judged by Pontius Pilate, He responded to Pontius Pilate's accusations with unbroken silence. Isn't that powerful? He could have called down a legion of angels from heaven and destroyed Pontius Pilate, all the priests and indeed the entire city of Jerusalem with one single action or a mere word. But Jesus said nothing.

As His death drew near and Jesus was arrested in Gethsemane, He said to Peter, "Or do you think that I cannot now pray to My Father, and He will provide Me with more than twelve legions of angels?" (Matthew 26:53, NKJV). But Jesus didn't do that. In fact, He caused His accusers and His spectators to wonder in awe at the fact that He did not even try to defend Himself. It takes tremendous courage to say nothing.

Today as you go about your daily work, don't be so quick to justify your actions or to have your say. Ask God to give you the faith to be able to sometimes say nothing – and let your silence speak louder than your words.

Sail on

2 Corinthians 5:7

For we walk by faith, not by sight.

I believe every Christian should pray for the sick because it's a command from God. "Go ye into all the world" (Mark 16:15–18). We are to lay hands on the sick and pray the prayer of faith and God will raise them up. That is the critical part. That is what faith is all about. It's calling upon those things which "are not" as if they were.

So often when having our healing meetings and the sick come forward to be prayed for, some of them, seen with carnal eyes, look absolutely beyond any kind of restoration: totally emaciated by the ravages of cancer; snow white because of sugar diabetes; crippled by arthritis; blind; deaf; dumb; or in wheelchairs. And yet that's the time when we have to extend our faith. The defining moment for me is always when the sick are brought onto the stage. We pray for them on the stage before they are healed. We don't only call them onto the stage once they have been healed, because we want the people to see the power of God being demonstrated.

Two weeks ago, in Durban, we once again saw the power of God healing the sick and setting the captives free. That increases people's faith in Jesus Christ more than anything else.

The following poem by J. R. Miller, quoted from *Streams in the Desert*, is a tribute to that intrepid explorer, Christopher Columbus, who persevered through enormous difficulties and discovered America:

Behind him lay the gray Azores,
Behind the Gates of Hercules;
Before him not the ghost of shores,
Before him only shoreless seas.
The good mate said: "Now we must pray,
For lo! the very stars are gone.
Brave Admiral, speak, what shall I say?"
"Why, say, 'Sail on! Sail on! And on!'"

"My men grow mutinous day by day;
My men grow ghastly wan and weak!"
The strong mate thought of home; a spray
Of salt wave washed his sunburned cheek.

"What shall I say, brave Admiral, say,
If we sight naught but seas at dawn?"
"Why, you shall say at break of day,
'Sail on! sail on! and on'!"

They sailed. They sailed. Then spake the mate:
"This mad sea shows his teeth tonight.
He curls his lip, he lies in wait,
With lifted teeth as if to bite!
Brave Admiral, say but one good word;
What shall we do when hope is gone?"
The words leapt like a leaping sword:
"Sail on! sail on! and on!"

Then, pale and worn, he kept his deck
And peered through darkness. Ah, that night
Of all dark nights! And then a speck –
A light! A light! at last a light!
It grew, a starlight flag unfurled!
It grew to be Time's burst of dawn.
He gained a world; he gave that world
Its grandest lesson: "On! Sail on!"

We need not be concerned about the storms of life; not even when the stars are sometimes obscured by clouds. When we press on with the work God has given us, we will surely reach land. If we continue to sail forward with faith in Jesus Christ, we will eventually accomplish that which God has called us to do.

Watch!

Mark 13:33–37

Take ye heed, watch and pray: for ye know not when the time is. For the Son of Man is as a man taking a far journey, who left his house, and gave authority to his servants, and to every man his work, and commanded the porter to watch. Watch ye therefore: for ye know not when the master of the house cometh, at even, or at midnight, or at the cockcrowing, or in the morning: Lest coming suddenly he find you sleeping. And what I say unto you I say unto all, Watch.

Are you ready for the coming of the Lord? I don't hear too many people speaking about the Second Coming these days. People seem to be so busy building homes, putting money in the bank, making sure that they are physically presentable, aligning their qualifications for the work they're going to get when they leave university, or upgrading themselves, that nobody seems to be waiting for the coming of the Lord.

This morning, while having my time with the Lord, He clearly spoke to me through Mark 13:33, "Take ye heed, watch and pray: for ye know not when the time is." He tells us that our waiting on His return is like the Son of Man embarking on a long journey. He leaves His house, hands authority over to His servants and gives each one of them work to do, commanding the porter to keep watch. He says, "Now be watchful, for you don't know when the Master of the house is coming back, whether in the evening, at midnight, at cockcrow, or in the morning." He continues to say, "Be careful lest, when He suddenly comes, He finds you sleeping." All that He says to us in verse 37 is, "Watch."

Does that mean we have to stop living? Not at all! The great reformer, Martin Luther, was asked what, if he knew for sure that the Lord was coming tomorrow, he would do today. His answer was that he would plant an apple tree. In other words, he would carry on with his life.

I've heard someone say that we must be prepared for the Lord to come tomorrow – and we must plan ahead as if He is coming in a thousand years. In other words, continue to make your plans but always be ready. Be ready to give an account of what you're doing. You see, my dear friend, we keep talking about the Second Coming of the Lord but we don't know when the Lord is going to call us home – and for each of us that would be the most critical time. We don't know whether He'll call us even this very day. I can honestly say, like Paul in Philippians 1:21, that for me to live is Christ and to die is but gain. As they say, you cannot frighten a Christian with the prospect of heaven.

Let us get our lives in order today. Let us be sure that we have no grudges against anyone, that we have leniency in our hearts, and that there is no root of bitterness or envy in our spirits, so if the Lord were to call us today we could say, "Lord, I am ready."

Don't quit

Job 13:15

Though he slay me, yet will I still trust him.

In her book *The Hiding Place* the famous Dutch Christian author Corrie ten Boom (1892–1983) tells how, during the Second World War, she and her older sister Betsie, together with their old watchmaker dad, were sent to a concentration camp for harbouring Jews in their attic and hiding them from the Nazis. Later, when Corrie was nursing her dying sister in her arms, she cried out, "Lord, how could you let this happen to my sister?" Her sister, a very mature and strong Christian, whispered to her, "If you know Him, you do not have to ask why."

Sometimes things don't go the way we expect them to go. Job lost his farm, his family, his health, basically everything he owned. People even said to him, "Why don't you just go and die?" In spite of his desolation, Job never questioned the Lord. At the end of the book of Job, we read that things turned around completely. He was reunited with his family; God blessed him more abundantly than he'd ever been blessed before.

We need to press on. We need to run this race called life. If you know Jesus as your personal Lord and Saviour, you don't have to ask why you are finding yourself in the predicament you're in. It's quite sufficient just to know that He is Lord, that nothing can happen without His permission and that ultimately you will succeed.

Today we need that mustard seed of faith. We can endorse the words of the wonderful evangelist and master plumber, Smith Wigglesworth (1859–1947), who was used by God to perform numerous miracles, and say, "God said it; we believe it and that settles it!"

Peace

Philippians 4:6–7

Be anxious for nothing, but in everything by prayer and supplication, with thanksgiving, let your requests be made known to God.

I had a meeting recently with a young man used very powerfully in the world for the Lord. He is accomplishing things for God that most of us only dream about, yet after the meeting he asked if he could see me on his own for a few moments. He then proceeded to pour his heart out, telling me that he had lost his joy and his purpose for living. I could not believe what my ears were hearing. He has been actively involved in many different facets of life for many years and yet he was filled with anxiety and begged me to help him. And then the Scripture Philippians 4:6–7 came to mind, which says: "Be anxious for nothing, but in everything by prayer and supplication, with thanksgiving, let your requests be known to God and the peace of God which surpasses all understanding, will guard your hearts and minds through Christ Jesus."

Jesus asks in Mark 8:36, "What shall it profit a man, if he shall gain the whole world, and lose his own soul?" This is what I think was starting to happen to the young man I mentioned above. He was working so hard doing the work of the Lord that he had forgotten the Lord of the work! Some of us in Christian ministry have been working so hard that we have actually lost the peace and the joy of this wonderful noble profession that Jesus Christ has given us.

I really want to encourage you this year to "smell the roses"; to take time out and let the peace of God restore everything that the locust and the canker worm have tried to take away from you in the past year. François Fenelon (1651–1715), that wonderful man of God, said: "It is the religion of Jesus alone that can bring peace to a man." Don't even be concerned about the future because as Jesus said, today has enough troubles of its own, without having to worry about tomorrow. Who knows, maybe the Lord will come and take us back to be with Him in paradise before then. Meditate on the things of God, spend time with your family and your loved ones. Enjoy your farming, go out on that ride, and check the cattle. Take your wife or husband, your son or daughter with you. Enjoy the time God has given to you, enjoy His creation and let the peace of God which passes all understanding comfort your heart. You cannot be expected to transmit that peace to other people if you don't have it yourself.

I think one of the biggest obstacles preventing people coming to Christ is when they see people who profess to be Christians but there is no peace, no joy, no tranquillity in their hearts. You need to spend time with the Prince of Peace.

That is the main reason why He came down to earth. If you spend time with the Prince of Peace, that peace will fill your heart and it is so contagious that it will flow over and touch others. I really believe that God wants to exhort you to rest in Him so that you will be well prepared for the coming year.

Remember, where there is peace, God is. Give Him an opportunity to make a difference in your life and in the lives of those around you as you transmit the love of Jesus Christ. As the saying goes, "Peace rules the day when Christ rules the mind."

Betrayal

Mark 14:18

One of you which eateth with me shall betray me.

Surely the most important reason for us to have faith (that is if we need a reason) is to ensure that we do not betray our Master. It is so sad to hear that mighty men and women of God who started out so strongly on the road of faith with Jesus Christ as Lord and Saviour have lost their way because of the pressures and temptations of this world. And more often than not, they have betrayed the Lord by denying Him. The greatest sin in the Bible is the sin of unbelief. When we say, "Lord, You can't really help us: this mountain is too big, this problem is too great," we are actually betraying the Lord. We're actually telling the Lord that He is not up to it.

We often speak about Judas Iscariot's betrayal of the Lord, but we seldom mention Peter! In Mark 14, the Lord says to Peter, "Before the cock crows twice, you will deny me three times" (verse 30). Denial is betrayal. The only difference between Peter and Judas Iscariot is that the one repented while the other devised a plan of his own.

God forbid that you and I should make our own plans today! If we did something that caused us to deny the Lord, let us repent as Peter the big fisherman did. After his repentance Peter was reinstated as the leader of the first church in our world. Let us not be like Judas Iscariot. I do believe that, although Judas also loved the Lord, he denied Him because of various factors having an adverse effect on his life. Tragically Judas then took his life into his own hands and hanged himself. Praise God for the fact that if we confess our sins, He will forgive us, for He is faithful and just and cleanses us from all unrighteousness (1 John 1:9).

John Newton, that great hymn writer best known for the hymn "Amazing Grace", knew what it was to betray the Lord through his lifestyle. Born in 1725, he was the captain of a slave ship. I cannot think of a worse profession and yet, because he repented, God reinstated him and he could write, "Amazing grace, how sweet the sound, that saved a wretch like me. I once was lost but now am found, was blind but now I see."

Today, let us not deny the Lord Jesus Christ and betray Him by our lack of faith. He is asking you and me today, "Is anything too hard for Me?" (Genesis 18:14).

Rainmaker

Matthew 17:20

If ye have faith as a grain of mustard seed, ye shall say unto this mountain, Remove hence to yonder place; and it shall remove; and nothing shall be impossible unto you.

I've just returned from a campaign in Harare, Zimbabwe, where we saw the power of God manifest in signs, wonders, and miracles. We saw many first-time commitments to Christ. We saw people healed of back problems, people's eyesight restored, and broken hearts mended. We saw people who were suffering from depression and hopelessness receive the hope of Jesus in their lives.

On the Sunday morning there was a combined service where all the churches in Harare united to praise God in spite of the terrible situation in the country where inflation has reached levels of over 1,000 per cent. In Harare I saw people standing in line to buy bags of maize meal, the staple food of Southern Africa. The Zimbabwean currency has depreciated to such an extent that it is almost worthless. Luckily Jesus' Word will never be declared null and void.

After our return from Harare I received an email informing me that it had started to rain in the Zimbabwean city shortly after our departure. They, like most of Southern Africa, have been experiencing what we call a green drought. Everything looks green on the surface but there is no moisture in the ground. The maize that I saw growing there was stunted and bleached snow-white by the intense sun. The people were saying that the dams were at the lowest levels in the history of Harare.

Jesus clearly states that these signs and miracles (rain) will follow the preaching of the Word of God.

We rejoiced with the people of Harare. I wish I could have been a fly on the wall so as to be able to hear what some of those farmers were saying!

Our God is a faithful God!

Friend of God

James 2:23

Abraham believed God, and it was imputed unto him for righteousness: and he was called the Friend of God.

God calls Abraham His "friend" a number of times in the Bible (see also Isaiah 41:8). Was Abraham known as the friend of God because of his impeccable lifestyle? Not at all! Abraham was very much a man of flesh and blood just like you and me. He had many shortfalls and he slipped up many times. So why did God call him "My friend, Abraham"?

Everybody wants to be God's friend. No one wants to fight with the Creator of the universe. Not anybody in his right state of mind anyway. The Bible states that God looked down and saw Abraham and said, "He is My friend." Abraham became God's friend because he believed God. As simple as that!

To reward Abraham's faith, God gave him a son who was called Isaac. It was through Isaac that Abraham became the father of many nations. However, God subjected Abraham to severe tests on more than one occasion. The greatest test of all was when young Isaac, a beautiful child, came of age (he was about thirteen years old) and God said to Abraham, "I want him back." Abraham never once doubted God. Genesis 22 relates how he took the young boy to the top of a mountain and was about to offer him as a living sacrifice when the Lord sent an angel to intervene.

The Lord was so touched by Abraham's willingness to give back his most precious possession that He told him, "In blessing… and in multiplying I will multiply thy seed as the stars of the heaven, and as the sand which is upon the sea shore; and thy seed shall possess the gate of his enemies" (Genesis 22:17).

Even though Abraham was a sinful man, even though he was very human, the mere fact that he trusted in God and had enough faith to believe that God could raise his son even from ashes, meant that he found favour in God's eyes.

Whatever you may do today, deal with it in faith and God will honour you.

Who is this man?

Matthew 8:27

What manner of man is this, that even the winds and the sea obey him!

Today we need to ask ourselves whether we are following a denomination, a church group, a religious club, or if we are following a man.

Jesus said, "If you've seen Me you've seen My Father." Jesus is God. Many of us forget that sometimes. Yes, we believe in the Holy Trinity, the Father, the Son and the Holy Spirit, but ultimately Jesus says, "If you've seen Me, you've seen My Father." The Holy Spirit is Jesus in the Spirit.

In the archives in Rome there is a report that is purported to be written by a Roman consul – Publius Lentulus – to his emperor, Tiberius, which is nearly 2,000 years old. This document reads as follows:

> There has appeared in Palestine a man who is still living and whose power is extraordinary. He has the title given him of Great Prophet; his disciples call him "the Son of God". He raises the dead and he heals all sorts of diseases.
>
> He is a tall, well-proportioned man, and there is an air of severity in his countenance which at once attracts the love and reverence of those who see him. His hair is the colour of new wine. From the roots to the ears, and thence to the shoulders, it is curled and falls down to the lowest parts of them. Upon the forehead it parts, after the manner of the Nazarenes. His forehead is flat and fair, his face is without blemish or defect and adorned with a graceful expression. His nose and mouth are very well proportioned; his beard is thick and the colour of his hair. His eyes are grey and extremely lively.
>
> In his reproofs, he is terrible, but in his exhortations and instructions, amiable and courteous. There is something wonderfully charming in his face with a mixture of gravity. He is never seen to laugh but has been observed to weep. He is very straight in stature, his hands large and spreading, his arms are very beautiful. He talks little, but with a great quality and is the handsomest man in the world.

That is a description that I received through a newsletter from the Bible Society. When I first read it, it brought me to tears because we keep forgetting that God is not just a mystical spiritual being. He is also a person. He has fingerprints, personality, and a character. He's not a Scotsman, nor a Zulu: He is a Jew.

Do you have an impression of this Nazarene who walked the shores of Galilee performing miracles 2,000 years ago? Do you have a vision of Him coming back to take His own to be with Him in heaven? It has to be very soon, because there are so many signs indicating that His coming is near. My prayer is that you and I will recognize Him when He comes.

Pioneer or settler?

Hebrews 13:5

I will never leave thee, nor forsake thee.

In one of his books, A. W. Tozer (the great Canadian preacher and author) says, "God works as long as His people live daringly. He ceases when they no longer need His aid."

Are we walking by faith or by sight (2 Corinthians 5:7)? Through reading Tozer's book, I was reminded that whenever God's people were on the move, God moved with them. When they stopped, God also stopped. Remember the great exodus from Egypt into the wilderness? God led the Israelites by a pillar of fire at night and by a cloud during the day. It's exciting to serve the Lord, but the Lord likes to move with His people as they are walking the walk of faith.

It's sometimes a very dangerous thing to get too comfortable when you're serving God. Tozer uses the example of a fallow field and a ploughed field. He suggests that in a fallow field everything is nice and calm; nothing moves but nothing changes either. It must be comfortable in a fallow field but it's actually going nowhere fast. However, the ploughed field can be compared to the confessions of a Christian. The plough of confession turns the soil and prepares the new field. This allows for seed to be planted and a beautiful new crop to grow. But it can be painful and it can be scary. The fences of security have to be knocked down for the tractor to gain access to the field.

The Lord has called us to an exciting life. I once read about a man of God who wanted to be an evangelist. He felt the Holy Spirit tell him that if you want to be an evangelist you have to be "reckless" with your reputation! That's why God loved Abraham so much. Abraham was prepared to go to an unknown destination leaving the secure environment of his farm behind in what is now modern-day Iraq. Moses had to leave his shepherd's job with his father-in-law and lead God's people to the Promised Land. But God went with them.

You and I, if we're going to live a life worthy of the walk of faith, need to attempt great things for God and expect great things from Him in return. Remember, my dear friend, we pass this way but once and then follows the judgment.

Trust God and He will never, ever let you down. God always honours faith.

Running the race

Philippians 3:12

… that I may apprehend that for which also I am apprehended of Christ Jesus.

The Lord is not interested in good starters. He is interested in good finishers. That is what is implied in this Scripture. Paul says, "not that I have been perfected, but I press on to lay hold of that for which Christ Jesus has laid hold of me."

There is a saying: "Every morning in Africa, an antelope wakes up. It knows it must outrun the fastest lion, or it will be killed. Every morning in Africa, a lion wakes up. It knows it must run faster than the fastest antelope, or it will starve. It doesn't matter whether you're a lion or an antelope. When the sun comes up in Africa, you'd better be running."

I often say to my colleagues that there is no such word as "retirement" in the Bible. We have to run the race and we have to persevere all the way to the finish line. If you consider the athletes taking part in a competitive race you'll find that the winner is known by everybody but nobody knows who came second. The sad thing is that nobody is really interested either.

We're not competing in a track event or even an ultra-marathon such as the 90-kilometre Comrades Marathon of South Africa; we are running in the real race of life. Paul says, "Not that I've apprehended, nor been perfected, but I press on to lay hold of that for which Christ has laid hold of me."

Today, by faith, get up if you have fallen down. Dust yourself off and get back into the race. Whatever you do, don't look behind you, because if you do you're sure to trip and fall again. Put the past behind you, as the Lord says in Luke 9:62, and focus on the finish line.

You might say today that the finish line is too far away. Well, do what all seasoned runners do: just look to the next lamppost or the next mark on the road and concentrate on covering those short distances. Before you know it, through the power of the Holy Spirit and by the assistance of the greatest runner who's ever lived, Jesus Christ, you will finish the race.

Don't hang around at the back of the group but run right in the middle. Get right into fellowship with fellow believers. You've heard it said many times that the best form of defence is attack. There's no such thing as a solitary Christian. The laws of the bush state that the roaring lion (the devil) is running to and fro, seeking whom he may devour – and he will always take out the straggler, the one that is loitering at the back, the one that is not totally committed and the one that is not running with the herd.

Keep your eyes fixed on Jesus and run the race of life **by faith** in God.

Feeling weary

Matthew 11:28

Come unto me, all ye that labour and are heavy laden, and I will give you rest.

It is an absolute fallacy and untruth to say, "Come to Jesus and all your problems will be over." There is no Scripture in the Bible to support remarks like this – believe me I have tried many times to validate such claims. What Jesus does promise, though, is that He will walk with us through the fire. Nowhere in the Bible does it say, "Come to Jesus and He will take away all your problems, all your ordeals and all your fears and anxieties." What He does say is that if you come to Him, He will give you rest. He says that His yoke is not heavy but easy and His burden is light. Nevertheless, to carry a yoke is to carry a burden. The Lord does not promise to take your yoke off you. He says, "My yoke is easy and My burden is light."

If we read 1 John 5:3 we see that the Lord says, "For this is the love of God, that we keep his commandments; and his commandments are not grievous." His commandments are not burdensome, not heavy. Why has the Lord given us the Ten Commandments? To help us to walk this road without collapsing, without stopping, without coming apart at the seams and without breaking down.

I don't know how many times I counsel people in the office who have picked up all kinds of heavy yokes and burdens, people carrying 50-kilogram bags of cement. Some seem to have a blacksmith's anvil tied with chains to their backs and can hardly walk. It is obvious that many – not all – are not obeying the Ten Commandments. They're not submitting to the easy yoke that the Lord has given us to carry. If we do things God's way, the burden suddenly becomes bearable. When we try to make our own plans and start cutting corners, we pay a tremendous price.

Let us start doing things God's way again. Not only will we find that the road that He has called us to walk in this life is not burdensome, but it can become full of joy and peace. Get back to basics today – back to the grass roots of your faith – and start doing the things which God told you to do in the first place. Then you will find that all the things you have been struggling with will fall into line.

Smelling the roses

Matthew 14:23

And when he had sent the multitudes away, he went up into a mountain apart to pray.

How does one get faith? Romans 10:17 says, "Faith comes by hearing, and hearing by the word of God" (NKJV). Our faith will not increase by doing good deeds, but by living closer to God. That's why Jesus, before He performed great miracles and wonders, always went up to the mountain to pray. He isolated Himself. He took time out to sit and smell the roses. So often Christians grow weary and lose their faith in God by working themselves to a standstill in order to increase their faith instead of sitting in the presence of God and allowing Him to enhance their belief in Him.

Consider the case of the woman who was suffering with blood problems. She'd been bleeding for twelve years and had spent all her money on the doctors. She was desperate; dying. Amid the huge crowd that was following Jesus she stretched out her hand and said, "If I can just touch the hem of His garment, I'll be healed." As soon as she had touched His garment, Jesus swung around and asked, "Who touched Me?" The disciples said, "Lord, You must be joking! There are people pressing against You from all sides." But Jesus knew that the woman had touched Him, because virtue had drained out of Him. When He turned around and asked the question, a very embarrassed woman confessed what she had done. Jesus said, "Woman, go in peace. Your faith has made you well."

Every time Jesus performed a great miracle, be it feeding the five thousand with two small fish and five barley loaves or calling the dead man, Lazarus, out of the tomb when he'd been dead for four days, you will find that He had spent some time smelling the roses first. Jesus spent time with His Father and by doing this, His faith grew.

I find that the more I read the Bible, the more my faith increases. The more I read the newspaper, the more my faith decreases. The more time I spend with negative people, the more my level of faith drops. When I look to Jesus, the Author and the Finisher of my faith, I find that my faith grows. If you want to have faith in God, spend time with God. You will find that you become like the Person that you spend time with.

Left alone

Genesis 32:24

And Jacob was left alone.

To be left alone can be experienced in two ways. It can either be a time of loneliness, which is possibly the worst thing that could ever happen to a person in this life, or it can be a time of enrichment if spent in God's presence.

Many years ago I had to go to Scotland for three months with my oldest daughter Lindy. Although I was preaching to many people during those three months, there were times when I was overwhelmed by utter loneliness, being without my wife and the rest of my children.

I remember walking down a road in the beautiful estate where I was staying in the south of Scotland. There were 600 red deer in this magnificent forest. It was autumn (September) and the oak trees were shedding their leaves, all in splendid hues of gold, brown, and amber. There was a wonderful stone bridge, just like in the film *Brigadoon*, with fresh, sparkling water running underneath and brilliantly coloured pheasant were crossing the road. All I wanted to do was to share this sight with my wife Jill. But she was 6,000 miles away in Southern Africa with my children. It was then that I experienced true and utter loneliness. Don't let the super-spiritual people tell you that if you have Jesus in your life you will never be lonely. That's a lie. Jesus Himself felt completely alone when He was in the Garden of Gethsemane in His time of great testing.

But to be alone with God is a good thing. As I write I am preparing to go down to Cape Town where I have to present a series of meetings. There's a tremendous sense of expectation: people are anticipating nothing less than Holy Spirit revival. Right now I'm not completely sure what the Lord wants me to preach about. I know, however, that as I arrange my life and spend time alone with God, He will speak to me both through the Scriptures and through His Holy Spirit talking to my heart. Purely by spending time with Him will I be able to hear His voice. Therefore I will be able to go to these meetings with confidence, knowing that I am teaching the true Word of God.

If you need to get answers from the Lord today, you need to spend time alone with God. Do not say that you can't afford to set aside time for this kind of solitude. You can't afford not to! Instead of running around in a circle like a headless chicken you need to seclude yourself and be alone with God. During this alone time we might even wrestle with the Lord as Jacob did, in order to obtain the answers we are looking for. Even Jesus found it necessary to spend time away from the crowds and only be with His Father.

John, the beloved one, was alone on the island of Patmos when God revealed the subject matter of the book of Revelation to him, which he then wrote. Moses was on his own when God spoke to him from the burning bush. Peter was on top of the house in Joppa when God showed him in a vision that he was to preach the gospel to all of the people.

God speaks to us when we are alone. Once we have the answers we were looking for, we need to return to the bustling crowd and tell them what the Lord revealed to us while we were spending time alone with Him.

Have faith in God

Mark 11:22

And Jesus answering saith unto them, Have faith in God.

This was the favourite Scripture of a mighty, mighty man of faith, James Hudson Taylor (1832–1905). When he was in his early twenties he was called by God to go to China, the most populated country in the whole world. This young man, at that stage not yet even a qualified doctor, greeted his mother with the words, "The next time I see you will probably be in heaven," and sailed away because he was in love with Jesus Christ.

Once settled in China, Hudson Taylor adopted Chinese dress and learned to speak the Chinese language fluently. In those days most of the Christians used to live on the coastland of China. He was responsible for bringing some 1,000 families from Britain into mainland China to preach the gospel. A tremendous rebellion took place in China just after those families had arrived and many of them perished, dying a martyr's death for their faith. It nearly broke Hudson Taylor physically, mentally, and spiritually.

At Shalom we have a saying: "Good seed doesn't cost, it pays". We're talking here, of course, about the Word of God, which never, ever returns void. Hudson Taylor has long since gone to be with the Lord Jesus Christ. Yet today the biggest revival that the world has ever seen is taking place in mainland China. People are being born again more quickly than people are having babies. Their house church movement is the largest in the whole world. People are in love with Jesus because a young man had faith in God and went to sow good seed. Now the Holy Spirit is reaping an awesome crop.

As I write, I'm sitting in the western part of the Cape. It is a beautiful morning and gentle rain is falling. I'm thanking God for what took place last night. We saw thousands and thousands of people coming to this little farming town, many camping outside in tents because they wanted to meet with God.

One feels so terribly inadequate at times such as this. But, while spending quality time with the Lord early this morning, God reminded me through His Word that He had chosen me, and that always brings me great solace and peace. I know, just as Hudson Taylor did, that by my own strength I can do nothing.

The Lord spoke to me, as He so often does in the early hours, through the Scriptures. I always read the Bible in the first person. Luke 1:66 says, "And the hand of the Lord was with him." Yes, the Lord was speaking about John the Baptist at that time, but I believe the Word of God is called the Living Word and we need to read it with a heart of faith. I believe that the hand of the Lord is with me. This weekend I will just keep sowing good seed, trusting God for nothing less than a Holy Ghost revival in our beloved South Africa.

Guidance

Luke 1:79

To give light to them that sit in darkness and in the shadow of death, to guide our feet into the way of peace.

The Lord Jesus Christ has called upon us to reach out to those people who "sit in darkness and in the shadow of death" and direct them to the path that leads to eternal life. He has called us to guide the feet of those who do not know Him to the way of peace. The only way we can do that is by setting the right example.

Francis of Assisi, a great man of God, was a soldier. While going off to war in 1204, Francis had a vision that directed him back to Assisi, where he lost his taste for his worldly life. He gave up all his worldly possessions and made a commitment to Jesus Christ to serve Him for the rest of his life by guiding people out of darkness into light. He maintained that the gospel must be preached at all costs but words should only be used when really necessary.

We have a favourite saying at Shalom: "Faith has feet; it's a doing word". Kathryn Kuhlman (1907–76), that incredible "country corn-bred farm girl", as she was known, was a woman used greatly by God to heal the sick. She used to say that if you felt sick you should go and find someone sicker than you and pray with them, and you would suddenly find that you're much better off than you thought you were.

Do you know the story of the little boy who was always complaining because he had no shoes – until he found the little boy who had no feet? Then he stopped complaining. Our worst enemy is not the devil but ourselves. Only when we start to forget about ourselves and live will peace and light shine in our lives.

Today, let us talk less and rather live our faith. The amazing thing is that the more we speak to others about having faith in Jesus and direct them in the ways of righteousness, the more God will direct us and encourage us.

Unknowing

Hebrews 11:8

… and he went out, not knowing whither he went.

Abraham left his home in Ur of the Chaldees and travelled to an unknown destination because God told him to do so. God honoured him; God always honours faith.

As I'm busy with this book I am about to leave and attend yet another meeting. The rain is pouring down and I'm thousands of kilometres away from my dear wife and best friend, Jill. I'm doing this by faith and not by sight. In 1989 I made a covenant with the Lord and He made a covenant with me. He said that if I had the faith to go out He would bring the people, the anointing, and provide the answers. Last night we saw people being healed and getting saved because God honours His word.

You might not feel like getting out today. You might not feel like going to work today. You might not feel like persevering in your marriage. You might not see any physical improvement in your loved one who is terminally ill today. But go forth in faith. Carry on. You will be so pleasantly surprised when you see how God will step in and manage the issues on your behalf.

Confident

Philippians 1:6

Being confident of this very thing, that He who has begun a good work in you will complete it until the day of Jesus Christ. (NKJV)

This morning we went to the last scheduled meeting in a little town called Hopefield on the west coast of the Cape. It's a minute little town with one shop and one bank (the bank does not even have a bank manager). In spite of the size of the town we saw 5,000 people waiting expectantly in a tent on "the manifestation of the sons of God" (Romans 8:19). It had been raining on the tent since last night.

I phoned my dear wife on the farm in KwaZulu-Natal, a great distance away from where I was, to ask her about the weather conditions back home. She said, "The sun is beating down. The maize is turning into onions. There's no sign of rain and it is very, very hot." I asked God, "Lord, once the plane has landed at half past eight tonight, and I am driving home from Durban airport, please may I drive home all the way in the rain and find that it's been raining on the farm, on my son's crops."

We saw many people come to Christ this morning. We saw first-time commitments, recommitments and healings like I haven't seen for a long time. The service started at half past ten and finished close to one o'clock. We drove the three hours to the airport and got onto the plane. No sign of rain. As we approached the airport in Durban, the rain started! It did not stop and we drove home all the way in the rain. Thanks be to God!

Our confidence is not in ourselves. Our confidence is in God. We are confident that whatever He starts to do in our lives He will follow through with, until the day of Jesus Christ. That's what gives us the faith to run this race.

Favour

Luke 2:52

And Jesus increased in wisdom and stature, and in favour with God and man.

As Christians we don't have to work at making enemies. If we live the Christian life and preach the gospel of Jesus Christ through our actions, the gospel not only draws people to God but it also offends them! All we have to do is do and be what God has called us to do and be, and the rest will happen automatically.

A while ago I was quite sad to receive a couple of letters – and indeed there might have been a little self-importance involved – speaking harshly against the story of the novel *Faith like Potatoes*. The two groups who compiled the letters have appointed themselves as "God's watchmen" and go about looking for anything remotely negative pertaining to Christian work. Yet they profess to be Christians themselves. All I sensed from these letters was bitterness, envy, jealousy, and obviously a lot of anger.

This is so sad because the Bible states that Jesus grew in wisdom and stature and He found favour with God and with men (Luke 2:52). Earlier in the chapter we read that Jesus was left behind in Jerusalem by His parents Joseph and Mary as they were on their way back home to Nazareth. His mother and father were a day's journey down the road when they realized He was missing and they had to turn back to find their son. After three days they found Him in the Temple, learning from men (this is the Son of God!) and discussing issues pertaining to the Word of God. There He was, in the Temple with the scribes and the Pharisees – the very people who would later crucify Him – learning, finding favour, and discussing the things relating to His heavenly Father.

Let us make a point today of finding favour with God and with man, without compromising our stand or our Christian values. God has called us to be His ambassadors (2 Corinthians 5:20). He has called us to a ministry of reconciliation, of calling man back to God and God to man. That is our sole objective. We don't have to be the prosecutor and the executioner. God does that. We need to concentrate on drawing people to God and on finding favour with Him by maintaining a lifestyle of humility, love, and understanding.

Focus

Galatians 6:9

And let us not be weary in well doing: For in due season we shall reap if we faint not.

Completing the Christian walk in this life is absolutely vital. The last part of a race is often the hardest. From doing a bit of running I know that it is just as you are getting to the end of a race, just before the finish line, that the pressure is really on. The legs just don't want to move any more, you're running out of breath, and are absolutely exhausted. That is when you have to focus like never before. The same can be said about the Christian walk. Jesus is not interested in good starters. He's only concerned about the finishers. That's why, when we get to heaven, He'll say, "Well done, good and faithful servant. Come and enter into thy rest." He doesn't say that during the race.

A survey of motorcar accidents revealed that many drivers will, after a very long trip, have an accident literally around the corner or a couple of blocks away from their home. They seem to go faster because they want to get home and are not as diligent or observant as when they started on their trip. They throw caution to the wind and make poor decisions because they are tired. They'll either go through a red light, exceed the speed limit, or take the corner too quickly and end up having a serious accident a stone's throw away from home.

Far be it from us that, after having run the race for so long, we capitulate just before the finish line. In South Africa we have encountered many sad stories of men and women of God who were used extensively by our Lord Jesus Christ to win souls, to teach the Word of God and to do wonderful Christian works. Yet, right at the end of their race as it were, they slipped up, committed adultery, stole money, or simply burnt themselves out.

As a new Christian I used to like the phrase "Rather burn out than rust out", but as I get older I'm realizing that burning out for Jesus, in that sense of the word, does not bring any glory to His name. Burn up for Jesus if you must, but don't burn out. If we're spending time with God every day by reading His Word, meditating and praying, we'll never burn out. John Wesley never burnt out. He preached the gospel until he was almost ninety. George Müller never burnt out; he preached the gospel into his late eighties. Martin Luther never burnt out. These men finished the race because they didn't panic.

God would say to you today: Walk or run the race by faith – but be careful as you get closer to the finish line. The pitfalls and the snares will become greater, because the reward you receive when you get to heaven is going to be absolutely awesome. Run the race with faith, keeping your eyes fixed on Jesus, the Author and the Finisher of your faith (Hebrews 12:1–2).

God's faithfulness

Lamentations 3:23

Great is thy faithfulness.

Jesus said to the woman with the blood problems, "Go in peace. Your faith has made you well." However, today we want to focus on God's faithfulness and not so much on our faith.

Firemen are amazing people who risk their lives every day, rescuing helpless victims from burning buildings and disaster areas. They lift the victims to safety using a special grip; they reach out and ask the victim to grab hold of their forearms. The fireman, while firmly holding on to the person's forearms, is then able to pull the victim to safety. If that poor person – who could be injured and exhausted – lets go, the fireman is usually able to maintain this grip. This is the scenario that comes to my mind when I think of Jesus. He is the faithful One and remains faithful even when our faith waivers.

One of my heroes, James Hudson Taylor – a man God used to introduce Christianity to mainland China and started the China Inland Mission – was responsible for bringing some 1,000 families from Britain to China to preach the gospel. Shortly after the relocation of the British, the horrific Boxer Rebellion broke out. The Chinese people turned on the European immigrants and a bloody massacre resulted. At that time James Hudson Taylor was recuperating in Switzerland after a long illness and was unable to return to China. He only received a letter every six months and didn't know what was happening. Sometimes he had such a sense of grievance for his people that he didn't even have the strength to pray or read his Bible. It was his good friend George Müller (1805–1898) who wrote to him and said, "Just have faith in the faithful One." That is what kept him going until the end of the ordeal.

And, as they say, the rest is history. Right now the biggest revival in the world is taking place in mainland China, where the number of house churches is amounting to hundreds of thousands. A vast number of people are being born again because of the faithfulness of God.

As you go out today, remember that even if your level of faith seems to be running close on empty, God remains faithful.

Wait

Lamentations 3:25

The Lord is good unto them that wait for him.

We often say that faith is a doing word. Faith is not just talking; faith should amount to action. For me, one of the hardest actions to undertake is that of waiting, especially waiting on the Lord. I read in *Streams in the Desert*: "Yet without trusting God, even great riches will leave us in poverty." What profound words; waiting on the Lord, trusting the Lord to steer our "car of life" to a better place when we take our hands off the wheel. The days of us acting like a bull in a china shop are over. We cannot do that, for the time we have left on earth is too limited. We have to sit quietly like the wise craftsman and figure out the best way to tackle the job at hand and then with clinical precision do it correctly the first time round.

I remember how full of strength, exuberance, and enthusiasm I used to be as a young man! Yet often during my early years of farming I would have to do the same job a dozen times in order to get it done correctly. I would find myself absolutely exhausted at the end of it.

One of our farm workers who started working with me in the early days was slow-moving, slow-talking, and slow-thinking but probably the fastest worker on the farm. I remember after instructing him to put up a fence to keep our cattle in, how he would dig the holes for the quarter posts, probably a good metre deep. I asked him why he was taking so long, saying "Just get the fence up so that we can get the cattle in." He would ignore me completely. The only reason I put up with him was because he was such an incredible craftsman. The top line of that fence looked like a piano wire. He would measure each gap between the wires and, by the time he put the fifth strand up, nothing could get past that fence. Because everything was done so immaculately, no cow, sheep, or human could push through that fence. I have fences on this farm that he erected almost thirty years ago. He would never be bullied into hurrying and once the fence was finished, it was something to be proud of.

The Lord says we need to wait upon Him. I have been confronted many times on my preaching tours by people asking, "Why did the Lord allow this to happen to me? Why has this calamity crossed my path?" If, however, they were completely honest with themselves, they'd realize that nine times out of ten they'd brought the calamity upon themselves because they would not wait upon the Lord.

I've known people who have emigrated on a whim from my beloved country of South Africa because they thought it was a good idea, because they wanted to get on with their lives, and because they were bored with what they were doing. They wanted better opportunities. They thought that the grass was greener on the other side. However, they were soon to realize (after selling all their possessions and relocating) that the grass wasn't greener. The going was much tougher and there's no place like home. Unfortunately, because of their financial situation, they couldn't return home.

Rather wait upon the Lord today than take action that you might regret. He says in 1 Thessalonians 5:24, "Faithful is he that calleth you, who will also do it." There are no quick fixes in the kingdom of God.

Burden

Psalm 55:22

Cast thy burden upon the Lord, and he shall sustain thee…

The Word of God is very clear on the fact that God will not allow us to be tempted beyond that which we are able to handle. He will never let us carry a burden that is too heavy for us even if some of us might be feeling that our burden is too much to bear this morning. The amazing thing is, though, that we really do grow stronger because of our burdens. When I look back upon my own life, the times when the Lord Jesus was nearest and sweetest to me, the times that I remember with great relish and cherish as very special memories, are the times when I was carrying my heaviest burdens.

I have a dear friend who prays with me every Wednesday morning. He is an athlete of note and since he is entering the sixty-year bracket, he is considered a veteran. Currently he is training for the world championships in a couple of months' time where he will be taking part in the discus, javelin and the hammer throw. Because he has his sights on the gold medal, he is training with a much heavier weight than he will actually have to throw at the championships. When he then takes up the lighter weight at the athletic games, he will undoubtedly excel.

I've never in my life met a worthy man of God who has not been through a fiery trial. I've never read about one of the patriarchs, the saints in the Bible, who did not have to carry heavy burdens. Each and every one of them was given the strength by the Lord Jesus Christ to carry their burden and finish their race. When the burden is eventually lifted, we can literally fly like eagles. David says, "Oh that I had the wings like a dove! for then I would fly away, and be at rest" (Psalm 55:6).

Even today, bear your burden like a good athlete. Give your utmost attention to carrying that burden with courage, sometimes sweating and having to grit your teeth, knowing that it's only for a season. And when that burden lifts, you will indeed be the better for it.

The athlete, who is training with a weight that is heavier than he actually needs to, is training to get his body into shape so that on the great day of the contest the hammer, the javelin, and the discus will feel like a paperweight as he throws it, hopefully to gain the gold medal. Your gold medal today is to live your life as a testimony to Jesus' goodness over you. All of creation is waiting with expectation for the manifestation of the sons of God (Romans 8:19).

Hold fast

Hebrews 10:23

Let us hold fast the profession of our faith without wavering; (for he is faithful that promised).

The best place to exercise our faith is out on the wild waters, away from the harbour where the boats are safely stowed from the storms. Out on the wild waters, on the big open sea, is where faith is not only tested but it grows. Most of the great men of faith that I have read about were men who were tested on the wild waters. Their faith never grew in the quiet cove of the little harbour behind the breakwater, but out on the wild waters.

James Hudson Taylor, that young Englishman who went out by faith to preach the gospel in China, once experienced a time in his life when everything seemed to be falling apart. When the Boxer Rebellion broke out and the missionaries were being slaughtered because of their faith, he was so desperate that he couldn't even pray or read his Bible. His dear friend George Müller – who started the huge orphanage in Bristol, England, where some 121,000 children and £6,000,000 went through his hands without him ever asking for a penny – wrote to him and said, "Faith is resting in the faithfulness of God."

Perhaps you are feeling so low this morning that you can't even pray. Maybe there is something that is really troubling you. Today you can rest assured that God is faithful. Even when your faith level is at its lowest, He is still as faithful as ever.

Matthew Henry, a great Christian theologian who lived from 1662 to 1714, said, "When I cannot feel the faith of assurance, I live by the fact of God's faithfulness."

If today we cannot trust in our feeling of faith, we can however trust in the faithfulness of God.

Waiting

Isaiah 40:31

But they that wait upon the Lord shall renew their strength; they shall mount up with wings as eagles; they shall run, and not be weary; and they shall walk, and not faint.

As I'm writing this daily reading, I'm sitting in a bed and breakfast in Stellenbosch in the Western Cape, waiting to be picked up and taken to an auditorium to preach the gospel of Jesus Christ. For me, this is always the hardest part in the process of delivering a sermon. It reminds me of when I used to play rugby many years ago, standing in the tunnel, the crowd shouting outside, butterflies the size of albatrosses flying around in my tummy, not knowing what's going to happen, who's going to win, and whether I will have a good game or not. There is one difference between my rugby and preaching days though: this time I know that the Lord Jesus Christ goes before me and the score is already on the board: 44–0 in favour of God's people!

The Lord promises that if we wait on Him, He will do the rest. So, that is exactly what I'm doing at the moment: just waiting on Him, knowing that He is going to do the rest. It is almost as if I am sitting in the passenger seat of a racing car, waiting for the Lord to start the engine and accompany me on the Formula One drive of my life! How special to know even before our exciting race has started, that the chequered flag will be waved for us today.

Today, I want to encourage you to wait on the Lord. Whether you have a financial decision to make today or a decision regarding your family, do not attempt to do so without spending time with God. To me this is the most precious time of all, waiting to see what God is going to do. Lamentations 3:25 says, "The Lord is good unto them that wait for him, to the soul that seeketh him."

As I am waiting for my host to come and collect me and take me to the auditorium, I am patiently waiting to see what God is going to do tonight: to see the healing that will take place, the souls that will be saved, to see people's lives changed forever, to see marriages coming together, to see people freed from depression, and to see people who have lost their vision regain it tonight. This is going to be the greatest night of many people's lives, not because of me, but because of Him.

This can be the greatest day of your life if you'll just wait on Him before you go to work, before you go about your business, before you go to school or college. Before you even go to the hospital to see your loved one, commit that person into God's hands. Go with the blessed assurance that Jesus goes before you. Expect the best.

William Carey, that great man of God who founded the Baptist Union in 1792 and who took India by storm, said, "Attempt great things for God and expect great things from God." So go today in the knowledge that the Lord is faithful, and that He goes before you.

Astonished

Luke 5:9

For he was astonished…

Jesus is the miracle worker. Simon Peter listened to God and cast his net back into the lake in exactly the area where he had not caught anything for a whole night. He obediently said, "Lord, I'll do it because You told me to." Of course you know what happened next: his net started to tear because of all the fish he had caught and he had to call the other boats to come and help him bring the catch in. The boats were so heavy with fish that they literally started to sink. The thing that touches me most about this story is that when Peter got back to the shore he fell down at Jesus' feet and said, "Depart from me, Lord, for I'm a sinful man."

We serve a miracle-working God. One thing that hurts the Lord terribly is the heart of unbelief. When we start to doubt or disobey Him, He can't work through us. He can only grant us the desires of our heart when we act in obedience regardless of how impossible the task at hand appears to be. In Peter's case his desire was to catch fish in order to earn money to feed his family. God gave him such a big catch that he could hardly bring it back to shore. Peter was so overwhelmed by God's goodness that he fell down at Jesus' feet, consumed by the awesomeness of Jesus Christ – and his own total unworthiness.

That's how it is with me today. I've just returned from Stellenbosch, where I saw over 16,000 people stand up and commit to Christ. Even as I am compiling this message, I am still overwhelmed: first of all by the awesomeness of God and secondly, that God uses a simple farmer like me (or a semi-literate farmer, as I like to call myself).

You see, God is no respecter of persons. He can use you too, if you will just go out once more and cast your net, even if it is in exactly the same spot that is supposedly barren. He can make fish swim wherever He wants them to. He can make your business successful. He can turn your marriage around. He can heal that sick child because He is God. He is the miracle worker. He is the One who is for us and not against us. He is the One who loves us so much that He actually died for us on the Cross of Calvary.

Today, go out and cast your net one more time and see what Jesus Christ will do for you.

Withdraw

Luke 5:16

And he withdrew himself into the wilderness, and prayed.

How often, when God has done something absolutely amazing in our lives, do we run around telling everybody about it but forget to give thanks to God? Often a drought situation in my district forces us to have a prayer meeting in Greytown's town hall to ask for rain as we did again this year. God always answers prayer. The rain comes, we have a thanksgiving prayer meeting and hardly anybody attends. That's so sad. It must really break our Father's heart.

Every time God's Son, Jesus, performed miracles – remember when He healed the leper, or filled the boats of Peter, James and John with fish after they'd been out fishing all night and had caught nothing – He secluded Himself, went into the wilderness and prayed. I believe that He did so for two reasons. The first was to give thanks to His Father for what had taken place and the second was to equip Himself through the power of the Holy Spirit for the next leg of the journey, for the next campaign that God had organized for Him.

As a new Christian I used to hear, "I'd rather burn out for Christ than rust for Christ." Only now, having walked the road for a longer period of time, do I realize that neither option brings any glory to God. To rust in the name of Christ, in other words to just do nothing, is not a good thing. Neither is pushing yourself to the brink of a complete burn-out.

We need to take the time and withdraw from everyday life, as Jesus did, to regain our physical, mental and, most important of all, spiritual strength and also to give thanks to Him and to seek His face with regards to the direction He wants us to take.

No matter how busy you are today, remember to take time out and withdraw. You can withdraw to the quietness of your bedroom, your garden, or your office. Just close the door and ask not to be disturbed. Spend a couple of hours in His presence and you'll be absolutely astounded at how much more work you'll be able to do after giving those few hours to God. "Seek first the kingdom of God and His righteousness, and all these other things shall be added to you" (Matthew 6:33, NKJV). You'll start to hear more clearly, you'll get direction, you won't be so tired and you'll be much more effective in your doing.

Faith has feet

Luke 5:19

... and let him down through the tiling with his couch into the midst before Jesus.

Faith is a word of action, a doing word. Many times people get despondent with the Lord because they say He does not answer their prayers. But when Jesus tells you to come, you actually have to take the step. When Jesus told Peter to get out of the boat and walk on the water, it was Peter's faith that made him obey the Lord. Then the Lord undertook for him. Peter took his eyes off the Master and, looking at the huge waves round about him in the storm, his faith wavered and he started to sink. He cried out to the Lord and the Lord was there for him.

At Shalom, we often find that when we step out in little faith, things don't seem to gel. We cry out to God and He enters onto the scene at the eleventh hour, often at the very last minute. Very clearly, though, God responds to the act of faith.

These men in today's reading loved their friend and knew that he would never get an opportunity to have Jesus lay His hands upon him because of the multitude waiting at the door of the house. That was why they carried the sick man up onto the roof, made a hole in it and let him down, right into the midst of the throng around Jesus. Immediately, when He saw the faith of the man's friends, He said to him, "Man, thy sins are forgiven thee" (verse 20). The man was instantly healed and he carried his bed out of the house.

No matter how difficult your circumstances may be today, take the step of faith, trust in the Lord Jesus Christ, and He will bring it to pass.

Unbelief

Numbers 14:11

And the Lord said unto Moses, How long will this people provoke me?

At Shalom we continually say that the greatest sin in the Bible is not murder, theft or adultery, but unbelief. There is nothing that dishonours Christ more than when we disbelieve the promises that He has spoken over us. C. H. Spurgeon, that great prince of preachers, said, "Strive with all diligence to keep out that monster, unbelief." He said that unbelief so dishonours Christ that He will withdraw His visible presence if we insult Him by indulging in it.

John Bunyan (1628–88), author of *The Pilgrim's Progress*, says that unbelief has as many lives as a cat. It seems to persist and continually rear its ugly head. We need to oppose it with all our hearts. My dear friend, start every morning by thanking God for His promises spoken over you. Let the Holy Spirit remind you that all the cattle on a thousand hills and the hills themselves belong to your Saviour. All the silver and gold belong to the Lord Jesus Christ. There is nothing that He will withhold from those who love Him. The only problem is that when we doubt our Lord we tie His hands behind His back and He cannot help us.

Today, let us repent of a heart of unbelief. Let us start to ask the Lord Jesus Christ to help us to believe the Word of God written about each one of us. Then we will go out in faith and conquer the world for God.

You've heard it being said that we should read our Bibles as we do the newspaper, because we seem to believe everything that is written in the newspaper but we always seem to question the Word of God, the authenticity of the Word and the promises regarding our lives contained in the Word. We would (sadly) have no problem with unbelief if only we trusted the writings in the Word as much as we do those in the daily paper.

Today, as we would continue with our rounds and toils for the Master, let us do it by faith. Let us turn our backs on that heart of unbelief and start to speak out the promises of God over our lives. Remember, there is power in words. What you say is what you will get.

A new man

2 Corinthians 5:17

Therefore if any man be in Christ, he is a new creation: old things have passed away…

To me, the most miraculous aspect of the Christian faith is how our precious Lord and Saviour, Jesus Christ, can take someone who is broken, someone whom the world has given up on, and not only patch up, but totally and completely renew this person's life that was shattered for whatever reason, mostly through sin.

Many years ago, a top American preacher came out to South Africa and we went to some of his seminars. In a heavy American accent he said, "You will never, ever, make a racehorse out of a donkey." But even as a brand new Christian there was something that didn't gel in my heart and I thought, "Lord, he's got it the wrong way around. The Lord Jesus Christ delights in taking donkeys and transforming them into international race winners!"

I can testify to that because that's exactly what He did with me. He took a broken-down man who had slipped up in so many ways and He gave me a second chance. He told me that the old things have passed and all things have become new in Christ.

He took that worm, Jacob, and made him into "a new threshing sledge with sharp teeth" (Isaiah 41:14–15, NKJV). He changed his name from Jacob to Israel. We should remember that Jacob was a terrible man. He was a thief, a liar, and he did his brother out of his inheritance – yet he loved God. He repented and God restored him.

King David, the greatest king that Israel ever had up until the time that our Lord Jesus Christ came to earth, was a murderer, an adulterer, and a liar. Yet when he truthfully repented, God forgave him and turned him into a new man. The same thing happened with the disciples. They let the Lord down. Every single one of them ran away; denied Him. Yet as soon as they repented, God forgave them.

Repent this morning. Ask God to forgive you for ungodly behaviour in your life. Turn around, walk in the opposite direction, don't go near that place, never do that thing again; and God will give you a brand new life!

Strength

Ezekiel 3:8

Behold, I have made thy face strong against their faces, and thy forehead strong against their foreheads.

Nowhere in the Bible is it suggested that we should be doormats for the unbeliever. In fact, the Lord says in 2 Timothy 1:7, "I've not given you a spirit of fear but of power, of love and of a sound mind." We have not lost our manliness or womanliness because we have become Christians. On the contrary! We have become humble, yes indeed; very meek, yes. But remember, meekness is controlled strength.

Moses was regarded as the meekest man in the world. Yet I would not have liked to double-cross Moses – would you? For forty years he commanded 2.5 million Israelites who moaned and whined in the desert… I don't think he was a soft man by any means, yet he was meek. A man with controlled strength…

You have to stand up for what is right. If something is wrong you need to confront it in the name of the Lord Jesus Christ and deal with it. If someone is short-changing you at work or a partner is doing you in, you need to confront them. You cannot say, "Well, that's in the Lord's hands." The Lord has given you the responsibility to rectify unjust situations, so don't try and wangle your way out of confrontation. No one likes confrontation, some people even less than others. Yet, as Christians, we need to stand up and be counted.

Many a time the Lord Jesus Christ, our mentor and our champion, was tested. There were times when He said nothing, for example when He stood before Pontius Pilate. But there were other times, like when He made a whip, went into the Temple, and cleared it of the moneychangers. He was not afraid to confront the Pharisees, the church pillars – "caterpillars" – of those days and call them "whitewashed sepulchres", meaning whitewashed graves. All nice and clean on the outside and full of dead men's bones on the inside! Yet He was so gentle, the Bible says, that He would not break a bent reed, or extinguish a smouldering flax (Isaiah 42:3).

The Lord makes us strong so we will be able to stand up for what we believe in on the day that it will be required of us to give an account of what is right and what is wrong. He has promised us that we need not be concerned about what we should say at that time, because He will place the words on our tongues. Go out today and trust the Lord to undertake the difficult situations on your behalf.

Miracles

Luke 5:26(b)

We have seen strange things today.

At Shalom we have the saying, "One genuine miracle equals one thousand sermons". Once, a few men who were concerned about their terminally ill friend carried him on his bed to the small house packed with people who wanted to see Jesus. They tried to get their friend into the dwelling through the door but couldn't because of the huge crowd. They climbed onto the roof, broke a hole through it, and lowered their friend down to Jesus, who healed him.

The church hierarchy is quite comfortable with the delivering of powerful sermons or even a prophetic word, but when it comes to miracles there is basically one of only two reactions: belief or disbelief. It's amazing. When Jesus started to perform miracles, the church started to work against Him.

We've seen it so often in our own campaigns. Everybody is happy until the miracles start and then you get opposing opinions such as, "It's just a circus." "What are they trying to prove?" The bottom line is that we're not trying to prove anything. We are simply being obedient. Look at Mark 16:20 and you will see that when the Lord went out to work with the disciples, He confirmed the Word with signs.

The most powerful thing about a miracle is that nobody can dispute it. The man who once was blind is now able to see; he who was lame can now walk. People must work out for themselves who did it. All we know is that there's only one power that operates on this earth, and that is the power of the Holy Spirit manifesting through the sons and daughters of God. The Bible clearly states in Hebrews 13:8 that He is the same yesterday, today, and for ever.

Three weeks ago in Hopefield, a small town in the Western Cape, we saw 5,000 hungry farmers and country folk who came from miles and miles away gathering in a tent to hear the gospel of Jesus Christ. One night I prayed for a young deaf girl and I believe that God opened her ears. I asked her to go and stand on the other side of the platform, maybe some twenty paces away from me, and face the other way. I asked her what her name was and said, "When I call your name, Sarah, I want you to turn around." Five thousand people were watching. The air became heavy with anticipation. Absolute instant attention!

I turned off the microphone and whispered her name. Nothing happened. Again I whispered her name but she couldn't hear me. I continued to pray for her again and explained to the crowd that Jesus once prayed for a blind man, who still couldn't see properly after the first prayer. When Jesus asked him what he could see he replied that he saw people as trees. Jesus prayed for him a second time and he was healed. I applied the Word of God and prayed a second time, went back, whispered her name, and she spun around. The atmosphere in the tent became electric. The levels of the people's faith rose.

People need to see miracles in this day and age because they are grasping at straws. They are looking for peace, purpose, and friends in every place that they can find: horoscopes, tarot cards, New Age doctrine, and teaching.

There is only One who can heal and His name is Jesus. He is the Christ. He is the Son of the living God. Why? Because He is the only One who gave His life for you and me. He says, "By My stripes you have been healed."

Stand fast

Isaiah 59:19(b)

When the enemy shall come in like a flood, the Spirit of the Lord shall lift up a standard against him.

Preachers often say that people are so busy boarding up the front door in order to keep the devil out that he walks straight in through the back door. That means that you can do the work of the Lord and it's almost as if the devil allows you to carry on. Then he enters through the back door and plays havoc among your family. I would encourage each one of you who are walking by faith at the moment, especially if God is using you in a powerful way, to be careful, to make sure that the back door is also bolted.

Faith is the substance of things hoped for; it's the evidence of things not yet seen. So by faith we run this race. If the devil can shift your attention, if he can cause you to falter because there's a member of your family who is taking the strain, or maybe you're having a problem in your family, he will stop you dead in your tracks. You need to take the problem that you are experiencing (maybe with a wayward son, maybe a rebellious daughter, maybe a husband or wife who is not supportive of what you are doing) and put it in God's hands. You pray for them and love them, but press on with the work that God has put before you.

The Lord says, "The enemy comes in like a flood," and sometimes he does, doesn't he? It just floods you. You can't see the wood for the trees. Maybe your production line is at its limit and the bank is saying it wants to foreclose. You start to panic. As soon as you panic, fear appears and fear is the opposite of faith. Fear gives you a distorted view of the big picture. You see, nothing has changed in the heavens. You're going through a skirmish at the moment. You might be losing one battle but if you keep your eyes on Jesus you will win the war. The Spirit of the Lord, the Holy Spirit, will lift up a standard against the enemy and he cannot come closer than that.

I would encourage you today by faith not to look at your circumstances but to keep your eyes fixed on Jesus, the Author and the Finisher of your faith. He will ensure that your work comes to fruition provided that you do not stagger at the promises of God through unbelief (Romans 4:20). Remember Abraham? He became the father of many nations. He was a hundred years old and still childless and yet his faith did not falter. He remained faithful and God gave Sarah a son, Isaac. If you love Jesus, Abraham is your father and he's my father too.

In this Christian walk we cannot afford to be directed by our feelings or emotions or else we'll be going like a train today but tomorrow we'll be ready to throw in the towel. I've just come back from one of the most successful campaigns I've ever had in thirty years of preaching and yet, as I am recording this story now, I am being severely tested. I have a choice to make. I can either throw in the towel – which is what you do when the boxer you have trained is taking such a hammering during a boxing match that you feel they can't carry on any more – or I can get up and keep fighting.

If you know any boxer who is worth their salt, they will tell you that it's not the person who can pack the biggest punch who is crowned as champion. The person who actually wins the fight is the one who can take the biggest punch and get up again smiling. Later the opponent doesn't know how to hurt them any more and starts to lose heart.

Rocky Marciano is the only heavyweight champion ever in the history of the sport to have fought forty-nine fights and remained undefeated. When he fought "Jersey" Joe Walcott at the world championships in 1952, Rocky looked to be the underdog. He was a man half the size of Jersey Joe. He was one of the smallest heavyweight boxers ever, but he was absolutely focused, disciplined, and was known to be the fittest man in boxing. He had an attitude of relentlessness. Despite being knocked down in the first round and suffering blurred vision in the sixth, Rocky eventually came back in the thirteenth round to knock out "Jersey" Joe Walcott and he became the heavyweight champion of the world and he never lost that title until he retired in 1956.

As Christians we might be taking a bit of a pounding at the moment and the devil might be coming right through the back door. But we will not surrender. As a good farmer I'm telling you that you will not plough a straight line if you keep looking behind you. Let's put the past to rest, press on, and receive that victory crown which Jesus has for each one of us who remain faithful and just to the end!

Fact, not feeling

Job 13:15

Though he slay me, yet will I trust in him.

How are you feeling today? Are you feeling on top of the world or maybe not quite so good? Your faith has got nothing to do with your feelings. That is why Paul says in 2 Corinthians 5:7 that "we walk by faith and not by sight". In today's reading, Job says that even if the Lord should kill him, he will continue to serve Him. Job was going through hell. He'd lost his family, his farming business as well as his health. Yet he trusted in the faithful One. That is why he could be so optimistic amid such a depressing situation.

Often after witnessing the sick being healed, the captives set free, broken hearts restored and, most of all, people coming to salvation, people come up to us after a meeting and ask, "Please will you pray that God will increase my faith?" We always tell them that we won't pray for God to increase their faith but instead that God will give them a hunger for His Word. Romans 10:17 says that "faith comes by hearing and hearing by the word of God" (NKJV). It's when we start to trust in the faithful One that our faith level is increased. The Word says in 1 John 5:7 that "there are three that bear witness in heaven, the Father, the Word and the Holy Spirit". So Jesus is the Word of God in print! If you want to get closer to Jesus, you need to spend more time reading His Word.

Don't be so concerned about what the newspapers or weather forecast say. Don't even be so concerned about what the specialist's report says. Be more concerned today about what Jesus has to say about you.

As you go out today, remember that your circumstances do not determine your outlook. You've heard it before: your attitude will determine your altitude. If you adopt an attitude of certainty today, certain that nothing can happen to you without God's permission because He is sovereign in your life, you have nothing to worry about. So keep on keeping on for the Lord and you will see, by the end of this day, what He has done for you.

Watchman

Ezekiel 3:17

Son of man, I have made thee a watchman unto the house of Israel: therefore hear the word at my mouth, and give them warning from me.

The Lord Jesus Christ has appointed you and me His watchmen. What does that mean? In the old days the watchman was seated at the rampart of the castle. He normally had a huge trumpet or bugle. When he saw the enemy approaching he would blow the trumpet or the bugle and all the people would leave their vegetable gardens, their market stalls, and abandon their activities to flee to the safety of the castle. The big iron gate would be closed behind them and they would be safe from harm.

Being a watchman is a huge responsibility. As you read this book today, and if you are a child of God, you have an obligation to warn the people. The fact that we are walking by faith and not by sight does not nullify our calling by the Lord to be watchmen and to warn the people of what is to come. We are coming to the last days and people need to be made aware of this as they need to get their house in order.

Our life and walk of faith does not mean that we are blind to the enemy standing before us. When we pray for the sick, we pray for their healing without denying the fact that they are sick. When we pray for the broken-hearted, we do not deny the fact that the person we are praying for has a broken heart. All we do is pray that God will heal the broken heart and make it strong. In other words, the only way by which we can combat the evil one and the powers of darkness is by acknowledging the fact that we are at war. The enemy is real, but "greater is he that is within you, than he that is in the world" (1 John 4:4). We are not leading a life of denial. We are real people. Our feet are on the ground and yet we know in Whom we trust.

Remember today that you have been called to be a watchman. You should warn the people of the impending darkness; the darkness that will cover the people (Isaiah 60:2). But the glory of the Lord will arise upon us and it shall be seen in us. It is time to blow your trumpet loud and clear today, to sound the warning that the enemy is approaching. After having done that, we must remind the people that if they trust in the Lord they have nothing to worry about because He promises us in Hebrews 13:5, "I will never leave you nor forsake you" (NKJV). That's wonderful news!

Cost

Psalm 55:22

Cast thy burden upon the Lord, and he shall sustain thee.

If your faith is not costing you anything, then it's worth nothing. The fact that Jesus promises to sustain you if you cast your burden upon Him does not imply that your problems will disappear when you come to Jesus. In fact, and I say this tongue-in-cheek, I have yet to find a Scripture (and I have been searching for it for some time), which states, "Come to Jesus and all your problems will be over." There is no such Scripture.

In Matthew 11:28–30 the Lord says, "Come unto me all of ye that labour and are heavy laden, and I will give you rest. Take my yoke upon you, and learn of me; for I am meek and lowly in heart: and ye shall find rest unto your souls. For my yoke is easy and my burden is light." A yoke is made to carry a burden. Yokes are put on oxen to pull the cart that carries the load.

Many years ago I heard a story of a young couple who got married and had a beautiful baby son. Immediately after the baby's birth, the young life started to cost Dad and Mum. As the baby grew into a little boy and went to school, it cost his parents even more money. He was a bright student and eventually graduated and went to university. That cost them a lot of money.

After a couple of years at university, the young man had proved himself to be a good student and a good sportsman and his parents were very proud of him. In spite of the fact that the university fees amounted to so much, they were paying it with happy hearts because he was doing so well. Later they even bought him a little motorcar so he was able to come home during vacations.

One Christmas he got into his little car and drove home. As he was coming down the highway, the driver of a huge 30-ton pantechnicon lost control over his vehicle and crashed head-on into this young man's vehicle, crushing the car and killing the student. They contacted his father and mother and informed them about their son's death. From that moment on their son didn't cost them a single penny any more: he was dead. If your faith is costing you nothing it is dead.

Today, if you are feeling as though you're under the whip and wondering why your faith is taking a pounding you might be asking the question: "Lord, where are You?" Rest assured, He has not left you nor forsaken you. He is with you. Your faith is intact. The reality is that we are living in a world that is not perfect. God has called us to walk by faith and not by sight. He will see us through the fire no matter how hot it might become, because He is a faithful God who will not allow us to carry a burden that is too heavy for us.

The enemy

Isaiah 59:19(b)

When the enemy shall come in like a flood, the Spirit of the Lord shall lift up a standard against him.

Jesus expects us to walk the walk of faith today. No matter how big the enemy might seem, no matter how high the mountain might be, we know that we can overcome it by having the power of God in our lives. I want to ask you today – who is the enemy? I want to submit to you that the devil had his neck broken on the Cross of Calvary. When Jesus was about to go into heaven He shouted, "It is finished!" In other words, the work had been completed. Three days later He rose from the dead. He broke the curse of death on our lives. Because He lives – as the beautiful song which you have heard so many times before, goes, – we can face tomorrow.

Sometimes our biggest enemy is not the devil at all, but ourselves. Today I would encourage you to concentrate on the faithfulness of God. Not on your own abilities, but on God's ability in you. Colossians 1:27 says, "Christ in you, the hope of glory." It's not you or me. It's Christ in us which is the hope of glory. That is good news!

Our faith must be focused on God, not on ourselves. That's why the Lord Jesus says that if you want to be His disciple you have to deny yourself daily, take up your cross and follow Him.

Today, as you focus on the faithful One, on the goodness of God, you'll find that He has never left you. He has never forsaken you. When the enemy approaches, He will raise a standard against him.

Have a glorious day today, knowing that your destiny is in God's hands and not your own!

Faint not

Galatians 6:9

And let us not be weary in well doing: for in due season we shall reap, if we faint not.

Walking the walk of faith is not an impulsive thing. You cannot have faith today, none tomorrow, and then your faith returning again the day after! No; faith is a lifestyle. The walk of faith is not determined by your circumstances or by whether you are succeeding or apparently failing. It is purely trusting in God, His Word and His faithfulness over you.

I don't know how many biographies I've read of men or women of God whose lives initially appear to be a continuous failure, but in the end their stories result in a glorious breakthrough and an incredible victory.

The Lord says that many are called but few are chosen. My friend, the Lord is not interested in good starters; He is interested in strong finishers. It's like the good farmer who sows good seed. He waits and in due season he reaps the crop – if he does not grow weary. Many a time a crop of maize that I have planted initially appears poor, yet by nurturing, weeding and fertilizing, it eventually grows into a bumper crop.

We have a children's home on our farm Shalom. We have been sowing good seed there for many years. On Sunday it felt as if we were reaping a good crop. What a joy it was to my heart! I was sitting among the crowd while a youth was handling the service in the church on our farm.

One of our young Zulu sons who came to us as a baby, young Levitt, who is now a young adult, was called to the stage. He took the guitar in his hands, put his notes down on the lectern and started to sing the most beautiful songs. He wrote the words and the music himself. I don't think there was a single person in that whole auditorium whose heart was not strangely warmed by the words that came out of this young man's mouth. He sang to us from his heart, and lives were changed. Our Zulu people at Shalom are still speaking about his songs. Yet who would have dreamed that this young man would be ministering to the very people, namely my wife and myself, who took him into our home and loved him as a son?

Do not give up. Today you might be struggling with your own children in your own home, you might be struggling with your husband or your wife, but the Lord says that if you do not grow weary in well-doing, in due season you shall reap. So persevere by faith with that relationship, that job situation, or with that good work and Jesus says He will not fail you. He will reward you out in the open; not only in heaven but during this life as well.

The call

1 Thessalonians 5:24

Faithful is he that calleth you, who also will do it.

Jesus called me when I was a mere sixteen years old. I remember it clearly and yet nothing happened until some sixteen years later when, at the age of thirty-two, I heard His voice calling me yet again in a little church in Greytown. He called me to preach to the multitudes. When I was sixteen years old I used to sit quietly in a little bit of scrub bush behind our home in Zambia on the top of an anthill. I used to dream of speaking to multitudes of people though I never had the courage in those days to speak to more than two. If I saw a girl I would run a mile!

What happened? Faithful is God. When He calls us, He will accomplish what He says He will. Within three months of the call on 18 February 1979, I was preaching the gospel in the little Methodist church in Greytown where I initially accepted God into my life. Ten years after that day, on 17 November 1989, I was called yet again. God showed me clearly that if I have the faith to trust Him, He will fill town halls and sports stadiums; He will fill huge tents with people and they will come and listen to the Word provided I have the courage and the faith to see it through.

By His grace, and to God be all the glory, it is over thirty years now and I am still preaching the gospel. God has filled stadiums, town halls, and tents. People have been responding to the gospel, have been healed and set free. He is a faithful God.

Has He called you, my dear friend? Be encouraged. If He has called you to do something, He will also see it through. Just listen to His still small voice speaking to you and start to move by faith to accomplish what He has called you to do. You will succeed in your life because God is not a man and does not lie (Numbers 23:19).

Like Moses, go out and use what you have. When Moses was complaining about how he was going to set the people free from Pharaoh, the most powerful ruler in the world, God asked him, "What do you have in your hand?" Moses answered, "A stick." God said, "Well, use it." Remember, that stick became a serpent!

God is asking you today, "What do you have in your hand?" Use what you have, and He will add to it. Like the little boy with the two small fish and the five barley loaves. He gave Jesus what he had; Jesus took it, multiplied it and fed 5,000 people, not including the women and children.

Priorities

Luke 6:9

Is it lawful on the sabbath days to do good or to do evil? to save life, or to destroy it?

So often we get our priorities mixed up. We are so concerned about the trivialities of life that we forget the main point. Praise God for our Saviour, Jesus Christ, who is such a practical person. I love Him so much. Being a farmer, I can relate to His teaching.

The Pharisees were so concerned about keeping one specific law, namely honouring the Sabbath as a time of rest, that they missed the whole point, which was that the Sabbath is there to worship God and to spend time with Him. They made the Sabbath an even higher priority than the Lord God Himself. The Lord Jesus Christ had to bring the people back to basics, to grass roots levels. That is why He healed the man with the withered hand on the Sabbath. He did it on purpose. He wanted to show the Pharisees that the Sabbath was created for us and not us for the Sabbath.

When I go to a farm, the first thing I look at as I drive through the gate (assuming that it is a livestock farm), is the condition of the cattle. If they are sleek and fat and every one of the cows has a calf at foot and the bull is looking imposing, I know that the head of the farm is a good farmer. Their facilities might not be the best but the animals are well looked after. This is a person who has their priorities in order.

Then I'll go to another farm and the facilities are immaculate, the barns are absolutely impeccably kept, the fences are beautiful, the gates are strong and well kept, but the cattle are standing in a corner – only skin and bone. This farmer has their priorities wrong. They're spending their money on the facilities and not on the animals. A person like that is destined to go bankrupt.

Jesus says that He's made the Sabbath and all the laws in the Bible for the well-being and benefit of His children. When you go out today, don't be so concerned about upholding the law. Be more concerned about God's people. I'm not for a moment suggesting that you need to break the law for the benefit of the people. God would never do that and neither did Jesus. But if it means that you have to miss your Bible study in order to watch a rugby match with a friend who is seeking God, you've probably got more chance of leading him to Christ by serving him in this way than you have by preaching to him.

Never, ever change your standards to please the world. Never compromise, but by the same token put your neighbour's interests first and foremost, and you will see how God will honour you. Like Jesus of Nazareth, make sure today that tending to the people around you enjoys more attention than any other Christian activity. I always tell intercessors that the best form of spiritual warfare is to lead a person to Jesus Christ!

Wait

Psalm 46:10

Be still, and know that I am God.

The following quote is from *Streams in the Desert*:

Don't steal tomorrow from God's hands.
Give Him time to speak to you and reveal His will.
He is never late – learn to wait.
He never shows up late; He knows just what is best;
Fret not yourself in vain; until He comes, just REST.

We know that faith has feet, that faith is a word of action, a doing word. Even James says, "Show me your faith, I'll show you my faith by my action." Waiting is a verb as well, a doing word. So often men and women who are called by God to do great things have a season during which they purely have to wait.

Are you waiting on God while you are doing this daily reading? Maybe you are extremely frustrated because you are not seeing the fruit of your labours? Perhaps you feel that God has forgotten you? Even if you do feel that God has forsaken or forgotten you, it is not the truth. God has a mighty task in store for you to accomplish on His behalf and He is preparing you for the last days. Remember, Jesus is no respecter of persons. He will use any man, woman, boy, or girl who will make themselves available. In fact, He has a habit of always choosing the weakest, the youngest, the most unqualified to do His bidding for Him.

Moses spent forty years waiting in the desert before God called him. Joseph also waited for many years. He was falsely accused by his brothers, then falsely accused in the courts of Pharaoh, and then thrown in jail. And still he waited. When he was released from jail he became the prime minister of Egypt, the mightiest nation in the world. He was able to save his own people from starvation.

Then, of course, the greatest example of all is our precious Lord and Saviour, Jesus Christ, who waited thirty years before His Father released Him to do the ministry He had called Him to do. That ministry spanned a brief moment in time – three years on this earth. Yet it impacted on the history of this earth as no other has ever done, or ever will do. He waited; He humbled Himself and allowed mere mortals to prepare Him for the greatest work that this world has ever seen.

Dr David Livingstone, the most famous missionary Africa has ever known, was raised in a very humble home in Blantyre, Scotland. While working at the cotton mills of his native country, he educated himself and persevered as he waited on God. Despite many hardships, he became a medical doctor. God was preparing him for one of the hardest tasks that any Christian missionary had ever been subjected to.

When he eventually came to Africa, he walked the length and breadth of sub-Sahara. He was subjected to about sixty bouts of malaria, an attack by a lion, and was nearly killed by militant slave-drivers. He died at the age of sixty, having fiercely opposed that horrific trade in human flesh, slavery. He opened Africa up to Christianity. He is known by the African people as the "good man". He was prepared to wait for God to use him in a powerful way.

Be encouraged today. Isaiah 40:31 tells us that those who wait upon the Lord shall renew their strength, mount up with wings like eagles, run and not be weary; they shall walk and not faint.

Unquestioning faith

Luke 7:9(b)

I say unto you, I have not found so great faith, no, not in Israel.

Jesus was in Capernaum (Peter's home town) when the elders of the Jews came and begged Him to go to the home of a centurion and heal his dying servant. The centurion was a good man. He had helped the Jews to build a synagogue although he was an unbeliever, a Gentile. He wasn't one of the chosen people of Israel. The elders of the Jews were obviously trying to help him.

When Jesus came down the road, the centurion sent some friends to meet Him and to give Him a message: "Please do not trouble Yourself to come all this way, because I'm not even worthy for You to come under my roof. Just say the word and my servant will be healed. I understand authority because I am a man who is under authority, giving orders to the soldiers, telling them to go this way and that way, to do this and that and they obey me." When Jesus heard these things He marvelled at the man's faith and told the people that He'd never, ever seen faith like this in all of Israel.

I want to say to you today that nothing, nothing, touches God's heart like when His children start to believe Him and His promises. We release the Lord to do great and mighty things in our midst if we only believe. He is not interested in good works. He's interested in our faith – calling those things that "are not" as if they are. And Jesus said that no one in all of Israel had the faith of that centurion. He was deeply touched and the centurion's servant was healed immediately.

Exercise your faith today if you want to please God. Start to believe in His promises spoken over you and your family, your business, your future, and your health. Then Jesus will step in and do exactly what He did for the centurion. He will solve the problem that you are burdened with.

Heavenly help

Luke 9:30

And behold, two men talked with Him, who were Moses and Elijah… (NKJV)

Even as I am writing this book I'm about to embark on a major campaign. Soon we will host the biggest men's conference ever to take place on this farm. Over 4,200 men have already registered and we are trusting God for nothing less than 5,000 men. A daunting task indeed, just considering the provision of parking for some 3,000 plus cars on this farm, toilet facilities, sound systems, seating accommodation, and feeding such a multitude. As I am writing it's early morning and the rain is falling. I also trust the Lord Jesus Christ to bring us calm, dry weather.

Jesus was reflecting on the biggest test of His earthly ministry. He was contemplating going to Jerusalem to die the death of a common criminal on behalf of man. He was on the top of the mountain and had taken His closest friends, Peter, John and James, to be with Him. After Jesus' friends had gone to sleep, Father God sent two of His mightiest men, Moses and Elijah, who had accomplished outstanding feats while walking on this earth. They appeared in glory and spoke of what Jesus would accomplish in Jerusalem (verse 31).

This day, as you go out to fight the good fight, to run the race, be comforted by the knowledge that the Lord has sent His angels with you and ahead of you. If Jesus Christ is your Lord and Saviour, you will never, ever be alone again. The Lord will never give you an impossible task to perform, a task that you are unable to handle, without giving you the wherewithal to do it.

Be encouraged. You are not alone. God is with you. Go in faith, knowing one thing; if Christ is for you there is no one that will ever be able to stand against you (Romans 8:31).

Be still

Psalm 46:10

Be still and know that I am God.

Are you experiencing a period in your life where nothing seems to be happening? Rejoice in the opportunity that the Lord is giving to you. I've just read the account of a very famous child of God, Frances Ridley Havergal, one of the most famous hymn writers of all times. In 1860 she was told by her doctor, "You must choose between writing and living, for you cannot do both." She was a very sickly person and waited in isolation for nine years before she wrote her book *Ministry of Song* in 1869. Afterwards she said that she could appreciate the distinct wisdom of having been kept waiting by God for nine years in the shadows.

Maybe today you're feeling as if God has cast you aside, that you are of no use to anyone? Maybe your ministry has dried up? Maybe your business is stagnant? Maybe that relationship is not even active any more? But the Lord is saying to you, "Be still."

There's a reason for being still. He has a plan for you and He wants you to regroup, reassess, and to re-strengthen yourself physically and spiritually, so when He opens that door you will be ready to accomplish whatever He's called you to.

As I am writing this I am waiting in great anticipation for a huge door to open. I used to feel this way many years ago when I played rugby. I can still distinctly remember the waiting in the dressing rooms before a game. I could smell the wintergreen ointment that sportsmen put on their bodies to warm their ligaments and muscles; young men strapping up knees that had been weakened by previous battles on the rugby field. Some were tying their bootlaces, making sure that they had everything they needed, some talked non-stop while others sat quietly. A few paced up and down as the trainer was reassuring everybody – all in preparation for the Cup Final. That waiting was not only difficult but also extremely important before we could venture through the tunnel and onto the battlefield, as it were.

Nowadays I am experiencing those feelings of anticipation to an even greater extent as I prepare for a huge preaching engagement, sitting waiting quietly on God to call me into the arena to do battle with the powers of darkness, to win souls for Christ, to heal the sick, to set the captives free, and to be an ambassador for the Master. What an awesome privilege and, more importantly, responsibility!

The same principles apply to you today – you don't have to be a sportsman or a preacher. Being a child of God requires you to be still and wait, because we know one thing: He has work for you to do! So rejoice if this is a time of quietness for you and make the most of it. We are definitely living in the last days and the Lord is looking for men and women He can trust and depend upon.

Quicken

Romans 8:11

But if the same Spirit of him that raised up Jesus from the dead dwell in you…

We thank the Lord as we remember that our Saviour Jesus Christ has no grave on this earth. My dear wife Jill and I have been to the tomb in Israel popularly believed to be that of Christ and I can guarantee you that the tomb is empty: there is no coffin in that tomb, no bones to be found, no relics left. Jesus Christ was raised from the dead.

Paul states in his letter to the Romans, if you have the same Spirit in you as the One that raised the Master from the tomb after having been dead for three days, your feeble, physical, mortal body will also be quickened.

The Word of God is the same yesterday, today, and forever (Hebrews 13:8). It doesn't matter what you're faced with this morning. All you have to do is ask the Holy Spirit to fill you with His power. We are no longer people of the flesh but people of the Spirit. Romans 8:14 says, "For as many as are led by the Spirit of God, they are the sons of God." That is your qualification.

As you go out today, allow the Spirit of God to lead you. Remember, the life of a believer is not dependent on feelings but on facts. If you put your trust in the Holy One of Israel today, you have nothing to fear. We walk by faith and not by sight. As you focus your attention on the Holy Spirit, He will quicken your mortal body and that mountain that you are facing at the moment will be transformed into a molehill. Trust in the Lord. He will never leave you, nor forsake you.

We serve a miracle-working God. In fact, He specializes in miracles. The bigger the impossibility, the greater the miracle! Don't give up.

The future of the world

Romans 8:19

For the earnest expectation of the creature waiteth for the manifestation of the sons of God.

As you set out today, Christian, remember one thing. You have an awesome responsibility, not only towards God but also towards your fellow man and woman.

The future of our nation, indeed the future of the world, does not depend on the Muslim, the heathen, or anyone else, but solely upon the Christian. As we go out to work today, let us remember that people are hanging onto every word, listening to everything the Christians say and watching everything we do. They will receive your message as if it were coming from God because you are representing Him – even if the message is negative. It is stated in no uncertain terms in 2 Corinthians 5:20 that we are His ambassadors. Be careful what you say today. Be careful about the attitude you display towards others, because we are representing the Lord.

He says in 2 Chronicles 7:14, "if My people, who are called by My name, will humble themselves… then I will…" (NKJV). The future lies in our hands. That is a huge responsibility and privilege!

People are not interested in your opinion, Christian, nor in mine. They are actually only interested in God's opinion. We need to be speaking what God says. That is why that nugatory old master plumber from Bradford in Yorkshire, England, was used in such a powerful way by Jesus Christ. I'm talking about Smith Wigglesworth; a simple man used by a profound God. His favourite saying was, "God said it. I believe it, and that settles it."

I believe God would say to us as we go out into the world today, "Keep it simple." Just keep telling people what Jesus means to you. That was the advice that Gypsy Smith, the famous British evangelist who lived from 1860 to 1947 and who preached off the back of his painted wagon, gave to a lay preacher who was totally exhausted and disillusioned. The lay preacher said, "I've preached everything from Genesis to Revelation. I have nothing more to tell the people." [Rodney] Gypsy Smith, a Romany gypsy, replied, "Just keep telling them what Jesus means to you." That is what we need to do. All of creation is waiting to hear from us. All we can do is to keep telling them what Jesus means to us.

New creature

2 Corinthians 5:17

If any man be in Christ, he is a new creature: old things have passed away; behold, all things are become new.

How are you feeling now as you are preparing to have your quiet time? Are you feeling as if you were beaten around a bit yesterday? Did you slip up yesterday? Did you forget yourself? Did you lose your temper? Did you shout at somebody when you shouldn't have? Did you let the banner slip? Are you feeling a bit disappointed in yourself? Did you react in a way that a Christian is not supposed to?

Be encouraged. The Lord says that old things have passed and all things have become new. This morning, while you are having your quiet time (and this is the reason why a quiet time is so critical), confess your sins to the Lord (1 John 1:9) and get back on the road. Remember that this is the reason why Jesus died for you and me on the Cross of Calvary; to nullify those things that happened yesterday and to be able to start a new day today, knowing that "good people don't go to heaven, believers do". That does not give us a licence to live like the devil. It does, however, give us the freedom to put the past behind us and press on with the new life.

Luke 9:62 says, "No man, having put his hand to the plough and looking back, is fit for the kingdom of God." It is impossible to plough a straight line if you keep looking behind you. I know; I'm a farmer. It is vital that you don't look behind you. You set your plough and you keep your eyes focused on a point on the horizon. Normally tractors have an arrow on the bonnet. You aim at the church steeple, a tree or hill, and plough a straight line by faith. After that, when you turn the tractor around you put the front wheel in the furrow you've just ploughed – and the tractor will plough by itself.

Put the past behind you today. Set your face, like a flint, towards Jerusalem (Jesus), and don't look behind you.

Abundant life

John 10:10(b)

I am come that they might have life, and that they might have it more abundantly.

As an unbeliever I always used to think that the poor Christians were so short-changed. They couldn't have any fun because they couldn't get drunk, they couldn't go wild, they couldn't do anything immoral or underhand and they were totally hamstrung. How wrong I was!

I can honestly tell you that since I've become a Christian, my life has been one of continual abundance. Sometimes God has blessed me so much that I have had to say, "Lord, please stop, because if You carry on You're going to kill me with Your love!" That's what happened to the great evangelist Charles Finney (1792–1875) – an American lawyer who had an encounter with the Holy Spirit one night.

It was as though a shaft of light penetrated his body. He said it was a shaft of love from God and he cried out, "Lord, if You don't stop You're going to consume me because I just cannot handle this incredible love!" The thief comes to steal your joy, your hope, your vision, and your future, but Jesus says, "I have come that they might have abundant life."

As you start off today, you need to focus on what God says about you. You need to focus on the fact that He loves you so much that He died for you. John 15:13 tells us, "Greater love hath no man than this, that a man lay down his life for his friend." If Jesus loves you that much, surely He has a plan for your life? Don't allow the lies of the devil to accuse you.

Go out today and live an abundant life for Jesus. Remember, it might be the last day that you are required to live in this world before He calls you home to be with Him. We are confident of this very thing: that He who has begun a good work in you (and me) will perform it until the day of Jesus Christ (Philippians 1:6).

Lord, You've got to do it

Zechariah 4:6

Not by might nor by power, but by my spirit, saith the Lord of hosts.

Today, as I am writing this reading, it is the eve of the 2007 Mighty Men Conference. Last night I spoke to the registrars, who informed me that 6,500 men from every corner of this nation and also from overseas are attending. It was with a lot of fear and trepidation that I spent time with my Master this morning. Like never before, I realized, "Lord, unless You take control, I'm powerless to do anything." This conference is not going to be successful by my might or preaching – I've been preaching now for almost thirty years – or my physical strength. Even if I've been jogging up and down the road every day this week to keep fit, none of it is going to help one little bit. All the fancy stories that I've told are of no consequence at this moment. "Holy Spirit, unless You do it, no one will win those souls over to Jesus Christ."

I've heard that there are dignitaries from very high political offices, international sportsmen, and CEOs of big companies coming. The more I hear stories such as this, the more I realize that unless God takes control of this conference, it's not going to happen. I console myself with the Scripture where the Lord Jesus tells Paul, "My grace is sufficient for you: for My strength is made perfect in weakness" (2 Corinthians 12:9, NKJV). Paul's response is simply, "Most gladly therefore will I rather glory in my infirmities, that the power of Christ may rest upon me."

I would encourage you today not to look at your own abilities because, if you do that, the mountain will surely crush you. Psalm 121:1–2 says, "I will lift up my eyes unto the hills, from whence cometh my help. My help cometh from the Lord, which made heaven and earth." When I look at the magnitude and the power of Almighty God, the One who said one Word and this whole universe came into being, the mountain becomes a very small insignificant molehill. Today as I go out, I am armed with the weapons of the Lord Jesus Christ and I know for sure that as I aim at the heart of Jerusalem (Isaiah 40:2), the Lord Jesus will bring in a mighty, mighty harvest.

My dear friend, you go and do likewise.

Walking the road

Daniel 3:25

... walking in the midst of the fire...

George Matheson is the wonderful blind Scottish preacher so often quoted in Mrs L. B. Cowman's incredible daily reading book, *Streams in the Desert*. This is one of the greatest daily devotional books I've ever read and I can really recommend it to my readers. George Matheson says that even through sorrow, hardship, and fiery trials, the road is still leading home – and we need to keep walking by faith and not by feeling.

Smith Wigglesworth – often referred to as the modern apostle of faith – was a man who trusted God with his very life. At one stage he was physically weighed down by extreme pain caused by kidney stones. He never flinched; he just kept walking the road. After a period of six long, painful years, he had passed over a hundred kidney stones. Sometimes he was so sick, in so much pain because of infection and the loss of blood, that he was more ill than the people he was praying for. Yet he pressed on.

Sadly it is often true that when a man is going through a fiery trial similar to that of Shadrach, Meshach and Abednego (Daniel 3:25), the "Job's comforters" will say, "There must be sin in your life." This is very often not the case. The fact of the matter is that we are living in an imperfect world and there are challenges that we need to face. The advantage that we have over the unbeliever is that the Lord Jesus Christ walks with us on that road of fire.

You know the poem by Mary Stevenson entitled *Footsteps in the Sand*? A man had a dream that he was walking along a sandy beach with the Lord Jesus Christ. But every time things became difficult there was only one set of footprints and he asked the Lord, "Why did You leave me every time the going got tough?" The Lord replied, "I never left you. I was carrying you." I can honestly testify to that in my own personal life. In my darkest moments, in my most fiery trials, the Lord was closer to me than at any other time.

Keep moving. Don't stop. Keep walking in the fire as the men of God did in Daniel's time. Remember, when King Nebuchadnezzar looked into the fire, there was a fourth man walking around with them. The fourth man had the form of One who was likened unto the Son of God. Yes, Jesus was walking around in the fire with them! Today, no matter how hard the trial might be, no matter how hard the going might be, remember that the Lord Jesus Christ is walking with you in that fire.

Dependence

Luke 16:17

And it is easier for heaven and earth to pass, than one title of the law to fail.

The Lord says that it's easier for heaven and earth to pass away than for the Word of God to change. The Bible tells us, "But the Word of the Lord endureth forever" (1 Peter 1:25).

If ever we were in need of something or someone to depend upon it is now, during these last days. Everywhere we look, we find that things are crumbling. The integrity of the men we once looked up to is shattering. The organizations where we invest our money are collapsing. Sporting icons that we really emulate and encourage our children to look up to are turning out to be poor role models. If ever we needed something concrete to put our hope in, it is now.

The good news is that our hope is in the Lord Jesus Christ. He remains the same: yesterday, today, and forever. The Lord says, "If you've seen Me, you've seen the Father." He says that He is the Word. And 1 John 5:7 says, "For there are three that bear record in heaven, the Father, the Word, and the Holy Ghost: and these three are one." Therefore Jesus is the Word. He is the One we can depend upon, no matter what happens, no matter how hard the going gets. Jesus is dependable.

I've just returned from a trip to Western Australia where I've seen the devastation of long-term drought. I've seen the spirit of the people who are really struggling. Yet I was able, with confidence, to preach the Word and tell them about Jesus Christ. I'm so in love with the Lord because He's so faithful. No sooner had I returned home to my beloved South Africa, than I heard news on the radio that good, heavy, penetrating rains, the best rains in ten years, were falling in Australia. Praise be to God! He can be depended upon.

Today, no matter what your circumstance may be, put your trust in the Word of God. Do exactly what He tells you to do; no more, no less. Don't try to change the Word of God. Don't even change a dot, or try to uncross a "t", because it is all-sufficient and everything that you will ever need. What He says, He will do and you can depend on Him.

Abide

2 John 1:9

He that abideth in the doctrine of Christ, he hath both the Father and the Son.

Whenever we have our open-air campaigns or meetings for the public we make the statement that we are not interested in public opinions and the public should not be interested in ours. Our only interest during these meetings is the opinion of God. Feel free to challenge us if we step out of line when we are preaching – but be sure to challenge us only with the Word of God.

It is so wonderful to know exactly where it is that you're going. I've heard the saying "The world stands aside for a man who knows where he is going." If you are following the Word of God and living according to His statutes, you will find that people are following you, because at the moment the world has no compass. There is no standard according to which people can build their lives and base their principles. There is no foundation strong enough to withstand the pressures of this world. It is with confidence that we can say, "Thus says the Lord…."

What I love about the Word of God is that it continually strengthens my faith. The Word is a very clear-cut statement. There is no room for compromise or misinterpretation. If the Lord says that the just shall walk by faith (Romans 1:17), then you'd better believe it. That's exactly how it's going to be. Who are the just? The just are those who have been redeemed by the blood of Jesus and made righteous in His sight.

I recently read a great book called *Moving Mountains* by Paul L. King. Every single man that King writes about is one who took the Word of God literally – as it was written – applied it, and God did the rest. I believe the Lord wants to tell you today to simplify your life. Get back to basics. Go out and take on the world. Live your dream and do exactly what the Holy Spirit tells you through His Word.

Forgiveness

Luke 17:4

And if he trespass against thee seven times in a day, and seven times in a day turn again to thee, saying, I repent; thou shalt forgive him.

Sometimes one of the hardest things is to forgive someone and then having them do the same thing again. Peter asked, "How many times shall I forgive my brother? Seven times?" Jesus answered, "Seven times seventy." It's not an easy thing to do, especially when the forgiven party does not respond.

Luke 17:4 is a very interesting Scripture because in the very next verse the apostle Peter asks of the Lord, "Increase our faith." We need faith to walk the Christian walk. It's not just the faith to see signs, wonders and miracles; to see the Lord sending rain when there's drought, to see the Lord raise the dead and get people up out of wheelchairs, or restoring blind eyes.

I saw that happen to a dear old lady once when I was preaching in Bergville. She came forward for prayer and said, "I've lost the sight in one eye and the other eye is deteriorating steadily." We anointed her with oil, prayed a simple prayer of faith, and God healed her. It's a wonderful thing to see.

What the Holy Spirit is speaking about today is the faith to walk the Christian walk; the faith to trust God to give you the compassion, the mercy, and the love to forgive someone who has trespassed against you – not only once but repeatedly. God says that His grace – His undeserved loving-kindness or unmerited favour – is sufficient for you and me. His strength is made perfect in our weakness. Forgiveness is therefore not optional for the Christian. We must forgive, so that Christ can forgive us.

Our prayer today is, "Lord, give us the love and the grace to forgive those who have hurt us, so that You might forgive us for the way in which we have hurt You." Then let us press on.

Often when I pray for people who are sick and come to me for prayer because they're suffering from migraine headaches, arthritis, and various other physical ailments, I ask them if they have aught against their fellow man. They admit that they have and say that they can never forgive them for what they have done. It might have been an abusive father, a business partner who called themself a Christian but purposely defrauded them of money, or a love affair that was breached because of unfaithfulness. That type of forgiveness takes a tremendous amount of faith.

When I am asked to pray for them, I often don't pray for the ailment but I pray that God will give them a heart of compassion to be able to forgive that loved one, so that they can press on and be healed. Many times, as soon as they ask God to give them the faith to forgive that person, their headaches, arthritis, and other physical ailments literally disappear.

Make a decision today to obey the Word of God. God has said to you that you must forgive. Just do it and let Him do the rest.

Faith in action

Mark 2:12(b)

We never saw it on this fashion.

Four men, filled with compassion, brought their paralyzed friend to be healed by Jesus. When they arrived at the house it was jam-packed. They had no way of getting their friend to the Master but they knew in their hearts that if He could only lay His hand upon their friend, he would be healed. They climbed onto the roof (very likely either a thatched or a tiled roof) and broke open a part of it. They lowered their friend down to the Master through the broken roof. How is that for love and compassion? At Shalom we say that faith has feet. It's not just a noun like a table or a chair. Faith is active.

When Jesus saw their determination to see their friend healed, He said to the lame man, "Arise, and take up thy bed, and go thy way into thine house" (Mark 2:11). The people were absolutely amazed and they glorified God. They said that they had never, ever witnessed anything like that before. They had never seen the power of God demonstrated through Jesus Christ like that until now.

"One genuine miracle equals a thousand sermons." I've seen it happen so many times during our meetings when the crowd is not listening to the Word of God. But then the Holy Spirit prompts me to call for the sick. We lay our hands upon them, pray the prayer of faith and God performs yet another mighty miracle. The people are astounded. "What do we do to be saved?"

Even today as you go out into the world, remember that God has anointed you. He has given you the ability and the power through His Holy Spirit to anoint the sick with oil, to pray the prayer of faith, and to release the Lord's miracle-working power in their lives.

Power

Acts 1:8(a)

But ye shall receive power, after that the Holy Ghost is come upon you…

We cannot expect to operate through faith in the name of Jesus Christ if we do not have the power of His Holy Spirit. That is exactly what Jesus told the disciples to do; they had to go to Jerusalem and wait to be anointed with the Holy Ghost. He said, "For John truly baptized with water; but ye shall be baptized with the Holy Ghost…" (Acts 1:5).

What a difference this made in their lives! A group of fear-ridden disciples cowered in the upper room because the Romans, the Jews, and the Pharisees were hunting them down to destroy every last one of them after the Master had been crucified. They were absolutely petrified. Then the power of the Holy Spirit came upon them with tongues of fire! A rushing, mighty wind filled the house, they all began to speak in other tongues and the disciples immediately received power from on high. They were the same people, yet totally transformed through the baptism of the Holy Spirit. They went out into the streets without any fear whatsoever. Peter preached his first sermon and approximately 3,000 people gave their lives to the Lord that day as a result.

The evidence of the baptism of the Holy Spirit is not only speaking in tongues; it is the power that is brought into a person's life in general. My dear friend, do you have that power within you today? You ask, "What do I need to do?" You just need to ask Him and then wait. Receive the anointing of the Holy Spirit by faith to run this race and finish it strongly for Jesus Christ.

That is what happened to John Wesley. He sought the power of God everywhere. He even went to America to preach to the Native Americans, thinking he would find the Lord in that service. He came back to Britain sorely disappointed. Then, in a little Bible study group in Aldersgate, London, he found what he had been searching for. He said, "A strange warmth came over my heart. Scales fell from my eyes." I believe he was baptized with the Holy Spirit, as the disciples were in the upper room nearly 2,000 years before.

John Wesley proceeded to preach 40,000 sermons and he rode 225,000 miles throughout Britain on horseback. The revival he initiated turned Britain from a drunken state into a godly nation. God can use you in exactly the same way if you trust Him by faith and ask Him to fill you.

Jesus' telephone number

Jeremiah 33:3

Call unto me, and I will answer thee.

Many of us Christians don't realize the power and authority that we have in Jesus Christ. In Matthew 16:19 Jesus says to us, "I will give unto thee the keys of the kingdom of heaven: and whatsoever thou shalt bind on earth shall be bound in heaven: and whatsoever thou shalt loose on earth shall be loosed in heaven." The Lord tells us in Acts 2:21 that "whosoever shall call on the name of the Lord shall be saved".

I have been reading the life story of John McMillan (1752–1833), a very quiet, gentle, and unassuming Presbyterian layman, who exercised dynamic authority and power. Every Christian has the authority in Christ over the powers of darkness and evil. We have the Lord Jesus Christ as our protector and deliverer.

I don't know how many mighty preachers have had grannies or mothers who continually prayed God's protection over them and claimed them for Jesus when they were young, wayward men and women. Many of these men and women entered into the kingdom as a result and became mighty witnesses for Jesus Christ. One such man was a twentieth-century Canadian preacher by the name of Ern Baxter. He was a wild young man whose granny prayed for him. He came to Christ and God raised him up in a mighty ministry.

Unfortunately he made the mistake so many of us make. He started to believe that it was his preaching ability that brought the large crowds to his meetings. One day his old granny died and went home to be with Jesus in heaven.

The following Sunday morning when he walked to the pulpit, he looked down and the chair in the front row where his granny used to sit was empty. He was quite sad as he had loved his granny, but he cleared his throat and greeted the congregation. However, when he tried to preach, nothing came out of his mouth. He couldn't speak. It was only then that he realized that it had never been his preaching ability, but his granny's calling out to God on his behalf that had given him the authority to preach the Word of God. He put his head on the pulpit and started to weep. He told the congregation what had happened. An old African–American granny with snow-white hair came running from the back of the church, shouting out, "Pastor, I'll be your granny!" He says he has grannies all over the world praying for him now.

Begin now to exercise the authority that God has given you in the name of Jesus Christ and stand against the powers of darkness and watch the Lord bind the strong man in the lives of your family and your loved ones.

Know the word

Romans 10:17

So then faith cometh by hearing, and hearing by the word of God.

We have tremendous authority in the Word of God but do we apply and believe it? When Jesus was tempted in the desert by the devil, He could simply have told the devil to go away, because He is God. But He didn't. He used the written Word of God to combat the evil one. If Jesus did that, how much more should you and I? As a Christian, it is so important to memorize the Word of God. I would encourage you, Christian, to make a decision to memorize at least one Scripture verse per week or month. Then, when you get into that tight spot, you can call out to the Lord and actually remind God, like Moses did, of His own Word. The Word of God never, ever returns void. If you use the Word of God in times of dire straits, for example when you are battling with depression or experiencing anxious moments, or when you are in need of help, the Lord will undertake for you. He promises you that.

Read about the great men of God; for example, David when he fought Goliath. If I were a betting man I would never have bet on David. It was a 1,000-to-1 chance that David could defeat Goliath. But that is how faith works! Faith is the substance of things hoped for; it's the evidence of things not yet seen. David was a man of great faith and God was on his side.

Moses stood before the Red Sea. Pharaoh's army was thundering down onto him from behind, the mightiest army in the world in those days. There was no hope. But, by faith in God's Word, Moses cast his rod out over the sea and it parted.

That is a fact, my dear friend. Jesus fed 5,000 men with two small fish and five bread rolls. That is a fact. And they even filled twelve baskets with leftovers.

I recently saw the same thing happen on our own farm. We fed 7,400 men for a full weekend although we had only catered for 5,000 men. We collected thirty-six baskets of leftovers. Thirty-six baskets divided by three equals twelve. We fed them three meals; supper on Friday night, a mid-day meal on Saturday and supper on Saturday night.

When we learn the Word of God, our faith increases. When we speak the Word of God by faith, God answers. Today, take the Word of God wherever you go. Wherever I travel, the Word of God, the Bible, accompanies me. That's my sword and my protection against the enemy. You do the same.

Overcomers

1 John 4:4

… greater is he that is in you, than he that is in the world.

John reminds us that God has overcome the powers of darkness.

Many people are talking about the Antichrist, about evil spirits, about demons. Those things do exist but we need to remember that He who lives within us – the Holy Spirit – is far greater than he who lives in the world (the devil, the evil one).

If you regard the great animal migrations that take place in Kenya and Tanzania every year, when literally millions of wildebeest, zebra, and various species of antelope migrate by following the rain pattern, you will see that prides of lion and packs of hyena and jackal follow these vast herds.

The lion always picks off the straggler or the animal on the outside of the herd. If we keep close to Jesus and keep Him in our hearts; if we keep close to the brethren and don't start straying to the things of the world, we'll be safe and able to finish the race. It's when people say that they've been saved by grace – and that's so true; no one knows that better than me – and then think that they have a bit of poetic licence to go back into the world and revisit those sleazy places which they know in their heart of hearts they shouldn't, or when they start to dabble in the occult, that they are overcome by fear and depression. That's when the devil attacks like a roaring lion and devours us.

If you spend enough time with the Word, God will never allow you to be stolen by the devil. Many people suffering from stress, depression, anxiety, or fear come to me for counselling or for prayer. The first question I ask them is, "Do you have quiet time? Are you spending time with God?" They usually reply, "No, because of the pressure I haven't been recently."

That is the first problem. What are you taking into your spirit-man every day? You have to be careful with the type of literature you read, the type of programme you watch on television, the type of friends you spend time with, and the language that is coming from your mouth, because all of that can pollute your spirit-man and can open the door for the evil one to enter with his accusations.

Remember that although he has no power – his neck was broken on the Cross of Calvary – he still remains a liar and a deceiver. Even before you go to work this morning, ask God to forgive you for compromising and to give you strength to keep your eyes fixed on Him and His promises, His love, His power and the future that He has for you. You will find that your situation will begin to change dramatically.

Lifestyle

Revelation 12:11

And they overcame him by the blood of the Lamb, and the word of their testimony; and they loved not their lives unto the death.

How did the early Christians overcome the devil? Very simply: through pleading the blood of Jesus over their sins. There are so many of us who are walking around feeling totally condemned by our previous lifestyle. All we have to do is to confess our sins and believe that God has washed them away with the blood of Jesus. Then we can press on. That takes faith and commitment.

I always say to friends that my biggest enemy is not the devil, but Angus Buchan. It's me. The Lord revealed to me a while ago that when He forgives, He forgets – unlike many of us, who forgive as long as it suits us but then when we want to, we revisit the old offences and say, "Remember, you did this or that." When Jesus forgives, He forgets. When you wake up in the morning and say, "Lord, remember what I did yesterday," He replies, "What did you do yesterday?"

I love Him so much. The blood of the Lamb is like that big blackboard duster. It simply wipes off all the writing, all the accusations. Our debt has been paid by Jesus. Yes, paid in full! Then we are able to carry on living by the word of our testimony.

Lifestyle… How are we living today? Is our testimony bringing glory to Jesus? Once we've prayed for an alcoholic we tell them, "Don't even frequent a pub or bar ever again"; to a person who has been set free, delivered from pornography, we say, "Don't ever go into a bookshop that keeps pornographic material again. Don't go anywhere near it. God has set you free. And when He sets you free, you shall be free indeed" (John 8:36).

"And they loved not their lives unto the death" (Revelation 12:11). In contemplating this Scripture, I think of the passage in Galatians 2:20, which says, "I have been crucified with Christ; it is no longer I who live, but Christ who lives in me" (NKJV). When we can die to self, we can live again. There's total freedom. We don't fear death. We look forward to heaven. You cannot frighten a Christian with death. Paul says, "For me to live is Christ, and to die is gain" (Philippians 1:21).

I remember a nursing sister telling us how, when she walks into the ward where an unbeliever is dying, there's the most incredible feeling of anger, pain, fear, suffering, gnashing of teeth, swearing, cursing, and blaspheming in that room. She can't stand to stay in a place like that. But when she goes into the ward of a saint who is going home, the fragrance of Christ lingers in that room. There's peace, joy, love, and tremendous expectancy as the family is bidding their loved one farewell. A Christian has no fear of dying, because to die is to be "absent from the body and to be present with the Lord" (2 Corinthians 5:8).

Today, let your lifestyle be one that is worthy of the title "Christian". Remember, Francis of Assisi said, "Preach the gospel at all costs and, only if you really have to, then use words."

Free as an eagle

Romans 8:1

There is therefore now no condemnation to them which are in Christ Jesus.

I remember walking in my green cathedral (my maize field) some years ago. We'd grown a crop of seed maize and I was working with a large team of Zulu ladies. We were pulling out the flowers of the one variety so that we could get cross-pollination from another. It was hot, it was hard work, and it had been a long day. I remember walking up and down those lines, concerned that if we were to have a hailstorm – and in the part of the world where we are farming hail is very common on hot summer days – my entire crop would be wiped out. It was so vulnerable. The young maize cobs were just pushing out from the stalk. The crop was standing amazingly beautiful but, you see, up to the time of my conversion, my hope and my trust had been in reaping a decent crop so I could repay my production loan to the farmers' cooperative, to the bank and put food on the table for my wife and children. I was starting to feel pretty condemned: if this crop was to fail we would have been finished.

It was only then that I realized that Jesus had promised me that if I cast my cares upon Him, He would care for me (1 Peter 5:7). As the penny dropped, the cares literally dropped from my shoulders as well. Absolute joy flooded my soul. I realized that if I'm in Christ, I'm a new man. All the old worries have passed away. I realized that if a hailstorm did come (because the Bible says very clearly that the rain falls on the righteous as well as on the unrighteous and that goes for drought and hailstorms too), then my Jesus would have a better plan for me. My heart lifted and I realized that there was no more condemnation, no more accusations that the devil could bring against me. All the sins that I'd committed in the past, all the bony fingers that pointed at me, were gone. I was a new person in Christ. With great joy and liberty I carried on working that day.

Even now, many years later, the accuser comes every now and again – he's so clever, but that's the only thing the accuser of the brethren can do – and reminds me of something I did, somewhere where I slipped up or fell short, maybe even as recently as yesterday. However, Jesus is very clear on this. He says that if we confess our sins He is faithful and just to forgive you, to forgive me and to cleanse us so we can press on (1 John 1:9). That's the way we'll finish this race, reminding ourselves that there's no more condemnation for those who are in Christ Jesus. Guilt is one of the biggest killers of anyone, especially when they grow older.

They say that John Newton (1725–1807), writer of "Amazing Grace", which is probably the most popular hymn in the world today, was so weak on his deathbed that he could only whisper. He was trying to say something and his friend came and put his ear to John's mouth. He whispered, "What a great sinner I am." And then, after a moment's pause, he added, "But what a great Saviour Jesus Christ is!"

Fear

2 Timothy 1:7

For God hath not given us a spirit of fear; but of power, and of love, and of a sound mind.

The opposite of fear is faith. Often, when people tell me that they are fearful, I tell them to really embrace the Word of God, to think about things which are positive, to trust the Lord in all circumstances, and to remember that the love and faith that we find in Christ automatically cancels out all fear.

Fear is not determined by your situation or circumstances. It is an attitude of the heart. Often people are in dire straits and yet there is no fear in them. There are others who, in spite of the absolute peace, security, and tranquillity surrounding them, are filled with fear. If Jesus is in your heart, fear cannot come in.

The early believers went to the gallows, dying a death of martyrs for their faith while singing hymns. After soldiers tore their baby away from his mother's breast, a husband and his wife were tied together at the stake. As the fire was lit the woman encouragingly told her husband, "Don't worry, my darling, tonight we'll have supper with Jesus." Her faith was so strong that circumstances could not interfere with the attitude of her heart.

On the other hand, we have King Saul, the king of Israel who was constantly plagued with demonic fear to such an extent that young David, the shepherd boy, was regularly called to his side to sing psalms in order to calm his nerves and try to bring peace to his heart.

Again, my dear friend, I want to reiterate that what you take in is what will affect you. Be careful of what you watch or read. It does affect your heart's attitude. The more time you spend in the presence of the Lord Jesus Christ through His Word, through prayer and fasting, the more peace will come upon you and the more faith will be birthed inside your heart. That will cast out all fear.

For many people, when diagnosed with cancer, the word itself strikes immediate fear and death into their lives. At times like these we as believers need to pray the prayer of faith and believe in God for a miracle and a turnaround. Jesus can heal cancer if he wishes to. Jesus can heal anything.

A story is told of a man who was lying on his deathbed. He had a problem with his heart. He overheard two specialists saying that he had a galloping heart disease, which I believe is supposed to be terminal. He misunderstood and thought galloping meant that his heart was one hundred per cent, so in the middle of the night he got up, and got dressed, discharged himself from hospital, and went home. He lived to a ripe old age!

As we start believing the promises of God, He will dispel any kind of fear that the devil might try to attack us with.

Trust God

Psalm 34:19

Many are the afflictions of the righteous: but the Lord delivereth him out of them all.

There's a fallacy going around in many Christian circles that if times are tough there must be sin in your life. I get so angry when I hear that because there is no scriptural foundation whatsoever to warrant an accusation like that. In fact it's far from the truth. If that were the truth, then it implies that for Jesus Christ to have been crucified on the Cross of Calvary, He must have done many bad things. We are faced with hardships in this life for many different reasons. One thing that we do know is that every hardship that a believer faces stimulates his growth in his walk of faith.

The one thing we must never do is question God. That leads to a road of defeat. We need to trust Him, to love Him, to know that He is for us and not against us, and most of all, we need to know, as the Scripture says, that He will deliver us from every single situation, no matter how hard it might be.

That is where faith comes in. Faith is not a case of walking by sight. It's a case of believing God's promises (2 Corinthians 5:7). If a Christian's faith is going to be determined by the highs and lows in their life, they will be on a spiritual roller coaster. We can agree with Paul that we know that all things work together for the good of those who love the Lord and are called according to His purposes (Romans 8:28). And that's why, Paul says, we rejoice in our tribulations. Tribulation produces patience; patience, experience; and character, hope.

When I lost my little nephew in a tragic accident after he fell off the tractor that I was driving, I was devastated and didn't really know how I was going to carry on. But I never once questioned God. I knew God and His character. I knew His personality. I have learned to love and trust Him with everything I have. I knew that He would not cause a thing like that to happen in order to punish me, or even to make me grow. I continued to trust in His goodness and I can honestly say, as a living testimony, that He delivered me from the darkness and seemingly bottomless pit in which I found myself in that time. In retrospect, some of the closest moments I've ever had with the Lord Jesus Christ were during the times when no one could help me, only God. And He never forsook me, nor did He leave me (Hebrews 13:5).

No matter what your challenge is at this time, remember that being a Christian gives us no guarantee that our problems will be over. However, what it does guarantee is that we will become more than survivors through Him who loves us.

Are you ready?

Luke 17:26(b)

So shall it be also in the days of the Son of man.

The Lord says that in the last days people will carry on like they did in the days of Noah. If you remember, Noah built his ark and everybody mocked him. They laughed at him until he entered the ark, the door was closed, and it started to rain. Before that time it had never rained on the earth. The water used to come up through the soil. It started raining and it rained until the greatest flood that the world has ever seen, manifested. People were wiped off the face of the earth.

My friend, are you ready? If the Lord were to come today, would you be prepared? The same thing happened to Lot. Lot went out of his house, and fire and brimstone from heaven rained on Sodom, destroying everyone. The Lord Jesus says that when He comes again people won't even have a chance to go back and get their clothes. There will be two people sleeping in a bed and one will be taken to heaven and the other one will be left behind.

In the very last verse of the Bible, Jesus says, "Surely I come quickly," and John responds, "Even so, come, Lord Jesus" (Revelation 22:20). In the back of my Bible I have written, "Keep short accounts with men and with God." I feel led to say to you today that the Lord is asking, "Are your accounts all square?" If you have aught against any man or woman you need to settle it because the Lord says that He will come unexpectedly like a thief in the night. We can't then say, "Lord, give us a couple of days to get our house in order." We need to live as if He's coming today and prepare as if He's coming in a thousand years' time. Carry on making plans, because we need vision, but at all times be ready for the coming of the Lord. It will be a fearful day for those who don't know Him. But for those of us who are believers, it's going to be a glorious time of reunion and of going home to be with Him in heaven.

If you are reading this book and you have not made peace with God, or a wrong attitude is ruling your life, I believe God is counselling you today to repent, to get back to your first love and to be found by the Master to be prepared and ready to go home. Indeed, in Mark 8:36 the Bible very clearly states, "What does it profit a man if he gains the whole world and loses his soul?" Let us put more effort into preparing for eternal life today and maybe less effort into this very temporary life that we are now living. I just thank God for every person, including myself, who is reading this book, because we still have time to make amends and put things right. There are some who have gone before us whose time of reconciliation, of repentance, of putting their house in order, has already passed. Those people are already standing before the judgment seat of God.

May the Lord bless you today as you sort out all your debts and make sure that, if He comes today, you have no problem in welcoming Him to take you home.

Seasons

Ecclesiastes 3:1

To every thing there is a season, and a time to every purpose under the heaven.

As I am looking through the window this morning, I can see the result of the first winter frost on our farm, Shalom. Literally two days ago, the paddock that I'm looking at now was a bright emerald green with the graze standing knee-high for our cattle to feast on. Now, a mere forty-eight hours later, it has been bleached by the frost. I can see that the cattle are desperately trying to put on that last bit of weight by eating greedily before the long nights and short days of winter are upon them. It's as if I am reminded by the Holy Spirit that time is definitely of the essence. That Scripture, "Do not say there are yet four months…", comes clearly to me. Time is marching on.

When I was a young man I was familiar with older people saying that the older you get the quicker the time goes. These days I'm noticing that there are young people coming to me, amazed at how short the days seem to be. In Matthew 24:22 the Lord says that He will shorten the last days for the sake of the elect. There is so much suffering in the world today and so much persecution of Christians by this worldly system, that I believe the Lord is doing just that. He is shortening the days for the sake of the Christian. I'm very excited about this, because I cannot wait to meet my Saviour face to face. On the other hand, I'm also very concerned because there are many people who still need to make peace with God and come into the kingdom of heaven.

Use your time very wisely, my friend. Also, do not take the opportunities that God has given you for granted.

The good Shepherd

Ezekiel 34:31

And ye [are] my flock.

The Lord says that if you love Him and acknowledge Him as your personal Lord and Saviour, you will become a member of His flock. He says that you will be a flock of His pasture. I farmed with sheep for many years and I understand the principle of taking care of them. Sheep need sufficient grazing, good quality pasture, and lots of protection. The Lord is saying to us today that if we are a part of His flock, He will be our God.

We need more reassurance than ever before during this uncertain day and age in which we are living. I've just returned from Australia, where I saw hundreds of thousands of sheep everywhere I looked. The tragedy is that many of the young shepherds are no longer able to take care of their flock because of the pasture being destroyed in front of their eyes due to the parching drought they have been experiencing. As the emaciated sheep start to die, their shepherds sometimes take their lives into their own hands and commit suicide.

There is no shortcut to heaven. There is no short way home. We have to do it God's way or not at all. Our Father promises and reminds us that if we are His flock then He will make sure that we will always have enough to eat. He undertakes that no ravenous wolf will devour us, no wolf in sheep's clothing will infiltrate our pen and that we will no longer be consumed by hunger in the land. He also promises us that we will never be ashamed like the heathen so often are (Ezekiel 34:29).

As we go out into the world today, we need to understand that when God enters into a covenant (a two-way agreement) with us. He will always honour His side thereof. He promises us that He will never leave us nor forsake us; He promises us that, as a good shepherd, He will ensure that we and our families have food to eat. All we have to do is acknowledge Him, follow His example, and love Him with all of our hearts. Let us therefore be assured that the Shepherd of our flock, Jesus Christ, will never see us wanting for anything.

A Friend

Proverbs 18:24

... there is a friend that sticketh closer than a brother.

What a wonderful promise from God today: to have a friend who sticks closer than a brother! Jesus promises in John 15:13, "Greater love hath no man than this, that a man lay down his life for his friends." Jesus died for you and me. The ultimate price that any person can pay for their friend is to shed their lifeblood for them.

That is exactly what Jesus did on the Cross of Calvary. He went the whole nine yards. He saw that we could never get past the sin of this world, so He died in our place. Because He died, we can live for ever.

John Newton, a ship's captain, did some horrendous things in his life. I recently saw the film *Amazing Grace*, a film which portrays Newton as a man plagued by his deeds. He said that he was haunted in his dreams, every single night, by the 20,000 faces of the slaves who perished on his ships as they were taken from Africa to the West Indies and the Americas. Then he found Jesus Christ, a friend who sticks closer than a brother – and Jesus gave him a reprieve as he repented. That is why he wrote that most beautiful and well-loved hymn, "Amazing Grace": "Amazing grace, how sweet the sound, that saved a wretch like me. I once was lost but now am found, was blind but now I see." In the movie he actually goes blind in his old age and says to young William Wilberforce, "Now that I'm blind, I can really see."

My prayer for each one of us today is that we will really see who our Friend, the One who sticks closer than any brother, is.

Power

Acts 1:8

But ye shall receive power, after that the Holy Ghost is come upon you…

Martin Luther, John Wesley, John Knox, John Calvin, St Augustine, and many other mighty men of God tried their hardest to earn their way to heaven and failed miserably. Martin Luther used to beat himself with whips. He used to chain himself to try and put the flesh down. He used to wear horsehair garments to try and punish his body, but he failed. It was only when he realized that "The just shall live by faith" (Romans 1:17) that he was liberated. The power that each one of these men received did not lie in their own strength. It came from heaven. That power is not the power we perceive in the world. It is the power that comes through Christ living in us. The Holy Spirit in us gives us the power to be witnesses for Jesus in Jerusalem, Judea, Samaria, and to the uttermost parts of the earth.

I can give testimony about the power of Christ transforming my own life. When I was a young lad I was very easily embarrassed. I could not speak to more than two people at a time and if I saw a girl I ran a mile. I weighed maybe 45 kilograms, had a face full of blotches and pimples and no self-confidence. When I met Jesus Christ and was born again, baptized in the Holy Spirit and in water, my life underwent a 180-degree turnabout. You see, Angus died and Jesus was born into Angus's life. It's no longer I who live but Christ who lives in me. That's the power that I have. I would not exchange it for anything.

You too can have that power, even today, if you bow the knee and acknowledge that without Christ you can't do it. Remember that He is called the Holy Spirit. He is not "the Spirit", He is the Holy Spirit. He cannot live inside a house that is dirty, wretched, or unclean. It was only when I repented of my sins that the Lord came to live within me and gave me eternal life, a life full of excitement and challenges.

"Attempt great things for God and expect great things from God" was William Carey's famous saying. He went to India as a young cobbler with his wife and children and, by the power of the Holy Spirit, proceeded to turn India upside down, not so much by his preaching but by his writing and his translations. You can do it as well. Like never before, the church is looking for men and women who are filled with the power of the Holy Spirit.

The prodigal son

Luke 15:13(b)

… and there wasted his substance with riotous living.

The *New Collins Dictionary* defines the word prodigal as "recklessly wasteful living". This prodigal was not a heathen in my understanding. He was part of the family, the youngest son of his father. He was not an outsider but a backslider.

Jesus is not only known as the Shepherd of the sheep, the Great Ploughman, the King of kings, the Lord of lords, the Lion of Judah, the Bright Morning Star or the Lily of the Valley. He's also known as the Friend of sinners, a title that I love more than any other. That is one of the reasons I am so in love with Him.

The young man in today's reading had claimed his inheritance from his father. The Bible doesn't say that he took the profits that his father had; it states that his father took and divided his living with him. In other words, he took a portion of his farm and gave it to his younger son. His son must have sold it – whether it was cattle or equipment we cannot say. As a result his father struggled quite a bit. That's probably why the older brother was so angry when the prodigal came home and his father fussed over him so much. He took his inheritance and squandered it. It cost his father dearly.

Maybe some of you reading this passage this morning are in that position. You have turned your back on God and are making your own plan. The Holy Spirit wants to tell you today to repent and return to your first love while there is still time. You say that you can't, you have gone too far. The good news is that you can never go too far away from God! If you go up the highest mountain, He's there. If you go into the deepest valley, He's there because He is living in your heart. He's asking you to repent today and come back home (Revelation 2:4). He says that He has one thing against you and that is that you have forgotten your first love. Many Christians, after a season, just go through the motions. It's not good enough. There's got to be a real love, a commitment.

After the prodigal son had squandered all of his father's money and was living in worse conditions than any one of his father's hired hands, he decided to humble himself and go back. This story is so encouraging for you and me today because it says that when his father saw him a long way off and recognized him (he was filthy, full of the sin and the stench of this world; he was degraded, had no self-confidence, was thin, sick, and totally disillusioned with this world), he ran to him, brought him home and loved him, put his best robe around him, a ring on his finger and slaughtered the fattened ox, because, he said, "My son was lost but now he's found." How's that for love?

Let us never allow ourselves to reach such depths of degradation and despair that we cannot return home. The Lord is waiting for you and me today with arms wide open, saying, "Come home. Let us bury the hatchet and let bygones be bygones. Let's press on together." Jesus came that we might have life eternal (John 10:10). Let's start living it today for Him.

Perseverance

Luke 18:1(b)

... that men ought always to pray, and not to faint.

What a beautiful parable this is! Through it, Jesus invites us to persist with our requests to Him. He speaks of a judge; a very hard man who feared neither God nor man. An old widow wanted his help with justice against her adversary. She wanted justice for something that someone had done to her. Eventually, because she persisted and troubled him, he capitulated and agreed to assist her in achieving justice. Jesus says that if the unrighteous judge was moved by the widow's persistence, how much more will God not avenge His own elect who cry to Him day and night?

A very dear son in Christ of mine has been used by God in such a powerful way during the last couple of months. He organized a men's conference for me with the number of delegates exceeding 7,000. Seven battalions if you're a military person. It was the biggest event we've ever had on Shalom. He organized everything and it worked like clockwork.

He's also a farmer and a businessman. Just subsequent to the conference two of his trucks were involved in accidents and, as you can imagine, he is very disillusioned at the moment. I was able to encourage him this morning with this Scripture.

My dear friend, do not give up. Persevere, because the victory is yours. You don't know how close you are to the victory. You might lose the battle but you can rest assured that you will definitely win the war. Jesus Christ has promised us that the victory is ours. Today as you go out to live your life for Him, remember to persist like the old widow. God has promised you that He will be coming to avenge you very speedily.

In closing, He asks you the question: When I come back will I find faith on earth (Luke 18:8)? Faith is not subject to feelings, circumstances, or situations. Our faith is in the faithful One. He has promised us that He will never disappoint us.

Praise

Numbers 21:17

Then Israel sang this song, Spring up, O well…

The people were dying of thirst because there was no water in the hot desert and the Lord told Moses to call the people together. Moses got them together and they began digging in the sand with their sticks. As they were digging they started to praise God in advance, thanking Him. They must have hit an underground stream and the water gurgled up almost in a supernatural way. They then had plenty of water to drink.

I want to ask you today, are you praising God enough in your circumstances? You don't praise Him for your circumstances if you are in dire straits right now, but you praise Him in your circumstances. If you have a sick child, you can start to praise God this morning that the Lord Jesus will undertake for that child. If your business is taking tremendous strain at the moment, you can praise God because we know that all things work together for the good of those who love the Lord and are called according to His purposes (Romans 8:28). It's going to turn around. If you are struggling in your marriage, with your family, start to praise God today for turning the tide. He's a good God. He's for you, not against you. He loves the family unit more than life itself. He will undertake. Just give Him an opportunity. And praise Him; praise Him unconditionally.

Job was regarded as a giant of faith. Irrespective of his situation, although he was sitting on the ash heap, his house had burnt down, his children had died, his farm had gone bankrupt, he still praised God. He said, "Though He slay me, yet will I still trust Him" (Job 13:15, NKJV).

Today, go out and praise God because He's worthy of receiving praise. Continue digging. Continue working and doing whatever God has told you to do. He will change your situation.

Responsibility

Genesis 4:9(b)

Am I my brother's keeper?

Early this morning, while spending time with the Lord and reading one of Smith Wigglesworth's daily devotionals, the Holy Spirit reminded me once again of our responsibility towards our fellow brothers and sisters to tell them that they must be born again, that Jesus Christ is the answer to all their problems, that there is a better way, that there is hope, no matter how bleak things may look.

As I am writing this I'm getting ready to go to yet another campaign, this time in Rustenburg, situated in the north-western part of South Africa. I have to leave my best friend in this life, my dear wife Jill, once again.

Sometimes I get tired and weary. Sometimes I say, "Lord, I don't feel like it." Then I'm reminded, like I was again this morning, of what He did for me. He died for me on the Cross of Calvary. He gave me a second chance when I was in a hopeless situation, when there was no future for me. He stepped into the gap. Maybe He didn't feel like leaving heaven either. Maybe He didn't feel like leaving the comfort of His Father, or the Holy Spirit. Yet He came to earth and laid down His life so I may have eternal life. The least I can do is to go this weekend and tell people the good news about Jesus Christ being the Friend of sinners, that He is the miracle worker and that if you give your life to Him you will have eternal peace, joy and fulfilment.

Over thirty years ago, when I had just invited Jesus Christ into my life and was born again, I was challenged by a dear friend to go and tell the first three people I saw the next day what I'd done. That was the start – and I've never stopped since. I challenge you to go out today and tell at least three people that Jesus is the answer. Why? Because you are your brother's keeper!

A new heart

Ezekiel 36:28(b)

… ye shall be my people, and I will be your God.

We can be confident that the Lord still has some work to do in our lives because He told the children of Israel outright – and that includes each one of us who believes in Him – that He is not finished with us. He says that because He is our Lord, and it is He who will give us a new heart for His own name's sake. He says that He will show the heathen that He will save His people.

We can be confident this morning that we will make it to the finish line but then we need to trust God by faith and He will do the rest. He says that He will save us for His own name's sake, for His own reputation.

If you've been going through the fire today or during this past season, the Word promises you that He will bring it to an end. He will bless you. He says that He will put a new heart in you. He will take your stony heart, and enable you to praise Him so He can bless you. Why? Because He is the Lord; because He is committed to bringing that which He has started in your life to fulfilment! He created you. As long as you keep walking by faith and trust, He'll take you right to the end of the road.

The confidence that we have today is not in our own goodness but in the faithfulness of Jesus Christ. A. W. Tozer said, "Don't even have faith in God's faithfulness, but have faith in God Himself." God, by nature, is a good God; He is for you and not against you. Philippians 1:6 says, "Being confident of this very thing, that he which hath begun a good work in you will perform it until the day of Jesus Christ." Be confident today. As long as you continue to walk by faith, as long as you continue to trust Him, He will ensure that you finish strongly for His own name's sake.

Humility

Luke 18:14(b)

… for every one that exalteth himself shall be abased; and he that humbleth himself shall be exalted.

Jesus very clearly states in Luke 18:9 that the people who trust in their own goodness will never see God, but God will exalt the humble. He tells the story of a Pharisee (a temple-goer, one who thinks he is good in his own right). This man goes to the temple every week, gives his tithes, thinks he lives a holy life but he trusts purely in his own goodness. The sinner goes to the temple and is filled with repentance to such an extent that he cannot even lift up his eyes. He cries out to God and says, "Lord, be merciful to me, a sinner." The Lord says, "I tell you that the man who exalts himself will be put down and he who humbles himself will be lifted up."

When Jesus walked on earth He was often found among the down-and-outs, with the prostitute, with the publican, with the sinner. He said, "I came for the sick and not for those who are healthy." In 1 Peter 5:5 the Lord says that He resists the proud but He gives grace to the humble. That's good news for a sinner like me. When we go to the house of the Lord, let us not start reminding God of all the good things we've done for Him. Let us rather appeal, like the publican, and say, "Lord, I'm a sinner. Please have mercy on me." He will.

At Shalom we have a saying that good men don't go to heaven; believers go to heaven – those people who have faith and believe that Jesus Christ is the Friend of sinners. I said that at a funeral once and one man was very angry with me. "How can you say that good people don't go to heaven?" I replied, "Quite simply because if that was the case, people of other faiths, like Muslims, Hindus, and other religions, would go to heaven before us because they do more good works than Christians do. But with the Lord Jesus Christ, it's a case of acknowledging Him as Lord and Saviour and knowing that in our own strength we can do nothing good, but that in Him we can do all things."

Today He says to you and me that if we confess our sins, He is faithful and just to forgive us and to cleanse us from all unrighteousness (1 John 1:9). Before you go out today, come before Him and ask forgiveness. Humble yourself and say that there's no good thing within you. He will forgive you and allow you to walk out of your home today a brand new person.

Clinging

Genesis 32:26(b)

I will not let thee go, except thou bless me

The great American preacher J. R. Miller says that Jacob won the victory and the blessing not by wrestling with God but by clinging to God, holding on to God in faith. The Lord is too big and too strong for any man to try and wrestle with. He is God. He is so big that by saying one single Word, this universe came into being. There is no man that has ever lived who can wrestle with God and win. Jacob's hip was displaced but, as Miller says, he got the Lord around the neck, as it were, and he hung on. The Lord was so impressed with his perseverance, that He said, "Thy name shall be called no more Jacob, but Israel: for as a prince hast thou power with God and with men, and hast prevailed" (verse 28).

Christianity is not a once-off experience. Sometimes we need to hang on by the skin of our teeth until God comes through for us. And He will. He's come through for me and He will come through for you. Sometimes, because the going is so tough, you cry out, "Lord, where are You?" Maybe you feel like that today. God says, "Cling on to Me and I'll carry you through."

When my younger son Fergus was a little boy, he had an obstruction in the bowel. The doctor said that he was in a very serious state. He was running a high temperature and needed to be operated on immediately. I was absolutely shattered. My life came to a standstill. I was busy harvesting maize at the time. I was dirty, covered in chaff and dust, and when I was called to the phone, I asked, "Well, do I have time to take a shower?" He said, "No, you don't. Go to Pietermaritzburg immediately," (this was the nearest city) "and they will be waiting for you at the emergency entrance. If the boy is not operated on immediately, he will die."

I will never forget driving those 40 kilometres with my son lying on the front seat. The doctor had inserted a drip into his arm and sedated him. The little sachet was stuck to the windscreen of the car. My wife and other children were weeping when I left them behind on the farm. On that road I cried out to God. I wrestled with God. When the wrestling no longer had any effect, I clung on to God.

I remembered that just the week before at Bible study we had talked about Abraham and the incredible faith he had and that, after a hundred years, God gave him his heart's desire, a little boy named Isaac. When Isaac turned thirteen God said, "I want him back." Abraham didn't hesitate. At that moment a peace came over me and, in the Spirit, I gave my son back to God. I just remained clinging on to Him.

When we got to the hospital they examined my son. They were going to operate the next morning. I sat by his bed the whole night, totally at peace, clinging to God. The next morning the doctor could not believe what had happened. The obstruction of the bowel had spontaneously cleared. There was nothing to see on the X-ray. He said, "You can take your son home."

Just cling to God today. He won't let you down.

The Word is alive

Ezekiel 37:4(b)

O ye dry bones, hear the word of the Lord.

I have just returned from Rustenburg in the north-western part of South Africa where we've had a weekend of preaching. Yesterday was Pentecost Sunday. We saw the power of God come down during that meeting. The facility was packed. There was not a single seat available; the people were sitting on the floor right up to the pulpit. There was a sense of expectancy burning like a fire amongst us. We could sense the Holy Spirit brooding over that place.

God did not disappoint us. Many people were filled with the Holy Spirit, speaking and singing in tongues. People were healed; people gave their lives to Jesus Christ for the first time ever. Just about everyone in that hall recommitted their lives to God, asking God to forgive them for a heart of unbelief.

How is it with you this morning, my dear friend? Are you dry, like the dry bones in the valley? Are you in a situation where you don't even want to read your Bible any more? The Lord has a message for you today. He says, "Dry bones, hear the Word of the Lord."

When you've finished today's reading, ask the Holy Spirit to fill you with His joy, His peace, His excitement, and His effervescence. Then read the Word, because the Word is Jesus Christ in print. He will quicken your mortal body. The Bible is very clear that the letter kills but the Spirit gives life. If there is no life in those dry bones, they cannot digest the Word. In order to digest the Word, we need to have the Holy Spirit in us.

As for me at the moment, I'm in love with the Lord all over again! You see, to be baptized by the Holy Spirit is not a one-off thing – it's receiving a continual top-up all the time. That's what's happened to me this weekend. As I shared the Word with the people in Rustenburg, the Lord topped me up. The Word came alive to me again today. The same thing can happen to you. Ask the Holy Spirit to put flesh onto those bones, an excitement in your heart, and then revisit the Word of God. Read it. He will feed you every day. That's why the Bible is called the Living Word.

It was so wonderful to see the young people weeping before God this past weekend, to see marriages restored by faith. A young couple who couldn't have a child came forward by faith. Like Abraham and Sarah, they are trusting God for a baby. It is the Holy Spirit who quickens people. A mother (and I'm talking faith when I say that) came forward, weeping, knowing that God is going to do something in her life.

Jesus is alive, I tell you. He's alive! Speak to Him, spend time with Him, share fellowship with Him, and He will direct your paths.

Childlike faith

Luke 18:16(b)

... for of such is the kingdom of God.

Do you remember this passage in the Bible telling of when parents brought their babies to Jesus for Him to lay His hands upon and bless them? Today we still dedicate children in a similar fashion into God's care until they are old enough to make a full commitment to Christ and to be born again. In today's reading the disciples saw that the Master was weary when the mothers brought their children to Him. They tried to turn the children away but He said to them, "Don't do this because unless you become as one of these little children, you'll never see the kingdom of God."

What God is saying is that He doesn't want us to become childish, but to have childlike faith. When my son was young, if I had said to him that the moon was made of cheddar cheese, he would have gone and told his science teacher, "My dad says that the moon is made of cheddar cheese." If the science teacher had replied that Neil Armstrong had walked on the moon, and that he said the moon is made of dust, my son have would responded, "I don't care what Neil Armstrong did or said, I'm telling you that my dad says that the moon is made of cheddar cheese and that's it."

That's childlike faith. That's how God wants you and me to be. That's why God used Smith Wigglesworth in such a powerful way. His favourite saying was, "God said it; I believe it and that settles it." If we have childlike faith today, not questioning God all the time but just believing what He tells us, then we too will have faith that can move mountains.

Although his wife was a wonderful Christian until the day she died, Charles Darwin questioned God and the Bible. He tried to prove that man descended from apes. Darwin was a very clever man but a miss is as good as a mile. To this day they cannot prove the direct link between the ape and man. There's still a gap that cannot be bridged and never will be, because we were not made as apes that evolved into men. According to the Bible, we were made in the image of God.

Today, let us be childlike. Let us take the Word literally, as it is written, and believe it, because "God is not a man, that he should lie" (Numbers 23:19).

Peace of God

John 14:27

Peace I leave with you.

May I ask you today whether the peace of God is ruling in your heart? What is happening inside your heart is what you are going to display to the world.

If ever the world needed peace, it is now. There is so much anger, so much hatred and so much war in the world today, that to see a man of peace is like seeing an oasis in a desert. This is truly one of the fruits of the Spirit. I trust that before you leave your home today to go into the world, you will calm your spirit and allow our Lord, Holy Spirit, to speak into your life, so that you may convey a spirit of peace wherever you go.

Many of us thump the table and demand that people be saved and come to Christ. That, if anything, chases people away from God. When you portray the peace of God in your life, you will draw people to you like a honey pot draws bees. It is totally and completely alluring. Your surroundings should not determine the attitude of your heart. You can find yourself in a hectic situation, but still be totally at peace.

I often speak of a *postina* – the Russian word for a little house built down in the bottom of the garden where the Russians go to have their quiet time – which I heard a preacher speak about many years ago. You can have that *postina* in your heart. Whether you're sitting in your office, are at home or on the farm, driving a big truck or flying an aeroplane, you can have that *postina*, that place of peace; a place where you can go and speak with God.

I'm not speaking about positive thinking. I'm not at all an advocate of positive thought. I am talking about the peace that is within the spirit of a man who knows God. You can go to that place at any time. I can actually describe my *postina* to you. It's a little path, leading through a forest to a wetland. There's a log on the side of the path. I sit on that log and can feel the peace of God in my heart. I can hear the doves singing in the trees and feel a gentle breeze blowing. There are ten- or twelve-foot tall reeds rustling in the wind. I allow the Holy Spirit to minister to me and I also speak to Him, not even audibly, just in my spirit-man and I am totally refreshed. That peace will come over me and then I go into the world and tell others about the Prince of Peace.

The lost

Luke 19:10

For the Son of man is come to seek and to save that which was lost.

For me, one of the most encouraging stories in the Bible is the story of Zacchaeus. Zacchaeus was a very wealthy sinner, a man who had made it to the top of his field in spite of being despised and hated by the people, especially the authorities. Yet, when Jesus came to town and saw Zacchaeus, He told him in front of everybody, "Hurry up and go home because I'm coming to stay at your house today." Can you imagine the uproar of the people? How could the Lord associate Himself with such a sinner? Nothing has changed through the ages. It is still happening to this day.

Zacchaeus was touched by God to such an extent that he did a 180-degree turnaround. He told the Lord he would give half of his goods to the poor and if he had taken anything from anybody, he would repay it to that person 400-fold.

When a man comes to Christ his life will start bearing fruit. Jesus says that we can judge a man by his fruit. There are some people who have been in the church all their lives and yet they've never come to the saving grace of Jesus Christ as Lord and Saviour. You can see it by their fruit. They do nothing for anyone. They're selfish, vain, and self-centred; they will not get involved in anything that does not benefit them directly. I've even seen that with some church leaders, especially in the realm of evangelism where I work. On various occasions I've asked men to come together to conquer a city for Jesus but sadly, if it did not benefit their particular fellowship or church, they backed out.

I remember booking the King's Park Rugby Stadium for a huge peace gathering that we held in 1997. It could hold over 50,000 people. Alan Kruger, the manager of the stadium, said to me at the time, "Do you realize this is going to cost you a fortune?"

I said, "Well, we have to do it, Alan."

At that stage Alan had not committed to Christ. We walked out onto the centre of this huge rugby field to where the kick-off takes place and looked around. I saw thousands and thousands of empty chairs and realized the magnitude of this step of faith. This man, who had yet to meet Christ, then said, "Do you have a sound system?"

I said, "No."

He said, "Well, we have one. We can help you with that. Do you have a security company?"

Again I said no.

He said, "We can help you with that too. Do you have a first aid company that you can employ?"

I replied, "No, we don't."

He said, "Well, we have one."

As we walked off the field, I said to him, "Alan, why are you doing this?"

He said, "Well, it's time for me to acknowledge what God has done for me."

Needless to say, on the final night of that huge campaign, Alan gave his life to Jesus and accepted Him as his personal Lord and Saviour on the 22-metre line of that rugby field. The Son of Man came to seek and to save that which was lost.

Correction

Job 5:17

Behold, happy is the man whom God correcteth: therefore despise not thou the chastening of the Almighty.

If you're going through a hard time at the moment, rejoice in your tribulation. The Bible says that tribulation produces patience; patience, experience; and experience, hope; and our hope is in Christ.

As long as the Lord is busy moulding you, it means that He still has time for you. The most dangerous season to be in is when you don't hear from God, when the heavens are quiet, your prayers bounce off the ceiling unanswered, and you don't feel the presence of God. You can be going through the most arduous trial of your life but if the Lord is still talking to you and correcting you, sorting you out, that's a healthy place to be. When everything goes quiet and you're not hearing from God, when He has as it were closed the door on you, then you're in severe trouble. That's not a good place to be.

I firmly believe that the Lord Jesus does not mind if sometimes we get angry or start complaining. I am sure that He understands if we, be it out of sheer frustration or maybe fear, demand answers from Him. He doesn't mind as long as we keep talking to Him. It's when we stop talking to Him and turn our backs on Him that His heart is sorely distraught.

You'll find that a child loves their parents most in times when they stand to be corrected by them. I've often seen how a child runs across the road to collect a ball that's been kicked out of the garden and a car swerves out at the last minute, nearly knocking the child down. The mother runs to her offspring and the first thing she does is give the child a good telling-off even though it was only an accident. The child has a good cry and the two of them hug each other before they go back into the garden. So it is in times of correction.

I remember a man once saying that the Lord is the Vinedresser and that He prunes back the vines He loves the most so they will produce more beautiful, sweeter grapes. But it's a painful thing, being pruned. This brother in Christ asked me, "How painful do you think it must be for God? Jesus has the pruning shears in His hands. Those are the hands that were nailed to the Cross. Even as He is pruning us, He's doing so with bleeding hands, with hands that have a hole through them where the spikes nailed them to the Cross. So it is even more painful for Him to prune us than it is for us to be pruned."

We rejoice that the Lord has not given up on us; that He is perfecting us to be that beautiful bride that He wants us to be on the day when He returns to take us back to be with Him.

Great faith must first endure great trials

Mark 5:36(b)

Be not afraid, only believe.

I've never heard of a man or woman of God who has not been subjected to fiery trials. George Müller was the man who started the huge children's homes in Bristol, England. A total of 121,000 children and £6,000,000 went through his hands without him ever having asked for a penny. He trusted God by faith. When asked how to have strong faith, the great preacher A. B. Simpson quotes him as saying, "The only way to learn strong faith is to endure great trials. I have learned my faith by standing firm amid severe testing." So, the greater the faith, the greater the test!

When we start the faith walk, there is no turning back. Remember, in God's economy, two plus two equals seven. Faith is what moves the hand of God. Without it, you cannot please God. You can't learn faith at Bible college, from a book, or even from other people. It has to be experienced. Romans 10:17 says that "faith comes by hearing, and hearing by the Word of God" (NKJV). That is so true.

People don't exercise faith if they don't need it. It's when you're out on the water like Peter, who cried out, "God help me!" He took his eyes off the Master and focused on his situation. That's when he started to sink. But the Lord saved him as he was sinking. How many of us are in the same situation today?

One thing I have experienced in my walk with the Lord Jesus Christ is that God always honours faith. Not presumption, but faith. We are in the process of booking, according to the internet, the biggest tent in the world. It is over two hectares in size. We are trusting and believing that 23,000 men will come to our small farm, Shalom, next year to hear the Word of God. This is a great step of faith for me.

Often, after God has blessed me and I've managed to do something by faith, I think, "Lord, that's enough now." But I had to realize that faith is not an event. Faith is a lifestyle. I must admit I'm getting more comfortable on the water now than sitting in the boat. I also understand that to have great faith I must first endure great trials.

God has a habit of choosing the weak, the nobodies, the so-called dropouts of this world to do His bidding for Him. I'm convinced that the reason for this is that He doesn't want anybody to share in His glory. It's by faith that we, like William Carey, the humble cobbler from England who changed the face of India for ever, set out again to "attempt great things for God and expect great things from God".

Mark 11:22 says, "Have faith in God." If you're going through a time of tribulation and things are hard for you, you can rest assured that the Lord is using it to strengthen your faith. The greatest times in my spiritual life have always been when I needed God the most. The good news is He has never, ever let me down, not even once. He won't let you down either, if you walk by faith.

Iron

Proverbs 27:17

Iron sharpeneth iron; so a man sharpeneth the countenance of his friend.

A young man came to visit me a couple of months ago. He set out on the two-hour drive from the coast with his wife and two beautiful children, only to arrive at the service when it was already finished. When I asked him if I could help, he said that he wanted to give his life to Jesus. Right there and then together with all the leaders of the church, including our pastor and his wife, we prayed the sinner's prayer. We gave him a few of our books and a movie that was made about us. With that, he left. He's a helicopter pilot. He spends a couple of months away from home and then a couple of months at home.

The Bible says, "Iron sharpens iron." This young man has just written me an email from Nigeria that has set my soul soaring. He told me that he's telling other people about Jesus. Although he hasn't even read the Bible yet, there's such a passion and a love for the lost in his heart since Jesus saved him that he can't restrain himself. He has a friend who comes from Peru, South America; the other side of the world. He started talking to him about Christ. By the sound of it, this man is coming through for the Lord now. He says he praises God every day because the Lord has given him new life and a new reason for living.

Peter Böhler (1712–75) was one of the early Moravians. He told John Wesley, one of the greatest modern-day evangelists who ever lived, to "preach faith until you have it, and then you'll preach faith". Faith is contagious. Jesus is contagious. As this young man is speaking to others about Christ, Christ is becoming more of a reality to him. As he has written to me, I can share with you this morning that this young man, literally a babe in Christ, has encouraged me in an incredible way to keep on preaching the gospel for Jesus Christ.

Go out today and sharpen another brother in Christ by telling him about the wonderful things that God has done for you.

Everywhere

Mark 16:20

And they went forth, and preached every where.

I've just read a wonderful letter from a group of young men who went to preach the gospel of Jesus Christ to groups of people in Central Africa who could not have been reached before.

On their way there, everything that they could possibly think of went wrong. The trailer that they used to carry their diesel and fresh water supplies, as well as their PA system, collapsed twice, as the stub axles sheared off.

They felt as if the devil was trying to discourage them. However, they carried on. While driving at 3.30 in the morning, the right wheel of the trailer came off and disappeared into the black African bushes. They couldn't find it and slept the rest of the night in the pickup. When daylight came they searched and found it. God undertook for them.

It reminds me of the disciples when Jesus told them to go across to the other side of Lake Galilee. They encountered a terrible storm on the way but that didn't sidetrack them. It actually strengthened their faith. The Lord didn't desert them or allow their boat to sink in the middle of the lake. They got to the other side.

These young men reached their destination and I was told that their trip was a resounding success, with over 4,000 people attending their meetings in the dusty marketplaces of western Zambia. They told me that every night hundreds and hundreds of people – over a thousand in total – gave their lives to the Lord. We thank God for these young men. They came to our conference and told me that they were fired up to get out there and spread the Word of God. As we sow good seed, we see that it doesn't cost, it pays! Just keep sowing good seed. What is that seed? It is the Word of God.

Man's chief end

Philippians 3:10(a)

That I may know him…

In A. W. Tozer's book *The Pursuit of God* – one of the all-time modern classics that I recommend to all my readers – the question is asked, "What is the chief end of man?" The answer is, "Man's chief end is to glorify God and enjoy Him forever." Isn't that beautiful? In Revelation 4:11, the four-and-twenty elders worship the Lord in heaven and take pleasure in worshipping Him day and night.

Today the question we need to ask ourselves is whether we are glorifying the Lord Jesus Christ through our lifestyle. If not, we need to adjust our lifestyle – today still. Are we good examples? Are we good ambassadors for Him? When we walk down the main street in town, do people know that we represent God? I know that not one of us reading this book today is without sin, but that does not give us a licence to carry on living a life which does not bring glory to Jesus Christ. The Bible tells us that we need to mend our ways. Indeed, we need to glorify God and enjoy Him forever.

Are you enjoying God? In this season of my life I am enjoying God like never before. Yesterday I had the privilege of watching a DVD of the men's conference that we recently had on the farm. To sit there and see God's glory portrayed through men giving their lives to Jesus, men fellowshipping, men getting baptized (there were 7,400 men in all), was something I'll never forget as long as I live.

A man called André managed to capture in a photograph a supernatural event that took place outside the huge 5,000-seater tent that I didn't see at the time because I was preaching inside. It was a rainbow, but a rainbow that was ascending straight into heaven as it were, into a golden mushroom-shaped cloud, with the sun shining from behind it. When I looked at the photograph, it was as if I was seeing God in Person.

Yes, indeed, I was – and am – enjoying Him immensely. He is more real to me now than He has ever been since the day I met Him. The more I see Him working supernaturally, not only in my own life but in the lives of others, the more I realize that my Redeemer lives. If I know that He lives, I can enjoy Him irrespective of what is happening around me. Those mountains automatically become mere molehills as I focus on glorifying my God and enjoying Him.

As you go out today, focus on the goodness of God in your life and you will start to enjoy Him as you have never enjoyed Him before.

The veil

Matthew 27:51

And behold, the veil of the temple was rent in twain from the top to the bottom…

In his book *The Pursuit of God*, A. W. Tozer says, "This veil was not a beautiful thing. It's not a thing about which we commonly care to talk. This veil is the partition which kept man from the Holy of Holies."

While reading this book, God really opened my eyes. Tozer says that the veil wasn't woven with fine threads, but it was rather woven with "self-sins": sins of self-righteousness, self-pity, self-confidence, self-sufficiency, self-admiration, self-love, and many others. He says that things like egotism, exhibitionism, and self-promotion are commonly found among Christian leaders. These are the things we need to deal with so that the veil may be torn in two and we may enter into the Holy of Holies and enjoy very close fellowship with Jesus Christ.

My friend, what kind of veil is keeping you from the Lord today? This book is committed to speaking about issues of faith. Faith cannot operate in a life full of sin. The only way that we can get faith is by walking with God. He gives us that faith.

Even as I'm writing this reading, I'm convinced that I have to deal with issues of sin in my life, the main one being self-centredness. If I deal with that, God will give me the ability to understand His Word and grow in faith.

These are not issues we can deal with ourselves. We cannot do a course or go to a college and learn about tearing away this veil that keeps us from Jesus. It comes solely by crucifying it at the Cross of Calvary. We need to deal with sin as the Holy Spirit reveals it to us, put it behind us and press on.

But be of good cheer today. He who is faithful has promised us that He will do it for us – if we will allow Him to. Just open your heart today and say, "Lord Jesus, deal with these terrible habits and attitudes in my life, so that I may walk into the Holy of Holies with You."

God bless you today as you go and face the day in the power of God's Holy Spirit.

14 April

Use it or lose it

Luke 19:13(b)

Occupy till I come.

One of the sports that I used to play as a young man, and still enjoy watching, is rugby. We watched a beautiful game on Saturday when the English team played the South African team. It was a very engaging and exciting game to watch, both sides giving their full 100 per cent effort. When I played, we used to tussle and wrestle for ages when there was a loose scrum. However, the new rule is that you only have a few seconds to get the ball out and feed it back to your team, otherwise you lose possession and the ball goes to the opposing team.

This morning, when reading the parable that Jesus told about the talents, the Lord reminded me once again of the immense responsibility you and I have to use whatever we might possess, to the glory of God. In the parable, the Lord gave each of His ten servants some money. When He came back, the first servant said that his coin had gained another ten coins. The Master said, "You've done well!" and gave him authority over ten cities. The next servant said that his coin had earned five, and he was given five cities. Unfortunately, the third servant was fearful to use what he had and kept it hidden away in a handkerchief. The Master said, "Why didn't you rather put it in the bank, where you could have earned a bit of interest? You're a wicked man!" and He took the coin that He had given the third servant and gave it to the man who already had ten.

I had a discussion some time ago with the Lord about this parable and speaking even as a Christian I said, "Lord, I think that was a bit unfair; You gave the one man so much while the other lost everything!" What the Lord was saying is that if you don't use the talent that He's given you – whether it be music, preaching, making money for the kingdom, taking care of people, or whichever other talent He has given you – God will take even that which you have and give it to someone else.

As we go out today, let us not be like the foolish servant who lost everything he had, but let us rather work hard. We know that if we use what we have for the Lord, He will increase our gifting, our abilities, and indeed our finances, so that we can be a blessing to the people in this world.

Try tears

John 11:35

Jesus wept.

General William Booth (1829–1912), a huge man with a beard and hooked nose, father of the Salvation Army, was a general in more ways than one. He was one of the old-school Englishmen; a great evangelist, one of Wesley's protégés and originally one of the Methodists' strongmen.

He was a man who disciplined himself physically, spiritually, and mentally. The story goes that every single morning of his life, he had an ice-cold bath when he got up in order to bring the flesh in line with the will of God. That is quite something to do during the winter in England, let me tell you!

To this day the Salvation Army is still the biggest army in the whole world. No army has ever had more soldiers than the Salvation Army.

William Booth sent out some of his best soldiers, many of whom were women, to far-flung heathen places. After a season they wrote to him very despondently, saying that they were having no success with preaching the gospel. He promptly wrote back a letter that contained just two words, "Try tears."

Needless to say, many souls were won for the Lord after that. The moral of the story is: Be Jesus to people, rather than speaking about Him to them.

Get on board

John 3:7

Ye must be born again.

There is a song that says, "Get on board for this is the last train to heaven." As mentioned previously, we often use an old cliché at Shalom, stating that good people don't go to heaven – *believers* go to heaven. We need to be ready in and out of season for the Lord to call us home, for time is definitely running out. The Lord is asking you and me today, "Do you have a ticket to board the last train to heaven?"

What is that ticket? Is it paying your tithe? Going to church regularly? Going to Bible study? Having regular quiet times? Taking care of the needy and the poor? Yes, it includes all of those things, but they won't get us into heaven. The only thing, ultimately, that will get us to heaven is knowing Jesus Christ as our personal Lord and Saviour.

I officiated at a funeral many years ago when a dear friend of mine was killed during a shoot-out in an army barracks. He was a wonderful man of God, full of excitement, fire, and the Holy Spirit. He got into an argument with another soldier who subsequently shot and killed him. I will never forget the Scripture that was delivered at his funeral. In it the Lord says, "I have no pleasure in the death of one who dies. Therefore turn [repent] and live!" (Ezekiel 18:32). When I asked the Holy Spirit to reveal to me what God meant, I understood Him to mean that God has no pleasure in the death of an unbeliever because he's on his way to hell. The Lord says to you and me today, "Get on board, make sure that you have the ticket." That ticket is the acknowledgment of Jesus Christ as your personal Lord and Saviour.

At the funeral I had a clear picture of a Victorian station somewhere in England, maybe King's Cross Station, with those huge girders and the see-through glass at the top. A big steam engine was approaching pulling many carriages behind it. People were hanging out of the windows of the train, looking to see if their loved ones were on the platform to meet them. The people on the platform were standing on their toes, looking to see if they could spot their loved ones on the train.

I believe that that is how it's going to be when we go home to heaven. The steam engine with white steam billowing from its chimney and wheels clattering on the tracks as it pulls into the station will be like the train that carries us to heaven. Our loved ones, those Christians who have gone before us, will be standing on the platform, looking to see if we're on that train.

My dear friend, we need to be on that train. The only way to do that is to make sure that we own a ticket. And a ticket can only be obtained through the knowledge that Jesus Christ is our Lord and Saviour and by having a personal relationship with Him.

Anything

John 14:14

If ye shall ask anything in my name, I will do it.

I've just been on the telephone with a very dear old friend who, at the age of seventy-six, is still regarded as one of South Africa's greatest sportsmen. He hurt his back and he's in pain. He phoned me and asked me to agree with him in faith that God would heal him so he could carry on preaching. That's what we've just done together. I believe by faith for a good report.

Many years ago a lady came to me from a good church – a church that cared for people, a church that had cake sales, that took care of the old and the needy, took care of its congregation, and preached the gospel every week, but did not believe in divine healing. This lady came to me, having already had three hip replacements. The specialist had said that there was no bone left to do a fourth one. She hobbled down the pathway on crutches and came to sit in my office. I asked her, as I always do, in the words of Jesus, "What do you want the Lord to do for you?"

She said, "I want Jesus to heal me."

I said, "Well, I'll stand with you on that one, because it's scriptural. Look at John 14:15. The Lord says, 'If you love Me, keep My commandments.' If you keep His commandments and you walk in the ways of the Lord, then you're going to ask in the correct manner and the Lord's going to answer you." We anointed her with oil, prayed the prayer of faith, and believed God for healing.

When I said "Amen," she said, "Thank you so much."

Her face lit up and then she started weeping. I asked why she was crying. She replied, "You know, the people at the church that I go to are such loving people, such genuine people, such caring people, but Angus, they will not believe with me for a divine miracle. Thank you for just agreeing with me." That was almost more important to her than the actual miracle.

My dear friend, the Lord Jesus says, "Anything…" and He means it! If we don't ask Him, we can't receive. Jesus asked the blind man Bartimaeus, "What do you want Me to do for you?" You and I would have thought, "Lord, why ask a question like that? You are God, You know everything." A blind man was standing in front of Him! He said, "Oh Lord, that I might receive my sight," and the Bible says he was healed immediately. Jesus said, "your faith has made you well" (Mark 10:46–52, NKJV).

Ask Him today. Ask Him! Get on your knees and ask Him and believe for that miracle. Then get hold of other people who will agree with you, and stand together in unison and believe God to answer that prayer so that you can give Jesus Christ all the glory. He is the same yesterday, today, and forever (Hebrews 13:8).

I have never yet met a person who has refused prayer. When I go to hospitals and ask people if I may pray, they say, "Please pray." A sick person will never refuse prayer, and God always answers prayer.

Bless you as you go out as His ambassador today.

The family

Joshua 24:15(b)

... but as for me and my house, we will serve the Lord.

Richard Baxter, the seventeenth-century English Puritan and theologian said, "Holy families must be the chief preservers of the interest of religion in the world."

Many years ago South Africa waged war against Angola. The Angolans brought in Cuban troops to fight against the South African forces. The young South African soldiers came home saying that the Cuban army had no power and indeed possessed a poor fighting spirit. They were ineffective against the power of the South African army. The problem was that the Cubans were not fighting for their families. Their families were back in Cuba. They were fighting in a foreign country in which they didn't have any real interest – they were merely sent there by their country.

But try to fight the Cubans in Cuba and it's another story. John F. Kennedy tried to do that. He pitted the might of the American forces against Cuba at the Bay of Pigs and they were repelled by Fidel Castro and the Cubans. Why? Because the Cubans were defending their families!

Strong families make a strong country. Charles Colson, the man who was the personal representative for President Richard Nixon and who went to jail for the president (but praise God, he got saved in jail), said, "No other structure can replace the family."

The devil is trying very hard to destroy families. You've heard the saying: "We bar up the front door and the devil walks in through the back door". The breaking up of families, an increasing divorce rate, sex before marriage, no loyalty or respect shown between parents and children are the order of the day. The elderly are simply abandoned at a care home and forgotten about. That's not how a family is supposed to function.

There's a saying: "The family that prays together stays together". If ever we needed to preserve the family, it's now. We need, by faith, to trust God every day for our families. The hardest place to be a Christian is at home because your family really knows who you are.

It says in Mark 8:36, "What will it profit a man if he gains the whole world, and loses his own soul?" (NKJV). What does it profit a man if he gains the whole world and he loses his family? Let us re-evaluate our standing today and see how things are with our family.

I remember as a young man, when I went to work on the eastern side of

Australia, I chose to stay in the home of one of the poorest families in town. The man of the house worked on the roads, his wife was a waitress in a café, and they had four or five children. They were battling to make ends meet and had to take in a lodger. I didn't have to stay there. I had taken some money with me from Africa and could have stayed in the local hotel. But I was loved and accepted by this family and truly experienced their warmth. That prevented me from becoming as homesick as I would have been if I'd stayed in a hotel and had my independence and my own room.

I slept in a room with a three-levelled bunk bed. One little boy slept on the top bunk, his brother on the bottom bunk and I slept on the middle one, but it was so good to be able to come home after a hard day's work riding horses and to have the family all sitting there, doing their homework. The food wasn't the greatest but the love was wonderful!

Hymn-writer John Bowring (1792–1872) said that a happy family is but an earlier heaven. Whatever you do, don't sacrifice your family, not even for your ministry. It's not worth it. Spend time today with that precious family of yours and remember it's never, ever too late to start all over again.

God bless you as you invest in your own family.

Overcomers

1 John 5:4(a)

For whatsoever is born of God overcometh the world…

I returned late last night from Mossel Bay, situated in the south-eastern part of the Cape. I was summoned by a family of sheep farmers. The husband is a new Christian who gave his life to the Lord at our men's conference about two months ago. He was on fire for the Lord.

A freak accident happened. His teenage twin sons were playing with friends and a rock was thrown, supposedly to be caught. It hit one of the twins against the head. He was in hospital on a life-support machine.

As that little private aircraft touched ground and I saw the desperate family standing there, I felt totally inadequate and without words. We embraced, were swept off to the hospital in the farmer's car and found that his wife's mother and father, sisters, nephews, nieces – the whole family – were there. We had a time of prayer in the outer room and asked the Lord to undertake for this young seventeen-year-old who had been certified brain-dead. We put on masks, washed our hands, and walked to his bedside in the ICU. I had a small bottle of oil and my Bible with me. It was then that I realized that the only people who can overcome are those who have faith and who believe that Jesus is the Son of God. I anointed the young man in the name of the Father, the Son, and the Holy Spirit and prayed a prayer of faith over him. I am by faith believing for a good report. When we left, there was much hugging and shaking of hands, "God bless," and, "Keep on keeping on."

Postscript: God took the young man home a week later. He is now perfectly restored and healed. Through this ordeal his twin brother came to Christ and, at the time of my writing, there is a mini-revival taking place at his school. Jesus said, "Unless a grain of wheat falls into the earth and dies, it remains… by itself alone. But if it dies, it produces many others and yields a rich harvest" (John 12:24, AMP).

I just know – the Lord has shown me again – that without faith we cannot finish this race. The only people who can overcome this world are those who choose to walk by faith and not by sight (2 Corinthians 5:7).

The Son of God

1 John 5:5

Who is he that overcometh the world, but he that believeth that Jesus is the Son of God?

Something I find very sad is to see how people almost try to explain away the miraculous conception of our Lord and Saviour and the miraculous birth in that stable in Nazareth 2,000 years ago. Every time we try to rationalize a miracle we take away the power of God to set us free.

I recently watched a programme on the National Geographic channel on television. I have no doubt that it was a quasi-Christian programme. What really saddened my heart was their attempt to explain every single miracle in the Old Testament to be a natural phenomenon: the walls of Jericho could have fallen down because of an earthquake; the River Jordan became dry for Joshua and the Israelites to walk through because of an avalanche which took place upstream and blocked the river. The parting of the Red Sea was also downplayed instead of accepting it as an act of God.

I have heard people saying that at a certain time of the year you can walk across the Red Sea in water that is ankle-deep. That means that the miracle of Moses and the Israelites crossing the sea was even greater than we had thought, because Pharaoh's whole army must then have drowned in ankle-deep water! That's kind of a joke and that's the way I would like us to treat these things.

If we do not believe that Jesus Christ is God made flesh then we have nothing to believe in. Many people talk about Jesus being the Son of God but Jesus is God made flesh. Remember, Jesus said, "If you've seen Me, you've seen My Father," and His Holy Spirit dwells in us even today. In all my life I have never been as sure of this one fact as I am now during these latter years of my life. I can honestly tell you that I know that my Redeemer lives (Job 19:25). That same verse goes on to say, "and that he shall stand at the latter day upon the earth". He is coming back in all His glory. Who is he that overcometh the world? Only he who believes that Jesus is the Son of God!

Whatever you do today, I encourage you to stop questioning God and start believing Him. Every other point of view and every other system in this world has given you cause for doubt, but Jesus never has. Believe that Jesus Christ is the Son of God and you will have life in abundance (John 10:10).

The temple of God

1 Corinthians 3:16(a)

Know ye not that ye are the temple of God... ?

I've been reading the book of Ezekiel in my quiet time. At the moment I'm reading chapters 38 and 39, where Ezekiel describes the holy Temple of God; its specifications, size, length, width, height, and depth. The Lord has impressed upon my heart that, because of the Holy Spirit who dwells in me, that Temple is no longer necessary or relevant. However, one thing that I have learned is that our God cannot dwell in a dirty place, because He is a holy God.

How does your temple look? Is it clean? Is it a fitting place for the Holy Spirit to dwell in? The Bible is very clear about the fact that we cannot serve two masters. Matthew 12:30 says, "He that is not with me is against me; and he that gathereth not with me scattereth abroad."

I often have people come to me and say, "But I don't hear from God. I feel so far from God. I feel as if my prayers are bouncing back from the ceiling. I don't feel the presence of God in my life." Maybe you need to search your life and see what your temple looks like. It's not a one-off thing; it's an ongoing exercise. What kind of thoughts do you entertain, what kind of books do you read? Will God find them acceptable? What type of programmes do you watch on TV? Are they pleasing to God?

Are you looking after your physical body? The food you eat: are you eating too much or too little? Are you exercising properly? All these things add up to keep the temple of the Holy Spirit clean and pure.

Your quiet times: do you spend time with God every day before you start or finish work? Don't say you don't have the time; you can't afford not to have the time. Get your mind and your spirit-man in tune with God before you go out and face the day. Then you can rest assured that the Holy Spirit will go with you.

John G. Lake, a great evangelist who came out to South Africa and started a huge revival, used to look in a mirror every day before he went to work and say, "God lives in that man and wherever that man goes today, God's going with him." Then only did he go out – and it's not a coincidence that the Lord used him to perform many signs, wonders, and miracles while he was walking on this earth.

Today, before you go out, make sure that you sweep your temple; that there's no dirt or filth that would prevent our Lord from coming and living in it. Watch the words of your mouth. Watch how you speak and what you say. The Bible says, "In the multitude of words sin is not lacking, But he who restrains his lips is wise" (Proverbs 10:19, NKJV). These are the fruits that come out of the man in whose temple the Holy Spirit is living. When he speaks, he speaks life and joy.

Wherever Jesus went on the earth He drew people to Him; multitudes followed Him. If you have no friends, if you have no one who is prepared to listen to you, maybe you need to have a good look at that temple of yours and see who is actually living there.

Come before the Lord this morning and rededicate your temple into His hands. Then go out and face the day, knowing that if Christ is for you, there is no one that can stand against you (Romans 8:31).

Humility

Acts 20:19(a)

Serving the Lord with all humility of mind...

There's nothing more beautiful than to see how God makes use of a humble man. James Hudson Taylor, who took Christianity to China and started the China Inland Mission, was just such a man. By the way, the greatest revival that the world has ever known is taking place in mainland China right at this moment. There are hundreds of thousands of house churches founded every single day in China, the most populated country on earth.

Hudson Taylor, the intrepid young missionary, sailed all the way back to England and was sitting in someone's house attending a Bible study one night when a reporter arrived from America. The reporter wanted to do a story on this young Englishman who was recruiting a thousand missionaries by faith and sending them out to China, not to stay in the compounds on the shore side of the coastal cities, but rather to go right into the heart of China where the gospel of Jesus Christ had never been heard before.

The reporter wanted to scoop a story about this incredible person. He walked into the room, was introduced to everybody and looked around to see this dynamic man. I don't know what he expected to find but I suppose he expected to see a well-dressed, charismatic person. He was so disappointed because he saw a small, timid-looking man, very pasty in colour and dressed in a huge dark overcoat, sitting in the corner and hardly saying a word.

When the Bible study commenced, the reporter probably thought, "Well, now great eloquence of speech is going to come from this man's mouth." The man never said a word. Towards the end of the evening the reporter was beginning to wonder why he'd even come, because he had no story to write.

Ah, but my friend, things changed when, right at the end of the meeting, the people said, "We're going to have a time of open prayer before we close." Then, the reporter said, the room came alive because this young English missionary from China started to speak to his God. He said it was as if the room fizzled with electricity. He'd never, ever heard a man talk with God like James Hudson Taylor did. His prayer was so powerful that there was no movement in that room until he'd finished praying. Then the reporter knew why he had come there: to observe a humble man who had a powerful relationship with God!

Another humble man of God was William Duma (1907–77), a Zulu Baptist preacher who pastored a Baptist church in Umgeni Road, Durban. He was used in a very powerful way by God, especially in the area of healing. The story goes that he was invited to Central Africa to preach at a Baptist church. The conventional Baptist churches have their entrance at the back of the church and the preacher enters the church after everybody is seated, then walks up the aisle to the pulpit. Everybody stands up as a token of respect and good manners. The guest preacher is introduced by the pastor, and then the service commences.

On the day of Duma's visit, the congregation waited and waited. The service was supposed to commence at nine. Nine o'clock came and the guest preacher from South Africa, this well-known, internationally renowned man of God, just didn't make his appearance. He was late. Ten past nine came and still nobody had arrived. Everybody was turning around in their seats, looking towards the entrance at the back of the church building to see whether this man of God was indeed going to arrive. Just then the pastor, who was waiting to give Duma a royal welcome up at the front of the church, heard a little tapping at the door in the vestry. That's the door where the cleaning lady comes in to wash all the communion glasses, to sweep out the pastor's office and to do some general cleaning on a Monday morning. He went to the door and there was the man of God standing at the servants' entrance. Needless to say, he preached up a storm in church that day! God resists the proud but gives grace to the humble (1 Peter 5:5).

One thing I've learned in my life is that when we humble ourselves God will exalt us. In fact, He warns us to always seek the lowest chair when we are invited to someone's house. Rather let the owner of the house invite you to sit on a higher place, before you go and sit there and he has to ask you to move because there's someone much more important than you coming. That can be very humiliating!

Smith Wigglesworth, preacher and man of great faith who was used by God to do many miracles, signs, and wonders, said, "The way to get up is to get down." We read in 1 Peter 5:6, "Humble yourselves therefore under the mighty hand of God, that he may exalt you in due time."

Pleasing God

Genesis 5:22(a)

And Enoch walked with God.

Enoch walked with God and pleased Him. As a result God took him home with Him to heaven. Enoch never died of sickness, disease, or even old age. God just took him straight home.

Do you have a desire today, my dear friend, to please God? Our chief end in this world is to glorify God and to enjoy Him forever. Are you enjoying God today? If you are enjoying spending time with Him then you will please God because you will walk with Him. That's what He wants to do with you. He wants to talk with you; He wants to spend time with you, to love you. He wants you to love Him. He wants to have fellowship with you. The main purpose of man's existence on this earth is to glorify God and to have fellowship with Him. That's what Enoch did.

In today's Christian walk there is so much emphasis on programmes, results, conferences, reading the latest book, watching the latest DVD, listening to the latest CD. But how much time do we spend walking with God? When was the last time you put on your hat, took your walking stick, called your dogs, or got onto your horse and went off to have a good heart-to-heart discussion with God?

Although only a young boy at the time, King David was used to destroy Goliath, the enemy of God's people. He did this quite easily because he spent time with God every day while he was looking after his father's sheep. When you walk with someone you become like that person. David communed with God and he had fellowship with Him; he knew who he was in God. So, when he went down to take lunch to his brothers who were fighting the battle against the Philistines and saw this blaspheming giant walking up and down the valley, challenging any man to come and fight him, he had no hesitation in telling King Saul, "Let me deal with this uncircumcised Philistine." We know the story; with one stone he felled that gigantic professional soldier like a good forester fells a tree with a sharp axe.

Who is your enemy? What is the Goliath in your life that you are struggling to defeat today? Can you pray with me: "Master, I desire to please You and the only way I can really please You today is to walk by faith. So, like the disciples of old (Luke 17:5), I would say, 'Lord, please today increase my faith.' Amen"?

Turn that mountain into a molehill

Hebrews 11:33(a)

Who through faith subdued kingdoms…

In Hebrews 11 you'll see that through faith the great men of God stopped the mouths of lions, obtained promises from God, and wrought righteousness. They subdued kingdoms, quenched violence, and escaped the edge of the sword. They were transformed from weaklings into strong men. They turned armies of aliens to flight. All through faith!

How do we get faith? Faith comes by hearing and hearing by the Word of God (Romans 10:17). Today, we need to stop making plans. There is an old South African farmer's cliché: "`n Boer maak `n plan" (a farmer always makes a plan). I've been farming for over forty years and not one of my plans has ever worked. We need to stop making our own plans today and start walking by faith. The same God, the same Jesus who enabled the saints of old to subdue whole kingdoms, will give you and me the faith to make the right plan, to undertake for our financial problems, to undertake for the health problems of our families, to undertake in the area of the political problems of our nation, to take care of our personal problems.

Faith is not a feeling. It is a fact. As you take the Word of God and apply it to your daily situation, that mountain looming over your life will be reduced to a mere molehill. I really believe that in these last days God is going to pour out His Holy Spirit in such a way that great men of faith will be raised up to conquer the kingdoms of darkness in order to glorify His Son Jesus Christ.

I've found that the safest place for me to be is out of my boat, walking on the water. Although we can't actually see it, that boat which we're clinging to with all of our might, the material, worldly thing, is in reality full of woodborer and is in fact sinking. The safest place to be is out on the water, walking the walk of faith and saying, "Lord, I cast all my cares upon You, because You care for me" (1 Peter 5:7).

All of a sudden you'll start seeing life through different eyes. You will not evaluate your life on the grounds of your circumstances any more but on the grounds of God's promises. This will strengthen your mortal body and you'll start attempting things that you've never, ever thought of before and expecting things that you've never seen before. Remember William Carey, that great missionary to India, whose favourite saying was, "Attempt great things for God and expect great things from God." Not because of his own ability, but because of his faith in God, he brought Christianity to India like no other man had ever done before.

Today go out in faith and put your trust not in yourself or your own abilities, but in Jesus Christ, the faithful One.

Hope

Romans 8:25

But if we hope for what we see not, then do we with patience wait for it.

My wife Jill will tell you that one of the virtues I battle most to acquire is patience. I'm an impatient person by nature. I'm impulsive. If we have to do something it must be done today, immediately. I'm sure I'm not alone in that. Actually though, if we are going to walk the walk of faith, we need to become patient people. You know the old saying: "Rome was not built in a day". I've studied many great men and women of God who were used by God in the area of faith and have found each one of them to be patient people.

When we are trusting God for something, He will give it to us in His time, not ours. We cannot demand anything from God. We cannot command the Holy Spirit to come down during a meeting. It's very offensive to me and I know to my wife as well, when we hear a speaker command the Holy Spirit to "Come now!". God is God and we are mere mortals. We can beseech the Lord, yes. We can ask the Lord, because we must; that's what Jesus said in Matthew 7:7, "Ask, and it will be given to you" (NKJV), but we cannot demand anything from God. We pray the prayer of faith, we believe God to do it and then we leave it in His hands because His timing is always perfect. We wait patiently.

That's why Abraham was regarded as the friend of God. He had patience. He waited almost a hundred years for an answer to a prayer. Some of us cannot even wait a hundred minutes! Then God gave him His promise – that he would have more sons than the stars in the sky, more than the grains of sand on the seashore. But he had to have patience and wait.

If farming has taught me one thing, it's patience. The farmer plants his field with his cereal crop and then he has to wait for the crop to germinate; he has to wait and be patient for the rain to come. Then he has to be patient for the crop to ripen; finally he has to be patient while harvesting that crop. Many times in my life, especially during years of drought, a crop that people thought to be an absolute disaster yielded a better return than a bumper crop because the price of the product had shot through the roof.

Today, as your hope remains in Jesus Christ and you go out to face the world, remember that He asks of you to be patient, so He can fulfil the promise that He's made you and the promise that you are hoping in. Faith requires patience.

The power of the spoken word

John 1:1

In the beginning was the Word, and the Word was with God, and the Word was God.

As you go out to do your daily rounds, be very conscious and careful of what you say. You've heard the old saying: "What you see is what you get", but I would like to introduce you to a new one – "What you say is what you get."

I recently undertook a five-hour trip in a light aircraft, which I must say was quite testing and trying. We flew almost two-thirds of the length of South Africa. Before the flight, as I got to the little airport right next to our farm and asked permission for the plane to land in order that I should be collected to go and tend to an emergency, a pilot came over and said to me that he had heard that there were terrible winds blowing down in the Cape. I'd heard nothing to that regard. Those words brought a murmur of unbelief and fear into my heart. I dispelled it immediately and said, "Well, it's an emergency. We have to go." He promptly replied, "No, no, obviously you must go. I just heard that it was going to be difficult." It wasn't at all, actually. It was a long trip but very pleasant. Be careful what comes out of your mouth. There's tremendous power in the spoken word. Father God spoke the Word and this universe came into being.

I've done a bit of long-distance running in my life. When you're running a standard marathon and you reach the 30-, 35- or 40-kilometre mark, in other words coming towards the end of the race (the race is 42.2 kilometres long), and someone standing at the side of the road shouts, "You're looking good; keep it up!" you have no idea what those words do for you.

I remember running one day with a young man who was about to become my son-in-law. He's a very fit young man. We'd already done about 25 km and were running up a hill. As we were reaching the crest of the hill, there were two ladies manning a watering point at the top. Tongue-in-cheek the one lady said to the other, "Well, there are two men running up the hill. The one looks fine…" In other words, the other one, me, looked half dead. Do you know what a devastating effect that kind of comment can have – even if it is made in jest?

At one stage The Carpenters, a brother and sister singing duo, took the world by storm. Their music was refreshing and very encouraging; they were the biggest-selling secular singing duo in the world. Their voices could be heard in just about every hotel, every airport, and every public place. However, just before her thirty-third birthday, Karen Carpenter died of a heart attack, the result of years of struggling with anorexia. The eating disorder had taken such a toll on her body that, when trying to cope with her hectic schedule, she died. The tragedy is that apparently someone had once said to her while she was on stage that she looked a little chubby. Those words started the eating disorder that later cost her her life. The power of the spoken word…

I would encourage all parents this morning to, in return, encourage their children. It doesn't matter what your children are going through; see them through God's eyes. Believe for that miracle. Believe for that turnaround. Believe for their salvation. Start speaking life over that husband or wife of yours who's so down at the moment. Start seeing them as God does and you'll find that suddenly the whole situation will turn.

I remember a businessman once telling me that he never backs a horse, he always backs the jockey. That means that he trusts people and sees the best in them. When he decides to buy a business, he doesn't base his decision on the turnover or appearance of the business; he bases his decision on the strength of the men and women, the employees of that business. He trusts people and not situations or circumstances.

Start speaking God's Word by faith over your situation and you'll see an incredible difference. In his book *The Pursuit of God*, A. W. Tozer says that "in the beginning God spoke to nothing and it became something. Chaos heard it and became order; darkness heard it and became light." He quotes Genesis 1:9, "God said it and it was so." God's Word in your mouth, spoken by faith, will accomplish the same thing. Be encouraged and go in faith today. Watch what you say.

The gaze of the soul

Psalm 46:10

Be still, and know that I am God.

In *The Pursuit of God* A. W. Tozer talks about being still and hearing the voice of God. When the Israelites were murmuring against God in the desert, He sent a multitude of snakes to bite them and as a result, many of the people died. When they repented, the Lord told Moses to make a bronze snake (which is still the emblem of the medical profession today) and put it on a pole. God told him that whenever the people got bitten by a snake, they would not die if they gazed upon that emblem (Numbers 21:8).

Faith comes by hearing, and hearing by the Word of God. We need to start spending time reading God's Word and meditating on His Word – something that is foreign to many Christians today. Meditation is not an Eastern religion. It's not something from another religion. To meditate is very important; to meditate on the goodness of God, the power of God, the greatness of God, the love of God, and the forgiveness of God is wholesome for the spiritual man and woman. If we want our faith to grow we need to repeatedly gaze God-ward. We have to continue washing ourselves with the promises and the reassurances of God. This automatically increases our faith and enables us to perform great feats for Jesus Christ.

Are you gazing upon God today? Tozer says that when we are gazing God-ward and inward, we will be ushered into a new level of spiritual life that will be more in keeping with the promises of God and the mood of the New Testament. What he is saying is that where you spend your time, and who you spend your time with, is who or what you will become like. If you spend an hour every day reading about all the bad news of this world in the newspaper, be prepared to become depressed, stressed out, melancholic, fearful, and weak. However, if you spend time gazing upon the promises of God, upon the prophecies of God in the last days, then you will operate in a different dimension. For example: "I will never leave you. I will never forsake you" (Hebrews 13:5); "The Lord is my helper; I will not fear. What can man do to me?" (Hebrews 13:6, NKJV). People will come to you from far and wide to ask, "What do you have, because whatever you have, I want!"

Spend some time today gazing upon God and you will find that your faith will increase a hundredfold.

Overcomers

Romans 8:28

And we know that all things work together for good to them that love God, to them who are called according to his purpose.

George Müller has become a great influence in my life. He was a Lutheran minister, a professional theologian, whose father had had to bail him out of jail every Monday morning after his weekend binges and womanizing, in order for him to get back to Bible college. It was a profession like any other. However, when he went to England he was gloriously saved in a little Bible study group. His life was changed for ever. He started the biggest children's home – orphanage – that I think the world has ever seen to this day. Something like 121,000 children and £6,000,000 went through his hands. He never asked for a penny; he was a man of great faith. He went through great trials and tribulations but God saw him through, right to the end. He said, and I quote, "In a thousand trials, it is not just five hundred of them that work for the good of the believer, but nine hundred and ninety-nine, plus one."

You might be going through a time of extreme testing at this moment, crying out to God, saying, "Lord, what is happening to me?" My dear friend, I want to say to you that nothing is happening to you that has not happened to the saints before you or will not happen to those that come after you. Remember, there is nothing new under the sun. We as believers need to understand that the end of the road, the result we are working toward, is not only in this life, it is also in the life to come.

I heard a beautiful story of a missionary who spent most of his life in darkest Africa. At long last he was on a ship, returning to New York harbour. As often happens, he was largely forgotten by most of the people who had sent him to the front line. He was standing at the back of the ship and as the huge ship drew into the harbour there was tremendous joy: people sang; danced; threw streamers onto the ship; and a brass band was playing. The people on the quayside were actually rejoicing over and praising a soccer team that was aboard this ship because they'd won a Cup Final overseas.

This missionary, who had spent most of his life overseas preaching the gospel, didn't have one single soul to welcome him home. He stood right at the back of the ship and cried out, "Lord, what's happening? These men played a simple soccer game and they receive tremendous accolades and praises. I'm getting nothing." The Holy Spirit said to him, "But my son, you haven't arrived home yet!"

When you go out today to face some tough fights or intense heat and you say, "I can't go on any more," you actually can. Understand that all things do work together for the good of those who love the Lord. All we need to understand is that God will never allow us to be tested beyond that which we are able to bear. We need to keep looking to Him, not behind us, but upwards and forwards, understanding that if we are in Christ we are more than survivors; we are victorious. Press on today; take on life one day at a time, thanking God, not for the predicament that you're in, but for the situation that He's going to free you from. He's promised that if you come to Him, He will take care of every single one of your needs.

God of the living

Luke 20:38

For he is not a God of the dead, but of the living.

Jesus was adamant about that. The Sadducees tried to trick Him because they did not believe in the resurrection. They asked, "What happens if a man has a wife, and dies. According to tradition, his brother must take his wife and bear children for his dead brother. Then he dies and the next brother takes the same wife, but also dies. When they get to heaven, which brother's wife will she be?" Jesus says that in heaven there won't be marriage because we will be like the angels. We will be the children of the resurrection because Jesus is the God of the living.

I want to tell you that this life is not the end of the road. It is just the beginning. We need to start storing riches in heaven where they cannot be destroyed by rust and moth, because our living God is coming back very soon to take us home to be with Him in glory. He is alive. He's not dead. The tomb is empty. I've been to the tomb in Jerusalem thought to be that of Christ, and there are no bones to be found. Nor is there a casket or a coffin. He's alive and on the move. He lives in my heart today and I trust that He is living in yours too. Are you concentrating purely on the efforts you are making on earth, or are you able to look beyond the here and now?

Are you serving a living God or a god that is dead? If you're serving a dead god (which might be an institution or some kind of club), that is not the Jesus Christ I serve. If you want to walk by faith you've got to get to know the God of faith, the One who calls those things which aren't into being; the One who says one Word and this whole universe comes into being. It doesn't matter how black things are becoming in these last days, they have to become darker in order for the Light to become brighter. Jesus Christ is on His way, I tell you. Be ready for Him. He is the God of the living. He is not coming back for those who worship idols like money, prestige or religion. He's returning to take home with Him the people who believe that He is alive, that He is the Son of the living God. I love Him so much. He is the same yesterday, today, and forever (Hebrews 13:8).

He is more alive to me today than He was when I gave my life to Him on 18 February 1979, because He has proved Himself faithful to me on many occasions. He has taken care of all my needs. He has taken care of my family. He is real to me. He is a Friend who sticks closer to me than a brother. In my darkest times He has been the closest to me. I can recommend Him to you. I can tell you today that God is not dead, He is alive. He is the God of those who are alive.

Today you should try to get close to those people who believe the same about Him. Keep away from the influence of those people who believe that He is just a figment of your imagination. Jesus Christ is more real than Julius Caesar ever was. There's more evidence that He's alive. Enjoy your day today as you serve the God of the living!

Faith honours God

Mark 11:24

What things soever ye desire, when ye pray, believe that ye receive them, and ye shall have them.

Charles Haddon Spurgeon says that we must be careful and take good care of our faith, for faith is the only way to obtain God's blessings. He says that prayer alone cannot bring down answers from heaven because it is the earnest prayer of one who believes that leads to answers. Faith indeed is the contact between God and man and without it we can do nothing.

How does one get faith? It comes by spending time with God, reading the Word of God, communicating with God. My dear reader, I cannot stress enough that the more time you can spend with the Lord Jesus the better it is for you.

My hobby, my passion, is to read biographies of mighty men and women of God who walked by faith and were used by God both in biblical times and beyond. All these remarkable people have one thing in common. They all spent lots and lots of time with God, reading God's Word, praying, and meditating. That is how faith is increased. The more time you spend with someone, the more you get to know them and the more you become like them.

Faith honours God and God honours faith. The Bible says that without faith we cannot even please God (Hebrews 11:6). Not faith in faith, but faith in Jesus Christ. When the sick woman with the blood problems reached out in the throng and touched the hem of Jesus' garment, He stopped and said to her, "Your faith has made you well." Likewise, He marvelled when a Roman centurion – an unbeliever, a heathen – said to Him, "You don't even have to come to my house. Just say the word and my servant will be made whole." Jesus said that He'd never seen faith such as that of the Roman centurion among the Jews in the whole of Israel.

Today, as you go about your business, if you want to please God (and I don't know anyone who doesn't want to please God), start interpreting His Word in a literal way, as it is written, and walk by faith, calling those things that "are not" as if they were. Trust God irrespective of your situation, not walking by your feelings but walking by faith, and the Lord Jesus Christ will do the rest.

Prayer of faith

James 5:15

And the prayer of faith...

Praying without faith will not result in obtaining answers from God. Any one of the mighty men and women of God will tell you that it's a fact that a prayer that is prayed in faith will move the heart of God. It's not prayer itself. Some people pray out of habit but they don't pray believing that they're going to receive anything. They don't pray with any expectation. They just go through the motions.

We know that in some denominations people pray out of habit. They pray day in and day out but it's basically just like a parrot imitating its master: it doesn't even know what it is saying. I once heard of people who had a parrot that could imitate the sound of a telephone and it drove its owners mad. They kept running to answer the phone only to find that there was nobody on the other side. Or a doorbell; they kept answering the door but it was the parrot making the sound of the doorbell.

Prayer without faith has the same effect. It's just going through the motions and God is not interested in that. He wants the prayer of faith. That's what He answers. It is written in Mark 11:2, "What things soever ye desire, when ye pray, believe that ye shall receive them, and ye shall have them." It's the prayer of faith that moves the heart of God.

There is a lovely story told about George Müller. He was on his way to a meeting in Quebec, using the same passage as the Titanic (the great ship that sank in 1912). Müller's ship was navigating through the icebergs off Newfoundland in 1877 when heavy fog descended upon the ocean. The captain, who was a Christian and who related this story, stopped the ship in mid-ocean and switched off the engines because he was afraid of running into an iceberg. An old man of German descent and with an upright stance walked up onto the bridge and asked why the ship had stopped. The captain looked at him and said, "Well, can't you see there's fog outside that's as thick as pea soup? We can't see where we're going."

The man said, "Have you prayed about this?"

The captain looked at him and wondered from which asylum this man had escaped. He said, "No, not yet."

The man said, "Well, let's go down to your cabin and pray."

They went to the cabin and got down on their knees to pray. George Müller prayed first. He said, "Lord, I've never been late for one of Your appointments in my life. I'm asking You now by faith to remove the fog so that we can get to our destination in time."

The captain was about to pray but felt a tap on his shoulder. He opened his eyes. It was George Müller. He said, "Don't pray! First of all, God has already answered my prayers and secondly, you don't believe." They got to their feet and walked onto the deck. Needless to say the fog had lifted, the engines of the ship started up and the ship arrived at its destination on time.

Today, when you go out and pray, remember to pray the prayer of faith. It's the prayer of faith that moves the heart of God.

2 May

The darker the clouds, the bigger the rainstorm

Ecclesiastes 11:3

If the clouds be full of rain, they empty themselves upon the earth…

Are you going through a time of darkness at the moment? Rest assured, my friend, there's going to be a storm and it will rain, which is how it works in life, but the sun will break through again to announce a new day. Without the dark clouds, there can be no rain. Don't be afraid of the storms that might come in your life. If you belong to Jesus Christ, each storm will be refreshing and bring life.

Remember, God will not allow the temptation to be more than you can stand.

Seek God's counsel

Revelation 3:20

I stand at the door, and knock: if any man hear my voice, and open the door, I will come in to him, and will sup with him, and he with me.

My dear friend, today the Lord wants to speak with you. He's actually standing right outside your door. All He wants you to do is to open the door so that He can come in and speak with you. Remember one very important thing: the handle of the door is on the inside. There's no handle on the outside. Our God is a gentleman. He does not force Himself on any person. He never has and never will. However, He loves you so much that He wants to come and comfort you today. He wants to give you counsel and guidance. He wants to forgive you. All He's asking you to do is to acknowledge that you need help from Him; to get up, open the door and say, "Lord, please come in and speak with me."

There's a saying: "Never speak to men about God until you've spoken to God about men". Today, if you have to do some counselling, to encourage someone, preach the gospel, address your workers, give counsel at your school, captain your sports team, and you are in need of godly wisdom and direction, why not sit down and ask God? He's standing right outside the door at the moment and He's asking you to let Him in. He wants to spend time with you!

You'll find that any man or woman who was used by God in marvellous ways always had their priorities in order. They would always have spent time with God before they spent time with people. They would always have sought the counsel of God before they sought the counsel of man.

Today, God says that if you seek the kingdom of God and His righteousness first, then all of these other things will be added unto you. Seek God's counsel. Do it God's way, and God will do the rest.

Decisions

Isaiah 30:21

This is the way, walk ye in it.

Today, there are many voices speaking to you, telling you to do this and to do that, to go this way, to go that way, to close down, to start up, to invest, to withdraw your investment, to look for new employment, to remain steadfast where you are – and you don't know exactly what to do. This is the time to step aside, to sit down and to wait; to calm yourself in the sacred stillness of God's presence. Spend time with Him and His Word and He will reveal Himself to you.

This morning as I am writing this devotion I am faced with huge decisions that I have to make regarding next year. When I think of the gigantic mountains that are standing before me, fear grips my heart if I look at them through the eyes of the flesh. Yet, if I look at them through the eyes of faith, they become mere molehills.

They say that your attitude determines your altitude. You need to get your attitude right. The only way to do that is by isolating yourself, to calm yourself and to wait on the Lord. Remember, my dear friend, that haste is not of God. When in doubt, then don't. The ploy of the devil is to keep us so busy that we cannot sit down and hear the voice of God. The modern day and age makes us believe that everything needs to be done immediately, faster and quicker. But that's not necessarily the best way to go.

The Lord says that whenever you turn to the right or the left, your ears will hear a voice behind you, saying, "This is the way. Walk ye in it." The only way you can hear that voice is by spending time with that Person. I'm talking about none other than the Good Shepherd. He requires of you, even today before you go out, to spend time with Him, to hear what He has to say and then to act upon it by faith.

Five years ago I spent time with God in a game reserve and was enjoying a laid-back time with my wife. The Lord spoke to me very clearly and told me to go home and cancel all the crusades and campaigns that we'd organized for that year. It sounded totally ludicrous and very unlike something that God would request, because He wants the gospel to be spread. But He had another plan for me. I cancelled all my appointments and then He said, "I want you to mentor men" (I thought maybe three or four men) "because I have a lack of spiritual fathers."

We had our first men's conference and saw 240 men arrive without any advertising of the event whatsoever. The next year 600 arrived. The following year there were 1,060. This year we had 7,400 men. They said that they're coming back next year, which will mean that the conference will be attended by 23,000 men. My dear friend, that's one **huge** army of God!

You know, when a person comes to Christ, their family often follow. We know that the Word of God never returns void, so had I pressed on and said, "No, I'm going ahead with my campaigns," there would have always been a measure of success – but not of godly proportions.

At the moment we are contemplating hiring the biggest tent in the world to stage the biggest men's conference this country has ever seen. All of it is going to be done by faith and I know that God will honour His Word. Why?

Because I heard the voice of God telling my heart to walk this way then that way, to stop and to wait. Now I am experiencing the most exciting time of my entire life.

Remember, the road to heaven has no shortcuts. Listen to God and He will show you the correct route.

Don't mock God

Luke 22:63

And the men that held Jesus mocked him.

Many men (before they enter into a personal relationship with Christ) like to refer to God as "the Man Upstairs" while they are spending time with their mates at a rugby game or in a pub. This can be excused if men who have never met Jesus Christ as Lord and Saviour call Him by that name. They don't really know how to express themselves. But the Bible says that it is a terrible thing to fall into the hands of the living God. Jesus actually says, "Do not fear those who kill the body but cannot kill the soul. But fear Him who is able to destroy both soul and body in hell" (Matthew 10:28, NKJV).

Many people fear the devil. They are very frightened and almost intimidated by the powers of darkness. When it comes to Jesus Christ, the Light of the world, though, they become very familiar. How often do you hear the name of our blessed Saviour used in vain? In these last days in which we are living, we need to be more careful than ever before that we do not mock God, because He will not be mocked.

Galatians 6:7 says, "Be not deceived; God is not mocked: for whatsoever a man soweth, that shall he also reap." God is sovereign. If you want to fight, the last person in the universe to try and fight with is God. You'll never, ever win that fight. He is omnipotent and no one has ever won a battle against God. He is the one person that we do not want to get on the wrong side of!

Job, a man from the Bible whom I have a lot of respect for – a farmer who literally went through hell on earth – said, "Even though He slay me, yet will I still trust Him." He lost everything. He almost lost his faith but he never mocked God. As we know, in the end God restored his fortunes and gave him twice as much as he had before he was so sorely tried. I want to encourage you today, even if there are things that you don't understand, even if you are feeling let down or maybe even far from God: don't mock Him.

I firmly believe that Mary Magdalene will have a special place in heaven because she never denied the Lord. She never mocked God. He'd restored her and she loved Him for what He had done for her.

Our God is the Friend of sinners like you and me. To me, He is more real than this book, and I know that He will not fail me. He will never leave me, nor forsake me. He has never failed me, He has never let me down and He is not about to do so today. Go out and face the day knowing that the God of heaven will never fail you. He's a good God and He is for you, not against you. Don't mock Him. There is no cause or reason to mock Him. He doesn't deserve it.

Hold your tongue

Proverbs 10:19

In the multitude of words there wanteth not sin: But he that refraineth his lips is wise.

This Scripture is one that stands out for me. I've just reread the account of our Lord Jesus Christ when He was brought before Pontius Pilate, then before Herod and then again before Pontius Pilate for the passing of judgment. He was accused of inciting the people and of disrespecting the Roman government. All these accusations were false. The Bible says that He never opened His mouth. He never said a word. He went like a lamb to the slaughter.

Being a farmer, I can tell you that there is only one animal that will hardly put up a fight when you slit its throat, and that is a lamb. A young calf will fight to the end. Even a chicken will kick and flap until it eventually dies, but a lamb offers no resistance. That's why our precious Saviour and Lord has so often been referred to as the Lamb of God that takes away the sin of the world. The Lord never spoke out for Himself.

Even today, I believe that the Lord wants each one of us to refrain from speaking too much. It is stated clearly in the Scripture in Proverbs that the more we speak the more often we incriminate ourselves and get ourselves into trouble. We are to let our lives speak for us. Yes indeed, there is a time to speak up and there is a time to keep quiet, but the Holy Spirit Himself will tell us when that time is.

My wife Jill is a tremendous example to me of one who speaks little and listens well. We argue very little, if at all. That's mostly my wife's doing. As the old saying goes, it takes two to tango. You cannot have an argument on your own. That's not to say that one must not stand up for righteousness. I think Jill is more prone to vindication than I am. But idle words spoken, especially in times of anger or frustration, are like a torn goose-down pillow on a windy day. Those feathers will be blown to a thousand places. It is impossible to catch every feather and put it back into that pillow. In a similar fashion it is almost impossible to retract the words that have been spoken.

An old saying I learned at school says that "sticks and stones will break your bones but words will never harm you". I think that this saying is totally wrong. Sticks and stones might break your bones, but they can heal. But when angry words are said in the heat of the moment, they remain in the heart. Only the Lord Jesus Christ can remove them.

Today when you go out, remember that when Jesus was falsely accused by the government and by the church, He never said a word. His actions redeemed Him. Go out today and be the salt of the world. Be Jesus to people who are in tremendous need. Love people. Words are cheap: actions speak much louder.

Purposed

Daniel 1:8

But Daniel purposed in his heart that he would not defile himself...

Daniel is a tremendous example of a man who stood his ground against the authorities of the day. As he was a highly favoured and obviously a good-looking child he was saved when Nebuchadnezzar invaded Israel and conquered Jerusalem. The Bible says he had no blemish, he was skilful in all wisdom, cunning in knowledge and understanding of science, and therefore the king wanted him in Babylon.

Daniel, however, was one of God's chosen ones. When he was tested and expected to conform, he resisted. He did not wish to drink the wine and eat the delicious food from the king's table. Instead, he kept his body in line with the Word of God. As a result, he was challenged by the chief eunuch who was called to look after the young men. The eunuch said that he would lose his head if the king saw that Daniel was looking more bedraggled than the others. Daniel promised the man that God would look after him.

Because of Daniel's faithfulness to God, God undertook for him physically, spiritually, and mentally. The Bible says that when it came to all matters of wisdom and understanding that the king asked of Daniel, he was found to be ten times better than all the magicians and astrologers that were in his realm. Daniel continued to find favour with King Nebuchadnezzar.

The moral of the story is: Do what God has told you to do, not what man tells you to do, and God will undertake for you in everything. Whatever decision you have to make today, ask yourself the question, "What would God do?" and then do that – as Daniel did. You will see that God will promote you, will give you answers, and will give you favour even among the men of this world.

Pleasing Him

Hebrews 11:6

But without faith it is impossible to please him.

Augustus Strong said, "Faith is God's measure of a man." That means that God does not measure us on our natural abilities, on our good works, on how many times we go to church, on how much money we tithe, or how many times we fast. He measures us on how much faith we live by. It took John Wesley and Martin Luther a long time to realize that "the just shall live by faith". These two men, who shook the world by the way they lived their lives, initially tried to live by good works. Martin Luther would beat himself with a whip and wear horsehair shirts (I can't think of anything more aggravating) to punish his body and try to bring his flesh in line with the Word of God. He tried to live a life of celibacy but failed miserably.

John Wesley tried to preach the gospel. To try and find justification he went all the way to America and preached to the Native American Indians. Again, he had no response, no results. In the end, in desperation, both of them found that it is only by faith in God that we will finish the race.

Even Paul said, "Oh wretched soul that I am. I do what I shouldn't do and I don't do what I should do." He also hung on to the grace of God, believing that through faith he would make it home. There's a very special Scripture for me, found in Ephesians 2:8, which says that we have been saved by grace through faith. And even that is not of us; it is a gift from God. This morning our confidence is not in our goodness, because we are wretched creatures. Our faith is in the Faithful One: He will not leave us nor forsake us.

Often I get myself into hot water when I tell people, especially older ladies, that man is sinful from the day that he is conceived in his mother's womb. They say, "You cannot tell me that a baby has sin in him." I reply that's exactly what God says and that's what David says. He said that from the time he was conceived in his mother's womb, he was conceived in sin. Have you ever had to tell a child to misbehave, or to be naughty? No? Exactly! We always tell children to behave themselves and to be good.

Today, we walk out into the world by faith in God's love towards us, knowing that if we trust Him He will ensure that we finish this race. I leave you with this quote from Augustine, truly a mighty, mighty man of God: "Trust the past to the mercy of God, the present to His love and the future to His providence."

Nonconformist

John 4:40(b)

... and he abode there two days.

One thing about our Saviour that touches my heart deeply is that He didn't go with the flow. He was a man for all people and for all seasons. He was not traditional in any way and definitely not religious. When the disciples went to buy Jesus something to eat, they came back to find Him speaking to a Samaritan; someone who was basically an "untouchable", a person one did not speak to, someone of another race, another ethnic group, but even worse, a woman of bad reputation who had been married many times before and was actually living with a man who was not even her husband (John 4:18).

This morning while we were having our quiet time, my wife Jill pointed out to me that not only did Jesus speak to the woman at the well but He actually went and stayed with the Samaritans for two days. When the disciples arrived, they were too scared to ask the Lord, "What are You doing talking to this woman?" but that's what they thought.

Yet Jesus came to save the lost. I find more critics in the church than outside of the church. Remember, my dear friend, it was not the alcoholic, the drug addict, the prostitute or the thief who crucified Jesus Christ but the religious people, the people of the church of that time. God forbid that you and I indirectly crucify our Lord again.

Respectability can be such a disadvantage to a believer. When you are newly saved and you come to Christ, you might still frequent places where a Christian wouldn't be seen dead, because people still know you there and accept you. After a while though, the danger is that you become so respectable that no one in the world wants to associate with you because they feel inferior. Jesus never had this problem. He said, "I came to save the lost. I came to save the sick, not the healthy." Even today as we go out, let us be very careful that we don't become aloof because we are believers. Let us be known to wash the dirty feet of the sinner so that he might be saved.

Many Samaritans came to Christ, not because of what the woman told them, but because of what He told them Himself. He took time out to stay with them for two days in their homes before He moved on. Today I leave again for another campaign in the Eastern Cape and the Lord is reminding me so clearly that my objective is to tell all people that Jesus Christ died for all sinners, especially for a sinner like me.

Acceptability

Luke 4:24

No prophet is accepted in his own country.

I don't know how many times, after giving their hearts to the Lord for the very first time, people come to me and say, "But please, I don't want to break with my old friends." I always smile because I know exactly what's happening. I don't say anything, obviously, but the truth of the matter is that we don't have to break with our old friends. They break with us. We are the ones that change, not them.

I remember inviting a couple to have dinner at our house after accepting Christ as Lord and Saviour. I was a very sociable person and, in those days, quite a hard-drinking man. One day, the Lord laid it on my heart that I didn't need alcohol any more because I had the Holy Spirit. I've always been an all-or-nothing person. I emptied my drinks cabinet and poured all the alcohol down the sink. When my friends arrived I offered them soft drinks. That was the last time they came to my house for supper. One thing I could be sure about was that I knew who my friends were.

It's very hard to convince people that you've changed. The Bible says that Jesus performed but a few miracles in His own home town because the people of Nazareth didn't accept Him as the Son of God. They knew Him as Joseph's young son who used to help His father in the carpentry shop. He was the brother of James and His sisters played with their friends. He was the young boy who ran errands for His mum and dad. When He wanted to pray for the sick they would not believe.

The hardest place to be a Christian is in your own home town because people always say, "We remember you," and, "We remember what you did." The more you try to tell them that you are a new person in Christ (2 Corinthians 5:17), the less they believe you. That, however, is no reason not to press on. I still find that the hardest place for me to preach – and I have the privilege of preaching all over the world – is in my own church on the farm. They've heard all the stories before. They know me. Yet I love them dearly and I know they love me. But to be a prophet in your own country, according to Jesus, is a very hard thing to be.

Therefore, as we go out today, especially when it comes to our loved ones, our own family, our husbands, our wives, our children, let us speak less and act more. Let our words be few and our love and actions show those in our town, in our home, in our business, on our farm, or on the sports field that we are indeed new people in Christ.

God's wisdom

Daniel 2:20

… for wisdom and might are his…

Here again is a case of desperation. All the wise men, the expatriates in Babylon, were summoned to King Nebuchadnezzar and told that if they could not interpret his dream they would be killed. Nebuchadnezzar was a very shrewd man and he said, "I'm not going to tell you what I dreamt. You have to tell me my dream first and then interpret the dream." That ensured that nobody could tell any lies! Not one of the men was able to grant the king's request. They were all ready to die, except for one man, Daniel.

Daniel spent lots of time with God. He knew God; he had the ear of God. Because he kept himself pure, secluded from the things of this world, he could apply the Word of God which says, "Ask, and it shall be given you; seek, and ye shall find; knock, and it shall be opened unto you" (Matthew 7:7). That's exactly what he did and God honoured His servant.

Many people are just too lazy to go and find God's will for themselves. It saddens me so much when people run after every visiting prophet who comes to town. I have no problem with prophets. Prophets are part of the fivefold ministry; they are ordained of God. But, to me, a prophet is there to confirm what God has already told you. If you are looking for wisdom, direction, if you need to hear from God today, why don't you ask God? God will show you. He will confirm it through His Word not once, but many times over if you really seek His face.

We often share the joke of divine cheating. A friend of mine was studying for the ministry but already pastoring a church. He had no time whatsoever to prepare. I do not condone this but I really believe his heart was for the people. After writing his final exams I asked him how it went, and he replied that, due to his lack of studying, he couldn't be sure. Yet, when he got his results, he had a number of distinctions. I asked how he'd managed it. He replied that he had asked God, and added, "I'm sure it was divine cheating!"

If you ask God today, like Daniel did, then nothing is left to chance. Spend time with God. Detach yourself from the world for a little while, sit down, and have a cup of tea. Read the Scriptures systematically. Pray. God will definitely tell you exactly what to do. Nothing is left to chance for a child of the Lord.

Angry with God

Job 38:4

Where wast thou when I laid the foundations of the earth?

Job was very upset with the Lord and was arguing with Him, demanding some answers that weren't forthcoming. Eventually God said, "Right, let's sit down and talk about this." The amazing thing was that the Lord never apologized or even explained to Job why he had to endure such afflictions. Instead, He asked Job, "Where were you when I created the earth? Do you know where the spring is in the middle of the sea that brings out all the water for the ocean? Can you cause the sun to rise in the morning and set in the evening? Can you keep the waves on the seashore intact and prevent them from exceeding their limit?" With that, Job became very quiet.

There are many things that I as a Christian don't understand. And I do sometimes demand answers from God, but when I sit down and realize who God is, and who I am, my whole attitude towards life changes. I realize that I am merely a humble creation of God. When I look at the lifestyle of our Lord Jesus Christ, who was God in the flesh, I see that He never broke a bent reed nor extinguished a smouldering flax. He was so gentle and completely fair. Yet He, who was totally innocent, died the most horrible death that anybody could die. How can I possibly be angry with God?

A couple of hours ago I went to pray with a lady who is in the last stages of terminal cancer. She had her whole family around her and she said to me, "Angus, I'm angry with God." Her family were quite embarrassed. They said they had never heard their mother speak like that before. I replied that it was perfectly all right and that they should allow her to speak her mind. I told the family that it is better to be angry with God than not to speak to Him, because one thing God cannot bear is when we turn our backs on Him. She retorted that she did love God but felt that His timing was all wrong.

After explaining to this dear lady about the love of Jesus Christ, peace settled in her heart. She recommitted her life to Christ and is now living in total submission to Him. There was a real joy that seemed to well up from within her. Her family said that up until that time they were very perturbed because she was very fearful of death, but now that she is no longer angry with God, she is totally at peace. She's not fighting Him, because she knows that in actual fact God is on her side.

As you go out today, remember that God is not against you. He is for you. The Bible says, "If God be for us, who can be against us?" (Romans 8:31).

Enough strength for your days on earth

Deuteronomy 33:25(b)

… and as thy days, so shall thy strength be.

People often say to me, "I hope I don't fail the Lord when the time comes for me to die." The Lord has promised that He's given us enough strength to live each day for Him. I also believe He's given us enough strength to die for Him.

I remember the life story of one of the New Covenanters, a group of Scotsmen who were being persecuted for their faith by the authorities of that time. They were being hunted down in Britain and executed. They were burned at the stake, beheaded, and generally died very painful deaths.

One of the leaders knew that he would eventually be caught. Although he was a very powerful man of God, he was a timid man by nature. He was very afraid that he would let the Lord down when it came to the crunch. He used to sit in his little farmhouse at night with a lit candle in front of him, and try to put his finger in the flame. He couldn't hold it there for very long because of the pain, and wondered how he was going to be able to stand up to being burned at the stake for the sake of his faith. Needless to say, they did catch him. He was tied to the stake and as the flames engulfed his physical body, he was singing hymns. The Lord gave him the strength to live, and the Lord gave him the strength to die. The Lord has promised us, "Your strength will equal your days." Therefore, believer, don't be afraid of not having enough strength to run the race and complete it.

When we look at our young families, many of us wonder whether we will have the strength to see them through their schooling and further education. I've got good news for you. If you keep your eyes fixed on Jesus, He'll see to it that you have that strength.

In a few days' time I will be marrying off my last daughter, the last of five children. I have the privilege of actually conducting the service. I remember how this little girl of mine, aged three or four, walked through the maize fields with me one day, holding on to my little finger with her whole hand. At that time I was under tremendous financial stress on the farm. I looked down at Robyn and tears filled my eyes. I said, "Lord, what's going to happen to this little girl if I don't finish the race?"

I can give you good testimony and tell you that she has finished her school career, she's been to university, she's qualified as a teacher, she's been running our children's home and she is a teacher at our school. She is marrying a fine young Christian farmer on Saturday. God has given me the strength to finish this part of my race and He can certainly do it for you as well.

Don't look at your problem; look at your Problem Solver and that mountain will become a mere molehill. He promises to give us the necessary strength. All we have to do is to believe Him.

Idle tales

Luke 24:11

And their words seemed to them as idle tales, and they believed them not.

It is a tragedy that so many Christians don't take the Word of God literally. According to 1 John 5:7, Jesus is the Word. If you believe the Word, you believe the Lord.

Today's verse, about the idle tales which were not believed, refers to the account of the women who came back from the tomb where Jesus had been buried, having found the tomb empty. They told the disciples, who battled to believe them. The problem is that as soon as you doubt, you don't have any more power or strength. That's why the disciples were cowering in the upper room. They had no power to go out, for they did not believe. Remember, Thomas said, "I'll believe when I can see." Of course, eventually he did see. In fact, Jesus said, "Put your finger in the hole in My hand and your hand in the gash in My side" – which was where the Roman soldier had pierced the Master (John 20:25–27).

The world says that seeing is believing. However, "seeing is believing" does not equal faith. For us Christians, who walk by faith and not by sight, believing is seeing. A problem you are facing now might be so huge that you don't actually believe that God can undertake for you in your current circumstance.

I want to tell you that in the time that I've been walking with Jesus I've learned that there is no problem that is too big for Him to solve.

When the ladies came back from the tomb, they told the disciples, "He is not there. He's risen." The disciples really struggled to come to grips with that. According to Luke, straight after that on the same day, Jesus walked with the two men on the road to Emmaus (Luke 24:13). Again, they could hardly believe that the Lord was walking with them. It was only towards evening, when He broke bread with them, that they realized that they were actually talking to the Lord. The two men went back to Jerusalem to tell the disciples that He was alive, that He had been walking with them, having a meal with them. As they were speaking, Jesus Himself stood in their midst and said, "Shalom" (Peace be unto you), and He opened their understanding of the Scriptures.

As you go out today, remember that believing is seeing. Don't doubt the supernatural, because the Lord Jesus Christ always operates in ways that we do not expect. Remember today that your attitude will determine your altitude and, if you walk the road by faith, you will finish the race.

Wisdom from above

Daniel 2:47

Of a truth it is, that your God is a God of gods, and a Lord of kings, and a revealer of secrets…

Here we have the account of Daniel being brought before Nebuchadnezzar, the most powerful man in the world. He was determined that his seers, his witches, his priests, his magicians, his astrologers, and his soothsayers would not only be able to tell him what he had dreamed but also interpret the dream for him. A very sly old fox Nebuchadnezzar was! Not only did he say, "Interpret my dream for me," but also, "Tell me what I dreamed." He made sure that they would have to know both.

In the whole of the kingdom, only one man was able to do what the king had requested and that was Daniel. He was a friend of God – a holy man – and God revealed the dream and the interpretation to Nebuchadnezzar through him. The result was that Nebuchadnezzar made Daniel a great man. He gave him many gifts, made him ruler over the whole province of Babylon, and allowed him to bring his friends, Shadrach, Meshach and Abednego, to oversee the affairs of the province while Daniel stayed in the palace.

God gives His children supernatural wisdom if they ask for it. Often, when we are experiencing drought in our area, I'll drive into town, pull up at a robot (traffic light), and a farm pickup will park next to me. The farmer will wind down the window and shout to me, "Angus, it's time for us to pray for rain. We need rain. You've got a hotline to heaven!" Sometimes, I must be honest with you, the old me feels like saying, "Well, why don't you pray yourself?" But I realize that it's a kind of backhanded compliment that the world is paying us believers, because they acknowledge that the Lord does hear our prayers. Invariably we call a prayer meeting in the town hall. When we pray the prayer of faith, God answers and He sends rain.

Many times we have people coming to us with complex problems – regarding their marriage, family or business – seeking our counsel because they know that we have a relationship with the Lord Jesus Christ. It's a tremendous honour and privilege.

We must, however, never take advantage of the relationship we have with the Lord or the privilege of having Him speak to us through the Word of God, through the Holy Spirit in our hearts, through meditation, through prayer, through fasting, and through confirmation by other Christians. Never take it for granted. Always remember that when we give a person godly counsel we are representing the Lord. We must not be presumptuous; we must be sure that we've heard from

God. And encourage that person, "You don't have to run around to get godly counsel. Just seek the Lord and He'll give you His counsel." Matthew 6:33 says, "But seek ye first the kingdom of God and his righteousness; and all these things shall be added unto you."

Often when people buy my books to read, I say to them, "If you're going to read my books instead of the Bible, I'd rather you didn't buy them." There's no substitute for the Word of God. When we start to read the Word of God for ourselves, we become wise men and women. Even today, make a pledge, a pact or a covenant with God to start reading His Word and to seek His wisdom through the written Word.

Marriage

Ephesians 5:31

... and they two shall be one flesh.

I am preparing myself for one of the highlights in my life. I have five children. Very soon, the last of my children, my daughter Robyn, will marry a Christian farmer, Dougal. They have very kindly given me the honour of conducting the service. I will walk my daughter down the aisle and then conduct the service, as I did for my other daughter, Jilly.

What has this got to do with faith? After having been married for more than half of my life now, I want to say to you that without faith a marriage cannot work. Not faith in faith, but faith in Jesus Christ. He is the third core of the three-ply rope that is spoken about in Ecclesiastes 4:12. That rope, that cord, cannot be broken.

I once heard someone say that marriage is like a triangle. The Lord Jesus Christ is at the top of the triangle and the bridegroom and the bride are in the two bottom corners. Humanly speaking they can only love each other and get as close to each other as those two points of the triangle. However, as they start to love Jesus more, they both go up the sides of the triangle and of course the closer they get to Jesus, the closer they get to each other. At my daughter's wedding, at the end of the service, I'll pray the words, "Therefore, what God has joined together, let no man put asunder."

The confidence that I have in praying that prayer is that both Dougal and Robyn love Jesus Christ very much. They are totally committed Christians. In my beloved South Africa it has got to that stage now where two out of every three marriages fail. As a result, I will not marry a couple who are not born-again children of God. The confidence I have in my daughter's marriage is due to the faith that they have in each other, but especially in Jesus Christ. The miracle of marriage – another miracle of God – is that the Lord says in Ephesians 5:31, "For this cause shall a man leave his father and mother, and shall be joined unto his wife, and they two shall be one flesh."

Today, as you face the challenges, remember to arrange your priority list in such a way that God is at the top, then your marriage, and only then does the rest follow.

As it says in the book of Proverbs, your marriage and your family will give you place to sit in the city gates with the elders. I don't know how many times when I'm travelling overseas and meeting people like church leaders, businessmen, sportsmen, and so on, the first question I am asked is not what degree I have in theology, or which Bible college I went to, but, "How is your wife? Is she a Christian? Are you still together? How are your children? Are they serving the Lord?" These are the credentials that grant me authority to speak.

Guard your marriage with your life because many people are boarding up the front door to keep the devil out and he's walking straight in through the kitchen door. Trust the Lord, day by day, to grow your marriage. Settle your differences; don't go to sleep without forgiving one another. And God will prosper not only your marriage but your life, your relationship with Him, and your business.

Broken heart

Psalm 34:18(a)

The Lord is nigh unto them that are of a broken heart…

I have just experienced one of the most horrific windstorms of the thirty years or more that I have been on this farm. The wind blew off many of the roofs of the houses at Shalom. And the dust! We were literally eating dust. The house is totally covered in it.

Fires broke out all around us, with many of our neighbours losing large tracts of commercial timber plantations. One young man lost a sawmill in the fire. Very tragic! Last night the wind changed and gentle rain started to fall. It extinguished the fire, settled the dust, and we continue to press through.

Are you suffering from a broken heart as you are reading this book? The Lord reminds you today that weeping lasts for a night but joy comes in the morning. That's what's happened with us on this farm, and exactly what can happen to you. The last part of verse 18 says that the Lord saves "such as be of a contrite spirit". Tell the Lord about your problems, your fears, your inadequacies and your mistakes – and He says that He will save you. Confess your shortcomings to Him; tell Him about that broken heart. He can heal you, and you will be able to carry on.

There's nothing worse than inadequate communication. If you can't tell Jesus what your problem is, He can't set you free. Before you go out today, sit down and have a good heart-to-heart talk with Him. You'll be amazed at how your life will change.

18 May

The Cross

Matthew 10:38

And he that taketh not his cross…

As I am writing this reading I am on my way to Pietermaritzburg to catch a plane to Johannesburg (Midrand) to preach the gospel at a Praiseathon (a praise marathon) that started last night. They have very kindly honoured me with the privilege of being the speaker and we believe that thousands of young people will attend.

As I am driving down this road to catch yet another aeroplane, it is a very cold, overcast Sunday morning. I have just been to the service in our own church on the farm and now I am once again on a lonely journey. My dear wife Jill is waiting for me at home. I'll be home late tonight. To be quite honest and brutally frank, I don't really feel like this today. But nobody feels like carrying a cross; it's a very uncomfortable object and it represents death to self!

Jesus says that unless we deny ourselves daily and take up our cross and follow Him, we cannot be His disciples. I am His disciple, not because I'm a good man, but because I'm a believer. He has told me to preach the gospel at all costs. That's exactly what I'm doing. I know that God will honour His Word today because He has never failed me, and His Word has never returned void. However, He does need a spokesman and I am that spokesman today. As you are reading this, you need to understand that I'm not complaining. I'm honoured, yet it is costly. Just yesterday my daughter got married and I'm feeling very melancholy at the moment. The fact that I am leaving my wife behind all by herself makes me feel even worse. Jesus says that unless a grain of wheat falls to the ground and dies, it abides alone, but if it dies it bears much grain. I know that when we die, we live. I know that souls will come to Christ today and people's lives will be changed because of God's faithfulness.

As a Christian it's essential to be honest. I have a problem with people who are always saying that if someone's unhappy, or taking a bit of strain, there must be sin in his life. That has nothing to do with it. It has to do with fighting a fight and running a race.

Don't go by your feelings today. Go by the facts. The facts are that God goes before us, irrespective of how we feel. So it is with great excitement that I go to do His work in Johannesburg but I am looking forward to coming home tonight to be with my wife and family.

Loneliness

Matthew 26:43

And he came and found them asleep again…

Are you feeling lonely today? I've heard some super-spiritual Christians say that if you're a Christian you should never be lonely. I understand where that is coming from but I want to say to you that even Jesus Himself was lonely. That's why He came to the disciples three times to say, "Please pray." He knew what was awaiting Him within the next few hours and He needed His friends to stand by Him. But they went to sleep and He was extremely lonely.

I don't think that there is anything worse in this world than loneliness. I want to exhort you even today to find a lonely person and go and have a cup of tea with them. There are so many lonely old people in this world and they have such a wealth of experience, so much to share with anyone who's prepared to listen to them. They've walked the road. All they want to do is share it with you. All you have to do is sit down and listen, but we are all so busy doing our own thing, aren't we? We often don't even have time to listen.

The job portfolio of an evangelist that I'm now attempting to fulfil can be very lonely. It is amazing that sometimes the loneliest place to be is right in the middle of a crowd of people. I've seen it many times at an airport, a railway station or at gatherings; amid crowds and crowds of people there will be the odd two or three people just standing there, totally alone with not a soul to speak to. It's so important to have a close relationship with the Holy Spirit at such times.

Don't be condemned if you feel lonely. It's perfectly natural. It's like when a loved one goes to be with the Lord. Obviously it's a tragedy if they are an unbeliever. If they don't make a decision for Christ before they die, the Bible tells us that they are going to hell. If they are a believer we know they are going to heaven, but there is still a time of mourning. A friend that passes leaves such a gap in our lives. It is someone we won't be able to speak to again until we go to heaven.

There's a natural loneliness that people experience. That loneliness is only temporary though, because when we meet face to face with the Lord Jesus Christ on the day that we go home, we will never be lonely again. Remember, the Bible clearly states that there is a Friend who sticks closer than a brother. His name is Jesus Christ.

Exploits

Daniel 11:32(b)

… but the people that do know their God shall be strong, and do exploits.

I'm sitting in the departure lounge at Oliver Tambo International Airport in Johannesburg, waiting to return home. I've just been at an amazing meeting. Two young men with hearts loyal to Jesus felt that God was telling them to stage a twenty-four-hour Praiseathon. Abiding by faith, they started at six o'clock this morning. It is half past five in the afternoon now and I've just been dropped off at the airport to go home. I'm just so in love with the Lord at this time!

I've seen something truly amazing happen. There must have been between 2,000 and 3,000 people attending and just because two young men booked the biggest conference centre in South Africa at Gallagher Estates, between Johannesburg and Pretoria, made the announcement and did not ask for money.

I thank God for the faithfulness of these young men. They were floating on air. As today's Scripture implies, God has promised us that He will be strong on behalf of those whose hearts are loyal towards Him, for the people who know their God shall be strong.

I really believe that we are living in the last days. Something like this would never have happened even five years ago. I made the altar call after a simple message and over 2,000 people responded. I asked for an indication of first-time commitments and there were hands going up all over the place. I didn't even have a chance to pray for the sick individually because there was no time. After the prayer for salvation we said a mass prayer for healing.

We thank the Lord Jesus for His goodness and His love and we really trust God for many, many more souls in the kingdom tonight.

Multitudes

Joel 3:14

Multitudes, multitudes in the valley of decision: for the day of the Lord is near in the valley of decision.

It is Sunday night and it is extremely busy. Everybody wants to get back home or back to work. I'm sitting in the departure lounge of yet another airport. The waiting room is jam-packed with people. My eyes are seeing a multitude of people and I am wondering how many of these young people, old people, black people, Asian people, white people, actually know Jesus Christ as their personal Lord and Saviour. God has given me such a heart of compassion for the lost.

I have just bumped into a young, strong Afrikaans man as we were both approaching the escalator. The young man was adamant that I go first. He looked familiar and on asking he replied that he was at the men's conference that we staged at Shalom Farm, and that his life was changed. He said that he will be attending again next year and that he will bring many men with him.

"Do you not say, 'There are four months and then comes the harvest'?… lift up your eyes and look at the fields, for they are already white for harvest" (John 4:35).

Ploughed

John 12:24

... unless a corn of wheat falls into the ground and dies... (NKJV)

There's an old saying that you have to be cruel to be kind. That doesn't always add up but it usually rings true in the life of a Christian.

Look at a beautiful field that's been lying fallow for a whole year. It is full of wild flowers, birds, bees, and other insects. Then a huge tractor comes along to plough it and everything that was looking so beautiful is turned over. A set of discs follows and levels the soil. The farmer comes along with his planting machine and plants the seed nice and deep. Everything looks barren and devastated. There's nothing. No life, no joy.

Everything looks brown and barren until the first spring rain arrives. Suddenly the field comes to life again, but even more abundantly (John 10:10). Then we see those beautiful green lines of maize or wheat just starting to sprout. Absolute abundant life! Three months later that field, which looked so barren when all the beautiful wild flowers and weeds were ploughed under, is producing a glorious golden crop of harvest. The birds are back. They are rejoicing, for they have food to eat. The wild animals have a place to hide and to live and the farmer can reap his crop to make some money to feed his family and his workers. A little later the urban population gets their food from the farm as well. So it is in the kingdom of God.

My dear friend, you might be going through a time when you feel like a ploughed field. You don't see any life or future. You don't see anything happening. Just wait on Him. He wants to produce a huge crop through you. Maybe you are merely in a season of your life where He's preparing you for the great harvest.

The furnace

Isaiah 48:10(b)

... I have chosen thee in the furnace of affliction.

Are you feeling as if you are in the middle of a raging furnace this morning? Are you feeling totally deserted, asking, "Lord, where are You?" He wants to answer you, "I chose you in the furnace of affliction."

If I had not been in a furnace, I doubt if I would have turned to God. I literally had reached the end of my tether when, in the midst of the furnace of affliction, I called out to God and He answered me. That happened on 18 February 1979. I am only now beginning to understand the Scripture which says that we rejoice in our tribulation, for "tribulation worketh patience; And patience, experience; and experience, hope" (Romans 5:3–4). It is through tribulation that we grow closer to God. I would encourage you today to remember that He has chosen you. If He has chosen you, He will never leave, nor forsake you (Hebrews 13:5).

No matter how hard the going might be right at this moment in your life, cling to the fact that He chose you. He will be faithful to you. He will see you through this time of tribulation. No matter how tough it might be, if Jesus has chosen you, He will guide you.

Charles H. Spurgeon says, "Dear Christian, do not be afraid, for Jesus is with you. Through all your fiery trials, His presence is both your comfort and safety. He will never forsake those He has chosen for His own. 'Do not be afraid for I am with you' (Genesis 26:24), is His unfailing Word of promise to His chosen ones who are experiencing the furnace of affliction."

I've never yet met a worthy man of God who has not been through the furnace of affliction. Remember, fire purifies us. It's the furnace that draws us closer to God and away from self. It's the furnace of affliction that burns away all the chaff, the hay, the stubble and all the dead wood, leaving only the pure material.

If you look at an old warrior of the Lord you'll see in the lines on their face that they've been through many trials and tribulations, but yet they look pure. When they speak, their words are true. They do not babble. They speak from their heart – from experience – and their words are normally encouraging, thoughtful, and full of wisdom. There is no shortcut to drawing closer to Christ. You have to walk through the fire.

Today, remember that no matter what affliction you are going through, the Lord Jesus Christ is in that fire with you. He promises you that He will never leave you, and that you will come out of that fire pure, clean, and renewed.

Weighed in the balances

Daniel 5:27

Thou art weighed in the balances, and art found wanting.

This has got to be one of the most frightening verses that I have come up against for a long time. Daniel, the prophet of God, told Nebuchadnezzar's son, "You knew the truth and yet you still challenged the Lord of heaven by following gods of brass, gold, iron, wood and stone, which cannot hear or speak, and you've denied the Lord. Therefore," he said, "you've been weighed and found wanting." The result was, of course, that he died.

I think that it is a good thing for a Christian to often reassess and re-evaluate where they stand with their Saviour. I'm not one for introspection or forever assessing personal issues, because self-centredness can be a killer. We do, however, need to reassess our spiritual walk from time to time, and I think this is what happened in the Scripture. The man of God challenged the king of Babylon and said, "You are found wanting. You have been following foreign gods and therefore you must pay the price."

Who, or what, is most important in our lives this morning? Is it our family, or maybe our farms, our businesses, our degree, or our sport? Is it our vision, or maybe our Christian work? My dear friend, if any of these comes before the Lord of heaven, the Lord Jesus Christ Himself, then we are found wanting. We need to repent today and ask God to forgive us, and get back to our first love.

In Revelation 2:2–3 the Lord says, "I've seen that you've done all these things." But He goes on to say, "Nevertheless I have somewhat against thee, because thou hast left thy first love" (verse 4).

This earthly walk is about a relationship with a man called Jesus Christ. Today, if we are found wanting, let us return to our first love. Remember, Jesus doesn't need you. He wants you. He doesn't need our expertise or even our availability. He said one Word and this whole universe came into being. He wants us because He wants to have fellowship with us. He chooses to speak with you and me. He loves us so much that He was prepared to die a hideous death for us. Today, before we go out to face the world, let us repent. Let us not be found wanting. Let us put God first, our family second and everything else third.

Excellent spirit

Daniel 6:3

… because an excellent spirit was in him; and the king thought to set him over the whole realm.

Daniel had an "excellent spirit" in him. Because he was a man of God who had God's Holy Spirit within him, the world, even the unbelievers, trusted him. How often does that happen?

I remember reading about Robert Moffat, the pioneer missionary in Kuruman in the Northern Cape. His son John relocated to Zimbabwe and mentored Lobengula, the son of Mzilikazi, who ran away from Shaka, king of the Zulu nation. Lobengula loved "Muffati", which was what he called John Moffat. Although he was very far from being a believer himself, whenever he got into trouble – and I believe he suffered from the DTs (more commonly known, perhaps, as "the shakes") because of his heavy drinking towards the end of his life – he would call no one else, none of his witchdoctors or *sangomas* (healer or diviner), but the man of God to come and sit with him, to pray with him and to comfort him.

Even King Saul, the first king of Israel, who suffered greatly from depression, would call for David, the man of God, to come and sing to him and comfort him. Saul did not like David and was insanely jealous of him, but still he recognized the excellent spirit within him.

Do you have an excellent spirit within you today? Sometimes we annoy members of our family who are not serving God, not necessarily by what we say, but simply by just being there. We are different. We are not of this world. A classic example is when they are having a big party and everybody is intoxicated. By staying stone-cold sober and minding our own business we become like salt in their wounds and they would prefer for us not to be there. The amazing thing is that when the tests and the tragedies of life strike, who do those selfsame members of the family run to first? To the children of God, who have an excellent spirit within them!

As both Nebuchadnezzar and his son knew, Daniel never compromised. They knew that they would always get the truth from the man of God. Today you and I should also pray that this will be our testimony. People don't have to love us but they will respect us as being people who are true to their word.

Today, be prepared for people to come and ask you questions, ask you to comfort and love them, because they can see Christ in you. When you respond, always remember to give an answer that the Lord Jesus Christ would give. When they see the Lord in you, they will take your counsel very seriously.

Don't interfere with God's plans

2 Samuel 6:6

... Uzzah put forth his hand to the ark of God, and took hold of it; for the oxen shook it.

Many a time we want to help the Lord. He doesn't want us to do that. He has everything under control and we get in the way.

When I was a young boy, my dad, who was a blacksmith, would do a lot of contract work away from home. During school holidays he would often take me with him. I remember that I was always getting in his way, because I wanted to help him. He wanted me to go and play and I was forever trying to get involved in what he was doing. He often became quite irate because I used to get myself into very dangerous situations while trying to assist him, for example getting underneath big boilers that he was trying to lift, never realizing that the tank could fall and kill me. I actually thought that he was being very inconsiderate for not allowing me to help him.

We must be careful that we don't get in God's way. As we often say at Shalom, a good idea is not necessarily God's idea, and a need does not justify a call. When Jesus walked on the earth He didn't heal all the sick. Remember the lame man at the Gate Beautiful? "Silver and gold have we none," said Peter and John, "but such as we have we give unto you. In the name of Jesus Christ of Nazareth, rise up and walk." The Lord healed the lame man at the Gate Beautiful through Peter and John's faith. Jesus walked past that lame man every day. The Bible says that the man had been there for many years begging for alms. God's timing is always perfect. I don't know why Jesus didn't heal him. I do know, however, that Jesus allowed Peter and John to heal him through His name.

We see many men and women going into the mission field because they think it's a good idea; because there are many AIDS orphans or many widows. They never last very long in the field if God has not specifically and directly called them.

We need to be called by God. God doesn't want us to help Him out. He wants us to be obedient to His call. God is more than able to undertake for each one of us. The story about Uzzah is very sad. He was trying to help God by steadying the ark, which was going to fall off the trailer that the oxen were pulling. The children of God knew that they were not to touch that ark under any circumstances because it was holy and the glory of the Lord was in it. As soon as Uzzah touched the ark he died. We keep forgetting that God is more than capable of attending to any problems that may occur. He could easily have steadied the ark Himself.

The preacher Charles H. Spurgeon uses the example of a huge lion inside a cage. There were naughty little boys throwing stones at the lion. One little child was trying to protect the lion, running up and down in front of the cage, taking the blows on his body in his attempts to save the lion. Spurgeon says that all the little boy had to do was open the cage and let the lion out. That's all we have to do – be obedient and do what God tells us to do. He will more than undertake for the rest.

The heart of man

John 2:24

But Jesus did not commit himself unto them, because he knew all men.

You've read the Scripture where Jesus says, "Don't cast your pearls before swine" (Matthew 7:6). I think one of the biggest mistakes that especially young Christians make is to divulge secrets to people they think they can trust and are then sorely disappointed when they hear their confidential stories being talked about in town.

Take your personal needs and problems to the Throne of Grace. That is what your quiet time is for in the early morning hours before you start your day's work. Spend time with Jesus. Tell Him about your problems and your needs. Cry out to Him and He will answer you. Jesus Himself shared very little even with the disciples because He knew what was in the heart of man.

I have to ask the Lord very regularly to help me. I'm a person who struggles to keep a secret. I love to tell everybody about everything. Maybe it's a weakness of evangelists. John Wesley, a holy man, one of the greatest evangelists who ever lived, could not keep a secret either. His brother Charles, the hymn writer, said of John, "If you ever want to keep a secret, don't tell my brother because he wears his heart on his sleeve." I would make a very unsuccessful poker player because people can read me like a book. Whether that's good or bad, I don't know.

Take your personal needs and those precious thoughts and plans to God first. Share them with the Lord. God will show you people you can really trust; people who can give you godly counsel. You'll find that those people will always direct you straight back to God. They might give you godly counsel, or a Scripture that you can meditate on, but they will never tell you what to do.

A man who is not walking in the Spirit of God will always give you his personal opinion. Remember, none of us should be interested in other people's opinions. We are only interested in God's opinion, because God's opinion is good for us.

Be not ashamed

Daniel 6:10

… and his windows being open in his chamber toward Jerusalem, he kneeled upon his knees three times a day, and prayed, and gave thanks before his God…

This is the story of King Darius, who really loved Daniel and gave him a top position in his government. The rest of his counsellors were jealous and told the king that Daniel was not worshipping their idols and therefore needed to be thrown into the lion's den. Daniel, by the way, never tried to hide the fact that he worshipped the one and only God. He made a point of opening his windows so that everyone could see him praying three times a day, facing Jerusalem. He knew what would happen but he was totally unashamed of his God. Daniel's openness got him into trouble.

We have a tongue-in-cheek saying: "There's no such thing as a secret agent Christian in the kingdom of God". If you're a Christian, you have to be outspoken. Think of the Scripture that says, "I am not ashamed of the gospel of Christ: for it is the power of God" (Romans 1:16). Time and time again I've seen that as soon as a man is ashamed of being a Christian, he has no power. The more outspoken a man is and the more he stands up for Christ, the more the power of God seems to be embodied in his life.

This is exactly what happened to Daniel. He was totally unashamed about serving God. King Darius was in a terrible predicament. He had issued a decree that any man who worshipped another god would be cast into the den of lions. He loved Daniel and didn't want him to be hurt but he could never act against his own regulations.

You know, it's an amazing thing. I've seen it myself, especially before I became a Christian. As a young student from Rhodes, my own brother-in-law would come home for the holidays. He would not drink; he was a teetotaller. He abstained from strong drink, as I do now. When we went to rugby practice he would sit out on the veranda and drink his soft drink. Even though people made fun of him, deep down I admired him because he had the courage to do it.

King Darius admired Daniel because of his openness and his steadfastness. He said to Daniel, "Daniel, don't be afraid; your God will deliver you" (verse 16). The Bible says that Darius couldn't sleep that night and went without food because he was so worried about his chief counsellor. The following morning he ran to the den, only to find that Daniel was alive and well. The lions had not hurt him. Verse 23 tells us that the king was "exceedingly glad" and commanded that Daniel be taken out of the den. Of course, Darius could see that God had protected His servant because he was not ashamed of Him. King Darius immediately promoted Daniel and allowed him to continue serving his God.

Be righteous in the name of Jesus Christ. Call sin by its name. Don't condemn people but don't apologize for standing up for the ways of the Lord. John 14:6 will get you into a lot of trouble, but I tell you now that God will never, ever abandon you when you can tell people unashamedly that Jesus Christ is the Way, the Truth, and the Life, and that no one will come to the Father but by Him.

Holiness, the end product of obedience

Hebrews 12:14

… and holiness, without which no man shall see the Lord…

Holiness is the end product of obedience. When we are obedient, we will become holy people.

Robert Murray M'Cheyne was just such a man. His life ended in 1943 when he went home to be with his God at the age of twenty-nine, but he was instrumental in starting one of the biggest revivals ever in Dundee, Scotland. The people loved him so much that his funeral lasted for three weeks. They filled his grave with roses and went from church to church commemorating him. Robert Murray M'Cheyne said, "My people's greatest need is my personal holiness" – meaning that people don't always listen so much to what you say as look at what you do.

Mr Harold Berry is now close on a hundred years old. I saw him a couple of weeks ago when I spoke at the Christian Praiseathon at Gallagher Estates, Midrand. Mr Berry prayed over me when I went to visit him at his home one day. I wanted to ask for his mantle and anointing, as Elisha asked Elijah for his. When he anointed me with oil and laid his hands on my head and started to pray over me, I felt the incredible presence of God in the room. I don't remember all the things he prayed over me, because he prayed in pure, unadulterated Scripture (from memory), but I do remember him saying, "It won't be so much what Angus says that will move the people, but rather what he is."

God needs us to be holy men and women in these last days; men and women that the people in the world will aspire to be like. That's not easy because it is against our nature. We must die so Christ can live within us. That's why the Lord Jesus Christ regarded John the Baptist so highly. In fact, the Lord said there had never been a man born out of the womb of a woman who was greater than John the Baptist. John the Baptist was the one who said, "I must decrease so that He can increase." That's exactly what you and I have to do.

I'll never forget the words an old man once said to me: "Preach so that we can see you." I didn't really understand what that meant until I meditated on it. What he was saying was, "We want to see your heart." Some people are very good at using words but never really allow you to get to know them. They always keep you at arm's length. When you become a Christian you have to become transparent. There are no secret agendas, no skeletons in the closet. What you see is what you get. That's what people are looking for. When people are able to see Christ in your life, they will turn to Him. The greatest compliment that any man can ever pay you is when he says, "I want what you have."

Some so-called Christians are so angry, so self-righteous, so damning. I know of some people whose sole objective in life is to prove everybody wrong, pull down every man and woman of God, sling mud wherever they can and cause trouble. The people in the world don't need that; they have enough of that already! That's what kept me out of the kingdom of God for so long: a man who raised his hands, saying, "Praise the Lord! Hallelujah," but was unable to keep a job or to feed his family. I used to say to myself, "If he's a Christian I'll get to heaven before he will."

Today, as you go out into the world, make sure that the sermon you preach is not delivered through the words you speak but through the life you live. "My people's greatest need is my personal holiness."

Keeping appointments

Isaiah 40:31

They that wait upon the Lord…

I have again been challenged by my dear wife, whom the Lord often uses to speak to me. She just came into my office to say that we have an appointment to get the motorcar serviced this morning, and that I am running very late. I said to her, "No problem, we'll be there soon," to which she replied, "That's not the Christian attitude. These people have taken time out to book the car in to be serviced." Because I am not honouring my appointment it is a bad testimony for the Lord.

Being late is actually an insult. My brother, who was a professional golfer in Bavaria for many years, told me that the German people greatly value their time. They take it as a direct insult if you are invited to a dinner engagement and arrive late, and it normally spoils the whole evening.

Are you keeping your appointments with the Lord Jesus Christ every day? The Lord is always waiting for you. Remember, God is never late for an appointment nor is He ever early. He is always on time. We need to do the same. When you seek His kingdom first you'll find that you cope so much easier with the rest of your day.

Spurgeon said towards the end of his life, "By attempting less, I trust that I'm going to accomplish more." That often happens. By doing less we sometimes accomplish that much more, because we don't rush. If we're rushing to keep an appointment we often forget half the things we need to take with us and what we want to say at the appointment. It becomes a disaster. Get up a bit earlier in the morning, spend time first of all with God, and then keep your appointments and be a good, honourable witness for Jesus.

Stepping off the edge

Romans 4:17(b)

... and calleth those things which be not as though they were...

We know the story of the eagle so well. There comes a time when the fledgling has to leave the nest. The parents slowly begin to take the down out of the nest. Then they remove the twigs, until there's nothing left. Eventually, they literally force the fledgling off the edge of the cliff. He steps out, as it were, into nothing. Are you in that position right now?

What the Lord wants you to do is to stretch your wings of faith today. Even as the little fledgling steps into so-called nothing his little wings start flapping. The air lifts him and he experiences the most exhilarating feeling he's ever had in his life.

Peter stepped out of the boat onto the water and literally started walking because his Saviour, our Lord Jesus Christ, called him to come. He was fine walking on the water, just like his Master, until he took his eyes off his Lord and saw the huge waves around him. As he started to sink he shouted out, "Save me, Lord!" The Lord saved him immediately.

If that fledgling's wings don't start flapping straight away and he starts to plummet to earth, his parents swoop down to catch him on their powerful wings. They don't, however, put him back into the nest but take him back high into the sky and give him another chance to try his wings. He never goes back into the nest.

Imagine if the boat that Peter stepped out of was full of wood rot and wood borer. It would have been disintegrating and sinking in any case. Jesus would surely not have placed him back into a sinking boat? Like never before, my dear friend, we cannot put our trust in the things of this world. One does not have to be a prophet to look around and see that things are disintegrating around us. The only thing that will stand at the end of the day is the Word of God.

Abraham "staggered not at the promise of God through unbelief; but was strong in faith, giving glory to God" (Romans 4:20). As an old man of 100 years (and the Bible says that his body was dead, meaning that he was too old to produce children) he stood on the promise of God, and called those things that weren't as if they were.

In closing, my dear friend, God is no respecter of persons. Any man, any woman, any boy, any girl who chooses to believe in Him will have life and have it in abundance. Just like that little fledgling eagle steps out into fresh air and starts to fly like his mother and father, step out today and fly. You will enjoy life in a way that you never imagined possible.

He IS

John 4:26

I that speak unto thee am he.

Many years ago, quite a number of students attended a sermon I delivered at a church in Pietermaritzburg, KwaZulu-Natal. During the service I mentioned that Jesus Christ is the Son of God but Jesus Christ is also God. Afterwards one of the students came to me and said that it was an absolute revelation to her. She had never realized that not only was Jesus the Son of God, but that He was God. You see, Jesus said to His disciples, "If you've seen Me, you've seen the Father." The woman at the well said, "I know that the Messiah is coming which is called the Christ, and when he comes he will tell us all things." Jesus answered her, "I that speak unto thee am he" (verse 26).

Do you believe that Jesus Christ is the Messiah? My dear friend, the bottom line of the Christian faith is that we acknowledge Jesus Christ as God. There are no other gods, there never were, and there never will be. Look at John 14:6. Jesus makes it very clear when He says, "I am the way, the truth and the life: no man cometh unto the Father, but by me."

That's why Jesus was able to heal the woman with the blood problem. She had been bleeding incessantly for many years. She'd spent all her money going from specialist to doctor, from doctor to specialist, and in the end she had nothing left. She told herself, "If I can just touch the hem of His garment, I'll be healed." Jesus spun around in that busy marketplace, surrounded with people, and said, "Who touched Me?" The disciples said, "Lord, You must be joking! There are people all around you." "No," He replied. "There's one person who touched me. I felt the virtue flow from My body." The embarrassed woman, who had been healed instantly, said, "It was me, Lord." He said, "Go in peace, woman. Your faith has made you well."

Stop asking so many questions, my friend, and start believing. The Word of God tells us, "For whosoever shall call upon the name of the Lord shall be saved" (Romans 10:13). Call upon His name today; believe in simple faith, and God will save you.

Standing in the gap

Daniel 9:17(a)

Now therefore, O our God, hear the prayer of thy servant...

Here we have the situation of Daniel pleading to God to show mercy to Jerusalem and, more importantly, to the Jewish people. Daniel was a godly man, a righteous man, a man of integrity, a man like Nathanael, of whom Jesus said, "This is a man in whom there is no guile." Yet Daniel interceded with God for the children of Israel.

Do you have family members who do not serve Jesus Christ? Do you have friends who have strayed from God's way? Maybe some are in a bad place. I want to exhort you to pray for them, for the Bible says, "For the effectual, fervent prayer of a righteous man availeth much" (James 5:16). Remember, my dear friend, if you are a believer, then you are righteous in the eyes of God because your sins have been forgiven and you have the keys to the kingdom of heaven (Matthew 16:19).

I believe in the power of prayer. That mighty man of faith, George Müller, prayed for loved ones for thirty, forty, fifty years. He persisted until they came into the kingdom. Some of them only came into the kingdom of God after he'd already gone home to be with the Lord. I exhort you to keep praying. I have heard so many wonderful stories of mighty men and women of God whose grannies and grandfathers prayed for them, praying them into the kingdom, into salvation.

There is tremendous power in prayer. As an evangelist the first thing I ask when going on a campaign is, "How is the prayer cover?" I'm not really interested in the advertising programme, the venue, the music team, or even the follow-up. My biggest concern is how much prayer has taken place before we go. Often while attending campaigns it feels as if I am preaching to a brick wall with no response from the crowd whatsoever. Every time this happens I find out afterwards that there was no intercessory prayer before that particular campaign started.

I've just returned from a wonderful campaign in Kidd's Beach, Eastern Province, South Africa; a little town with a population of between 200 and 300 people. We saw over 2,000 people per night and many souls came to Christ for the first time. Signs and wonders followed the preaching of God's Word. That's just because of the faithful prayers of the intercessors.

Don't stop praying. I once heard an old saying that when men work, they work, but when men pray, God works. Daniel, a righteous man, a holy man, had such a heart for the people of Israel that he kept praying for them. Let us do the same as we go about our daily rounds and business, and we will see miracles unfold before our very own eyes.

God bless you as you enter this day as a prayer warrior for Jesus.

Victory

1 John 5:4(b)

... and this is the victory that overcometh the world, even our faith.

Faith is not faith until it has been tried and tested. How I sometimes wish that one could just go to a Bible college and take an exam to learn about faith! Unfortunately there are no shortcuts in the kingdom of God. We have to live our faith. That's why Paul could say, "That I might know him, and the power of his resurrection, and the fellowship of his sufferings, being made conformable unto his death" (Philippians 3:10). Paul was growing in faith at that time. He was a man who was pressing on towards Jesus.

My dear friend, even today, if things are not going quite the way you planned and the going is really getting tough, rejoice, because God is working on your character. A beautiful poem from that wonderful book, *Streams in the Desert*, reads:

It is easy to love Him when the blue is in the sky,
When the summer winds are blowing,
And we smell the roses nigh.
There is little effort needed to obey His precious will,
When it leads through flower-decked valley,
Or over sun-kissed hill.

But what the Lord Jesus Christ is requiring from you and me today is to continue walking by faith even when the going gets tough. That is not easy. It's only possible if we have an intimate relationship with the Lord. It is during times of severe testing, when everything around us seems dark and black and there seems to be no light at the end of the tunnel, that we really have to walk by faith and not by sight, because our eyes deceive us. We see nothing but failure and pain and hopelessness. When we start to walk with eyes of faith, we see the future opening up and a new day dawning.

My dear friend, this is not our home. We are but passing through in a very brief moment, a wink of an eye. Seventy years, maybe a few more by His grace, is all that we have to live in this world. And then it's home; home to spend eternity with the Lord Jesus Christ.

Today, lift up those heavy arms, straighten that back, push your chest out and say, "By faith I'm going to have a good day today, because if Jesus Christ is for me, there is no one who will ever stand against me" (Romans 8:31).

Time factor

John 4:35

Say not ye, There are yet four months…

During my quiet time this morning I read Daniel chapter 9, where the Lord says very specifically that He's given the people of Israel time to repent of their iniquity, of their sin, and to reconcile with one another before the awful and terrible day comes. I also read the Lord's words in the New Testament that state that the harvest is white and it's time to reap (John 4:35).

As a farmer I realize that when it comes to harvesting, time is of the essence. If you do not bring the harvest in before the season changes, the rains come and the harvest is spoiled. I think one of the saddest Scriptures in the Bible that I've ever read is Jeremiah 8:20, which says, "The harvest is past, the summer is ended, and we are not saved."

As you are reading this today, I pray that God will put a sense of urgency in your heart to tell people what it means to be saved. I've just read one of the most beautiful emails I have ever had the privilege of reading. A young mother by the name of Mariëtte told me that she woke up at one o'clock in the morning to hear her husband, who had just turned forty, making strange noises. She thought he was having a nightmare and tried to wake him, but could not. She even sprinkled cold water over his face but he did not wake up. He died right there. He left behind a young wife and two beautiful young daughters.

That young man came to the Mighty Men Conference a couple of months before his passing and was touched by Almighty God. He had an opportunity to repent, to reconcile, to turn from his iniquity, and truly meet with God. She said that when he came home from the conference he was a changed man. We had a signature song called "New Day" that was sung by Joe Niemand. The chorus goes: "I am ready, come what may". After the conference her husband listened to that song almost constantly on his cell phone. As he was dying his wife took the cell phone, put it on his chest and as he went home to be with Jesus his favourite song was playing.

Today is the day of salvation. If you know of a loved one or someone at your workplace that needs Christ, maybe you need to speak to them about the time factor today.

The altar

Genesis 22:2

Take now thy son, thine only son Isaac, whom thou lovest…
and offer him there for a burnt offering.

I firmly believe that the reason why Abraham is known in the Bible as the friend of God (James 2:23) is because the Lord meant everything to him. If you continue today's reading in Genesis 22, you will see that Abraham never complained and never questioned anything that God said. The Bible says that he rose early one morning and took his son Isaac to the mountain to sacrifice him to God. Abraham loved God so much and knew God's character so well that he did not doubt that God could raise his son from the very ashes if He so desired.

That is what God is asking of you and me today. He asks whether there's anything in our lives that is more important to us than Him. If you can honestly say, first and foremost, that there is nothing more important to you than the Lord Jesus Christ, then God will honour you, my dear friend, as you have never experienced before.

The Bible says that the Lord tested Abraham. If you know the nature of God, you know that God would never have taken Isaac as a living sacrifice in order to hurt Abraham. The Bible says that Jesus is so gentle that He will not extinguish a smouldering flax nor will He break a bent reed. Abraham knew God so well that he never doubted that good was going to come out of whatever was going to happen. Romans 8:28 says that all things work together for the good of those who love the Lord and are called according to His purposes. Because of his relationship with God, Abraham knew that God would not hurt his son. That's why he could give Isaac back to God.

Give your loved one back to God today. Lay any situation that is getting the better of you – be it a shaky marriage or unsatisfactory circumstances at work or school – before the Master's feet. Put it back on the altar and let God deal with it.

God made Abraham the father of many nations. He had more sons than the stars in the sky or than the grains of sand on the seashore. Why? Simply because he was willing to give his one and only son, Isaac, back to God. Remember the little boy, in among 5,000 men, who brought his two little fish and five barley loaves to Jesus? Jesus multiplied his offering and fed 5,000 men as well as the little boy with it. All of them ate until they had their fill and twelve baskets of leftovers were collected.

Give that most precious possession – whether it be your ministry, your vision, or your heart's desire – to God today, and allow Him to multiply it for you.

Character

Ephesians 6:10

Be strong in the Lord…

Phillips Brooks says, "Never pray for an easier life. Rather pray to be a stronger person. Never pray for tasks equal to your power. Rather pray for power equal to your tasks. Then doing your work will be no miracle. You will be the miracle."

We will never become stronger by avoiding challenges or seeking to walk the comfortable road. "One only gets stronger by attempting great things for God and expecting great things from God" was William Carey's favourite saying. He was the English cobbler who went out to India to preach the gospel and ended up being one of the greatest translators of the Word of God that this world has ever known.

Right next to our farm we have the Lion Match Company, which makes matches. They grow poplar trees in the swamp areas. The trees grow very fast and very tall but when they're cut down and dried out they're like balsa wood and barely weigh anything at all. They are soft because they grow very fast.

Just a short distance away is what they call the Lowveld, where you will find hard, gnarled thorn trees. They're not as big as the poplar trees and have taken five or ten times longer to grow. When those thorn trees are cut down you see that the pith is almost right to the outside edge of the tree, whereas the poplar has no pith. When you try and pick up an eight-foot log of thorn tree wood, it is like trying to pick up a railway line. Why? These thorn trees take years to grow and do so in arid areas. The poplar trees, however, grow in soft, well-watered, sheltered land and are very weak. The first strong wind that comes along blows those poplars over.

Today, rejoice in your tribulation, because "tribulation worketh patience; And patience, experience; and experience, hope" (Romans 5:3–4). God is looking for men and women of character, hope, and experience that He can trust to finish His work for Him.

The power of praise

Psalm 92:1

It is a good thing to give thanks unto the Lord, and to sing praises unto thy name, O Most High...

There is definitely power in praise. I had the privilege and honour of praying for a very dear friend of mine who had just been told that he has cancer of the brain. We anointed him with oil, prayed the prayer of faith, and we believe for a good report. Already we are praising Him for what is still to come, because God is faithful.

My dear friend, no matter how depressed you might be feeling today, praise the Lord because there is power in praise. It is like medicine for the body. Jesus praised His Father before He delivered Lazarus from the tomb. The good farmer praises God while he's planting the seed for a harvest that is yet to be seen or reaped. God honours faith and He honours those who praise Him. Praise His name today because He is worthy to be praised.

I think that's why Job was such a special man to God. I spoke at a men's conference not so long ago on the subject of "The just shall live by faith". The example I used was not Elijah, nor Paul or any of the other miracle workers; it was Job himself, for Job was a man of great faith. Even in the depths of despair, after he had lost everything, he still chose to praise his Lord. He says very clearly in Job 13:15, "Though he slay me, yet will I trust in him." God can work with that kind of faith and praise.

Today, irrespective of your situation, go and praise Him because He is praiseworthy, and watch how the tide turns for you. Watch the crop become a bumper crop. Watch the dead being raised and new life come to pass as you walk in the path of praise.

Unmerited favour

2 Corinthians 12:9

My grace is sufficient for you… (NKJV)

I am celebrating my sixtieth birthday today. I feel as if I have reached a milestone in my life. God has been so good to me, especially in the last thirty years, and I thank Him for each experience; the good, the bad, and the ugly (the title of that old Western movie), because I've experienced all three of them. Yet I can honestly say that I am looking forward to the next season in my life with much excitement, expectation and trepidation.

We have huge expectations of what we believe God is going to accomplish through us. In times of weakness or fear, I remember this Scripture, "My grace is sufficient for you." The Lord has shown me so many times that His grace is sufficient. Not hopefully or maybe, or is going to be, but is. It is completed. The grace is already established; it is there for me to grab and put on like a garment. Grace is undeserved loving kindness, unmerited favour. I don't deserve it and yet God in His goodness and His infinite love and wisdom has chosen to give it to me. That's why we can expect great things from God and attempt great things for God, because His grace is always available to His children.

How about you today? How old are you? Or, more to the point, how old do you feel? It doesn't matter whether you're eighteen or eighty; His grace is still the same, available to each one who would accept it. There were times in the past sixty years when I thought I would never see sixty. Yet, by His grace, I've made it to the age of sixty. Now I'm looking forward with great excitement to see what God is going to do in my life. You need to do the same.

Colossians 1:27 says it is "Christ in you, the hope of glory." Christ is going to do it through me and you if we walk in humility and holiness. I firmly believe that the best is yet to come for us. I believe that the latter rain will be greater than the former rain – as the Word of God says. I believe that there will be a greater harvest of souls and a revival such as the world has never seen before. Then the return of the Lord will happen. Jesus is not coming soon, He's on His way. Time is of the essence.

My dear friends, as we go out today let us use the grace of God to do what we can, because we don't know what tomorrow holds. We do, however, know the One who holds tomorrow, and that's good news!

Our temptations

Romans 7:24

O wretched man that I am!...

Do you often do what you don't want to do, and end up not doing what you should do? If you read Romans chapter 7, you'll see that's exactly how Paul felt. Many Christians – especially me – find themselves in a daily struggle. The flesh is very strong and very inviting.

Sometimes when preaching at a campaign, I'll see a young couple that is madly in love and of a marriageable age. And, under the anointing of the Holy Spirit (I firmly believe that), I ask them, "Do you intend to get married?" Often the young girl will burst into tears and the young man will look quite sheepish and say, "Well... yes, we are." I usually tell them that I don't believe in long engagements because you leave yourself wide open to temptation. If you have met the girl or man of your dreams, get married. And then the reasons (excuses?) come: Yes, but we have to wait for family to come from overseas...We have to wait until we have enough money to put a deposit down on a house...We have to wait to do this and that. I don't believe that. I believe that you can get married and do all of that afterwards. We must not give the devil a single foothold in our lives. He is a thief and a tempter. The Lord tests us but He never tempts us. The devil is the one who tempts us, and he uses our human side to do so. On a positive note, if you are in a wrestling-like situation today, rejoice, because it means that your conscience is still sensitive to the sin in your life. If the Holy Spirit is still convicting you, you can praise His name for that. When your conscience is seared then you don't really care; you feel nothing. When that happens you are on your way out.

God forgives sin if we confess, but the result of the sin leaves a scar on our hearts for the rest of our lives. If you have an affair with a person you are not married to, and a child is born out of that relationship, God will forgive you if you repent. But every time you see that little child it will be a reminder of a time when you were unfaithful to God.

The moral of the story is: Don't do it. Wait on God. Get your strength renewed, as Isaiah 40:31 says. Then you'll think clearly, concisely, and you'll make sound decisions. Do not procrastinate! If God tells you to settle that account, and you have the money, settle it. Don't say you'll do it next time. Do it now. If God has shown you that someone is to be your wife, then propose to her and get married. Sort out all the other trivialities later. There's nothing worse than a procrastinator. You've heard the saying: "The road to hell is paved with good intentions". "I must do that tomorrow; I must do that ..." and you never do.

Let us not war against the devil. Rather, let us just be obedient to the Holy Spirit. Then we will lead a life of peace and victory.

Unpopular

John 7:43

So there was a division among the people because of him.

How often, when we come to know Jesus Christ as our personal Lord and Saviour, all we want to do is get on with our day-to-day living. I clearly remember saying to dear friends of mine once I'd become a Christian, "Nothing will change. I don't want to lose my friends and still want to socialize with you." You know, the bottom line is though that they actually left me because we had nothing in common any more. Jesus Christ became the focal point and the centre of my life.

Jesus said that if people say all manner of evil about you for His name's sake, jump for joy. You don't have to be controversial when you're a Christian, because Christianity is controversial anyway. The devil, the powers of darkness, the world, the demons, hate Jesus. If Jesus lives within you, my dear friend, then you must be prepared for these things.

John 7:43 says there was a division amongst the people. Some people said, "Surely, this is the Son of God." Others said, "How can the Son of God come out of Galilee?" That's where Jesus was operating from, preaching. They didn't realize He was born in Bethlehem. And we read that the people were divided because of Him. Jesus will always bring division. Just as oil and water cannot mix, righteousness and sin cannot live together.

I know a young lady who read our book *Hardcore Christianity*. She was living with her fiancé at the time. They were to get married three months later and she was convicted that they were living together unlawfully. She said to her fiancé, "We need to separate until we get married." He replied, "If you leave this flat, the relationship is over." "Well," she said, "then it's over."

She was able to come to me and say that she was a new person in Christ. Yes, she was very sad. They'd been going out for two years before she found out what kind of man he was. If a man can do a thing like that to a young girl before they get married, what will he do once they are married?

I would encourage you today to carry on loving people, to carry on being the fragrance of Jesus Christ wherever you go. But do not get discouraged if you find that you're unpopular in certain worldly circles. It is a natural thing. It happens because all of a sudden you have something other people want. You have joy in your heart when others are despondent. You have Jesus when the world doesn't. Continue to shine as a light. Don't go out of your way to make enemies. Just keep the love of Christ shining in your heart and the Lord will do the rest.

The King's mighty men – and women

Joshua 1:14

... all the mighty men of valour...

We need to claim the victory. It is ours. Whatever the Lord accomplished on the Cross of Calvary is ours because we are His children. So often the Christian walks around with an attitude of defeat, of a pauper, a beggar, and sometimes even a tramp. This has got to stop! We are not of those who are downcast and defeated. We are the victors through Jesus Christ, our Saviour, our Lord, the Commander of our army. We need to claim victory and not allow the devil in any way to steal it from us.

When we had our first Mighty Men Conference a letter was put in the newspaper criticizing us severely for calling it a "Mighty Men's Conference". Not only one letter, either. I had a couple. "Where does humility fit into all of this? Are God's people not supposed to walk in humility?" The answer is: Yes, very much so. But we cannot disregard the victory that the Lord Jesus Christ has given to us as children of God.

F. B. Meyer says, "Claim your share in the Saviour's victory." We are children of the King and therefore we have the victory. We are mighty men because we can do all things through Christ Jesus who strengthens us (Philippians 4:13).

Today, as go about your business and face the world, remember that God goes before you. Lift up your head, push your shoulders back, face the world and thank God that you are more than a survivor through Christ Jesus who died for you.

One God

Isaiah 45:21(b)

… and there is no God else beside me; a just God and a Saviour; there is none beside me.

The writer Isaiah describes it so beautifully when he says that those of us that would rather chase other gods shall be as the morning cloud, as the early dew that evaporates. Our lives shall be like the chaff that is driven from the floor by the whirlwind. As the very smoke that comes out of the chimney disappears, so shall our faith be.

In the book of Isaiah the Lord describes so clearly what happens to us when we start to follow other gods. He talks about gods or molten images of silver, of idols, of worshipping the work of craftsmen – and as soon as we read this we think that we have graduated from that type of idol worship. But we need to look very carefully to see if there isn't any other god in our lives. Anything at all that takes the place of the Lord Jesus Christ in our lives is a god. It could be our business, our sport, our very own family. Let us make very sure today that the Lord is our God, and that all these other things take a second place in our lives.

I heard a man preaching last night. He said, "Many people are climbing the ladder of success and when they reach the top they find that the ladder has been positioned against the wrong wall and their lives are totally empty." The Lord says to you that He is the One who has brought you out of the land of Egypt (out of tribulation and trouble and hopelessness). Why then, when you've started so well, are you starting to chase after other gods? Galatians 3:3 asks, "Are you so foolish? Having begun in the Spirit, are you now being made perfect by the flesh?" (NKJV). This very morning, before we face the new day, let us get our priorities back in order and let us serve the living God, for He will never forsake us, nor leave us.

Remember: we've been saved by grace through faith, and that not of ourselves, for it was a gift from God (Ephesians 2:8). When we get saved, so many of us are initially totally absorbed in the wonderful, undeserved loving-kindness of the Lord Jesus Christ but then, after a while, we start to build these little idols and we try to give back to God.

We can't give anything back to God. All He wants us to do is to worship Him in spirit and in truth, to put Him first in our lives, to acknowledge Him in everything, and to spend time with Him every day. That's all we can do. He just wants our fellowship and our love and the rest follows automatically. Yes, we know that faith has feet, but we can't earn our way into heaven and we certainly can't earn our way into heaven by making idols!

Spend lots of time with God. Continue to thank Him for the amazing love that He's extended to you.

Light

John 8:12

I am the light of the world.

Jesus tells us that any man who follows Him will not walk in darkness but will have the light of life. I can give real testimony to that. Many people come to me in states of depression, feeling anxious or fearful, and don't know the way out. I'm not a psychologist and have no medical training per se but I can share from personal experience. When I found myself in times of extreme darkness and I could see no light at the end of the tunnel, I looked to Jesus Christ. He led me out of that tunnel, placed me on a rock, and gave me a second chance. And He can do it for you today. He is the Light of the world. It doesn't matter how badly things are going for you at this moment; if you keep looking to Him, the Author and the Finisher of your faith, you will never walk in darkness again.

Earlier this year we completed a huge men's conference on this farm. Over 7,000 men gathered here for a weekend. We were speaking about the light of God and the presence and the glory of the Lord. A man called Bruno, whom I had never met before, arrived late at the conference. He had been travelling for many hours. We'd already gone into the tent to start the first session on the Friday night. He stood outside the tent and took a photograph with his digital camera. Even as I am writing now, I can't help staring at the photograph. Once again, I'm astounded at what I see: a shaft of white light coming from a dark sky, settling on top of the tent, and then just flowing outward. I can only say that it has to be the glory of God, because that very night we were speaking about the light of God dispelling darkness and how, wherever the glory of the Lord is, there can be no evil.

Many years ago Jill and I were taking care of the poor and the needy, and a young girl who had a huge drug problem came to stay on our farm. Much later, she related a story to us. She told us that there were some young men from Durban, the big city about two hours' drive away from our farm, who actually came to the farm to bring her drugs. But they could not get to the farm. They said that there was a huge light shining on the farm that scared them so much that they returned to Durban.

Jesus says, "I am the Light of the world." He says, "If you follow after Me you will not walk in darkness, but you shall have the light of life."

The valley

Psalm 84:6

Who passing through the valley of Baca make it a well…

The following poem is quoted from *Streams in the Desert*:

I've been through the valley of weeping,
The valley of sorrow and pain;
But the "God of all comfort" was with me,
At hand to uphold and sustain.

As the earth needs the clouds and the sunshine,
Our souls need both sorrow and joy;
So He places us oft in the furnace,
The dross from the gold to destroy.

The writer says that comfort is not given to us when we are light-hearted and cheerful. We must travel through the depths of emotion to experience comfort – one of God's most precious gifts.

Today if you're going through a trying time, understand that that's the time when the Lord will be closest to you. When I look back on some of the darkest and most challenging moments of my life, I can see that the Lord was closer to me at those times than in times of happiness, rejoicing and peace. That is why Paul says he rejoices in his tribulation, because "tribulation worketh patience; And patience, experience; and experience, hope" (Romans 5:3–4). I've never yet met a person with any kind of character who's not been through the valley of Baca – the valley of trials.

You say that you cannot cope with the trial you're going through now. I say to you that Jesus can. You say that you're being tested above that which you are able to contain. I say to you that God promised that He would never allow you to be tested above that which you can handle.

The Bible says that when we're weak, we are actually strong. The Lord says in 2 Corinthians 12:9, "My grace is sufficient for you" (NKJV). If you want to be used by God as a mighty warrior, you must be prepared to go through the valley of Baca. It's only for a short time and then the Lord will grant you sufficient time to recuperate. But if you can't go through the valley, then you cannot get to the mountaintop.

That is why it is so important to have quiet time with the Lord Jesus Christ every day, preferably first thing in the morning, in order for Him to strengthen you. I once read that to be effective in doing God's work, you need to get to the mountain first and spend time with God, just like Jesus did. Only then can you go into the valley and help those who are suffering or struggling, and those who are desperate. If you don't spend time on the mountain you cannot help those who are in the valley.

Today, as you walk through the valley of Baca, understand one thing. It is only for a season. And then God will send you back up the mountain to commune with His Son and to get strong, so that you can finish the race in style.

Good courage

Psalm 31:24

Be of good courage, and he shall strengthen your heart, all ye that hope in the Lord.

What a wonderful Scripture for today! If ever we needed someone to build our hope on, it is now in these last days. Be of good courage. Get up today, mighty man or woman of God, and in courage go forth to face the world. The Lord has promised you and me that He will strengthen our hearts.

Maybe as you are reading this, you don't know how you're going to face the day. There are so many challenges in this world. Things seem to be speeding by at a phenomenal pace. There's so much fear and hopelessness in the world today. But the Lord has promised us that if we put our hope in Jesus Christ, it is He and He alone who shall strengthen our hearts.

The early church did not refer to its members as Christians but rather as believers. It's according to our faith that we shall have the victory. That is why as believers we choose to walk by faith and not by sight (2 Corinthians 5:7).

Many of us are fearful and we worry about things that are actually never going to happen. Let us remember that if Christ is for us there is no one that can stand against us (Romans 8:31). That's why it's such a beautiful and special privilege to belong to Jesus Christ, because we know that nothing in this world can happen to us without His sovereign permission, for He is God.

You cannot frighten a Christian with death. The apostle Paul said, "For me to live is Christ, and to die is gain" (Philippians 1:21). If we live, we live for Jesus. If we die, we go home to be with Him in heaven. As we go in courage, believing that He will never forsake us, that He'll never leave us, we have absolutely nothing to fear.

Be of good courage today, believer. He will strengthen your heart if you put your hope in Him. Go and shine as a bright light and touch many souls today – just by your presence, by your fragrance, and by your very being. In these last days people are looking for lighthouses to keep them off the rocks of the world, and God has made you and me one of them. Go in peace, and may the peace of God go with you.

You can do it

Hebrews 13:5

… I will never leave you nor forsake you… (NKJV)

I have just received a text message early this morning from a dear friend who wrote: "If you take no risks, you will suffer no defeats. If you take no risks, you win no victories. When last did you gain a victory for God and His kingdom?"

My young son Fergie, also a farmer, said to me one day, "Dad, to have tried and failed is better than to have not tried at all." I think this is the bottom line. The good news is that when we're serving Jesus and we run onto that rugby field to play our game of rugby, the score is already on the board – 44–0 in our favour. There's no real risk.

Some people spell risk: F-A-I-T-H. That's not altogether true, because there's no risk when you walk by faith. Faith is the surest thing on this earth. But faith has feet. We are expected to get out of the boat and to walk on the water for the Lord. As we do that, God undertakes supernaturally and we pull off another mighty victory.

Get out of your comfort zone today and get on the road knowing that Jesus Christ will never leave you nor forsake you, and you'll see the difference that it's going to make in your life and to those around you, especially to your family.

God bless you today as you gain another victory for the kingdom of God!

Believing

John 8:24(b)

Jesus says: "… for if ye believe not that I am he, ye shall die in your sins."

At the end of the day, after all our debating and learning, after all our searching through the Scriptures and going to Bible college, university, theological seminary, and after reading volumes of theological discourses, it is astounding to conclude that the Christian faith is actually simple. If you believe that Jesus Christ is the Son of God, you shall be saved. However, if you believe that He is anything other than the Son of God, you shall be condemned and shall go to hell and burn there forever.

John Wesley was sorely rebuked by the theologians when he used to preach that when sinners go to hell they don't die there; they burn forever. But if you look at the Scriptures, that's exactly what they say. So the saying: "Let's eat, drink and be merry, for tomorrow we die" doesn't hold any water, because we don't die. We go to hell. However, if we slip up, if we make mistakes and we genuinely repent – which means to stop doing it – and believe that Jesus Christ is the Son of God, we shall be saved, just like the thief on the cross. He deserved to die. He was a common thief and a criminal. Yet, two minutes before he died, he acknowledged that Jesus Christ was the Son of God, because he said, "Lord, remember me when You get to heaven." The Lord said, "Today you'll be with Me in Paradise."

The good news is, my dear friend, that the Christian faith is not based on good deeds, or upon intellect, or even upon Christian service. It is purely based on our belief that Jesus Christ is God in the flesh. That's wonderful news for you and me. Remember the woman who was caught for committing adultery? As they were about to stone her, Jesus wrote in the sand and said, "You who have no sin, cast the first stone." They all dropped their stones and left, and the Lord asked the woman, "Where are your accusers?" She answered, "There are none." He told her, "Neither do I accuse you. Go and sin no more."

He has the authority to forgive us and to give us a second chance. Today you and I must do likewise and go and sin no more. Let us shout from the rooftops that Jesus Christ is indeed our blessed Saviour and Redeemer!

Unconditional rejoicing

Habakkuk 3:17–18

Although the fig tree shall not blossom, neither shall fruit be in the vines; the labour of the olive shall fail, and the fields shall yield no meat; the flock shall be cut off from the fold, and there shall be no herd in the stalls; Yet will I rejoice in the Lord, I will joy in the God of my salvation.

It is so easy to rejoice in the Lord when everything is going well. That is exactly what the devil said to the Lord about His faithful servant Job, the most righteous man on earth. "It's easy for him to worship You when things are going well, but take away everything and let's see what he will do." This is so true even in the world in which we are living in today. The world is waiting to see what we will do and how we will react when things are not going well. They will say, "It's easy for them to praise God when the going is easy."

It is when the going gets tough that the world wants to see how a Christian reacts. In the book of Habakkuk, even though the crops were failing, the farmer still rejoiced in the Lord. That is what God is expecting of you and me today, because at the end of the day the good news is that if we are in Christ we will gain victory.

That has been proven time and time again in my own life. When I thought that we were finished, God came through for us in the final hour.

I remember one year having an absolutely disastrous planting season. I obviously calibrated the planting machine incorrectly. Instead of planting 54,000 plants per hectare, I ended up with 25,000 or even fewer plants per hectare. In the early morning, when I used to walk through my corn to check the field, the plant population was so low that I could walk through the field without getting any dew on my shirt. I was so desperate and distraught. I truly felt that I'd failed completely that time. Yet, I chose to rejoice in the Lord, because He's a good God. That year we happened to experience one of the most horrific droughts ever. If I'd have had a proper plant population I would have reaped nothing, because the plants do not produce cobs of maize in drought. But, because we had the huge spacing, I was able to reap a crop that paid all my debt and put food on the table for my family and me.

Sometimes a situation might appear to be an absolute disaster and yet it turns out to be an absolute blessing.

Last night I heard a robin singing in the rain,
And the raindrop's patter made a sweet refrain,
Making all the sweeter the music of the strain.

I have learned your lesson, bird with dappled wing,
Listened to your music with its lilt of spring –
When the storm cloud darkens, then's the TIME to sing.

Eben Eugene Rexford

Sound the alarm!

Joel 2:1

Blow ye the trumpet in Zion.

Like never before, Christian, it is time for you and me to sound the alarm, to tell the inhabitants of the land that the Lord is coming – and indeed His coming is at hand. Like never before, there is a sense of urgency on earth. You can see it in nature and in people's lives, and people need to be prepared for the coming of the Lord. The Lord often talks about the great and terrible Day. It will be a terrible day for those who don't know Jesus Christ as Lord and Saviour. But for those of us who do know Him, it will be a day of great rejoicing and celebration. People need to know that it is time to return to God.

There's an old saying: "The road to hell is paved with good intentions". In other words, do not procrastinate. Make sure that you contact that loved one today; make sure that you mention to those people you work with or the people you are studying with as well as the people you are playing sport with, that the Day of the Lord is nigh. Jesus says, "Do you not say, 'There are still four more months and then comes the harvest'?… lift up your eyes and look at the fields, for they are already white for harvest" (John 4:35, NKJV).

Remember the foolish farmer who had a bumper crop. He said he was going to build himself a much bigger barn because he could not put the amount of grain he was harvesting into his existing barns. He said to himself, "I'll build a great barn, then I'll sit back and relax, and I'll eat, drink, and be merry." But the Lord said to him, "Foolish man, do you not realize that even this very night your life will be required of you?"

Even today, as we go about our business, let us keep short accounts with each other and shorter accounts with God. In other words, don't leave anything undone. If there's an issue that needs to be resolved, do so while there is still time, because the Lord is coming very soon. As God's watchmen and representatives on earth, we have an obligation to blow the trumpet in Zion.

Many years ago I made a banner of a watchman – sound asleep on top of the turret on the castle, the trumpet in his hand, and the enemy approaching over the hills to overrun the castle. The people inside the castle were sound asleep because they trusted the watchman to warn them if the enemy came. Well, the Lord is coming soon and He has told you and me to blow that trumpet like never before and to sound the alarm, for the Day of the Lord is at hand.

If you go out today, take every opportunity to tell people through your actions, deeds or word of mouth that Jesus Christ is not coming soon – He is on His way!

Observe the Lord

Ecclesiastes 11:4

He who observes the wind will not sow, And he who regards the clouds will not reap. (NKJV)

Many years ago, when my oldest son was still at university, he came home for the holidays and saw that his mother and I were very tired. We were going through a particularly trying time on the farm. The crop (seed maize) was suffering terribly due to a severe drought. The maize was 30 cm high and was going white, twisting, and starting to look like onions rather than maize because of the dry weather. My son encouraged his mother and me to take a break for a few days while he watched over the farm, which we duly did.

This young man, who loves the Lord very much, would go out and pray over the maize fields and cry out to God to send rain. He told us that he even tried to reason with God, reminding Him that his mother and father were serving the Lord with all of their hearts, and that the farm was dedicated to Jesus. Yet the drought was intensifying.

Then one day he went out in the pickup and was in the middle of the field when a huge black cloud approached. He was so excited because he could see the sheets of rain coming down over the mountains just in front of the farm. The storm started to break over the farm; huge drops of rain fell on the dusty fields. As each drop hit the soil, clouds of dust would billow. He was so excited. Just then a strong east wind came up and divided the storm in two. One half of the clouds went to the left, the other to the right.

My son watched the rain pelting down on the mountains to the left and right of him. He was absolutely devastated. Disillusioned he got into his pickup and went back to the farm office where he kept his Bible. He opened his Bible and the Scripture that opened for him was, "He who observes the wind will not sow; and he who regards the clouds will not reap." With that, he got on his knees and wept. He asked God's forgiveness. Needless to say, the next morning there was gentle rain falling on the dry dusty land; rain that the crop could absorb. There was no damage, no hail, and no floods. Just gentle, life-giving rain… . When we returned from our break the crop was looking magnificent. Today, don't trust the elements, or in your own abilities. Trust only in God.

Prepare to be ground

Isaiah 28:28

Grain must be ground to make bread... (NIV)

Are you going through a tough time at present? J. R. Miller says that the things that are most precious to us today came to us through tears and pain. You can't feed anybody unless you're prepared to be made into flour, which is then processed into dough, and then baked into bread.

John 12:24 says that "unless a grain of wheat falls to the ground and dies, it remains alone; but if it dies, it produces much grain" (NKJV). So often, we have to go through the suffering process in order to identify with those who are hurting. There's nobody who is more impatient with a person who is sick than someone who has never, ever been sick before.

If you want a coach to teach you how to play golf, soccer, rugby, tennis, or cricket, don't get a superstar, because nine times out of ten you'll find that they are very impatient. They usually show you something once and then expect you to do it, because they can. Often the best teachers are people who have hardly ever played or who haven't succeeded in the particular sport themselves.

The late Kitch Christie was the Springbok coach who led the Springbok team to the 1995 World Cup, which they won. I don't think Kitch Christie ever played a game of provincial rugby in his life but he was a people person. He had a heart for the young men. He lived up to their full expectations. While he was leading the Springboks to victory, he was suffering from terminal cancer and died shortly after the World Cup.

You'll find that a person who knows suffering is a person who has tremendous patience and is someone who has an impact on those who are struggling as well. Unless we are prepared to be ground and made into flour, we cannot expect to be of any benefit to those around us.

Today, if you are taking a lot of strain and suffering, don't think that it is strange. God will use your situation to bless others in time to come.

Believing is seeing

John 9:23

Therefore said his parents, He is of age; ask him.

People often say: "I'll believe it when I see it." What they should be saying is: "I'll see it when I believe it." Believing is seeing. This is the account of the young man who was born blind. Jesus made mud from His spittle, put it on the young man's eyes and told him to go and wash in the pool of Siloam. He did so and he regained his sight. The temple people, the Pharisees, asked his parents if the young man had been blind from birth, as they did not believe it. His parents were scared of how the Pharisees might react if they should confirm that he had been blind from birth, so they said, "He is of age; ask him." Eventually the young man was so tired of the nonsense that he said, "One thing I know, that, whereas I was blind, now I see." They still wouldn't accept it and so the young man sarcastically replied, "Why are you asking all these questions? Do you also want to be one of His disciples?"

We have said many times before that one genuine miracle equals a thousand sermons. We have seen that so often. I was recently sent a photograph taken at the Mighty Men Conference that was held at Shalom in April 2007, which shows a white light descending from a dark sky, and spreading out over the tent. I can only describe it as looking like hot butter melting and flowing over the whole roof of the tent.

I've not yet personally met Bruno, the man who took the photograph; he comes from Phalaborwa, a town in the northern part of South Africa. He wept when he first saw the photograph and he was reluctant to send it to me because he wasn't sure what my reaction would be. I choose to believe it was the glory of God over the tent, which was filled to capacity, numbering 7,400 men. We were speaking about the light of God, about the glory of God's presence at that time.

However, there are still those who, when they see the photograph, are sceptical. The intercessors were speaking about the light of God, and there it was! Yet there are still some who question whether it is authentic or not.

Today, my dear friend, believe! Believe and then you will see, and don't be like those Pharisees who said, "We will believe when we see." Believe first and then God will show you His glory. And He will give you liberty and freedom to trust Him like you've never had before.

It's not easy

Mark 16:15

... Go ye into all the world, and preach the gospel to every creature.

I am currently in Brisbane, in the north-eastern part of Australia. I arrived yesterday from my beloved Africa and once again I understand the Great Commission. But understanding it doesn't make it easy!

Our first problem is the time factor. I couldn't fall asleep last night, because it was still the middle of the afternoon in Africa, where I had just come from. I knew I had to sleep because we have a lot of work to do today. We are about to catch another plane and fly to the heart of Australia, to an area called the outback, and preach the gospel to people there who are devastated by the drought that has been raging for a number of years. The good news is that Jesus is going before me, and He will make a way for me where there seems to be no way.

I can encourage you today; just do what Jesus tells you to and He will do the rest. Remember the servants who came to Mary, the mother of Jesus, at the marriage feast in Cana? They said that Jesus had told them to fill the vats with water. They couldn't understand His reasoning. She told them, "Just do what He tells you to." They did so – and the first miracle recounted in the New Testament took place. Jesus turned the water into wine.

I know that He's going to work a miracle in Australia as well. He's not a man that He should lie, nor the Son of Man that He should repent. Has He not said it, will He not do it? As He has spoken, will He not make it good (Numbers 23:19)? So it is with great excitement that I am looking forward to serving the Lord again today and to see what He is going to do as we simply remain obedient to His Word.

So shall ye know!

Joel 3:17

So shall ye know that I am the Lord your God...

I'm sitting in western Queensland in the middle of the Australian outback, in a small town called Roma, which boasts of having the biggest cattle sale yards in the world and of being able to auction over 14,000 head of cattle in one day. This area had been drought stricken for several years. When we arrived here yesterday by aeroplane, it had already started to rain. As we continued praising God and repenting before Him last night, the heavens opened and it's been raining non-stop now for close on twelve hours. Gentle, persistent rain – just what the farmers and the grazers need!

Once again, I am so aware of the awesomeness, the majesty and the love of God. My dear friend, God loves you more than you could ever imagine. All He wants us to do today is what the people of Roma and Charleyville, a small town even further west, did. That is to repent and say sorry – and Jesus will literally open the heavens with blessings for you.

In this area it was so dry that they started using bulldozers to push the trees over, so the cattle could at least eat the leaves on the trees. But Jesus promised us that we shall know that He is the Lord our God. All the preaching that I've done over these last few days is not even a drop in the bucket when it comes to showing people that our God is alive and very much on the move. This rain is speaking volumes even to the sceptics, even to the agnostics, because they cannot dispute that the worst drought of this millennium has been broken. We know that He is the Rainmaker extraordinaire. There is nothing too hard for Him (Genesis 18:14)!

The Good Shepherd

John 10:11

I am the good shepherd.

In this day, when it's very hard to find someone that you can trust or look up to, it's wonderful to know that there is One who is faithful and true, who will never leave us nor forsake us. He is the Good Shepherd, Jesus Christ Himself. He refers to Himself by that title for a good reason. He says that He's not a hireling, because when the enemy, like a wolf, comes to scatter the sheep, the hireling will leave the flock and protect himself. But the good shepherd will remain faithful and will protect the entrance to the fold; not allowing any intruder to enter.

If you want to put your trust in someone today there is no one else who is more worthy than the Good Shepherd, the Lord Jesus Christ. I can honestly recommend this shepherd. Since the day that I first put my trust in Him, He has never failed me or my family. Jesus is known by many names. Amongst others, He is known as the Vinedresser, the Lily of the Valley, the Bright Morning Star, the King of kings, the Lord of lords, the Lion of Judah, and the Friend of sinners, but He is also known as the Good Shepherd.

In South Africa we herd our sheep from the back, mostly using sheepdogs. The shepherds in the Middle East, of whom Jesus was speaking, actually lead from the front and the sheep follow them. If there are any predators attacking the flock from the front the shepherd will always encounter them first. He is the one who looks for good grazing and water. King David understood that, because he was a shepherd himself. He said, "The Lord is my shepherd: I shall not want." That should be our confession today; that the Lord is our shepherd and so we shall not want.

I've just returned from Australia and once again reiterated to the people there that if God tells you to leave your country (for example South Africa) and go to a far-off land, then by all means go. But if it's for any other reason, such as safety, or peace of mind, or security, then it's the wrong thing to do. There's only One who can guarantee safety and His name is Jesus Christ. That's why it's really ironic that in the Garden of Gethsemane the disciples ran away from the only person in the universe who could have helped and protected them – Jesus Himself.

When you go out to work today, be sure that you don't put your trust in chariots, or in horses (Psalm 20:7), but put your trust in the Lord and He will not forsake you. Remember, however, that He is a holy God. You cannot serve two masters. If you are not walking in God's ways, you are exposing yourself to the enemy. Rather do it God's way and let Him be the shepherd who will stand in the gateway of the fold and protect you from the enemy who wants to attack your business, your marriage, and your vision of your future.

Seeing is not faith, but reasoning

Hebrews 11:8(b)

… and he went out, not knowing whither he went.

God reminded me again in my quiet time this morning that He always honours faith. But we need to wait on God to get a clear Word from Him, and then operate in faith. When we walk in faith – the substance of things hoped for, the evidence of things not yet seen – it doesn't always make sense. Two and two, in God's economy, can often equal seven. We cannot understand how it works, but by faith we continue to walk the road that He has laid out before us.

Think of NASA, with the most brilliant mathematicians in the whole world. They will tell you categorically that it is mathematically impossible for the bumble bee to fly. His wings are too small and his torso is too big. Have you never seen a bumblebee fly? I've seen many. That's what faith is about. God honours faith.

I heard a beautiful saying the other day: "Waiting on God brings us to the end of our journey much faster than our feet can". To me, that means that those who wait on the Lord shall first of all renew their strength. But secondly, faith comes by hearing and hearing by the Word of God (Romans 10:17), which means that the more time you spend waiting on God, the more clearly you are going to hear from God. And then you're going to operate in faith, not presumption. There's a big difference between faith and presumption. Presumption is something that you think God has told you. Faith is something that you know God has told you. It's better to wait and then to follow the direction God has shown you.

That's exactly what Abraham did. That's why he was the friend of God. Not because he was a good man, but because he obeyed the Word of the Lord. Abraham heard from God, who told him to go to an unknown destination. Being a farmer myself, I can really relate to Abraham. He left everything he had (he was an extremely wealthy man), and he went to a destination that he didn't even know existed. God went ahead of him and the rest of the story, as they say, is history. That's why you (if you are a Christian) and I have our names written in the Lamb's Book of Life, because Abraham is our father. God gave Abraham favour because he obeyed God – and He will do the same for you and me today if we choose to walk by faith and not by sight (2 Corinthians 5:7).

A man once said to me that faith is spelled R–I–S–K. That's quite funny but actually quite far from the truth. Faith is more secure than anything else in this world; more secure than the monetary system or your health, more secure than all your worldly wisdom and education, for God never makes mistakes.

That great preacher, Charles H. Spurgeon, the "Prince of Preachers", said at the end of his life, "By attempting less, I hope to achieve more." What he meant was that by spending more time with God and operating in faith, he would achieve a lot more for the Lord than by just working with sweat, blood and tears and no faith.

Today, let us bring pleasure and joy to the heart of God by trusting Him and walking by faith, rather than listening to the lies of the devil and the worldly system. By listening to the latter we usually get ourselves into all kinds of financial difficulties and trouble, and end up fearful, battling with depression and stomach ulcers and blaming God. Let us ask ourselves the question, "What would Jesus do?" and then do it. Get confirmation from God through the Bible and then move on by faith.

God's mouthpiece

Exodus 4:12

Now therefore go, and I will be with thy mouth, and teach thee what thou shalt say.

Maybe today you're getting ready to deliver a speech? Maybe you have to keep an appointment regarding a serious financial matter? Maybe you have to see a lawyer about an issue? Maybe you have to speak in front of your class at school and you are nervous? Be encouraged. The Lord says that He will be your mouth and He will teach you what to say. I can honestly give testimony to that.

I remember speaking at a farmer's day in the Eastern Cape many years ago. I was to be part of a panel one afternoon. The farmers were firing all kinds of questions at us. One farmer, obviously a very angry chap, stood up and asked, "Is it according to God's Word to pay taxes to a government that is ungodly?" It was a very contentious question. I must be honest that I was totally floored. I didn't know what to say. I prayed silently, asking the Holy Spirit to give me the words. The answer came straight to me. I asked him, "Whose name is on that twenty Rand note?" He said, "The South African government's." I replied, "Jesus says, 'Render unto Caesar what is Caesar's, and unto God what's God's.'" That was the end of the discussion.

Do you remember that that is exactly what happened in the Bible? The Jews came to test Jesus and they asked, "Must we pay taxes to Rome?" He asked, "Whose head is on that coin?" They replied, "Caesar's." Jesus said to them, "Render therefore to Caesar the things that are Caesar's, and to God the things that are God's" (Matthew 22:21, NKJV), and we read in verse 22 that they marvelled at His words and left Him and went their way.

God will give you the words to speak at that time. Many a time as I'm about to get up and walk to the pulpit or the platform to deliver a message, the Holy Spirit impresses upon me to change my sermon. Fortunately I've been obedient to Him, but it's very nerve-wracking when I've taken time out to prepare a word and the Lord then tells me, "That's not what I want you to tell the people." I don't do this very often but when He tells me clearly, I do it! I open my mouth and the right words come out. The response is always absolutely amazing.

I would encourage you today not to be so concerned about what you're going to say. Rather prepare your heart and the Lord Jesus Christ will give you the words. Psalm 81:10 states: "open thy mouth wide, and I will fill it."

Direction

Psalm 119:105

Thy word is a lamp unto my feet, and a light unto my path.

The other day I read, "There are no shortcuts to any place worth going to." Quite an appropriate quote for today's reading, I thought. The Lord has promised us that His Word is a lamp unto our feet. He is the One who gives us direction. There are no shortcuts to heaven.

I've just returned from the eastern side of Australia. I flew two hours from Brisbane to the outback. I had received a call from a pastor who said that the young farmers were committing suicide. He was trying to give them direction, trying to tell them that there was a better way, but he could see in their eyes that they were thinking, "What do you know about what we're going through?" He asked me to come and speak to them.

What I told this desperate community, and I believe this with all my heart, is that there are no shortcuts to heaven. We've got to go the whole nine yards if we're going to go home to be with Jesus. We need to pray for those who have taken their lives and ask for God's abundant mercy to be with them – but God does not look favourably upon suicide. We have no right to take our own lives, because it's murder in the eyes of God. To reach any place that is worth going to, we've got to be prepared to put our shoulder to the wheel and work hard. Then we'll get there. Nothing that is worth having in the kingdom of God comes easy.

Look at the lives of many of the great men and women of God in the Bible and you'll see that each one had to follow a long, arduous road. But it led to a wonderful place, to a wonderful conclusion, to nothing less than heaven itself. I would exhort you today: Don't take any shortcuts. Don't borrow money that you can't pay back only because you think that tomorrow will be different. Cut your cloth according to your pocket. Don't try and do the taxman in. Don't short-circuit anything. Rather take the long road and know that it leads to the place that's worth going to.

You know the story of the hare and the tortoise. The hare was always taking shortcuts, running as fast as he could. The tortoise was just going through his paces steadily. I have a very dear, blessed old mother in the Lord. She's well into her eighties. I call her Tortoise and she calls me Hare. She often jokes and says she'll get there before me – and I think she's right! She's a prayer warrior. I think that if it weren't for ladies like her, I wouldn't be in the race any more. She prays for me, insists that I rest and take time out, because she knows that shortcuts don't normally end up in any place worth being.

Today, take time out to smell the roses. Pace yourself and take the long route home. Often the shortcut ends up being the longest way, anyway. The best way to do it is to put your trust in the Lord Jesus Christ and keep asking Him if this is the road to walk. Then go for it!

A friend

Job 19:25

For I know that my Redeemer lives… (NKJV)

Job is possibly one of the greatest men of faith in the whole Bible. We say that because when Job was sorely tempted by the evil one, he did not respond by denying God but instead remained faithful to Him. Job is one of my heroes in the Bible.

Here in chapter 19, Job recounts the tremendous trials and tests that he is going through. He says that his brothers were removed from him, his acquaintances were completely estranged from him, his relatives failed him, and his close friends forgot him. He says that even those who dwelled in his house, and his servants, counted him as a stranger; that he was an alien in their sight. He says that even young children despised him. His close friends abhorred him and those whom he loved turned against him. He desperately cries out, "Have pity on me, have pity on me, oh you my friends!" It appears as if everyone has rejected him. Yet, in the midst of all this desertion, at the top of his voice he can say, "For I know that my Redeemer lives, And He shall stand at last on the earth" (verse 25). What faith!

Friend, maybe you're going through a similar ordeal today? Maybe you are feeling rejected by those who are close to you? Maybe you're going through hard times and at this stage it just seems as if everything and everyone is conspiring against you? The world loves a winner but has no time for a loser.

I encourage you today by faith to look at the book of Job, a man who refused to deny the Lord, even in times of great trials and tribulations. The good news is that in fact the Lord did not desert or turn His back on him. If you look at the last chapter of Job, you will see that the Lord blessed Job in his latter days with more than he had at the beginning. He had 14,000 sheep, 6,000 camels, 1,000 yoke of oxen, and 1,000 female donkeys (Job 42:12).

He also had seven more sons and three more daughters, who were the most beautiful women in the land. Job lived to 140 years of age and saw his children and grandchildren for four generations. Job 42:17 says, "So Job died, being old and full of days."

Have Your way

Psalm 19:14

Let the words of my mouth, and the meditation of my heart, be acceptable in your sight, O Lord, my strength, and my redeemer.

Those who know me well will know that I will never start preaching without praying this prayer to God. This might be a good prayer for you to memorize as well.

Before you go into that board meeting or that critical meeting with your bank manager, or have a family sit-down to talk about real issues, you need to pray this prayer: "The words of my mouth: Let them be words of faith, encouragement, of hope, of trust." Then echo the words of the psalmist and say, "And the meditation of my heart – the things which I think in my heart, those things that I store in my heart – let them come from God and be acceptable only to Him." He says, "For You, O Lord, are my strength and my Redeemer."

As you go into the world today with this prayer upon your lips and in your heart, you will do nothing but good. You will sow nothing but good seed, and you will be found honourable before the Lord. The men and women of the world might not necessarily like you, but they will respect you, as you literally speak the oracles of God. Remember: what you say is what you are. As you speak words of life today, God will build you up in your inner man or woman and give you your rightful place in this world.

Teach us, O Lord

Psalm 32:8

I will instruct you and teach you in the way you should go; I will guide you with My eye. (NKJV)

Today you might be in a state of indecision. You might need to make some serious decisions and are looking for guidance. The good news is that the Lord promises to instruct and teach you; He will show you the way and guide you. All you need to do today is to put your trust in Him. "Some trust in chariots, and some in horses but we will remember the name of the Lord our God" (Psalm 20:7). Our trust needs to be in Him and Him alone.

Very often people are totally amazed at and confused about how God uses semi-literate people in such pronounced ways. Abraham Lincoln, one of the greatest, if not *the* greatest president of the United States of America, was a country boy. He had very little education and seemed to be failing in every area of his life until he met the Lord Jesus Christ in a very real way. In spite of his poor formal education he made some profound decisions while governing the United States of America. He is the one who was partly responsible for abolishing slavery in the USA because the Lord was the One who instructed and taught him.

Don't despise your small beginnings. If you put your trust in the Lord today, He will instruct and teach you.

Agreement

Amos 3:3

Can two walk together, unless they are agreed? (NKJV)

I get very disturbed when I hear about the ever-increasing divorce rate while travelling both locally and internationally. I've spoken to some men who deal with this issue and they told me that the main cause for divorce is not a third party but purely the fact that the couple cannot get on together. They cannot agree on anything. They say that they are incompatible and this gives them legal cause to be divorced. This is a tragedy, because those same people prayed on their wedding day and made a covenant with God that they would stay together until death parted them.

Two people cannot walk and live together unless they are one in spirit. The only way to achieve this is to have the Lord Jesus Christ as the focal point in your life. The third member of a successful relationship is Jesus Himself. I know from my own experience that if I have a disagreement with Jill it will be fruitless to spend time in prayer until I have rectified the situation, because I know that God will not hear my prayers. He might hear them but He won't act on them.

This day, even before you finish your quiet time, make sure that you are in agreement with your loved one. Go and ask forgiveness – even if it's not your fault. Humble yourself, and your loved one will forgive you. Then you can walk together. The Bible says that one will chase a thousand, but two will chase ten thousand. When you stand together and walk in agreement, God will bless your union, your relationship and your friendship.

You might say, "But Angus, I'm already divorced." What you need to do is to repent and plead the blood of Jesus Christ, like all sinners do (me especially), and then press on. Luke 9:62 says, "No man, having put his hand to the plough, and looking back, is fit for the kingdom of God." Press on and don't do it again.

How do you walk in agreement with your partner? By spending time with your partner – whether it is your child, a good friend, or a partner at work. Spend time talking to each other and working through your issues, so that you can walk together in victory.

It's time to seek the Lord

Amos 5:14

Seek good, and not evil, that ye may live…

The Lord is forthright in this Scripture when He says, "If you seek Me, you'll live, but if you don't seek Me, you'll die."

Like never before, we need to start seeking the Lord. So often, especially with modern technology, it's tempting to seek everything else but God. In his book *Prayer* Philip Yancey says that it is getting increasingly difficult for the modern person to pray.

Some of the examples used by him are very good. For instance, the farmer who, instead of getting on his knees and praying for rain, consults the internet to see what the weather forecast predicts for the next few days or weeks, and then operates according to that. Or the mother with a sick child who, instead of getting down on her knees beside the child's bed and praying that God will undertake supernaturally, rushes the child off to the specialist and looks to the specialist for healing.

We are not saying for one moment that these things are wrong. Not at all! What we are saying, however, is that at the end of the day we need to remember that the specialist is only a vessel used by God and that the wonderful technology that can predict the weather is only a very rough guide as to what the outcome of the weather might be. In my own life, I've seen God bring rain when no rain was forecast. I've seen God heal sick people when the doctors have said, "There's no more that we can do for you. Go home and die peacefully with your family." And God raised them up.

The Lord says, "Seek good, and not evil, that you may live" (NKJV). Don't be foolish and try every remedy or method and only when there are no more options available, seek the Lord. Rather do it the other way around. Remember that faith has feet. It's a doing word.

The Lord relented

Exodus 32:14

So the Lord relented from the harm which He said He would do to His people. (NKJV)

The Israelites were in the desert and got tired of waiting for Moses to come down from the mountain with the Ten Commandments and they decided to make their own god to worship. Can you imagine such audacity? How often do you and I, when things are tough, promise the Lord that we'll never serve another god, that we'll never leave Him again, and never forsake Him? Yet, as soon as things start going well, the first thing we seem to do is to forget from whence our strength comes and we start to chase after other gods like money, pleasure, and self-indulgence. That's exactly what the Israelites did. They forgot God, the God who had brought them out of Egypt. They made an ordinary, golden image of a calf and started to worship it.

God was so angry that He told Moses that He was going to obliterate the people of Israel from the face of the earth. If He'd done that, you and I wouldn't be here today. Moses, small little Moses, just one little man, like a little ant looking up to the majesty of God, said, "Lord, You can't do that, because You will be the laughing stock of the world. You brought the people of Israel out of Egypt. Have You brought them out only to harm them? Remember Your sons Abraham, Isaac, and Jacob. You swore to them and to Yourself; You made a covenant with them, Lord, that You will multiply their descendants. Now You want to wipe them out." The Bible says, "So the Lord relented…" (Exodus 32:14, NKJV).

According to the *New Collins Dictionary* the word "relent" means to change one's mind about some decision, especially a harsh one. That's what God did. My dear friend, today, by faith, after we have repented, the Lord will forgive us because He is such a gracious God, and we can go out and start again. That's why I am so in love with our Lord and Saviour, Jesus Christ. What a gracious God He is, that He would even respond to His own creation, humble Himself, and change His mind! There is no sin that is too big for God to forgive. There is no sin so small that God cannot forgive it.

Today, before you go out to face the world, repent of any sin in your life and then, by faith, trust God that He has forgiven you and go. And don't commit it again.

Priorities

John 12:8

For the poor you have with you always; but Me you do not have always. (NKJV)

There were two sisters, Mary and Martha. Martha was a doer. She always kept her hands busy. When the Lord came to have a meal with them in their house, she was the one who was scurrying around, making sure the food was cooked and that the house was clean. Mary was sitting at the Master's feet, listening to what He had to say.

When Lazarus fell ill, the sisters sent for Jesus but their brother died before the Master got there. As Jesus was on His way to raise Lazarus from the dead, Martha ran out to meet Him but Mary waited in the house (John 11:20). I can only assume that she was praying.

The third incident took place after Jesus had raised Lazarus from the dead and returned to visit the family at their house. Mary came, and anointed the Lord's feet with the beautiful, fragrant oil and then wiped His feet with her hair. Judas Iscariot, an evil man – a thief actually – who looked after the disciples' money box, said, "Lord, surely she could have sold that perfume and got 300 denarii to give to the poor?" His motive was totally impure. Jesus replied, "Leave her alone. She has kept this for My day of burial. The poor you will have with you always, but Me you will not always have with you."

Mary sat at Jesus' feet and it was the best place to be at that time, because she knew He wouldn't be with them for very long. Are you so busy doing the work of the Lord that you have actually forgotten to spend time with the Provider of the work? If that's the case, my dear friend, you're in severe trouble.

I've seen it many times before: missionaries who went out to the mission field, supposedly to work for God, and who came back totally dejected. Some even turned their backs on God, completely disheartened by the lack of response from the heathen. Their motive for becoming missionaries was impure. They didn't do it for Jesus. They might have done it for many other reasons, but not for God.

Then there are the others, like David Livingstone, who went out to preach the gospel. In his whole life I think he only had one convert – and that was a chief from Botswana. Yet he was content, because he wasn't doing it for the heathen. He was doing it for the Master.

During the First World War, a beautiful young nurse with a peaches-and-cream complexion, amidst the stinking trenches and dead soldiers, sat with a man's head on her lap, her beautiful white uniform splattered with blood, mud, and dirt. An editor of a newspaper and the major of the army walked by and said,

"I wouldn't do that job for a million pounds!" The beautiful little Christian nurse overheard him, looked up, and said, "Sir, neither would I." She did it for Jesus.

Today, when we go out, let us remember: Whatever we do, whatever it might be, let's do it for Jesus because of the love that we have for Him.

My yoke

Matthew 11:30

For my yoke is easy, and my burden is light.

My wife told me the other day about a story she read about a little carpenter shop in Nazareth with a sign over the door: "The best yokes are made here". Of course that was Joseph's carpenter shop, where he and his son Jesus made the best yokes in town. That has never changed. The Lord says in Matthew 11:30, "My yoke is easy, and my burden is light."

Why do we always think that other people's yokes are easier to carry than our own? It's the same thing as taking up your cross. You always feel that your cross is heavier than those of the people around you. That's why the Lord says, "Come unto Me all ye that labour and are heavy laden, and I will give you rest. Take My yoke upon you … for My burden is light."

Being a farmer I know the importance of a yoke. If you've ever ploughed with oxen or horses you will know how important it is to have two animals of the same strength and the same height pulling together. If not, the one pulls faster than the other or carries a heavier load. This causes chafing and a lot of discomfort and pain and eventually the two animals cannot carry the yoke together.

It is so important to be evenly yoked in this life. If you are unevenly yoked in marriage – the one partner being a Christian and the other not – the marriage can never work. When two animals are yoked, they need to pull in the same direction. You can't have one animal pulling to the left and the other to the right, for they end up going nowhere and it causes a lot of discomfort and pain. The same principle applies to a marriage.

If you are reading this today and you're contemplating marriage, be sure of one thing: you need to be evenly yoked. One of the biggest mistakes people make is to think that they will change their partner and make him or her into a Christian once they are married. Unfortunately, normally the opposite happens. You need to be sure of whom you are going to be yoked with for the rest of your life. Be very sure.

I don't believe in long engagements. I believe that once a man and woman have decided that they are going to be married, they need to do so straight away because the temptation is great and the body is weak. Before they are married they can make mistakes that do not bring glory to God. However, having said that, never get married on the spur of the moment. It's a huge decision to make.

The same principle can be applied in the business world. Jesus says that we should not be unevenly yoked in our work environment. Before you go into partnership, make sure that your partner is a God-fearing man; that you are prepared to use the Bible as your compass and reference. Then your business will prosper and God will honour it. However, if one man is a believer and the other one is not, the believer will want to do things according to the Word of God, such as pay his taxes and charge a fair price for a fair product, while his partner will probably try to do the opposite. There will be continual friction and discomfort and the business will never succeed.

Today, find the carpenter shop with the sign "The best yokes are made here". Ask the Lord Jesus Christ to make your yoke so you can pull your load with comfort, joy, and patience and then you can be sure that you will get to your destination.

Take up your cross

Mark 8:34

Whoever desires to come after Me, let him deny himself, and take up his cross, and follow Me. (NKJV)

There's always a price to pay when you follow Jesus. It cost Jesus His life. The decision to follow the Lord is a serious one to make. The Lord says that you have to take up your cross. The cross is the symbol of Christianity but it is so much more than a fancy ornament to be hung around a person's neck. It is actually the symbol of suffering because Jesus paid with His life so we could have the privilege of becoming His followers. Jesus says we must be prepared to take up our cross if we are to follow Him.

In that beautiful book *Streams in the Desert* there is an article that is quoted from *Glimpses through Life's Windows*, which reads like this:

> The Changed Cross is a poem that tells of a weary woman who thought that the cross she must bear surely was heavier than those of other people, so she wished that she could choose another person's instead. When she went to sleep, she dreamed that she was taken to a place where there were many different crosses from which to choose. There were various shapes and sizes, but the most beautiful one was covered with jewels and gold. "This I could wear with comfort," she said. So she picked it up but her weak body staggered beneath its weight. The jewels and the gold were beautiful, yet they were much too heavy for her to carry.
>
> The next cross she noticed was quite lovely with beautiful flowers entwined around its sculptured form. Surely this was the one for her. She lifted it, but beneath the flowers were large thorns that pierced and tore her skin.
>
> Finally, she came to a plain cross without jewels or any carvings and with only a few words of love inscribed on it. When she picked it up, it proved to be better than all the rest, and the easiest to carry. As she looked at it, she noticed it was bathed in a radiance that fell from heaven. Then she recognized it as her own old cross. She had found it once again, and it was the best of all, and the lightest for her.

You see, God knows what cross we need to bear, and we never know how heavy someone else's cross is. We envy someone who is rich, who is carrying a golden cross adorned with jewels, but we don't know how heavy it might be. We look at someone else whose life seems to be so easy, and who is carrying a cross that is covered with flowers. Yet if we could actually weigh all the crosses that we think are lighter than ours, we would never find one better suited for us than our own.

So don't be concerned about someone else's cross but rather carry your own. Carry it with dignity, with pride and persistence and, most of all, carry it because of the love you have for Jesus Christ. Prefer others over yourself. Help those who are weary and heavy laden, and the Lord will give you more than the strength you need to carry your own cross.

Know God

Titus 1:16

They profess that they know God; but in works they deny him…

I was preaching at a campaign in the Eastern Cape and a grizzly old farmer came up to me and said, "Son, preach so that we can see you." I pondered on what he had meant: "Speak, so that we can see you." What he was trying to say was, "Actions speak louder than words." He wanted me to bare my heart so that they knew where I was coming from.

I think that is what the Lord is saying in this Scripture. There are many people who profess to know God but their lifestyle divulges the opposite. Unfortunately, this denies them entry into God's kingdom. We give our lives to the Lord Jesus Christ, not to a great speaker or even a denomination, but an unbeliever doesn't know these things. People automatically assume that a person is a representative of God when they stand up for the Lord – and our blessed Lord Jesus gets judged according to that person's works and lifestyle.

It's therefore a very serious thing when you nail your colours to the mast and say that you belong to Jesus, because from that time onwards, you are on display. You can no longer say, "It's my own life; I can do what I like with it." No you can't! Galatians 2:20 says, "I am crucified with Christ." Our life has got to measure up to our profession. If our profession is Jesus Christ, we must display the fruits of the Spirit. I've found that the more one spends time with the Lord, the easier it is to become like Him.

When you go out today, remember that you are an ambassador for Jesus Christ (2 Corinthians 5:20) and, as they perceive you, they'll perceive the Master. It's not really so much what you say, but who you are, that will persuade them.

One of the hardest things to do is to damage your reputation and then go back and ask forgiveness. Admitting you made a mistake usually makes a bigger impression on an unbeliever than when you walk around like a saint. It is then that the people will know that you are a real person but that you are trying your very best to walk in the footsteps of Jesus.

God bless you today as you go out and represent the King of Glory.

Living for Christ

Philippians 1:21

For to me, to live is Christ, and to die is gain.

We often talk about how the saints knew Paul and loved him. I read an article by Leonard Ravenhill, which points out that the demons also knew Paul very well and feared him, because he was continually upsetting them. Remember the story where the seven sons of Sceva tried to cast a demon out of a man (Acts 19:14)? The demon in the man attacked them and nearly killed all seven of them. They ran for their lives and left all their clothes behind. The demons said, "Jesus we know, Paul we know, but we don't know you."

I feel in my heart that the devil also needs to know who we are as believers. We are not there to be toyed with. We are there to be feared – if we walk in the power and the might of our Lord Jesus Christ. Paul had absolutely no fear of death because he had already died. He was broken and humbled when the Lord knocked him off his horse on his way to Damascus to persecute the Christians (Acts 9:4–6). The Lord said, "Saul, Saul, why persecutest thou me?" "Who art thou, Lord?" "I am Jesus." He was totally humbled, then blinded so that he had to be led by the hand. Ananias, one of the men that he was going to try and kill in Damascus, had to pray for him to regain his sight.

The demons couldn't kill Paul. He was already dead. That's why he had so much power. He feared nothing but sin and desired no one but God. He didn't have any personal possessions left, so he couldn't be tempted with anything. He had nothing to protect. Leonard Ravenhill calls him "A God-intoxicated man".

Does the Lord know you and me? If He came back today to take us home to be with Him in heaven, would He recognize us? Maybe a more serious question is: Does the world recognize who we are? When we frequent places where the men of the world are – and we should do if we are going to be the salt of the earth and the light in darkness – do they know who we are? Do they alter their conversation when we come onto the scene? Do they think twice before they tell those dirty jokes? Or are we just one of the boys?

Paul was known by his lifestyle. As with Jesus his Saviour, wherever Paul went there was either a riot or a revival. Friends, we are in dire need of men like that today. Men of faith, who can call sin by its name but who are also soft and gentle; who can sit with a drug addict or an alcoholic in the gutter and speak with them and not be concerned about what other people would say; who can have fellowship with a person of another race who is a believer and not be concerned about the status quo or how they are going to be branded; who are able to have fellowship with men and women who have fallen but are wanting to come back to God. Do people say about you, "That man, that woman is a child of God"? That's what Paul said in Philippians 4:9, "Those things, which ye have both learned, and received, and heard, and seen in me, do: and the God of peace shall be with you."

My dear friend, let's ask ourselves the question today: Are we Jesus' ambassadors or not? I trust that the answer will be that, by His grace, we are. We will no longer be one of those who sit on the fence. The Lord hates lukewarm people (Revelation 3:16). Let's be red-hot for Him today, just like Paul was!

Doubt, the killer

John 12:10

But the chief priests plotted to put Lazarus to death also… (NKJV)

The greatest sin in the Bible is unbelief. It's not murder, it's not adultery, it's not theft, it's not lying; it's unbelief.

The only reason that God could not use the Pharisees and the high priests to propagate His gospel was because of their unbelief. They could not believe that Jesus Christ is the Son of God. Even when Lazarus – a man who had been dead in the tomb for four days – was raised by Jesus, they could still not believe that Jesus Christ raised him. Or maybe they didn't want to believe it. Something that the Lord showed me in my quiet time this morning was that they had actually planned to put Lazarus to death in order to prevent the Jews from following Jesus Christ as Lord and Saviour. What a terrible, drastic thing to do in order to cover up the miracle-working power of our risen Saviour!

How did people know that Jesus Christ is the Son of God? Was it because of His fancy sermons? No. It was because of the signs, wonders and miracles that He performed. At Shalom we say that one genuine miracle equals a thousand sermons.

My friend, faith comes by hearing and hearing by the Word of God (Romans 10:17). Many people ask me to pray that God would increase their faith. I always say that I won't pray for God to increase their faith; instead I will pray for them to hunger after the Word of God and to read and believe the Bible. The more time you spend with the Word of God, the greater your faith will become.

Keep away from those people who, when they see a glass half-full with water, tell you that it's half-empty. Keep away from those people who, when they see the sun coming up in the morning, say, "It is going to be a dry season," and then at midday when the clouds come up, say, "Floods are on the way." You can never please people like that. They can never be happy because they are always negative. Start spending time with people who choose to believe the promises of God.

I've just returned from the outback of Australia, where I saw God work in very powerful ways. They hadn't had proper rain there for eight to nine years. Rain started falling on the Saturday in the area where we were preaching – and it rained right through to the Monday when I was leaving.

God is a miracle-working God. It's got nothing to do with you or me. All He asks you to do is to believe. He says, "If you have the faith of a mustard seed…"

Fair-weather faith

Matthew 12:30

He who is not with Me is against Me; and he who does not gather with Me scatters abroad.

(NKJV)

Charles Haddon Spurgeon, the great Baptist preacher, said, "Fair-weather faith is not faith at all."

At sea, the safest place to be is over the deepest part of the deep blue ocean, away from the shore where the rocks can turn a ship into splinters. Most sailors will tell you that they can survive almost any storm that breaks if the boat is over the deepest part of the ocean. It's when a ship's captain gets nervous during a storm and wants to keep the shoreline in sight when the wind will blow the ship onto the rocks and destroy the crew and the ship's contents. It is when the captain chooses to take the boat way out to sea when the storm comes that the ship will be tossed to and fro but will not sink because there are no rocks or obstacles to break it up.

The safest place to be is right in the middle of the storm. They say that right in the centre of a tornado – a twister – is absolute calm. The destruction takes place around the periphery. Likewise, I remember when I was playing rugby as a young man that the safest place to be was right in the middle of the loose ruck. I never seemed to get hurt then. However, if I hesitated and hung around the edges of the scrum, I always seemed to get a stray boot in my face or somewhere against my body.

It is exactly the same with us Christians. When things are going well, we keep one foot in the world and the other in the kingdom, if that's at all possible. Of course, when the pressure builds or when the storms blow up, we try to serve two masters and end up getting seriously hurt. I would encourage you to fully commit to the Lord. Hand every single aspect of your life over to Him, knowing that He will not leave you nor forsake you (Hebrews 13:5).

The safest place to be is right next to the Lord. The safest place that the disciples could have been was right next to the Saviour of the world. Yet, on that terrible evening in the Garden of Gethsemane, when the high priest's soldiers came to arrest the Master, the disciples ran away from the only person who could help them.

Don't seek the calm waters today. Any good sailor will tell you that the thing they fear most at sea is a calm where the water becomes like glass and there's not a wisp of a breeze. For a sailing ship that means that it is going nowhere. The calm can last for up to three weeks – and if that happens the crew can literally die of starvation and thirst. With a storm, even if the wind is blowing the wrong way, you can at least tack against it.

Sometimes the most dangerous place for a Christian to be is in a situation that is too calm. For it is then that he does not spend time with the Lord or in Christian fellowship or reading the Scripture and then it is so easy for him to fall back to his old ways.

Before you go out today, make a pledge to God that you will not be a fair-weather Christian, but that you will be God's man, God's woman, irrespective of the waves or the winds of the storms. Make a decision to get out to the deep waters, away from the shore. A man once said that he would rather be with Jesus in a little dinghy sailing around the Cape of Storms, with ten-storey high waves down upon them, than to be in the *Queen Mary* on a quiet lake without Him!

Glorify God

John 12:28

Father, glorify thy name.

Jesus' sole purpose on earth was to glorify His heavenly Father. He came for no other reason. If you read a little further in today's Scripture you'll see that some people said that the Lord's voice was like thunder that came from heaven and others said that it was like an angel speaking to Jesus. The Lord went on to say, "If you lift Me up from the earth, I will draw all peoples to Myself." The gospel of Jesus Christ is a very simple story, my dear friend. As you lift up Jesus today wherever you go, He will draw people to Himself.

I have just returned from a meeting in Bloemfontein in the heart of our beloved South Africa, where we saw the cricket stadium jam-packed to such an extent that we didn't even have the space to call people forward to pray for them individually for healing. There were hundreds and hundreds of sick people coming forward. All I could do was to pray one general prayer – but I knew that Jesus would do the rest. We saw the whole stadium recommit to Christ and renew their covenant, and we saw literally hundreds upon hundreds of people raise their hands, acknowledging Jesus as Lord for the first time.

This is indeed harvest time. We only need to be careful not to appropriate any of God's glory to ourselves, because even the Master Himself said that His purpose on this earth was to lift up the name of His heavenly Father.

As you keep telling people today that Jesus Christ is Lord, He is the healer, He is the deliverer, He is the giver of new life, the Lord will do the rest. That is basically all that preaching entails. It's just lifting up the name of Jesus – and you can do that today in the workshop, the schoolroom, on the farm, in the hospital, or wherever. You don't have to go to Bible college and get a degree to learn how to preach. You just need to exalt the name of the Saviour. That name is more than ample to undertake for every single need. Go today and just keep telling them what Jesus means to you.

Talking to God

1 Thessalonians 5:17

Pray without ceasing.

In his book on prayer, Phillip Yancey says that the main reason why we pray is to get to know God. I think that's so simple and so appropriate.

Getting to know God... How does one get to know someone? By speaking to them and spending time with them. Phillip Yancey uses the example of the film *Fiddler on the Roof,* where the main character cries out to God right through the film. At one stage he says, "I can understand You punishing me when I'm bad, or my wife because she talks too much, or my daughter when she wants to marry an unbeliever, but what do You have against my horse?" He's sitting on the side of the road and his horse has gone lame.

Very clever, very funny, and yet so true! God wants us to speak to Him in everyday language. The prayer that Jesus taught us is such a real prayer. It talks about all the common and day-to-day things that we require, like food, clothing, forgiveness of sin, taking care of our neighbour and so on.

Remember to talk to Him at all times. Once we were travelling in a Kombi to a campaign in a nearby town. There were seven or eight of us in the vehicle. We started praying, then we'd interject by talking to one another about something that came up, then we would carry on praying, just as you would talk to your best friend. Some of the men in the vehicle were astounded because they'd never, ever seen people pray in such a way before.

I'd encourage you to talk to Jesus as you are ploughing today, maybe taking cattle to the sale, maybe working at the till in a shop, or maybe sitting in a classroom studying. After you have been praying for many years, and you've known God for a long time, you don't even have to talk to Him verbally. You can talk to Him in your spirit. Personally, I often find that so soothing and helpful, especially when I am travelling a lot and I'm away from home, maybe sitting on an aeroplane. I can just close my eyes and talk to the Lord in my heart and get the answers I need. It's all about having a true relationship.

Today, when you go out to live for the Lord, pray relentlessly and see how much better your day will go, and how few mistakes you'll make.

God's people

2 Chronicles 7:14

If my people ...

I'm about to speak at an agricultural congress in our province, KwaZulu-Natal. There will be delegates coming from all over the province: black, white, Asian, emerging farmers and established commercial farmers. We've just heard that the National Minister of Agriculture will also be attending. I have been told that I am allowed to read from God's Word, say a prayer and may speak for fifteen minutes. Even as I'm sitting in my prayer room contemplating what to say, this Scripture (2 Chronicles 7:14) is weighing heavy on my heart. The Lord says, "If my people ..." and this is the message which I believe God wants me to give to these very precious colleagues of mine.

Farming is not for sissies. It is a wonderful way of life but not easy – one is dealing with the elements, the devaluation of the currency, labour problems, diseases and many other unforeseen factors. The Lord has impressed upon me to remind the delegates that it doesn't matter how well they can farm, it doesn't matter how well they plough, how well they fertilize, or how well they sow their seed; unless God brings the rain there will be no harvest. It doesn't matter how well they breed their animals; unless God protects their livestock and allows them to multiply, they will remain infertile, they will remain plagued by disease and their stud farming will fail.

What we need to remember is to put God first; then we need to be sure that there are no unresolved issues between us and our family, our workers, or our business colleagues. Then we can expect God to do a mighty work for us. I've seen God turn failure into success so many times before.

I've just had an email message sent to me by a farmer from Western Australia, where we were some few months ago. While we were there we prayed, repenting before God with the Australian farmers on the West Coast. They are now looking forward to harvesting a bumper crop of wheat. A photo was attached to the mail showing the farmer kneeling in the field with the sun rising behind him and the wheat standing higher than his shoulders. Incidentally, he was suffering from terrible back pain when we were there. We prayed the prayer of faith and God has healed his back as well! "If My people, who are called by My name ..." (2 Chronicles 7:14). That's the answer. The answer is in the hands of the believer.

Choosing not to choose

Isaiah 30:18

Blessed are all who wait for him! (NIV)

The hardest thing for me to do is to wait. I am neither a good fisherman nor a good hunter. I am too impatient. So this is the very aspect of my personality that the Lord Jesus Christ is working on as I am writing this book. But the Lord has really blessed my wife Jill in this regard. She has the ability – I believe the God-given ability – to be still and to wait on God. The Lord reveals tremendous jewels and nuggets of gold to her because she is content to wait.

One cannot work out one's own salvation by doing good deeds. Salvation is all about resting in the blessed assurance that Jesus Christ has saved us unconditionally, simply because we believe that He is the Son of God. The desire to always be doing things for the Lord is not necessarily placed in our hearts by Him. The Lord created us primarily for His own pleasure and to have fellowship with Him.

Some of us are so busy running around the countryside trying to do good works for the Lord that He can't speak to us. Maybe, just maybe, we are trying to run away from issues that He wants us to face up to. When Jill and I go away for a break, normally to the bush to spend time with the Lord, it is usually the most trying time for me because I have to sit down. There's nowhere to go, nothing to do, no cell phones, no radio, no television, no meetings to prepare for. Just to sit can be extremely taxing, because then God starts to speak clearly to my heart and shows me areas that He is not pleased with, areas that I need to brush up on.

The Holy Spirit also reveals things about me that I'm not happy with, that I am embarrassed about, issues that need to be dealt with. If you want to be used by God, you must be prepared to wait for Him so that He can speak into your life, so you have something of substance to tell the world.

Stand still

Exodus 14:13

Do not be afraid. Stand still, and see the salvation of the Lord. (NKJV)

After we've done everything we can in our strength by faith, then we need to be still and allow the Lord to complete the work. I've often been quoted as saying that faith has feet; faith is a doing word. And that is so true – but there comes a time when we need to stand back and see what God is going to do next. Moses told the Israelites to stand still, and of course the Lord did the rest.

Today you might have to make some serious decisions. Today you may even be saying that unless God takes over, you are in trouble. Well, I've got good news for you. God will do what you ask Him to, but He will do it His way and not your way. His ways are not our ways and His thoughts are not our thoughts.

I remember one specific year when we had the most horrific drought on the farm. I was planting seed maize at the time. I had leased the farm next door and we put in over 200 hectares of seed maize. We spent all our production line, our overdrafts were at the full limit, and in the end there was no crop to reap. The sheaves were bare. There was no corn inside. I had a huge labour force that came to work, to reap the maize, and we were staring bankruptcy straight in the face.

This was summer. Totally contrary to all weather patterns, we had a freak snowstorm that decimated the forests around our farm. Because the gum (eucalyptus) trees and the wattle trees come from the southern hemisphere, they are unable to carry snow. The pines were fine. All the gum and wattle trees were twisted and the branches were broken by the weight of the snow, to such a degree that the timber companies were at a loss as to what to do.

I had all these people on our farm looking for work. We went out, bought four chainsaws and begged the timber companies for a contract to help them clear the forests. They agreed, and gave us the forests that were affected the worst to start with because they knew we were farmers and not foresters, so we had to prove ourselves. My youngest son Fergie had just left school and we were able to start felling huge plantations. This took months and months.

Slowly but surely we clawed our way back. They paid us for the contract work that we did and we were able to repay our production lines and our overdrafts. As we were facing an absolute disaster the Lord brought a freak snowstorm – and that was our salvation.

Today, just do what you can and then stand back and see what God can do. He will never leave you nor forsake you.

Hold your peace

Exodus 14:14

The Lord will fight for you, and you shall hold your peace. (NKJV)

The image that comes to mind straight away is the Lord Jesus Christ standing before Pontius Pilate. Pontius Pilate was questioning Him at length and the Bible says, "And He answered him not." Jesus never said a word. He never opened His mouth. He did not have to defend Himself. His Father was doing that.

Sometimes, instead of arguing, the better response is to say nothing. I'm talking particularly in the event of a family argument. Sometimes rather just pray and don't say too much, because the Lord Himself will speak for you. Let your words be few and let people judge you by your actions rather than your words.

When you surrendered your life to Him, the Lord promised that He would take care of every one of your needs. He has a plan for us but sometimes we are so busy making our own plans that we can't actually hear what He wants to do. Read Exodus 14:15 and you'll see that the Lord said to Moses, "Why do you cry to Me? Tell the children of Israel to go forward" (NKJV). He said, "Lift up your rod, stretch it out over the sea, and divide it. And then the children will go on dry ground through the midst of the sea." If the Lord is on your side you truly have nothing to worry about. You will definitely gain a landslide victory.

Romans 8:31 says, "If God is for you, there's no one that will stand against you." The young David knew this very well when he took on Goliath. That young boy had such a sound perception of the person of God that he was not afraid of this huge giant at all – this professional killer who was going to swat him like a fly.

Goliath said, "Do you think I'm a dog that you come against me with sticks and stones?" Young David replied, "I come to you in the name of the Lord of hosts, the God of the armies of Israel, whom you have defied. This day the Lord will deliver you into my hand, and I will strike you and take your head from you, and this day I will give the carcasses of the camp of the Philistines to the birds of the air and the wild beasts of the earth, that all the earth may know that there is a God in Israel" (1 Samuel 17:45–46, NKJV). With that, David killed Goliath with a stone and a sling, and nothing else.

The Lord will fight for you as well today, and He will use weapons which you and I would never dream of; very simple ones at that, so that no one can touch His glory. Hold your peace today and go your way. Let the Lord go before you and wait and see how He will deal with the enemies that will confront you.

Have a wonderful day!

Walk the talk

John 12:19(b)

Look, the world has gone after Him! (NKJV)

Friends, we don't have to persuade people about the sovereignty and the miracle-working power of Jesus Christ. All we have to do is to keep exalting the Lord and He will do the rest.

When people saw Lazarus walking the streets they started to follow after Jesus Christ, because Lazarus was a walking miracle. However, the Pharisees (the church, as it were, in those days) said amongst themselves, "We are accomplishing nothing; but look, the world has gone after Him."

Are we walking the talk? When people see us, do they want to follow after the Lord Jesus Christ? When they hear our conversation, when they see our deeds, our humility, our love and our compassion, does it draw them to follow after the Man from Galilee? Do people come up to us and ask, "What do you have? Because whatever it is that you have, I want."? Then, of course, it's a mere formality to introduce them to the King.

We have to trust God to intercede in a supernatural way. We have to start walking by faith and not by sight. We have to see those things that "are not" as if they are, or else we become equal to the world – negative, depressed, without any hope. We have to start encouraging one another by speaking life to each other. That can only happen if we spend time reading the Word of God.

The world went after Jesus because He had something that this life could not offer, and that was hope. If ever the world was in need of hope, it's now. As we sense the Day of Judgment drawing closer, the words in the book of Revelation ring even more true: "The wicked shall become more wicked and the righteous more righteous."

I'm seeing with my carnal eyes the power of God like I've never seen it before – maybe because I haven't been looking for it before.

I urge you to make a decision today to believe the promises of God spoken over you, and not the lies of the devil. Then people will see Christ in you and follow after Him.

Holy God

Hebrews 12:14

Pursue peace with all men, and holiness, without which no one shall see the Lord.

So often I hear of people who have been gloriously saved by the Lord Jesus Christ, people whose sins have been washed away and who are free once again – new people in Christ. But sometimes it worries me when I don't see reverence and respect granted to our Holy God. He offered His only Son for us while we were still sinners; a tremendous price to pay, when you think about it.

If you are reading this book, and have a son or a daughter, maybe you'll understand. If you had to sacrifice him for a good man that would truly be a wonderful gesture. But will you be willing to sacrifice your own son for a bad man – for a sinner, like Angus Buchan? That is too much to ask, surely. Yet that's what our Father did. We need to respect Him as a holy God. He is a holy and righteous God. He is so holy that He could not even look upon His own Son when He was dying on the cross. Jesus cried out, "ELI, ELI, LAMA SABACHTHANI?" (My God, My God, why have You forsaken Me?) The Father could not look upon His own Son because He's a holy God, and His Son had taken on all the filth and squalor, all the sin of this world upon Himself.

If you look at the book of Leviticus chapter 16, you'll see that even Moses' brother, Aaron, who was the high priest, lost his two sons because they offered profane fire before the Lord, and they died. The Lord told Moses very clearly, "Tell Aaron your brother not to come at just any time into the Holy Place inside the veil, before the mercy seat which is on the ark, lest he die" (Leviticus 16:1–2, NKJV).

I really believe that although He is "a Friend who sticks closer than a brother", He is also God and we need to pay Him reverence and respect. He is not our "mate" or "the Man upstairs". He is God Almighty, the Holy One, who sacrificed His most precious possession so that we might have everlasting life.

Holiness can be defined as "the end product of obedience". We automatically become holy men and women when we start to obey the Word of God. Today, let us go out and show Him huge respect. If someone is using our Saviour's name in vain, we need to ask God to give us the courage to quietly say to him, "Please, I'd appreciate it if you didn't use my Saviour's name in such a way." Don't tell God that you love Him. Show Him that you love Him by the course of your actions.

Jesus is trustworthy

Numbers 23:19

God is not a man, that he should lie…

Unfortunately in this day and age we see companies drowning in financial trouble; we see the money market going up and down like a yoyo; we see devaluation of currencies. I ponder over the country just north of South Africa's borders where inflation is running riot. People can't even deposit their money into their bank accounts any more as the currency is devaluing too rapidly. Not only does the same state of affairs reign supreme in Israel as well, but sadly, wherever you go in the world. In America large corporations are going bankrupt due to corruption and unreliable top management. I'm talking about CEOs, "respectable" men and women. Who can you trust? In this world, no one really!

There is One, however, who is faithful. His name is Jesus. He always does what He says: He is entirely reliable. Many of us would not be walking the perilous roads we are now if only we had listened to His counsel. He speaks to us through His Word and through other Christians. To me personally, He speaks through nature. Through the elements. He confirms His counsel time and time again.

In Revelation 3:8 the Lord says, "I know your works… I have set before you an open door, and no one can shut it." He is saying that when the door opens, go through it. When it closes, don't try and break it down. So many come to their demise because they follow their gut feeling rather than listening to God's faithful Word.

The Scripture quoted today continues, "He's not even a son of man, that he should repent." God doesn't have to apologize, because He doesn't make mistakes. He delivers on His promises. If He said, "Come unto Me, all of you that are weary and heavy laden, and I will give you rest," you can be assured He'll do it, but we have to do it according to His plan, His Word, not our own.

How true the words of the proverb are: if you sow the wind, you'll reap the whirlwind. Many of us cry out, "Lord, Lord, why did You forsake me? Lord, why did You let me go through this? Lord, where were You when I called?" He says, "I was there all the time but you didn't trust Me. You trusted somebody else's counsel and so you have to bear the consequences." The good news is that if we repent, if we ask for God's forgiveness, we can always start anew.

God's counsel to you today is: Begin to seek His kingdom and His righteousness first, and all of the other things will be added to you (Matthew 6:33).

Spirit of faith

Numbers 14:24

But my servant Caleb, because he had another spirit with him…

Caleb is one of my heroes in the Word of God. If ever there was a man whom we could emulate and follow, it is Caleb. He was a man of great faith. There were only two men who went into the Promised Land out of all the millions of Israelites who came from Egypt. One was Joshua and the other was Caleb. Both of them were men of faith.

I want to emphasize the importance of walking the walk of faith. Jesus always honours faith. I've experienced this in my own life. If you get out of the boat and walk on the water, He will walk with you, just as He did with Peter. The secret is to keep your eyes on Jesus and not on the waves, or else you might sink.

Caleb was a man who kept his eyes fixed on God. When Caleb was eighty-five years old, a time when most men would have already retired and slowed down, Joshua offered him his inheritance. He said, "What would you like, Caleb? You've been such a faithful warrior of God!" Caleb replied, "Give me the big mountain where the giants live." A true man of faith!

Today, ask God to give you the faith so that you, like Caleb, can have a bold spirit. When the world around us is collapsing and falling apart due to a spirit of fear, it grants the children of God the opportunity to expand the kingdom of God.

In Romans 4:20 the Bible says that Abraham staggered not at the promises of God through unbelief, but remained strong in faith, giving glory to God. He was a hundred years old when God promised him that he'd be the father of all nations. In carnal eyes there was no hope for Abraham to have a family, let alone be the father of many nations. Yet, because he had faith, God honoured him and Sarah. Sarah bore the most beautiful son, Isaac, and Abraham became the father of all believers today.

God does not discriminate on grounds of age, gender, or qualifications. He will honour faith, as he did with Caleb. If you have a bold spirit and you follow Him wholeheartedly – which implies that you become a holy man or woman – He promises you a land of milk and honey for your children to inherit. What a promise! Let's go for it today.

Holy God

1 Samuel 3:4

… the Lord called Samuel: and he answered, Here am I.

The Bible says that the young boy Samuel had yet to meet the Lord. Yet when God called him, he answered, "Here am I." It reminds me of when Jesus called the disciples. Some of them said, "I must first go and bury my dead." He said, "Let the dead bury the dead." Some said, "I must go and say goodbye to my family." Jesus replied, "No, follow after Me."

There's always a price to pay when following Jesus Christ. The Lord expects nothing less than immediate obedience. Sometimes, He may not even ask twice. I've read of many mighty men of God – Billy Graham was one, Reinhard Bonnke another – who said that they didn't believe they were God's first choice. The Lord called many before them who didn't respond.

God does not need our ability. He needs our availability. He doesn't always choose the people that we would have selected to do the work. He chooses the weak, the young, the illiterate, the broken, those who have made gross mistakes in the past – and then He uses them to work miracles, because He is a jealous God and will not share His glory with any man.

God called a little boy by the name of Samuel, and used him in a very powerful way. He was probably one of the most famous prophets in the Bible; definitely the one who rarely, if ever, took a wrong turn. He was completely dedicated to his Master, who never faulted, and who had no fear of man.

Eli had grown cold towards the things of the Lord. He'd allowed his own sons to desecrate the house of God and he never said a word. Samuel was afraid to tell Eli what God had told him, but Eli knew that Samuel had heard from God and he demanded that he be told the truth. It's the truth that sets a person free.

We know how the story ends. Eli's two sons were killed and Eli was so fat and overweight that he, on receiving the dreadful news of his sons' deaths, fell backwards and broke his neck. The young man Samuel, who said to the Lord, "Here am I", was used in a powerful way by God to anoint both Saul, the first king of Israel, and his successor David, the greatest king Israel ever had until Jesus Christ Himself. What an honour. Why did God choose him? Simply because he obeyed!

Today, spend some time and remind yourself that God has called you as well. It will give you the courage not to compromise, or to become insipid and untrustworthy. Then, as you go out today, simply obey the Word of the Lord.

Your life will never, ever be the same again!

Open door

Revelation 3:8

Behold, I have set before thee an open door…

People come to me and ask for counsel: "What should I do? I don't know whether I should leave or whether I should stay; whether I should get married or not; whether I should start the business or not." My advice is very simple – keep going through open doors, but if the doors are closed, the option to enter through them does not exist any more. I don't think it can be any simpler than that.

The gospel is simple, so simple that even young children can understand it. Let's not complicate it. If you're seeking the Lord when making decisions, I encourage you to fast and to pray, to read the Word of God, and then to follow through with all your leads. God will honour you, and your ventures will be successful.

God does not make mistakes. He is the Alpha and the Omega, the beginning and the end. He knows all things and He is all things. He loves you and is on your side. He will use circumstances and even unbelievers to open and close doors for you as He used Balaam's donkey to warn Balaam.

Avoid going around asking everybody's opinion. You'll get a hundred different opinions. Seek the Word of the Lord. Seek Him, go through the doors and God will help you to make your dreams come true.

Servant's heart

John 13:4

He riseth from supper and laid aside his garments, took a towel and girded himself.

Once again, the Master puts so many of us to shame. A valuable lesson that I have learned with regards to preaching, is that one must never preach down to people. So often when a preacher begins working in their ministry they are very humble, but the more they preach, the more they run the risk of becoming arrogant and proud. Instead of feeding God's sheep, they start to judge God's flock. This is not what the Lord wants us to do.

One of my heroes is Pastor William Duma, a Zulu preacher who used to look after his father's cattle in the hills of the Umkomaas Valley. God used him to heal the sick; he had a tremendous reputation, especially in the area of physical healing.

Many years ago he was invited to preach at a Baptist church in Zambia. At nine o'clock the congregation was waiting for the man of God who had come all the way from South Africa. The church was packed to capacity. In a typical Baptist church, the preacher enters from the back and walks up to the altar. People were craning their necks, looking around to see when this mighty man of God was going to appear. There was no sign of him. They could see that the pastor was getting quite agitated.

Then there was a faint knock at the back door, the vestry door that is usually used by the cleaning lady to gain entry to the church. The pastor left the pulpit and went through to the back door, opened it, and there stood the man of God – at the back entrance.

Jesus said that if you want to be the greatest in the kingdom of God you must be prepared to be the least. He demonstrated this not by preaching, but by washing the feet of His own disciples.

We need to serve our brothers and sisters while we still can. Today, make sure that, as a servant of God, people perceive you not as dominating, but as a humble servant. You see, my dear friend, the word "minister" literally means "to serve". Humility is the sign of a great man or woman of God. Why? Because that is how Jesus is.

Obey the first call

Jonah 3:1

Now the word of the Lord came to Jonah the second time… (NKJV)

It is much easier to obey the Lord than to continually have to apologize. Often we get ourselves into so much trouble simply by not obeying the voice of God.

I look at my own life. I remember responding to an altar call when I was about six years old, in a movie house in a place called Ndola in Zambia. I put up my hand, went to the front and accepted Jesus Christ as my Lord and Saviour. Because of the temptations of the world, I strayed, only to return on 18 February 1979. If I have one regret in life (and I don't have many, I can assure you), it is that I didn't heed and obey God's call the first time. It would have saved me so much pain and disappointment.

So it was with Jonah. If Jonah had just obeyed the Lord the first time, gone to Nineveh and preached the gospel, he wouldn't have had to go through the ordeal of being in the belly of a big fish for three days, nor would he have had to face the humiliation because of what he did. Nevertheless, the important thing is that he was obedient, eventually.

If God has called you to do something for Him – it might be restitution (making right with someone that you've wronged) – just go and do it. Get it done with so that you can get on with your life. Even if you were asked by God many years ago to do something, do it now while you still have time. If you read the rest of chapter 3 of the book of Jonah, you'll see that when Jonah went to the city of Nineveh he found it to be such a huge city that it took him three days to walk through it. He preached the gospel, and the king and all the people heard the Word of the Lord and repented. The Lord saved the entire city as a result.

God called you for a specific purpose and He calls you again today to complete what He has laid on your heart, not only for the sake of the gospel but also for your own sake and peace of mind.

May God bless you today as you go out and obey! It brings so much joy, so much peace and so much contentment.

Turning from evil ways

Jonah 3:10

And God saw their works; that they turned from their evil way; and God repented of the evil that he had said that he would do unto them.

Reading the book of Jonah has brought me so much joy and hope. Our God is such a gracious and forgiving God. He was going to destroy the city of Nineveh, a city so huge that according to the Bible it took three days to pass through. God had said that in forty days He was going to overthrow (destroy) it. Yet, when He saw the people changing and turning from their evil ways, He repented (meaning He stopped) and gave them another chance.

My dear friend, as you are reading this today, stand assured that there is nothing that God won't forgive. He is a gracious God. If He sees that you are really bearing the fruit of repentance, He will save you. The Bible promises salvation: "If My people who are called by My name will humble themselves, and pray…" (NKJV). This is what the people of Nineveh did when Jonah came and told them what God was going to do. The Bible tells us clearly that the Lord gave them a second chance.

Jesus spoke to the accusers of the prostitute who was about to be stoned and said, "Let him who is without sin cast the first stone." Of course no one could, and they all left. Jesus said to her, "Go and sin no more. Your sins are forgiven." I love Him so much! He's the Friend of sinners like me. It doesn't matter what we've done today.

It doesn't matter what sins we have committed. If we truly repent, which means to stop doing it, and seek His face, He will forgive and save us. The only difference between Peter and Judas Iscariot is that Peter repented and Judas didn't. Judas Iscariot betrayed the Lord once. Peter betrayed the Lord three times. But Peter repented and Judas didn't.

As you start your day, come before the Lord, ask forgiveness for all your sins and let the Lord minister to your soul. It says in Romans 8:1, "There is therefore now no condemnation to those who are in Christ Jesus" (NKJV). So, if the Lord sets you free, you shall be free indeed.

Different people

2 Corinthians 6:17

Wherefore come out from among them, and be ye separate, saith the Lord.

If ever we needed to change our ways, it is today. When I see the temptation that the internet, cell phones, computers, advertising billboards, and ordinary television offer, I cringe and say, "Lord, please, just give us the strength."

The Lord says that we have to be different in order to be His children. It seems to be the order of the day for young men and women to be intimate before they are married. It's not even regarded as being wrong. It takes extreme courage and strength for them to stand up for Christ today. But the Lord says that if we stand up for righteousness and honour, then we shall be His sons and daughters.

The Christian businessman or woman has to face a similar challenge in order to become successful. They have to be very courageous because they cannot operate according to the standards of the world. They've got to do it God's way; then the Lord can honour them, and always will.

As it says in the Word of God, there is no doubt that in the last days the filthy will become filthier and the righteous more righteous. You don't even have to be controversial. You just have to be a Christian and you'll automatically become controversial.

Finding a Christian who stands up for his or her faith, that conducts him or herself in the correct way, honouring the name of Jesus Christ, is wonderful and encouraging. As a Christian it is so refreshing for me to see young professional sportsmen, whether they be soccer players, rugby players, tennis, or cricket players, honouring God openly on the sports field.

Today, whether you're a blacksmith, as my dad was, or whether you're a schoolteacher, a student, or a farmer, I believe God is challenging you to come forth and be a Christian. Be different. Do things God's way and see what God will do in your life. All of a sudden you'll become that ambassador of Jesus Christ. What a wonderful thing it is to pull your shoulders back, lift your head, proudly push out your chest – in a humble way – and go out and witness for Christ! Not even by word of mouth but by your very life.

Go out today. Be among the people, but also remain separate from the things of the world that would dishonour the Lord.

No shortcuts

1 Samuel 31:4(b)

Saul took a sword and fell upon it.

The death of Saul came about through pride. Pride always comes before the fall. In 1 Peter 5:5 the Lord says that He resists the proud but He gives grace to the humble.

Many people had to pay severely for their actions because of their selfish, foolish pride. The passage in 1 Samuel 31 describes how Saul was about to be captured by the enemy. Rather than being mocked by them, he instructed his armour bearer to kill him. His armour bearer refused, so he committed suicide.

You know, friends, there is no shortcut to heaven. Nobody is without sin. There's nobody in this world who has never made a mistake. All God wants us to do is to repent and to start again. It doesn't matter what you've done or what you haven't done. If you ask for God's forgiveness, if you confess your sin and make restitution, God will give you another chance.

Many a time, when I had to support couples who were experiencing marital problems, the problems were caused by pride. Neither party was prepared to apologize, nor to accept the blame, and as a result they lost a beautiful marriage. All they had to do was to humble themselves and God would have healed them and set their marriage free.

I heard a sad story about a man coming out of the divorce court after his sixth failed marriage. He said, "She tried so hard but she just couldn't make me happy." How arrogant is that? What he didn't realize was that a marriage is an interaction between two people, and not one-sided. His wife was not there to make him happy. His wife was there to be looked after and loved, to be cared for and protected by him. What you give is what you get.

Pride says, "It's either my way or no way." That's not the way God works. God humbled me in a profound way. I was a self-made man who was determined to do it again when I came to South Africa from Zambia. I refused to accept help from anybody. I tried to do it my way and wanted to pay for everything. I wouldn't accept any gifts or assistance. Eventually I had to beg God for mercy.

God healed me. As a result I will never start a meeting without prayer and I will never pray on the platform without getting on my knees. Why? Because I want the Lord to see and I want people to know that I'm not a proud man. I want to remain humble so that God can lift me up. I don't want to try and lift myself up. I can't. In fact, Jesus says, "If you lift Me up I will draw all men unto Myself."

Work out your salvation today with fear and trembling. Trust in the Lord and He will pave your road to success.

Seeking counsel from God

2 Samuel 2:1

David enquired of the Lord.

I was sitting in a car park, waiting for my best friend (my wife) to finish her shopping. This can sometimes be a long, tedious operation. It's one area that I'm still working on in my life. I've not yet mastered the art of shopping, and my wife knows it, so we have an agreement. I sit in the car and write my book and she does the shopping.

As I was contemplating the Word of God, one of my sons in the Lord came and asked me for godly counsel. He was faced with a situation where one of his managers wasn't sure whether to leave the operation, or to stay. He told me that he had noticed that my hair was starting to turn white (well, it's almost snow white now!) and to him that's a sign of wisdom and he was asking counsel of me.

David enquired of the Lord. Yes, we can seek godly wisdom from one another, especially from the elders of the church, those who have been walking with God for a long time. When he asked me for this counsel I remembered the Great Commission in Mark 16:15: "Go into all the world and preach the gospel to every creature" (NKJV).

I remember an incident in my own life where someone who was walking with me in the Lord could not make up his mind whether the time for him to move on had come, or if he had to stay. Early one morning God reminded me of a song written by Keith Green – that wonderful gospel singer who has since gone to be with the Lord – with the lyrics: "If He has not told you to stay, then you'd better go."

Instead of praying about going, I said, "If He has not told you to stay; then go." The next day this brother came into my office and said, "I'm leaving. God has clearly told me that my time is up."

I want to say to you today: like David, enquire of God. God will always give you an answer, but be prepared to wait. Be prepared to take counsel from other brethren in the faith and then act on it. His answer is always simple, basic, and very easy to understand. But you need to hear it and then you need, by faith, to act on it. So, whatever God is telling you today, just do it. If you are not sure of a decision, then don't act on it. Quite simple! If the door is not open, don't try to bash it down. However, if the door opens, enter.

When you belong to Jesus there is no risk involved. In fact, I believe that faith is the surest thing that there is. So by faith step out today and do whatever it is that God tells you to do.

A godly life

Deuteronomy 10:12

... what doth the Lord thy God require of thee...

I get to deal with a countless number of broken people at the campaigns where I preach: people who are disillusioned with life; people who have been hurt; people who have made wrong decisions; people who are casualties of the worldly system.

This simple verse for today is so refreshing. All that the Lord requires of us is to fear Him. That fear does not imply being frightened; it implies treating Him with reverence, love, and respect.

Secondly, it's to walk in His ways, to do things as God would want you to. Ask yourself the question: "What would Jesus do?" and then do exactly that. Many young Christians wear wristbands with WWJD printed on them. The idea is to look at that wristband when you have to make a decision and – whether it's breaking the speed limit, falsifying your income tax returns or taking advantage of someone – ask yourself the question, "Would Jesus do that?" The answer will be a clear "No", so don't do it. Walk in His ways!

Thirdly, it is to love Him. You see, my dear friend, if you love someone, it's not hard to obey their rules. God doesn't want you to serve Him without soul. He wants you to serve Him with a heart of love. The early Christians said that there were only two things that one had to do. One was to glorify God and the other was to enjoy Him forever. Right now, I am so in love with my Master. I am really enjoying every moment with Him.

The Scripture says, "And to serve the Lord with all your heart and with all your soul." It's very easy to serve someone you love. How do you love someone? By spending time with them and getting to know them.

Today, just obey the Lord and do what He requires of you – and ninety per cent of the hardships that you're going through will disappear. The Lord says, "I have come that they may have life, and that they may have it more abundantly" (John 10:10, NKJV).

God bless you today as you chase after Him with a real desire to love Him and to obey Him.

Took our sin

John 3:16

For God so loved the world, that he gave his only begotten Son, that whosoever believeth in him should not perish, but have everlasting life.

There's a tale of a mighty man of God by the name of Anil who lived in Russia many, many years ago. He headed up a tribe of nomads. They lived in tents, looked after their cattle, sheep, and horses and they loved the Lord Jesus Christ very much. However, the Russian leader at that time was an evil man who repeatedly tried to destroy this tribe, but he could never quite catch them. Their strength was in their unity and their togetherness. They would have a sentry with a ram's horn posted on the highest mountain. As soon as he saw the king's soldiers coming, he would blow the horn. They would pack their tents and move off with their cattle, sheep, and horses. When the king's men arrived at their camping site, there was no trace of them.

Unfortunately, thievery broke out in the camp. The leaders came to Anil in his tent, where he was praying, and said, "There's a thief who is stealing our belongings. The biggest concern we have is that it's going to bring dissension amongst the people. When that happens there will be no unity. That will cause us to fall into the hands of the evil king."

Anil called all the people together, gave them a stern talking to and said he didn't ever want to see or hear about the matter again. With that, it stopped for about three weeks; then it started again. Anil called his leaders together and said, "We'll have to make an example of this because it's got to stop. It's demoralizing the folk and sooner or later it is going to lead to a divide. When that happens, the enemy will definitely catch up with us." They agreed to set a trap. The leaders asked, "But what will we do with the culprit when we catch him?" Anil said, "We'll have to make an example of him. We'll strip him down to the waist, tie him to a wagon wheel and we will lash him with thirty-nine stripes." (Bear in mind that forty was the death penalty.) This was agreed upon.

After a week, sure enough they caught the culprit. The tragedy was that it was Anil's eighty-five-year-old mother who was the thief. All the people came to Anil's tent to see what the man of God was going to do, because he'd already made a decree that the thief would be lashed. He said to the members of his clan, "Give me three days to fast and pray", because he loved his mother dearly, "and then I'll tell you what the result will be." After three days they all came together. Anil came out of his tent. He said, "The sentence will be carried out, but I shall take the lashes on my own back for my mother."

My dear friend, do you honestly believe that Anil's mother ever stole again after she had to stand there and watch her innocent son take the thrashing of his life for her sin? Well, that's exactly what Jesus Christ did for you and me. He took our sin upon Himself, was crucified and died for us. Today let us go and sin no more.

Forgiveness

Jonah 4:3

O Lord, take, I beseech thee, my life from me.

This is an account of Jonah who ran away from God – and only when he received instruction for the second time did he obey the Lord, because he knew what the consequences were going to be. He knew that the Lord was going to save the people of Nineveh – 60,000 of them – from total destruction and death because our God is a merciful God, slow to anger and of great kindness.

Jonah went and preached the gospel message after receiving instruction to do so for the second time. The whole nation repented and God had mercy on them and saved them. Jonah was so angry at God for bestowing mercy upon these people that he actually wanted to die. He said, "Oh Lord, take my life from me. It is better for me to die than to live."

How many of us have feelings of hatred for a person who hurt or harmed us or our families in one way or another? What we would like is sweet revenge. I'll never forget speaking at a farmer's day some years ago when we were going through some very tough times in the Natal Midlands area. Nearly 270 farmers had been murdered at that stage. I was encouraging the farmers to come to the King's Park Rugby Stadium in Durban and join in a day of prayer for peace.

While I was encouraging them to come, one farmer stood up and said, "Doesn't it say in the Bible, an eye for an eye and a tooth for a tooth?" I said, "Yes it does." Then I was at a loss for words. This man's soul was obviously in pain. He was very angry and felt unforgiving. Then the Holy Spirit prompted me to ask him a question. I asked, "Tell me, Sir, do you have a wife and children?" He said, "Yes, I do." I said, "You're a very selfish man, aren't you? In order to have a bit of sweet revenge you're prepared to put your wife and children on the altar, because the killing won't stop until we, as the children of God, come before the Lord and repent." He went very pale and quiet, and sat down.

Jonah wanted the people of Nineveh destroyed but God wanted them to be saved. There might be somebody who's done something terrible to you and you cannot find it in your heart to forgive them. I'd encourage you on this day to hand them over to God. Let Him deal with it and then press on with your life. The person that you are battling to forgive is probably not even aware of it and getting on with his life, but your bitterness and inability to forgive are making you sick on a physical, mental and spiritual level.

Today, forgive those who have done aught against you, hand them over to God and start over.

A servant's heart

John 13:12(b)

Know ye what I have done to you?

Jesus was dining with His blessed disciples for the last time before He was taken away, interrogated, beaten, and eventually crucified by the high priest's soldiers. He got up from the table, wrapped a towel around His waist, filled a basin with water and proceeded to wash His disciples' feet, one at a time. After He'd finished, He asked, "Do you know what I have done for you? They call Me Master and they say well, for so I am. If I'm your Master and I've washed your feet then surely you need to wash each other's feet?" The Lord was truly a humble person.

Martin Luther was once asked what the three greatest virtues of a man of God are. He replied, "Humility, humility and humility." If you want to be used by God, if you want to be counted among those who are followers of God, you need to humble yourself today in the sight of the Lord – and He will raise you up. God resists the proud and gives grace to the humble (1 Peter 5:5).

William Carey was a young country boy from England who was prompted by the Holy Spirit to go to India and tell people about his blessed Redeemer. Someone mocked him once and said, "I believe you're just a shoemaker?" He said, "No, Sir, I can't make shoes. I'm a cobbler. I can only repair them." An answer like that diffuses any kind of argument or arrogance.

Today, let your actions speak louder than your words. Be prepared to walk the extra mile, even for those who are of the most humble station in this life.

A time to be born

Ecclesiastes 3:2

A time to be born… and a time to plant.

As I am looking out of my window, I can clearly see that spring has sprung on the farm. The new grass is starting to grow – a beautiful green is at last tingeing the lawn after a very hard, long, and dry winter. I look out at the garden and notice that the Barberton daisies, azaleas and rambling roses are producing new buds. There's a tremendous noise up in the trees as the new flock of weavers are busy building nests, preparing to breed. In the field, the cows are calving down their new crop of calves. I can smell hope in the air.

Dear friend, maybe you've been through a winter of suffering, maybe a winter of mourning? Perhaps you've just recovered from sickness, or experienced tragedy in your family or in your business? The good news is that the Lord brings about seasons in our lives. Without a winter you cannot appreciate spring. It almost seems like the harder the winter, the more precious and beautiful spring becomes. The fragrance of new flowers and the sight of the new leaves on the trees give us hope for new opportunities.

Be encouraged today and remember that the Lord is still in control. He's in control not only of every aspect of our lives but of what happens on this earth. At the end of the day, we're waiting for that final spring day, the day when the Lord will come to take us home to be with Him in glory. But until that day, enjoy smelling the roses, enjoy God's creation and thank Him, not only for the big things but for the little things as well; the fact that you woke up this morning; that you can see, smell, hear and that you can walk. You have people who love you, care for you and are looking up to you to be strong for them.

Let this be the first best day of the rest of your life.

What does the Lord require of us?

Micah 6:8

... but to do justly...

I have just realized that the farm is too quiet. There is no action and the work should have started an hour ago. The tractors are silent. The cattle are still in their paddocks. The normal noise of Zulu women singing and people getting ready for work is absent.

Then I remember; every Friday morning we go to the house of God from seven to eight o'clock to spend an hour in praise and worship, thanking the Lord for a new day with our families.

God requires us to respect those whom we employ – and indeed every fellow man. If your faith is costing you nothing, it's worth nothing. It's costing us time and money to go to the house of the Lord but it's the best invested time and money that we can ever spend. We need to do what is just.

Today, when you go about your daily rounds, be sure to do justice to your fellow man. Don't alter the scales. Pay a person exactly what he is worth, and no less. Go the extra mile for the widow and the orphan. Let your actions speak louder than your words. Let people know that you are part of Jesus Christ's flock, because you're a just person and because you live justly.

The whole world

Mark 8:36

For what shall it profit a man, if he shall gain the whole world, and lose his own soul?

I was watching a programme on the History Channel on television last night and was totally amazed at what a human being can accomplish. There's no doubt that we are made in God's image. It is sad though that often our abilities and gifts from God become our gods. When this happens we are in serious trouble.

Howard Hughes, an American with a brilliant mind, designed aeroplanes. He designed the biggest wooden aeroplane ever to fly. It looked like a flying boat and was able to land in the sea. Together with his engineers and all his scientists, he then began to develop the helicopter. Later he started experimenting with electronics – a word that was hardly even used in those days. He started sending satellites into space. His was just an ordinary man with his own private company that did not form part of the United States government. Eventually, he was ranked second only to the United States government in the development of missiles and the sending of satellites into space enabling communication to take place throughout the whole world simultaneously. It had never been done before.

In 1935 Howard Hughes broke the world record for the fastest trip around the world in an aeroplane. He was known as "The Aviator" and was a man who was admired by everybody. He became the wealthiest man in the whole of the United States of America. When he died it took years to work out exactly how much he was worth.

Yet, that man died of malnutrition. He isolated himself, became a recluse, and lived on the top floor of a hotel in a dark room. He became obsessed with germs and disease. Nobody was allowed to touch him. He eventually stopped eating and died a miserable man alone in a room. At the time of his death he weighed less than 50 kg. He had accomplished so much and yet he lost everything. Why? His priorities were all wrong. The Bible says, "What does it profit a man if he gains the whole world and he loses his soul?"

There is no problem with a man being successful. I know many Christian businessmen who are extremely successful. The problem arises when the business becomes more important than God and your vision changes. You are no longer doing your work for God; you're doing it for your own gain. Perhaps you should do a priority check in your own life before you go out to work today. Ask yourself the question: Why am I really doing this? If it is for the Lord Jesus Christ, then go ahead, but if it's for anything else, then reconsider. There's no future in working for your own self-satisfaction or ego.

Robert Le Tourneau, the man who invented most of the huge earth-moving machines, was just as famous as Howard Hughes in his own right, but he did it for the Lord Jesus Christ. He left a tremendous legacy, at which we are still marvelling.

First fruits

Exodus 34:2

In the morning... come up... and present yourself to Me there on the top of the mountain. (NKJV)

The Lord requires our first fruits and I know it's not always possible. When my son, Andrew, was studying at university he said that the best time for him to be alone with God was early in the morning, at two or three o'clock, when all the students were either sleeping or studying.

The Lord requires our first fruits: usually we can give Him that in the early morning when we wake up refreshed. All the cares and the troubles of yesterday are gone. Our bodies and minds are rested and we are expectant of God. We are waiting for orders from the Lord. It's a habit of mine to rise early every morning and give God the first fruits of the day.

Martin Luther, who was a very early riser himself, was asked, "What do you do when you get really busy?" He replied, "Then I get up even earlier." I would exhort you today to give the Lord Jesus Christ your first fruits. Hear from Him. Get your orders, your vision, and your direction from Him first thing in the morning and you will find that your day will be so much better.

A dear Christian once said, "Give God the fresh blossom of the day. Never make Him wait until the petals have faded." In the early morning, when things are quiet, you can give God your full attention without any interruptions. The phone won't ring, the children will still be asleep, and your loved one should be having a quiet time as well. My wife and I have our own separate quiet times after which we then spend time together.

Lastly, remember: before you speak to people about God, speak first to God about people.

In God's hands

Job 1:21

The Lord gave, and the Lord has taken away. (NKJV)

Do you know how liberating it is to commit your situation into God's hands? We actually have very little control over most matters, yet we fret, become fearful, despondent, and in fact depressed at times, because we don't know what the future holds. Job came to a stage in his life where he'd been severely tested and pressurized by the evil one. He said, "The Lord has given to me, and the Lord has taken away."

As you read this today you might be facing a situation where your business is in jeopardy of closing down; your child may be on the brink of death; maybe your loved one has just walked away; or maybe you've just been made redundant at work. You are devastated but, due to the circumstances, you are unable to do anything about it. Then it is time to start praying. It's the power of prayer that moves mountains. Not just prayer, though. As we've said before, it's the power of the prayer of faith that moves mountains.

Mark 11:24 says, "What things soever ye desire, when ye pray, believe that ye receive them and ye shall have them." Then you leave the rest to God. He, in His own infinite love, wisdom and compassion, will rectify your situation.

The amazing thing is that when you do survive this situation, you'll be like Meshach, Shadrach and Abednego. King Nebuchadnezzar had ordered them to bow the knee to his god and they refused, and were thrown into the furnace. Even the people who threw them into the furnace were burned, yet these men didn't even smell of fire when they came out of the fiery furnace. They were untouched, because there was a fourth Person that walked around in that furnace with them.

Today, trust God. Release your problem to Him and see the change that He will bring about in your troublesome situation.

Detachment

Philippians 1:21

For me to live is Christ, and to die is gain.

I've just read a lovely book by Paul L. King. He writes about the life of a mighty woman of God, Hannah Whitall Smith (1832–1911), who said:

> The old Bible teachers used to lecture on what they called "detachment". This referred to cutting the soul loose from all that could hold it back from God. This need for detachment is the lesson for many of our shakings. We cannot follow the Lord fully as long as we are tied tightly to anything else. It would be like a boat trying to sail out into the boundless ocean while it is still tied fast to the shore. We must be detached from every earthly tie. Those souls who abandon the self life and give themselves up to the Lord to be fully possessed by Him find that He takes possession of the inner springs of their being. Seeing God in everything is the only thing that will make me loving and patient with people who annoy and trouble me.

We will continually be tested and tried by people. Most of the time God allows these people to cross our paths in order to test our love for Him. That's what He's asking of you today. Are you prepared, like Paul, to detach yourself completely from this world; to be in the world but not to be part of it? Then God has a free agent that He can work through to move mountains, to perform miracles, signs and wonders – starting in your own life and your own home, then in your business, your farm, your community, and ultimately the rest of the world.

Merciful God

Micah 7:18

Who is a God like unto thee; that pardoneth iniquity?

My dear friend, Jesus is known by many names. He is known as the Lily of the Valley, the Bright Morning Star, the King of kings, the Lord of lords, the Lion of Judah, the Shepherd of the sheep, the Great Ploughman, but there's one title in particular which endears my Master to me; He is known as the Friend of sinners like us.

Remember today that there is no more condemnation for those who are in Christ Jesus (Romans 8:1). As you read this today you might feel condemned because of a mistake you made yesterday, maybe because of something you said or did that you're ashamed of. Confess to the Lord today and the God of mercy will forgive you. There is no God – never has been and never will be – who has more love and mercy, and who loves to pardon His children more, than the Lord Jesus Christ. The Bible says that He delights in mercy.

Don't continue to carry burdens of guilt with you today. Leave them at the bottom of the Cross. That's exactly the reason why Jesus died for you – so you can have life in abundance (John 10:10).

The evil one is known as the father of all lies, the deceiver of the brethren. Before I preach a sermon, the evil one will try for at least ten minutes to stop me from getting onto that platform. It is then that I have to confess my sins, for He is faithful and just to forgive me all of my sins and to cleanse me from all unrighteousness (1 John 1:9). Then, like an eagle that soars freely in the air without any encumbrances, I can take off and abandon myself to God – and stand back to see what God can accomplish!

Robert Murray M'Cheyne was a young man whom God used as an instrument to bring about a huge revival in Dundee in eastern Scotland. He used to say, "Rather than have been an instrument of the Lord, all I was, was an adoring spectator."

That is how it is for us today. Let us walk in mercy, let us walk in love, and in forgiveness. Let us go today in Jesus' name and do that for others as well.

Faithful lifestyle

1 Timothy 3:2

A bishop then must be blameless… of good behaviour, hospitable… (NKJV)

The theme of this book of daily readings is faith. We're not only talking about signs, wonders, and miracles. We're not only talking about the mighty works of God. Today I want us to ponder over personal holiness.

Paul says to Timothy that it's a faithful saying that if a man desires the position of a leader (bishop), he desires a good work, but he must be a man that is temperate, sober minded, of good behaviour, and hospitable. He must be a man who is able to teach the Word of God. He must be blameless.

All of these conditions apply to us. There is no point in casting out demons, praying for the sick, performing signs and wonders, if we don't live by what we preach: the Word of God. The Lord makes it very clear that a leader should not be given to wine; is not a drunkard or a winebibber; is not greedy for money; is not quarrelsome, and is not someone who covets what their brother has. They should be humble; without pride and arrogance.

A leader is someone who rules their house in such a way that their children are obedient and respectful. He must be respected among those around him as a person of God. If you want God to use you in the realm of faith, in the area of signs, wonders and miracles, you need to get your own house in order.

I was preaching to a group of farmers once when, during the interval, an old man came and stood next to me and said, "Son, we want you to preach so that we can see you." What did that mean? It meant that they wanted me to preach without a mask. It implied that I should be real. It meant to speak my heart. You will not be able to do those things if all is not well in your own life. Matthew 6:33 says, "Seek first the kingdom of God and His righteousness, and all these things shall be added to you."

Today, remember: First we need to get our house in order before we go out and tell others about our blessed Redeemer. That's when people will listen.

Let's work on personal holiness today.

Our dress code: It's so important to give a good impression for Jesus.

Our language: There's no place in the kingdom of God for a man who professes to be an ambassador for Jesus and yet uses filthy language.

Humility: Preferring others to yourself; always going the extra mile for your fellow man.

Work on your holiness and you'll see faith growing in your life!

The gardener

John 15:1

I AM the true vine and my Father is the husbandman.

Jesus says that He is the vine and His Father is the husbandman (gardener). He tends to His garden in an excellent manner. His most treasured vine in the garden is His Son, Jesus Christ. He says that He cuts away every branch from that vine that does not bear fruit.

I remember many years ago, in my early days as a Christian, hearing a man say, "Sometimes we feel very hard done by and almost neglected by the Gardener when He starts to prune us with those shears. But have you ever considered the fact that the Gardener, holding that pair of secateurs, has holes in His hands from the Cross of Calvary? The pain that He must be suffering while pruning our branches must be excruciating; much more painful than what we are experiencing when He cuts away all the rough edges of our lives, enabling us to bear better fruit."

As a farmer myself, I know that every winter we are supposed to prune our fruit trees and treat them with paint to guard against invasive insects laying their eggs in the exposed areas of the branch. When spring arrives the fruit trees or the vines produce new leaves and start to bear fruit. What beautiful fruit they bear!

If you are going through a difficult time, and you are feeling that you are getting a raw deal, or that God has abandoned you or maybe that He isn't hearing your prayers, you need to remember that God will never leave you, nor forsake you (Hebrews 13:5). I can guarantee this. He has never left me, nor has He abandoned me. He has allowed me to be pruned to ensure that I'll produce a good crop; a sweet, juicy, and heavy crop for the sake of the gospel.

Here is a beautiful poem that I found in *Streams of the Desert*:

I walked a mile with pleasure; she chatted all the way;
But left me none the wiser
For all she had to say.
I walked a mile with sorrow, and she never said a word;
But oh, the things I learned from her,
When sorrow walked with me!

Once again, I can honestly tell you: when I look back on my life, the times of my greatest trials have been the times when I've been most impacted upon by the Lord.

The flood

Nahum 1:8

But with an overrunning flood he will make an utter end…

This is an encouraging word for believers. The Lord promises us that He will put an end to the pursuing of the believers by the enemies. My dear friend, we don't have to do anything but stand firm, wait and see, and trust the Lord. The Israelites stood by and watched as Moses cast out his rod. The great Red Sea parted and 2.5 million Israelites passed through the sea on dry land. Then, when the mightiest army in the world tried to descend upon the children of Israel, God closed the sea and Pharaoh's soldiers perished. In the same way, the Lord promises us today that His mercy, goodness and power will protect us.

Isaiah 59:19 says, "When the enemy comes in like a flood, The Spirit of the Lord will …" A dear friend of mine, who is engaged in a great war with cancer, pointed out something very special to me. He said, "Move the comma in that verse so that it reads like this, 'When the enemy comes in, like a flood The Spirit of the Lord will lift up a standard against him'"(NKJV).

That is so true. If we are serving the Lord we are in the majority – and there is nothing but nothing that can stand in our way. The Bible says in Hebrews 13:6, "The Lord is my helper, and I will not fear what man shall do unto me." It doesn't matter how big your mountain is today. It doesn't matter how big the enemy seems to you today. Remember that the Lord has said to you that "with an overrunning flood" He will put an end to your adversaries and your enemies.

Today, like Noah, build your ark. Build it on the Word and promises of God. Do not look to the left or to the right or even behind you, because we are living in perilous times. If we try and follow our own plans they will surely be flooded by the power of God. When the rains come – the rains of testing; the rains of holiness; the rains of purity – your ark will be lifted.

Discernment

Matthew 7:7

Seek, and ye shall find…

Even as I'm writing this book, I am at a stage of my life where I really need to hear from God on a regular basis. It's an amazing thing. As a new believer you seek assurance from God as to what is right and what is wrong, what to believe and what not to believe. As you grow in your faith (and I am still growing on a daily basis), what you are searching for changes: you do not want to find out what is right and what is wrong so much any more (for as you grow in faith you learn that) but you want to find out what the Lord is planning for your future and how you can utilize your time to be more profitable for Him.

Once the Lord Jesus Christ starts to open doors for you, you suddenly have friends you never knew you had (and I'm talking within the kingdom here). The majority of these friends are genuine but you might still find that some have agendas that are not necessarily in line with God's plan. I place them in two categories – kingdom builders and empire builders. An empire builder is someone who is interested in their own vision and not necessarily God's. A kingdom builder is someone who wants to see people saved and to see God's kingdom growing in glory here on earth.

That is what I'm asking for at this time in my life: discernment to know who to trust; who to open my heart to; and who to guard my heart against. Sometimes that's hard. Jesus also experienced that because it was by the Twelve that He was so sadly let down and disappointed, and more than once as well.

At the end of the day the work belongs to God. It doesn't matter what it is, but if we ask, God will give us a spirit of discernment. That should lead us to make the right decisions regarding who to go into partnership with, who to get involved with and who not to. There's an old saying: "When in doubt, don't". I believe those to be pretty accurate words. The most important thing, however, is to seek the Lord. If you seek Him with all of your heart He will show you the way. Many people, even some who are reading this book now, can give account of getting themselves into serious trouble. If they'd only listened to God, if they'd only been obedient to the Holy Spirit, they would never have had to pay such an expensive price.

In some cases, if we know the Word of God, we don't even have to ask God. For example, if you fall in love with a young man who asks you to be his wife and he's not a committed Christian, the answer should be a very definite no, because God says we must not be unevenly yoked. If you've been offered a lucrative business position and it's all there in black and white but your soon-to-be partner is of another faith, the answer is quite clear. No! Yet, how often do we disregard God's counsel and end up having to go back and ask for forgiveness, and start all over again?

Now before doing anything, I seek the Lord. It makes life a whole lot easier. "Seek first the kingdom of God and His righteousness, and all these things shall be added to you" (Matthew 6:33, NKJV). It's not by coincidence that God blesses His obedient children. He is able to do so because they listen to Him and obey His instructions.

God gave me clear direction to rest my land on the farm once every seven years. I was unable to do that at the time, because if I had I would have gone bankrupt. What I did was to rest one seventh of my land every year. After seven years the whole farm has been rested at least once. That is a principle that God put into place and of which the Holy Spirit convicted me, and it's working. You need to ask God personally what you need to do and then you need to obey.

Seek Him while He may be found. Don't be in a rush to make decisions. If someone is pushing you to make a decision to buy a new motorcar, to sell your house, to get married, to go into a partnership, I want to encourage you; don't allow yourself to be pressurized. God is always on time. His timing is perfect. Nine times out of ten, that man who says, "If you don't buy it today it's going to be gone," will be back tomorrow and he still won't have sold it. Just take your time, seek the Lord and He will answer.

Knock on the door

Matthew 7:7

Knock and the door shall be opened unto you.

God wants me to speak about knocking on the door today. There's no such thing as false humility. When we approach Christ, He expects us to knock on the door, so it will be opened.

Revelation 3:20 says, "Behold, I stand at the door, and knock." Jesus is knocking on our door. Remember that the handle is on the inside. If we open the door He will come in and have supper with us.

Today He's asking you to knock on the door and ask, so that He can grant you your heart's desire. Some of us say, "No, we're not going to do that. We don't want to upset the Lord. We know how busy He is. We'll just wait until He comes to us." If you don't ask, He will never open that door. He wants us to seek and He wants to hear our requests. Just like your little boy or girl who wants to ask you something. Before they even ask, you actually know what it is that they want but you want to hear it from them. It is the same for the Almighty God.

I believe it's also so important to be specific when you ask. I remember when Yonggi Cho first got saved, he asked the Lord for a bicycle. He said he wanted a maroon three-speed bicycle. He specified the make and requested that the bicycle should have cable brakes and that's exactly what God gave him.

Get into the habit of asking God for specifics. Make sure that they are within His will. John 14:14 says, "If you ask anything in My name, I will do it" (NKJV), but John 14:15 says, "If you love Me, keep My commandments" (NKJV). So don't ask God for something that's not within His will for you or your family. I've asked God for specific things many times before and He has given me exactly what I wanted and sometimes even more!

Feeding your soul

Isaiah 40:31(a)

… those who wait on the Lord… (NKJV)

A missionary went to China. After spending some time there, a Chinese man was converted to Christ through his ministry. They became very close friends. This Chinese gentleman grew in stature as a man of God. The missionary left and went back to his homeland. Maybe five or ten years later he went to visit the converted Chinese man. He asked him how his Christian walk was going. The Chinese man said, "It's as if there are two dogs fighting in my heart – a black one and a white one. The one represents good and the other one evil." The missionary asked him, "Which one is winning?" He replied, quite interestingly, "It depends on which one I feed the most."

My dear friend, which dog in your heart is getting more food at the moment? If you are spending time with the Word of God, you will become a great man or woman of faith. If you're spending your time being busy with worldly things, then that's what you'll become: of this world. If you're spending time with negative people, talking about negative things, you'll become a negative person.

I would encourage you today, if you want to be a man or woman of faith, to get alongside people who are walking by faith, people who are calling those things that aren't as if they were, people who are prepared to move mountains for Jesus, people with faith like a mustard seed.

Jesus said, "If you have the faith of a mustard seed you can ask for that sycamore tree to be uprooted and removed into the sea, and it will happen." That's all you have to do. Spend time, feed your soul with matters concerning God and then you will become a mighty warrior of faith for Jesus Christ.

Be gentle

Proverbs 15:1

A soft answer turneth away wrath: but grievous words stir up anger.

As the old saying goes: "It takes two to tango." Often, married couples come to me and complain that they just can't get along. I say to them, "Don't respond with anger, because it just makes matters worse. Try to be gentle with one another." As the writer says in Proverbs, if you want that wrath, that fierce fire in your lives or in your marriage, to cease, you have to douse the fire with soft answers.

I have a new horse, Big Stuff. He's four years old and an American quarter horse cross thoroughbred. He is a feisty horse; a most magnificent animal. He has a beautiful long black tail and mane and I am convinced that he knows how magnificent he is! You could say that he's a juvenile.

Lately I have experienced a few "disagreements" with this beautiful animal. My children bought me a beautiful handmade American stockman's saddle which weighs a lot and Big Stuff doesn't like that on his back at all. I'm not exactly a featherweight myself. So needless to say the other day he tried to buck me off. He bucked me three times, and although I managed to hang on, I'm still sore and stiff!

The point I want to make is that I tried to use a heavy hand with Big Stuff. I put him in a ploughed field and gave him a thorough workout, but ended up making him more aggressive and full of wrath.

Now I'm using a different approach, a gentle approach. I'm talking to him. There's a man by the name of Monty Roberts, known as the "Horse Whisperer". He believes you can talk to a horse, win his trust and gain his confidence and love and then he'll do anything for you. His father was the direct opposite. He used to beat horses and literally "break them in", in other words, break their spirit and then the horse would succumb.

Monty Roberts has developed a method whereby he doesn't break the spirit of the animal, but brings out the best in him. That's what we need to do with one another: bring out the best in each other.

Knowing

Job 19:25

For I know that my Redeemer lives, And He shall stand at last on the earth.

At the moment I'm listening to a magnificent piece of music, Handel's *Messiah*. I love the way God uses young people to compose appropriate music for the time in which they live. As much as I love modern and contemporary music, it's wonderful for me to quietly sit and listen to the *Messiah*, which was written in the late 1600s but is still greatly admired today. Handel wrote the 260-page manuscript in the short span of twenty-four days. He said that when he began writing the Hallelujah Chorus it seemed as if heaven and earth opened to his gaze.

This magnificent piece of music brings glory to God because most of what they are singing is pure undiluted Scripture. The one psalm that speaks most to me is the song "I know that my Redeemer liveth". It is sung so beautifully that it truly touches my heart. The words go, "Even though my skin is destroyed, my flesh is destroyed, I know that I shall see my God."

I want to encourage you today, dear Christian. Lift up your eyes and concentrate on your soon to come Messiah and you will see the problems of this world fade into insignificance when you think of what is yet to come – the glory of the Lord upon you!

Let everything that we do today bring glory to Jesus Christ. After the London premiere performance of the *Messiah*, Handel was congratulated on the excellent "entertainment", to which he immediately replied, "I should be sorry if I only entertain them; I wish to make them better." It was during this London premiere that the king of England got to his feet during the opening lines of the triumphant Hallelujah Chorus and thus started a tradition that has remained for over 200 years. It is unquestionably the most beautiful choral music in history. And why not? It pays tribute to the King of kings and the Lord of lords.

For I know that my Redeemer lives. And that, my dear friend, is the only sure thing in this world that can keep us going; to know that He lives, and most of all, that He shall stand at last on the earth.

Endurance

Hebrews 6:15

After he had patiently endured, he obtained the promise.

I read the other day that believing faith leads to realization. Isn't Abraham such a perfect example of just that? God promised him that he would be the father of many nations. At a hundred years old he was still childless. Yet he stood fast. Romans 4:20 says, "He staggered not at the promise of God through unbelief; but was strong in faith, giving glory to God." He was a patient man and because of that, that which was promised to him came to pass. He received a son called Isaac and was ultimately the father of many nations.

I believe the Lord is asking if we are walking on the road of patience and endurance. It is not an easy road, but that's the road we have to walk if we want to realize our vision. Without faith, we cannot please God. Those who come to God must believe that He is, and that He rewards those who diligently seek Him (Hebrews 11:6).

If farming has taught me one thing, it's endurance. If you don't succeed the first time you have to go back and do it again. I don't know how many times I've had to redo a job in order to get it right. Then, once you plant that crop, you have to trust the Lord to send the rain. When it doesn't rain and the ground gets hard, one is tempted to dig up those pips and find out whether they've germinated or whether they've swollen and died. You leave them and then, at the eleventh hour, there's a beautiful shower of rain and the next day it's absolutely breathtaking to see a field that was brown and dusty suddenly full of beautiful young, tender plants, coming up row after row. Within a week there's a field of lush young plants and the beginning of a wonderful crop of food, given once again to us by our God, the Holy One.

On the other hand, I've seen farmers who lose patience. They don't believe that the rain will come and they put a disc into the ground, plough up all the seed and start sowing new seed. Effectively, they've already lost about two to three weeks of growth, because those seeds were swelling underground and they were starting to germinate. Those farmers never really make up that wasted growing time. It's so important to commit every aspect of your working life to the Lord and to believe by faith. That faith then eventually becomes a reality and God gets all the glory.

Today, don't listen to the doubt in your heart. Don't listen to the lies of the devil, who will try to tempt you to lose your faith. Just be patient and God will work with you to sort out that situation for you in His own time.

Be merciful

Micah 6:8

... to love mercy...

A dear friend and colleague, whom I love dearly, and who heads up one of the biggest churches in South Africa, came and graced me with his presence over a period of two days. We opened our hearts towards each other about the wrongdoings we were suffering at the hand of the people in the church, and indeed by those who were very near and dear to us.

We felt powerless to do anything about the people taking advantage of us because of the favour that God has bestowed on us. Things like basic ethics were being abused. The old man rises up and you want retribution. You want to put things straight and say, "You can't do that because it's unethical even in the world." Yet we keep our mouths shut and do nothing.

We remind ourselves of what Jesus said: "Turn the other cheek." He said, "Pray for those who oppress you and misuse you." This dear friend of mine wrote a little note saying, "Others are enjoying mercy at your expense!" Jesus says, "That pleases Me, because it's exactly what I've done for you'" (a prophetic Word from the Lord).

I think of David and his son Absalom. Absalom took advantage of his father. He sat at the city gate as people were coming to receive counsel from King David and told them that they didn't have to go and see the king as he had all the answers anyway. He undermined his father, not once but many times. People warned David of what was happening. He knew about it and he did nothing because he loved his son so much. At the end, of course, justice prevailed. Absalom was killed and his father still remained on the throne.

Be encouraged today. If you know of people that are taking advantage of you, just keep quiet. If Christ is for you there is no one that will ever stand against you (Romans 8:31). Love mercy, because that is what Christ wants you to do. Show mercy to others as He has shown mercy to you.

A little while

John 16:16

… a little while, and ye shall see me…

Maybe today you are saying to yourself, "I don't think I can go on much longer. I've literally come to the end of the road. I see no light at the end of the tunnel. I only see darkness. I see bankruptcy, death, despair." Be encouraged, Little One, for Jesus says that in a short while He's coming back again.

As a farmer I can tell you that the signs are clear, there for all to see. We know when the time for planting our crop of maize has arrived. We plant our crops in spring. When the fig tree produces its new leaves, the time is right.

So it is with the coming of the Lord. Signs on earth such as earthquakes, floods, tsunamis, pandemic diseases, HIV and AIDS, bird flu, uncontrolled foot and mouth disease amongst cattle, disregard for human life and immorality at its absolute worst, are actually Jesus saying, "I'm coming." I would encourage you today to just push on.

During the Second World War, that great orator Sir Winston Churchill was asked to address a school assembly. He stood up and said, "Never give up. Never, never, never give up!" With that, he sat down. That was the complete speech. To this day people quote that speech.

Jesus says, "I am coming in a short while." Don't give up. Persevere, because our reward is great in heaven.

Much fruit

John 15:8

By this My Father is glorified, that you bear much fruit … (NKJV)

As a farmer I can really identify with this Scripture. I have an orchard of deciduous fruit. We grow apples, pears, plums, peaches, and figs. The fruit trees that I love the most are the ones that produce the juiciest fruit in abundance. The ones that I find hard to tend to in terms of pruning and looking after are those that are reluctant to bear fruit. In fact, eventually I cut them down.

Jesus says that His Father is glorified when we bear much fruit. What fruit are we speaking about? We're speaking about the fruit of our lives. We're speaking about the fruit of the Spirit. We're speaking about the overflow of God's love from our hearts to our community, starting with our own families. We're speaking about things like patience, love, joy, and even longsuffering. We're speaking about feeding the hungry and taking care of the needy. We're speaking about preaching the gospel at all costs and, like Francis of Assisi, only using words if we really have to.

The fruit that people are looking for is actually your character. My dear friend, the greatest compliment that you'll ever get from anyone is when they can say to you, "I see that you've been walking with God." That comes by spending time with Him.

Some years ago I was preaching down in the Eastern Cape and a gentleman whom I regard as a great ambassador for Christ came to me and said, "I see you as a companion of Jesus." That brought tears to my eyes. I opened the flyleaf of my old Bible and asked him to write it in there. It's one of the most treasured compliments that I've ever received in my life, and I thank God for that. I will remember it always.

You see, if you're bearing fruit, people will recognize Jesus in you. That compliment was paid to me in 1998. I was so humbled by it. He said that I was connected with God. Only God can do that through me and only when I am committed to spending time with Him. I know that I'm a wretched sinner, saved by grace. It's only because of His life flowing through me that I can bear any kind of fruit.

Familiarity

Matthew 13:57

A prophet is not without honour, except in his own country, and in his own house.

There's a saying: "Familiarity breeds contempt". What a true statement. A very dear friend of mine, François van Niekerk, came to visit me. He heads up a large congregation in Pretoria, South Africa. We were talking about the things of God and particularly the area of ministry. He told me to be careful not to allow a spirit of familiarity to grab hold of me. Very interesting…

What he meant was that God anoints men and women. The Bible says that the gifts of God are without repentance, which means, in effect, that even if a person has fallen into sin they can still lay hands upon the sick and they will be healed if God has given them that gift. The same applies to the gift of prophesying or preaching. Of course we realize that, unless he repents, the man who has fallen into sin will pay the ultimate price. But the gift of God continues.

Sometimes you get to know somebody who has an anointing on their life of, for example, discernment but, as you become familiar with that person, you start to notice the flaws in their carnal life. Maybe they are not the tidiest person in the world; maybe when you go on tour with them, they're the person who's a bit careless and lazy. Whatever the case may be, as you get to know that person and familiarize yourself with them, you start disrespecting them in the flesh.

When that happens, and they bring a Word of correction or discernment to you, you don't receive it because you know the character of the person. However, the Word comes from God. When you don't receive it, you lose the blessing because you don't recognize the anointing of God on his life any more.

Be careful of familiarity. Sometimes it can rob you. A person can bring an accurate Word but you don't receive it. That's exactly what happened with Jesus. The Bible says that Jesus could hardly perform any miracles in Nazareth. Why? Because of familiarity! The people would say, "Oh, that's Jesus. He's the carpenter's son. His brother's in my class at school. His sister is married to my best friend." So they didn't receive His ministry and they lost out. Yet when Jesus went on half an hour's walk down to Galilee, signs, wonders, and miracles which have shaken the world for 2,000 years took place. Why? Because the people received Him as the Prophet of God!

Don't judge a book by its cover. Discern the Word of the Lord. Respect the anointing on a person of God and receive it, so that you too can be blessed. The bottom line is that, because of unbelief, we can't believe that God can use people whom we regard as sinful. Remember, my friend, we are all sinners; but by the grace of God do we stand.

Don't deprive yourself of a blessing. If God sends a Word that's appropriate, then receive it, even if you don't particularly receive the person who brings it. If the people in Nazareth had believed that Jesus Christ was the Anointed One, they would have witnessed miracles taking place in Nazareth as well. But they didn't; they said He was just the carpenter's son – and they lost out.

Don't lose out on what God has in store for you because of a spirit of familiarity.

Offence

John 16:1(b)

... that ye should not be offended.

Jesus tells us, "If people hate you because of Me, it is because they hated Me first." He asks, "Is a servant greater than his Lord? If they've persecuted Me, they'll also persecute you."

Maybe you offend a number of people on a regular basis because of your relationship with Jesus Christ. Maybe you offend them by not participating in the things they do. As a result they ridicule you, pull you down, and make a fool of you. The Lord says that we must jump for joy when people say all manner of evil against us for His name's sake.

The first campaign that I ever organized was in 1989, in a little town called Ladysmith in the Natal Midlands. I'll never forget that as I drove down the road into Ladysmith, the Holy Spirit spoke clearly to my heart. He asked me three questions:

"Are you prepared to be a fool for Me?"

I replied, "Oh, Lord, that's very easy, because I'm a fool anyway."

The second question was a little harder. "Are you prepared for people to say all manner of evil against you for My name's sake? In other words, if people mock you because of Me, will you not be offended?"

I said, "No, Lord. I won't be."

Then He asked me the third question, which is the one that I still struggle with to this very day. "Are you prepared to see less of your family for My sake?"

I had to say, "Lord, only by Your grace am I prepared to drink from the cup of suffering."

I have been confronted by these three questions time and time again over the years. The only people who can offend you are the ones who are very close and special to you. Today, if you have a loved one who is offended by you because of your stand for Jesus Christ, the Lord says that He will give you the grace to love them and to stand fast.

The Lord even says, "You might be put out of the synagogue (the church) for My name's sake." Some people will even think that if they kill you, they're doing God's service. In Acts 8:1 we read that, before he became Paul, Saul of Tarsus thought he was doing the right thing by organizing the killing of Stephen, the first martyr in the New Testament.

My prayer for you today, my dear friend, is that you won't allow offence to pull you down as you go about your work. Rejoice quietly in your spirit when people mock you because you don't drink; or because you've stopped participating in those filthy jokes; or because you won't take part in watching those blue movies. Don't be concerned. They mocked Jesus as well.

At the end of the day we have the victory – and those people will come to us and ask us to pray for them because they know what is right and what is wrong. You should be proud if you are offending people because of the presence of Jesus Christ in your life. Look to Him for your reward in heaven.

Strength

Habakkuk 3:19

The Lord God is my strength, and he will make my feet like hinds' feet.

Today, may I ask you whose strength you are trusting in? You can say flippantly, "The Lord's", but are you very sure about that? Are you sure that you're not trusting in the money market, in your physical strength, or in your reputation? Habakkuk says, "The Lord God is my strength, and He will make my feet like hinds' feet. He will make my feet sure and secure, like those of the antelope that can jump across the rocks and balance on the smallest outcrop of rocks, totally trusting his Creator."

Today, our strength is not in our feelings. They can be like a roller coaster. One minute you feel on top of the world, the next you feel as if you're going to die. Job understood those feelings, as do many of us, but today our trust is in God alone. In 2 Corinthians 5:7 it says that "we walk by faith, not by sight". Today, irrespective of what is happening in the political arena, irrespective of what is happening on the home front, we know that our trust and our strength are in the Lord God.

In verse 17, Habakkuk says, "Although the fig shall not blossom…" During the last thirty or forty years of farming I've seen farmers who were multimillionaires one day and paupers the next. The wonderful crop of today is ravaged by disease, insect damage, or weather conditions tomorrow. We cannot live by our feelings. Our strength needs to come from God; only then can we weather the storms and rejoice in the days of plenty.

Today as you go your way, remember the hind. His feet are firmly placed on the ground because his strength is in God.

No fear of man

Psalm 27:1

The Lord is the strength of my life; of whom shall I be afraid?

Today, remember that it's the Lord Jesus Christ who saved you. Not a man, not an organization, nor a denomination; it was the Lord Himself. He is the One we must continue to put our faith and our trust in and to look to for our reward, our comfort and our strength.

As I am writing, I am watching the Rugby World Cup, and I have noticed yet again how fickle man can be. A player makes a wonderful move and scores a try and he becomes an instant hero. Not even ten minutes later the very same player fumbles with the ball, potentially loses the match for the team, and is regarded as an absolute villain. It is therefore fatal to put our trust in man. Our trust is in the Lord.

The Word of God says in Hebrews 13:6, "The Lord is my helper; I will not fear. What can man do to me?" (NKJV). You will find that your life will be a lot less turbulent if you put your trust in God. With the kind of work I do, people's expectations can put tremendous pressure on me if I allow them to. I've realized that the more I trust and look to Jesus, the more amazing my life becomes.

I think of that wonderful poem "If" written by Rudyard Kipling, where he looks at every stage of a man's life and says that he has learned to treat praise and criticism as the same enemy. Our dependency must never be upon man's expectations of us but on Jesus Christ alone. In spite of knowing our shortfalls and our weaknesses He still loves us very much. He will see us through if we keep on keeping on for Him.

That's what that great orator Sir Winston Churchill said. He was a man who saw Britain through its darkest days during the Second World War, when everything was pointing towards defeat and disaster as the might of the German Third Reich was bearing down upon Britain. He stood firm. The shortest speech he ever made was at a private school during the war, where he stood up and said to the boys, "Never give up."

Today I encourage you to keep on keeping on for Jesus Christ. Remember, if Christ is for you, there is no one who will ever stand against you (Romans 8:31).

Indifference

Zephaniah 1:12(b)

The Lord will not do good, neither will he do evil.

The Lord says that He will punish the men who say in their hearts, "The Lord does no good and the Lord does no evil." How many times have you met folk like that, especially people who are totally indifferent towards the things of God? As a preacher I find that the hardest audience to speak to is people who are indifferent. The opposite of love is not hate; it's indifference. I would rather someone shake his fist at me and ask, "Can you prove that?"

That actually happened to me down at the Orient Theatre in East London in the Eastern Cape many years ago. A young man arrived as I was preaching. He had on his Stetson, his cowboy boots, and was carrying a bottle of beer. He sat in the back row with his boots on the seat in front him. There were about a thousand people present. He started to heckle me as I was preaching, saying things like, "Can you prove that? Where does it say that in the Bible? I don't believe you." He caused such a commotion that some of our workers had to escort him out. But do you know – that young man gave his life to Jesus two weeks later! You see, he was desperate for the truth. He was not indifferent.

I would rather someone be angry with God (although that's not a good idea) than be indifferent. I think the Lord feels the same. Think of your child. You'd rather have your child throw a tantrum than just be indifferent. Although the tantrum is not the answer, at least there's interaction with your child. It is the same with God. God cannot stand someone who is indifferent towards Him.

My dear friend, the Lord has no time for lukewarm Christians. He clearly says in Revelation 3:16, "So then, because you are lukewarm, and neither cold nor hot, I will vomit you out of My mouth" (NKJV).

A man or woman who is indifferent can be a great asset to the devil. They will neither speak up for nor attack the things of God. They're like a drone. A drone, if you've ever studied beekeeping, is an absolute passenger. He's not a worker, he holds no office in the hive, and is of no consequence. He is, in fact, a burden to the rest of the hive. God forbid that you and I become like that today. If you have any issue with God, rather speak to Him about it, settle it, and press on. But bury that indifferent, complacent spirit. It is very dangerous and it leads to destruction and hell, starting with you and then with your family.

The Lord prefers you to be excited and inspired. I can honestly say that since I've met Jesus, my own life has been completely transformed. I have a reason to live. I'm following after my dream. For the first time in my life everything I do makes sense. I want to tell you one thing. The Lord is still doing plenty of good in this dying world of ours.

One last thing: there is a consequence for those who do evil. There is a price that they will pay. Do not be concerned about when the evil are going to receive judgment. They will receive judgment in due course when the Lord comes again. In the meantime be sure that your own life is in order.

Job 21:15 says clearly, "Who is the Almighty, that we should serve Him? And what profit do we have, if we pray to Him?" So many people say that. I've heard farmers say, "What can God do for me?" because they happen to be successful. What they don't realize is that they can plant a crop, they can till the land, they can fertilize it, they can do everything according to the book – but if Jesus doesn't send the rain they will have no crop to harvest.

Today, let us remember that our God is a good God and He will not tolerate evil.

Guide

John 16:13

He will guide you into all truth…

If you go for a walk in a game reserve you are accompanied by a game ranger. They will be armed with a high velocity rifle and will walk in front of you. You will walk behind them and follow their instructions. If suddenly 200–300 metres ahead of you a rhinoceros appears – which probably weighs in excess of two tons – and with a newly born calf, you have a dangerous situation on your hands.

The guide will tell you to stop in your tracks and not to take photographs. You will follow the instructions as they would have been trained to handle a situation like that. The fact that the game ranger might be a young person does not matter. They will have the relevant experience and instructions from the highest authority in the game reserve. You need to obey the ranger if you don't want to jeopardize your well-being. They know that although the rhinoceros has very poor sight, its sense of hearing and smell are exceptionally good. The game ranger will make sure that you move downwind from the animal and its calf and will stand still so that the animal can relax and carry on grazing, and then they will walk quietly around it.

Jesus said, "I am going so that I might send a Guide. He will tell you everything that you should do, because He doesn't speak of Himself but only those things which I will tell Him to speak of."

Today, as you go about your daily chores, know that the Holy Spirit is with you. If you listen carefully, He will give you instructions. He will tell you not to buy those shares on the stock exchange. He will tell you clearly not to exceed the speed limit as it is dangerous.

You can choose to believe Him, or you can say, "No, I'm going to do it my own way." If you do that, you are risking your life. He will give you instructions, which you need to follow. They might be life-saving instructions. Be obedient today to your Guide and you will have a wonderful day.

Humility

Micah 6:8

… to walk humbly with your God… (NKJV)

This subject has enjoyed a lot of attention in this book. If you want to be a man or a woman of faith, you need to walk humbly with God. The Lord says that He resists the proud man but He gives grace to the humble (1 Peter 5:5). The hallmark of a man or woman of God is humility, nothing else. When God sees your humble heart He will entrust you with good things. The more humbly you walk with God the more He will exalt you. It doesn't matter what other people think. In the world we are always trying to prove a point, always trying to prove ourselves, but in Christ we humble ourselves and He exalts us in His good time.

To walk with your God is so important. Those quiet times every day are absolutely vital and you need to walk even more closely with God when He starts to use you more powerfully. When you walk with God you will be a humble person, because you will realize that it's all about Him. It has nothing to do with you or me. The more He exalts you and puts you in high places, the more humble you will need to be.

Remember the parable where the Lord says that when you are invited to a marriage feast, rather sit in the lowest seat so that the lord of the house can come and move you up to the high place (Luke 14:10).

There's nothing more embarrassing than to go to a house and sit in the top seat and the lord of the house has to come and ask you to please go and sit down at the bottom!

In the world you are taught that only the fittest will survive, but in the kingdom of God the exact opposite is true. God exalts the humble and uses them for His kingdom. Walk with God today in humility and you will have a wonderful season in your life.

Youthfulness

Job 33:25(b)

He shall return to the days of his youth.

Jesus Christ in you makes all the difference. Colossians 1:27 says, "Christ in you, the hope of glory." I want to say to you today that God has renewed my very being, not only my spirit, not only my soul, but also my actual, physical body. I feel stronger today than I did ten years ago.

We have the privilege of praying for the sick. The gift of healing is part of the tools of the evangelist. At our meetings we say that about ninety per cent of all sickness is psychosomatic – it starts in the mind. When someone becomes unhappy, when they become troubled or fearful, then they become sick. But when the Lord Jesus Christ comes into a person's life like a ray of sunshine, forgives them of all their sins, gives them a vision, a dream to pursue, that person receives a new lease on life, which I believe affects them physically as well.

I've just been on a five-kilometre run, not because I felt like it, but because I've got to keep myself in shape. God has work for me to do. Ten years ago I wasn't as keen on running as I am now and I didn't have the urgency to serve the Lord that I have now. The Lord says that we are to use our renewed youthfulness profitably for Him.

A. B. Simpson says, "The same Christ, with all His attributes and mighty power, belongs to us. We are members of His body, His flesh, and His bones, and if we will only believe this and receive it, we may actually draw our life from the very life of the Son of God." He says, "Dear God, help me to know and to live this verse: 'The body is for the Lord, and the Lord for the body' (1 Corinthians 6:13)."

Today, take that which God has offered you. Take it, receive it and get up this morning. Speak to yourself. Even David used to do that: "My soul, why art thou so downcast?" Remind yourself that when Jesus said on the Cross, "It is finished!", He meant it. He had overcome all sin, all evil and destruction, sicknesses and diseases. Lay your hand upon that part of your body that's giving you trouble today, pray over it and ask God to heal it and to set you free.

He says He will renew your youthfulness. The only reason for that is so that you can become a more effective witness for Him in the marketplace.

Intimacy with Jesus

Psalm 27:4

One thing I have desired of the Lord…

David loved the Lord with a passion. Yes, he made many mistakes but one thing that overruled all of that was his intimacy with God. He knew God in a special way that few other people ever had the privilege to. He spent time with God. He wrote songs and psalms about God. He played music to God in the fields when he was watching over the sheep of his father Jesse.

If there's one thing that God is impressing upon my heart at the moment, it's to experience Him in an intimate way. Do you have an intimate relationship with the Lord at this time?

One of the great religious and social giants who lived in the 1700s was Count Nikolaus von Zinzendorf, a very wealthy man, who was one of the leading religious and social reformers of Europe. He had an insatiable desire to know God more intimately and he spent all his money and all his worldly possessions on sending out missionaries. He was the first man of the Protestant faith to ever send out missionaries.

Apparently, as a four-year-old boy, he would write letters to his beloved Jesus and throw them out of the window believing that the Lord would collect them. Later, he said, "I have loved Him for a long time but I have never actually done anything for Him." He was talking about Jesus. "From now on I will do whatever He leads me to do. I have but one passion and that is Christ." This took place after he had been to an art gallery and saw a portrait Jesus with a crown of thorns. The inscription below the portrait read, "I did it for thee. What hast thou done for Me?" His life was never the same again.

My dear friend, do you have an intimate relationship with Jesus today? It's no good being a professor of theology and knowing all the history as recorded from Genesis to Revelation in the Bible if you have never met the Author of the Book.

Another man who had an insatiable hunger and desire for God was George Frederick Handel. He was a German-born composer. Sitting at a table with tears streaming down his face, he commented to a servant after composing the Hallelujah Chorus from the *Messiah*, "I thought I saw all heaven before me, and the great God Himself." He'd been working on the composition for twenty-four days without leaving his house. A man who had an intimate relationship with Jesus Christ indeed!

My Helper

Hebrews 13:6

The Lord is my helper; I will not fear. What can man do to me?

The other day I was reading one of Philip Yancey's books on prayer. In a chapter entitled "Disciplines for Emergency Workers", he writes that after the deadly Christmas 2004 tsunami disaster, workers rushed to that devastated area in Asia to help those who were lost. It was one hellish sight: homes decimated and literally wiped off the face of the earth; children lost; men walking up and down the streets in an absolute daze, not comprehending that they'd lost their wives, their children, and all their possessions. Absolute devastation; dead bodies lying everywhere.

Yancey reports that an acquaintance who was helping to organize the relief work in Sri Lanka wrote him an email, entitled "Disciplines for Emergency Workers". He mentions that it is a very appropriate title for anybody who's involved in God's kingdom because in times of extreme stress and disaster we tend to push ourselves beyond what is considered to be normal. Are you doing that at the moment? If you are involved in the work of the Lord then you need to pay attention.

Yancey then went on to give some practical advice which I would like to share with you: number one, get enough sleep; number two, don't neglect your family; and number three, tend to your emotional needs. This, he says, is the most important piece of advice if you wish to stay strong in order to help others. Finally, he says, as Mother Teresa has shown us: anyone who wants to do long-term crisis ministry must have a healthy devotional life.

Isaiah 40:31 says, "those who wait on the Lord…" (NKJV). Every one of us who loves Jesus Christ is in effect in His service full-time. Remember the saying: "Don't speak to men about God until you've spoken to God about men". In other words, your quiet time that you spend with Jesus in the morning is absolutely vital, before you go out to face the day.

A good friend of mine, Bruce, came to see me one day. He got hold of a pen and a piece of paper and drew a wheel. In the wheel he put a whole lot of spokes. He entitled this "The balanced wheel". Every one of those spokes represented a different area in our lives. For example: quiet time with God; time spent with husband / wife; time spent with family; time spent exercising; time spent relaxing; time spent smelling the roses.

Remember William Carey, the founder of the Baptist Union; a mighty man of God whom I think had a greater impact on India than any other missionary?

He had a rose garden. When he was under extreme pressure, he would take some time to go and tend to his roses. Smelling the roses for me entails riding horses. I find it very relaxing, especially if I've been away on a campaign for a long time.

I want to remind you again: be careful that you are not so busy fighting the devil, as it were, and barring the front door, that you do not notice him walking in through the back door and causing havoc within your family.

Lastly, keep the flame fuelled. You can only give of your overflow – never of your substance – otherwise you'll have nothing left. How do we keep it fuelled up? By spending time with the Lord, who is our Helper!

Taking stock

Haggai 1:7

Consider your ways.

There are many of us, as the saying goes, who are chasing our tails. A number of people are holding down two jobs, working day and night to put food on the table. This is evident all over the world. Recently, I returned from Australia where I noticed people working eighteen to twenty hour days just to be able to meet their obligations.

The Lord says, "You've sown much but you have brought in little." He says, "You eat but you don't have enough. You drink but you're not filled with drink. You put clothes on yourselves but you're not warm. You earn wages and you put your wages into a bag with holes."

It is time to take stock today. If we start to put Jesus first in our lives we will experience a calmness within us. Many of us might be working too many hours and for the wrong reasons. Just because your next-door neighbour has a new car, you feel that you need one too, when there's actually nothing wrong with the car you are currently driving. You may want to send your child to a specific school because of an old family tradition but your child would probably rather be with you anyway than in a boarding school. You may be buying new clothes while there's nothing wrong with the ones you are wearing.

If you should sit down and take stock to see what you really need versus what you would like to have, you'll find that what you have is quite sufficient. You don't have to be running around so much, as the Lord will give you clear direction as to what He wants of you.

If you begin to sow good seed – that is in the kingdom of God, in the house of the Lord and into His work – you'll find that you will reap an abundant crop. If you start asking God to prioritize your life for you, the drought will end and the fig tree will yield its fruit. There will be cows in the stall. There will be health and joy in your home.

Get out of the madding crowd! I'm not saying that you have to leave your job, or the area in which you are living, but I am saying that if you begin to take stock and put Jesus Christ first in your life again by faith and do what He is telling you to do, you will find all of these other things will be given unto you.

Sometimes we need to be ruthless and drastic when making our decisions. You have to stop, sit down, take stock with your family, and then do what you have to do. If you have to cut your losses, so be it. The sooner the better, or else that rust, that cancer, will just continually creep up and consume everything you have. Cut it off, settle your debts; get back to basics.

Put Jesus' principles first in your life, your family, and your business. And God will do the rest!

Loneliness

Haggai 2:4(b)

I am with you, saith the Lord of hosts.

I was preaching at the Pretoria North High School a few months ago. Some parents were also attending the sessions that we hosted for the students. At the end of the sessions, an old lady came up to me and told me that she had come to Pretoria from Durban in KwaZulu-Natal many years ago with her family. They had since died and she was alone without any friends. She confessed that, more than once, she had stood in front of her mirror with a handful of tranquillizers, wanting to put an end to her life. That morning she made a recommitment to Christ and realized that He will never leave her, nor forsake her (Hebrews 13:5). She decided to continue with God.

This morning the Lord reminds us in His Word, "'I am with you,' says the Lord of hosts." Even in Mark 16:20 it says that the Lord walked and moved with the disciples. The disciples preached the gospel everywhere and the Lord validated their work with signs, wonders, and miracles. This was after He'd gone home to be in heaven. Obviously, it was through the power of His Holy Spirit.

Whenever I get onto a platform to preach to a large crowd, I remind myself – and the Holy Spirit reaffirms it when I spend time in prayer – that I'm not alone. It would be a terrible nightmare for me to stand on a platform addressing a huge crowd of people and realize that the Holy Spirit was not present. Quite simply, it would be hell for me!

He has never forsaken me and He has never let me down. And He will not forsake you either. Whatever you have to do today, and wherever you have to go, commit it to the Lord and know that He's going with you. In Exodus 3:10, God says to Moses that he should go and tell Pharaoh to release the children of Israel and allow them to leave. Moses says, "Who am I that I should go to Pharaoh?" and the Lord replies, "Certainly I will be with thee" (verse 12). That is reassurance indeed! If Christ is for us, there is no one who can stand against us.

The power of personal testimony

Acts 7:54

When they heard these things, they were cut to the heart…

This is what took place after Stephen gave his testimony. The power of personal testimony is incredible. There's nothing that will convict a man (or anger him) like the power of personal testimony. You see, with a personal testimony you can either agree or disagree but you can't argue because you weren't there. They were so angered by Stephen's testimony that they stoned him to death.

I encourage you today: you might not be a great preacher; you might not be a theologian; but you do have a testimony. If you don't have a testimony, I have to question whether in fact you have been born again.

George Whitefield (1714–70) was one of the greatest evangelists of all time. He said, "I must bear testimony to my old friend, Mr Charles Wesley. He put a book in my hands called *The Life of God and the Soul of a Man,* through which God showed me that I must be born again."

I can relate to that. Whenever I go to Oxford, I cannot help but go to the spot where Jesus Christ first revealed Himself to me. I learned that a person can go to church, say their prayers and receive the sacrament and not be a Christian. "How my heart did rise and shudder like a poor man who is most reluctant to look into his ledger, for fear that he will find himself bankrupt. Oh, what a ray of divine light did then break in upon my soul!"

I can honestly tell you that Jesus is more real to me today than He was the day I met Him. The one thing that I'm guarding with my life is my personal intimate relationship with my Saviour. I trust today that you will do the same.

Solitude

Mark 1:35

He went out, and departed into a solitary place…

Are you in a very rushed mode today? I would encourage you to take time out. Spend time with the Lord before you attempt anything else and you will find that things will go well for you. Basically, spend time in solitude, spend time with the Lord, and hear what the Lord wants to say to you.

During my quiet time this morning, the Holy Spirit reminded me that all the men and women of God who have ever attempted or accomplished greatness for Him, were people who spent time in solitude.

Spurgeon, that great British preacher known as the "Prince of Preachers", had a church built for him and was preaching to crowds of up to 10,000 people when he was twenty-one years old. But, towards the end of his life, he said, "By attempting less, I hope to achieve more." I'm doing the same myself.

If you read this morning's Scripture you'll see that Jesus rose very early in the morning after having prayed the night before for people who were sick. There were multitudes of people at the door of Simon Peter's house, waiting to be healed. The Bible says, "In the morning, rising up very early, before the day started, He went out and departed into a solitary place." That's where He prayed. Simon and the disciples came looking for Him, saying, "All men are seeking You."

Twenty years ago I had the habit of running backwards and forwards and it took me ten times as long to do the work as it is taking me now. Now I sit down, I wait to hear from God and then I make the right decision and do the right thing first time round – not because I'm any wiser, but because I'm spending more time with the Lord.

Don't neglect the time you spend every day in solitude with the Lord before you go into the marketplace. Jesus was not a crowd pleaser. He was a God pleaser. The more time He spent with the Lord, the more power God gave Him to perform amazing miracles, signs and wonders. This book is dedicated to encouraging people to walk by faith and not by sight (2 Corinthians 5:7). However, faith comes by hearing and hearing by the Word of God (Romans 10:17). You cannot hear the Word of God in a noisy marketplace. You need to climb up a mountain and spend time in solitude. Then you will be able to hear the Lord clearly when He speaks to you. I firmly believe that you don't speak to man about God until you've spoken to God about man.

The Firstborn

Colossians 1:15

… the image of the invisible God, the firstborn of every creature.

As I am sitting in my prayer room on this Sunday morning, I am so excited. The rain is falling gently on our dry and dusty farm. I've been reminded again that Jesus Christ is God.

I'll never forget preaching to a number of young students in a nearby city many years ago. That night I said that Jesus Christ is not only the Son of God; He is God. Again, this Scripture brings it to reality. He is the image of the invisible God. If you see Jesus, you see God. If you see God you see Jesus, because He is the same person. What an honour and a privilege to come into my prayer room this morning and to have Him meet me here and speak to me through His Word!

Oh, my dear friend, do not neglect these first fruits, this time spent with God. He is the only One who can truly help you. He is the only One who can guide you and give you advice that will never falter. He can heal your broken heart and renew your vision. He is the only One who can heal you physically, because He created you. He loves you so much that He gave His own life for you. "Greater love hath no man than this, that a man lay down his life for his friends" (John 15:13). God did that for you and for me. The very least we can do is to glorify Him and place him first in our lives.

Spend a lot of time with God and you'll find that everything else will fall into place.

Our heavenly intercessor

John 17:9

I pray for them…

The main reason why I have such great respect and love for intercessors is not only because my wife and many of the men and women with integrity who are nearest and dearest to me are intercessors, but because my Saviour, Jesus Christ, is an intercessor. That is His full-time occupation in heaven today. He is praying for you and me. He says, "I pray for them." He says to His Father: "I don't pray for the world but I pray for those that You have given Me, because they are Yours."

Prayer means more to me than a million dollars would. Often people will approach me at meetings and say, "Angus, I wish I could give you some money for the ministry but I don't have any. But I can pray." I always say, "Thank you! That means more to me than a million rand!" The Bible says in James 5:16 that the effective fervent prayer of a righteous man (or woman) availeth much.

As I'm writing this book today, I'm holding a prayer cross in my hand. It's a small bronze cross, a replica of the one that was found in the catacombs of Rome in AD 450. It's a candid image of the Lord Jesus Christ crucified on the Cross, but it's probably one of my most precious possessions.

It was given to me many, many years ago by a pastor from Australia by the name of Rick Burley. He came to say goodbye to me after we'd had a three-week campaign in Newcastle, Australia. He said, "Angus, I don't have any money to give you to thank you for coming, but there are two things I am going to give to you. I'm going to give you my prayer cross. Put it in your hand every morning when you pray. Squeeze it and the corners of the cross will bite into your fingers and remind you of what Jesus Christ did for you and me on the Cross of Calvary. Secondly, I've made a covenant with God that I will pray for you every day for the rest of my life." Rick Burley prayed for me this morning.

Remember today that you never have to feel lonely. You never have to feel isolated or discarded or disregarded in any way, because the Master is continually praying for you.

Have a wonderful day!

Shameless

Zephaniah 3:5(b)

… but the unjust knoweth no shame…

I can remember how my nature as an unbeliever used to be; I was a man who had no shame. I thank God that my sins are covered by the blood that was shed by Jesus on the Cross of Calvary. Nevertheless, I did things which I'm not proud of.

You see, when you don't have the Holy Spirit within you convicting you of your conduct and your behaviour, you have no shame. You will do anything for attention, love, and acceptance. So, you may sell your soul for a plate of lentil soup, as Esau did with Jacob. In order to satisfy his flesh, he gave away his inheritance. God forbid that you and I do that today.

You don't have to have a shameless past in order to have a good testimony. You don't have to sow your wild oats before you come to Christ. As one great preacher said, "God will forgive you for all of your sins, but the scars remain on your heart." Wherever I go, I remind people of this. Rather fear the Lord from the beginning, and you will be a wise man – or woman. Job 28:28 says, "the fear of the Lord, that is wisdom; and to depart from evil is understanding."

The unjust know no shame because they are uninformed. They do not have the Holy Spirit directing them in their hearts. They do things which the believer would never dream of doing.

I thank God for giving me the strength I need not to swear any more. As a tough farmer, a man of limited education and very poor vocabulary, every second word I said was blasphemous. God set me free from that when I gave my life to Him almost thirty years ago, and I thank Him for that.

May God embrace you with His sensitivity today, preventing you from hurting a person with idle words. May He ensure that you don't bring shame upon yourself or God, through your actions or your lifestyle.

Mighty God

Zephaniah 3:17

The Lord thy God in the midst of thee is mighty…

Next to the scripture that I am reading this morning, I see that I have written in the margin: "MMC 07" (Mighty Men Conference 2007); a conference I will never forget for as long as I live.

I met a fellow evangelist at a meeting last week. He said that after attending that conference, where 7,400 men bowed their knees before the living God, the anointing of God was so strong on his life that for three weeks afterwards he felt as if he was covered by God's cloak.

To experience the Lord our God amidst us is a powerful sensation! There's no doubt about it, my dear friend: when 7,400 men worship God unashamedly, the Holy Spirit never fails to arrive. I have the photograph in my prayer room that was taken by a young man from Phalaborwa, who arrived at the meeting very late that night. When he went back home to develop the picture, a shaft of white light descending from the black sky and spilling over the tent like melted butter was visible in the photo. We were talking about the glory of God that weekend.

The Lord is always in the midst of His people. The Bible says that He will save us and that He will rejoice over us (Zephaniah 3:17). The Lord must have been delighted that weekend; He took one of His sons home to be with Him. A Mr O'Brien went home to meet with Jesus that weekend.

The Scripture continues, "he will rest in his love; he will joy over thee with singing." Yes, indeed, we could hear the voice of angels singing. Many men were so overwhelmed that they could hardly talk. The presence of the Holy Spirit amongst us was overwhelming during the time of worship. Even when my son Andy led us into praise and worship, I battled to bring myself to preach. God was in our midst.

This coming year we are believing for no fewer than 30,000 men to attend that same weekend conference (in actual fact, 60,000 men came in total).

He shall do it

Psalm 22:27

All the ends of the world shall remember and turn unto the Lord…

Often we are struck by the enormity of the task of preaching the gospel of Jesus Christ with time running out. We think, "Lord, how are You ever going to do it? How are You going to save this world?" Everywhere we look, we see devastation and destruction.

Just north of our border we see our Zimbabwean neighbours suffering. There is nothing left in their country. There is no work, no food, no means of communication, no self-respect and people are literally begging. And we ask, "Lord, how are You going to do it?"

We see the Islamic nations rising up against us. We see the New Age movement with a total disregard for moral standards in our world. And, most of all, we see people randomly murdering each other for no reason at all. We ask, "Lord, how are You going to save this world?"

He reminds us this morning that the "ends of the world shall remember and turn unto the Lord: all the… nations shall worship before" Him (Psalm 22:27).

We thank God that the biggest revival the world has ever known is taking place in China today. We praise God that young people are worshipping Him more than ever before. We thank God that there are unprecedented miracles, signs, and wonders taking place every day. We thank God for my very own South Africa. And, in the midst of all the violence and upheaval, a steady revival is still taking place among the different cultures, different races, different genders and people from different walks of life.

People are returning to God. I firmly believe that before the coming of the Lord, we are going to live to see the greatest revival that South Africa – and indeed the world – has ever witnessed.

The good news is that we don't have to do anything differently. We just have to obey the Word of God and make sure that our ways, those of our families as well as our professional conduct reflect the ways of our Father. And God promised us that He will turn the very ends of the world to Himself, and that all the families of the nations will worship Him!

Growing in God

Deuteronomy 32:11

As an eagle stirreth up her nest...

Just as the eagle will take her young and literally push them out of the nest and off the edge of the cliff, so the Master does to us, because He wants us to use our unrealized power of flight.

Today, you might be reading this while thinking, "Lord, I can't take much more of this", or "Lord, I don't understand what's happening." The Lord says, "I will never leave you, nor forsake you" (Hebrews 13:5, NKJV).

The Bible says that just as the eagle spreads its wings, so does the Lord. Even as we would tumble towards certain death and destruction, He will lift us up on His wings, take us high up into the sky and let us go again. Our heavenly Father will continue to do this until we have perfected the art of flying.

That's how the Lord allows us to grow. Often, just as we start to settle down, He shakes our nest, making sure that we carry on moving. God loves us so much that He's determined not to keep us in the same place.

He wants us to grow in faith from glory to glory.

Remember, faith is a doing word. Faith has feet. Faith grows through exercise. Just as the young eaglet has to flex those wings and start to fly, so do you and I.

Today, go out knowing that He will never allow you to fall and be crushed on the rocks below. He is right next to you. He knows exactly what He is doing. You just keep walking in faith and He will see you through.

Soldiers of the Cross

Psalm 34:19

Many are the afflictions of the righteous…

Are you feeling that you're going through really trying times at the moment? Are you feeling that maybe even the Lord Himself has forsaken you? Dear Christian, be encouraged. I've just read an article written by Charles H. Spurgeon, where he says:

> Dear believer, do you understand that God may take away your comforts and privileges in order to make you a stronger Christian? Do you see why the Lord always trains His soldiers, not by allowing them to lie on beds of ease but by calling them to difficult marches and service? He makes them wade through streams, swim across rivers, climb steep mountains and walk many long marches carrying heavy backpacks of sorrow.
>
> This is how He develops soldiers; not by dressing them up in fine uniforms to strut at the gates of the barracks, or to appear as handsome gentlemen to those who are strolling through the park. No, God knows that soldiers can only be made in battle and are not developed in times of peace. We may be able to grow the raw materials of which soldiers are made, but turning them into true warriors requires the education brought about by the smell of gunpowder and by fighting in the midst of the bullets and exploding bombs, not by living through pleasant and peaceful times.
>
> So, dear Christian, could this account for your situation? Is the Lord uncovering your gifts and causing them to grow? Is He developing in you the qualities of a soldier by shoving you into the heat of the battle? Should you not then use every gift and weapon that He has given you to become a conqueror?

So today, go forth in faith, knowing that the Commander of the armies of heaven and earth goes before you and that He will never allow you to attempt that which you are not able to handle. He has trained you to be one of His mighty warriors!

Meek

Matthew 5:5

Blessed are the meek: for they shall inherit the earth.

The definition of meekness is controlled strength. A prime example of a meek man in the Bible is none other than Moses. I think he was referred to as the meekest man known to the world. You can imagine; leading 2.5 million Israelites who were whining and moaning for forty years in the desert without any food, water, clothing, or housing, took some doing. No one could ever accuse Moses of being timid or weak. That's for sure!

Often, especially among men, if someone is considered meek he gets labelled as being weak or emotional. Nothing could be further from the truth. The Lord says, "Blessed are the meek: for they shall inherit the earth."

I believe God will encourage and welcome men and women who walk in meekness.

A meek person thinks before they speak. They wait their turn before giving an opinion, which is usually always worth listening to. I regard my own, dear wife Jill as a meek person. She is anything but a weak person. She has a very strong personality but she is the one who thinks before she speaks and always listens. She will say in one sentence what I do in a whole paragraph.

Consider the boxing fraternity. They will tell you that a counter puncher is a man you need to look out for. Who is he? He's the one who will back off while the aggressor throws his punches. Then, when the aggressor is off balance, the counter puncher comes back with the knockout blow simply because he reads the situation and makes his punches count.

Let us aim to be like that today. Let us be known as meek people; as people who are able to control their tempers and emotions and as those who are able to wait on the Lord, to hear the Word of the Lord and deliver the Word of God at the right time. We can rest assured that conducting ourselves in such a way is like delivering a telling blow and the victory will always belong to Jesus Christ.

If we are impatient and very impulsive people, we need to ask God today to fill us with meekness so we can find goodwill and inherit the earth. That includes witnessing to unbelievers.

The proof of the pudding

John 14:21

He that hath my commandments, and keepeth them, he it is that loveth me...

Today we need to understand that, as the saying goes, we can fool most of the people most of the time but we cannot fool all of the people all of the time! You will never fool God.

God is saying to you and to me today, "Stop telling Me that you love Me and start showing it. You can't tell Me that you love Me and then disobey My commandments." It's like your children. You can tell that your children love you by the way they serve, honour, and obey you. Talk is cheap and actions speak so much louder than words.

The Lord is asking us to love Him with all our hearts and to love our neighbours as ourselves. He's asking for us to surrender unconditionally. It doesn't matter how others respond to us. What does matter is how we respond to God and to our fellow man. It is impossible for me to have quiet time in the morning if I have aught against my brother or sister. I have to love them. Why? Because it's a commandment that Jesus gave me. Jesus loved even those who persecuted Him.

Do you remember that Peter denied the Lord three times before the crucifixion? Yet He is such a merciful and gracious God that when He was raised from the dead, the angel in the empty tomb told Mary Magdalene and the women with her to "tell His disciples – and Peter – that He is going before you into Galilee; there you will see Him, as He said to you" (Mark 16:7, NKJV). Why did he say that? Because Jesus knew that Peter probably felt so ashamed for letting the Lord down three times, that he wouldn't have gone.

The Lord loves us so much. Today, He says to us, "If you love Me, obey My commandments." Do you know that after that Peter never denied the Lord again? Do you know that Peter's actions spoke louder than his words? Do you know that Peter was the one who was crucified upside down – so was his wife, who was crucified before him – for the sake of the Lord Jesus Christ?

Let people see your love for Christ today by the way in which you serve Him and His creation.

Mercy

Matthew 5:7

Blessed are the merciful: for they shall obtain mercy.

The *New Collins Dictionary* defines the meaning of the word "mercy" as compassionate. Jesus wants us to be compassionate so that He can be compassionate towards us. When I gave my life to Jesus Christ, I suddenly changed from being an arrogant, self-centred, self-made man to being a very humble creature. I realized how much I had to rely on God's compassion to forgive me for the lifestyle that I used to entertain.

When that happens, you'll think twice before casting stones at other people. Remember the saying: "People who live in glass houses shouldn't throw stones". If God has forgiven you much, then you will love Him all the more. That's what they said about Peter. Then you'll find that you have a lot more compassion for others.

Unfortunately, what tends to happen is that after a period of walking in God's grace and mercy, arrogance starts to rear its ugly head again. You experience the need to place yourself first again and find that you become less patient and less understanding towards those who are struggling around you.

My late mother was a sickly woman. Although she suffered a lot of pain and discomfort, she was a wonderful, patient, and caring nurse whenever my brother, sister or I fell ill. My mother would sit up all night and make sure that we took our medicine. She would sit by my bedside and read me stories, or just sit and be there for me. She knew what it was like to feel unwell as she battled terribly with asthma.

The Lord says, "Blessed are the merciful: for they shall obtain mercy." Today, try to be more compassionate with that person at your workplace or at home (maybe even a child of yours?). Remember that God has been extremely merciful towards you. You might think, "It's not fair, I don't deserve this", and you are probably quite right. Neither did Jesus deserve to be crucified for our sins. Yet, He did it gracefully.

Remember today that others are receiving mercy at your expense. Consider it a tremendous privilege and blessing.

A forked tongue

John 17:17

Sanctify them through thy truth: thy word is truth.

There's an old Native American saying, "Don't speak with a forked tongue." A person who speaks with a forked tongue is a liar. We praise God for the fact that His Word is true.

I've just received a very sad phone call from a young South African farmer who's been struggling with his marriage for some time. His wife went to visit her sister overseas. When she left, she was happy and totally at peace. He stayed behind to run the farm. When she returned, he said, he knew that something was wrong. When he tried to embrace her she didn't respond. Shortly afterwards, she asked for a divorce. He tried to find out why and she gave a whole lot of untruthful reasons. He has just found out that there's a third party involved. The young husband is devastated. She has been lying to him and that's the part that's hurting him more than anything else.

I can say to you this morning, my dear friend, that Jesus Christ is not a liar. Numbers 23:19 tells you that God is not a man, that He should lie. In this day and age, it is so hard to find honest people. Therefore, it is so refreshing to know that the Word of God never, ever lies. Everything that God said in His Word has either come to pass, or is busy coming to pass.

Maybe you are feeling disillusioned today? Maybe someone has let you down – maybe your partner in business, a child, maybe your spouse? But I can assure you of one thing: God will never, ever let you down. Do not put your trust in man. Put your expectation in God and in Him alone. Psalm 62:5 says, "My soul, wait thou only upon God; for my expectation is from him." Sometimes, we put tremendous pressure on our partners instead of putting our ultimate trust in God, who is all truth.

We prayed the prayer of faith over the telephone and the young man is going to let his wife go. We prayed that God will work in her heart and that she will return home, because her husband still loves her. We are believing for a reconciliation in this marriage. His love for her is so strong that if she should return home and truly repent, he will forgive her and show her much grace, just as the Lord Jesus Christ did for him. It might take some time, but we have faith that it will happen.

The great I AM

John 18:5

I am he.

Often, we forget who we are serving. We forget the true identity of Jesus Christ. My dear friend, He is more than a conqueror, more than the King of kings and the Lord of lords, more even than your Saviour and Redeemer. He is indeed the great I AM.

This morning during my quiet time I read a beautiful account of the high priests' soldiers coming to arrest Jesus. Isn't it amazing how Jesus immediately puts the attacker on the back foot, turning him into the defender! As you read John 18, you will see that when they arrived, Jesus asked, "Whom seek ye?" (verse 4). They answered, "We are seeking Jesus of Nazareth." The Master replied, "I am he." As soon as He said this, the Bible says that they fell to the ground. There was suddenly a power, a force that they had come up against.

In Exodus 3:14 we read about Moses, who is told by God to go and set His people free. Moses said, "When I go to Pharaoh" (the most powerful ruler who was regarded by the Egyptians as God) "who shall I say has sent me?"

God answered, "Say I AM has sent you." This same I AM was in the Garden of Gethsemane praying when the unruly force that served the high priests, Caiaphas and Annas, came to arrest Him.

Maybe you are feeling totally inadequate today, maybe unarmed or too small for the job? When you go out today, remember that the great I AM is going with you.

John G. Lake, the great American evangelist who in five years caused a huge revival in South Africa, used to say, "Get up, look in the mirror and you'll see yourself. Say to that person in the mirror, 'God lives in you. Wherever you go today, He's going with you.' Then go out and face the world."

The Lord says to you today that He, the great I AM, goes with you. There is nobody on this earth that can stand against you if He goes before you. Romans 8:31 states that if God be for us, who can be against us?

Powerless without God

John 19:11

Thou couldest have no power at all against me, except it were given thee from above.

This is the story of Pontius Pilate. He was basically a good man, an innocent man as it were, brought into conflict and caught in the middle of the Jews and our Saviour. When Jesus did not speak to him, he said, "Do You realize that I have the power of life and death over You?"

Jesus very firmly corrected him and said, "You have no power at all against Me. It's only because it's been given to you from above." We need to understand that without the Lord Jesus Christ you and I are powerless.

A few weeks ago all the experts and leaders of this area gathered for a farmers' congress. Good, professional men and farmers who know their trade very well and have been voted to represent groups of farmers from all over the province, came together to discuss issues like the price of commodities, the political situation, land distribution, the planting of crops, marketing of crops, and so forth.

They asked me to open the congress with prayer and a Scripture reading from the Holy Bible. Once again, I had the privilege of reminding them that "the earth is the Lord's and the fullness thereof" (Psalm 50:12), and that on our own we can do nothing.

It doesn't matter how educated or qualified we might be in agriculture. We can do everything according to the book, but if the Lord doesn't provide the rain, we're in dire straits. He is, at the end of the day, the Alpha and the Omega.

This is what Jesus was saying to Pontius Pilate, "You might be the governor and the ruler. You might even have the authority to allow men to live and to die. But the only reason that you have that authority over Me is because My Father gave it to you."

Today, it might do us well to remember that without God nothing can happen. Let's place Him first today before we go forth to conduct our business.

It's all His

Haggai 2:8

The silver is mine and the gold is mine, saith the Lord of hosts.

We're living in an era where bankruptcy is rife. People are tricked into taking on debt that they cannot afford to repay. They are enticed to borrow money with the promise that no down payment is required. They are lured into buying houses and expensive motorcars that they cannot afford and to take luxurious holidays that they have not budgeted for. As soon as money gets paid into their accounts, they are hounded by the creditors to pay their dues, threatening them with jail if they don't. People end up with two to three jobs to repay money that they have spent on luxuries that they didn't need or want at the time.

Today, God reminds us that all the silver and the gold is His. The Lord is saying to us that He is sufficient for you and me; and that He will make a way for us where there seems to be no way. He says, "If you ask anything in My name, I will do it" (John 14:14, NKJV), but He says in verse 15, "If you love Me, keep My commandments" (NKJV). That means that if you ask anything in His name that is according to His will, He'll give it to you.

Maybe you're a farmer and the rain this year hasn't been adequate. You owe the co-op or the bank money for fertilizer, seed, herbicide, and insecticide, which you bought with borrowed money. If you are feeling anxious about your financial situation today, call out to the One who owns all the silver and gold in this world; and I promise you that He will undertake for you. It's happened to me, not once, but time and time again.

Please don't allow yourself to be enticed by the evil one to buy things which you don't really need with money that you don't really have, and then cry out to God and ask Him to undertake for you. He didn't say that. He said He'd make a way for you if you obey His commandments.

Go and speak to your creditors today. Tell them that you'll pay them as soon as you can and then start working towards settling those debts. Suddenly you will have a new lease on life. You'll find that you won't feel sick any more and that you won't be carrying burdens, cast iron anvils on your back, because of unnecessary debt.

If you have a need today, ask the Lord Jesus Christ. He owns the bank of heaven!

Obedience

Mark 16:15

Go…

Keith Green was a rock 'n' roll star in the 1960s, a time fraught with drugs and known as the "hippy era". He was a young man who was seeking the truth – like most drug addicts do – and he got saved. He was a pianist who had an incredible love for God. The Lord was very real to him. At the age of twenty-nine he tragically died in an aeroplane crash but he is still remembered for the impact he had on this world, especially on the young people.

Keith Green wrote in one of his songs, "If God has not told you to stay, You'd better go." This is so profound. I want to reiterate that today: if God has not told you to stay, you'd better go. Many years ago I had an incident with one of our team members who couldn't decide whether his time with us at Shalom was up, or whether he should stay. He struggled with this decision for about a year. One morning he came into my prayer room and said that he still hadn't heard from God. I said, "Well, if God hasn't told you to stay, you'd better go." The very next morning he came and said he was leaving.

If God has not told you to stay at home, you'd better go into the mission field and preach the gospel. That applies to any decision you make in your life. Some of us are forever waiting for a prompt or a sign. We are always waiting to hear the word "Go". But if you have no peace in your heart with what you're doing at the moment, then you need to make that decision.

My late dad was a humble blacksmith but he had great words of wisdom. One day he said to my brother and me, "When you get up in the morning and you don't feel like going to work, change your job because most of your life is spent in the workplace." I know that's easier said than done but many times when I pray for people who are sick in their bodies, the Holy Spirit will reveal to me that they are actually very unhappy in their lives and that's what's bringing on the sickness. When they deal with that situation, whether it be unforgiveness or unhappiness in the workplace, suddenly their health starts to improve as well.

I encourage you today to hear from God for yourself. If He hasn't told you to stay, then you'd better go.

Small voice

1 Kings 19:12

… but the Lord was not in the fire: and after the fire a still small voice.

So often we want God to answer us in miraculous and huge ways. We want a ticker tape message broadcasted across the sky to hear what God wants us to do. The Bible clearly states that when Elijah was looking for an answer from God, he didn't see it in the strong wind that rent the mountains and broke the rocks in pieces. He did not see Him in the wind, the earthquake or in the fire. But a still small voice spoke to him and gave him clear direction.

Poor Elijah thought he was the only one left in the whole of Israel who had not bowed the knee to the two other gods they worshipped. After the Lord had given him direction, He reassured him, "I still have 7,000 men who have not bowed the knee."

Some days you might feel that you are the only one in your workplace, in your school or in your community who is a Christian. My dear friend, do not be deceived. I was under the impression that there were no Christians on my farm, but the Holy Spirit convicted me many years ago to deliver services (entailing prayer, singing, and the delivering of testimony) to our farm workers before we start with the day's work. When I initiated this early-morning service, I was pleasantly surprised to see how many of our workers were believers. That service continues to this very day.

Jesus will sometimes speak to you through a small voice in your heart of hearts. I want to encourage you to take the time and to sit and listen.

Wait for Him to speak to you. Often we are so busy with our computers, cell phones and our programmes that the Master does not get an opportunity to speak to us.

We say to people that we haven't heard from God. It's because we haven't waited to hear from Him. That still, small voice demands absolute concentration and commitment to God before our hearts will be able to hear Him. You say you don't have the time. You cannot afford not to have the time if you want to lead a life that is going to be successful, prosperous and full of purpose. You have to make time to receive your directions from the King of kings and the Lord of lords.

Chosen

Haggai 2:23(b)

… for I have chosen thee, saith the Lord of hosts.

When you are doing God's work, it is a privilege and honour to be reminded by the Holy Spirit through God's Word that He has chosen you! The same Scripture is found in John 15:16. I'm on my way to the airport to catch a plane to Pretoria, where I will be speaking at a large conference. To have the reassurance that He has chosen me means more to me than anything else.

Robert Murray M'Cheyne said that if he knew that Jesus was praying for him in the room next door, he would not fear a thousand enemies. He said, "With the Lord, time and distance make no difference. Jesus is interceding for me; therefore I need have no fear of any man." I can honestly say this morning that I have no fear of man because I know that my Jesus is praying for me right now.

The same can apply to you. If Jesus calls you He will anoint you. He will give you the strength and the ability to complete the work that He has called you to do. Go in peace today knowing that He goes before you. He will never leave you, nor forsake you.

Drinking of the cup

John 18:11(b)

… the cup which my Father hath given me, shall I not drink it?

I'm on my way to yet another appointment in the early hours of the morning. The sun has not yet risen. The same question that the Lord asked me in 1989 arises: "Are you prepared to drink from the cup? Are you prepared to see less of your family for My name's sake?" I said at that time, "Lord, only by Your grace." Now, even more so! "By Your grace alone…"

My children are all grown up and have left home. This morning I left my wife. I made her a cup of tea, kissed her goodbye, and I'm on my way to preach the gospel. There is a price to pay. It's drinking from that cup of suffering. A very, very small cup to drink from in comparison with others; nevertheless the hardest thing for me to do is to leave my family in order to be obedient to the call on my life.

Jesus did the same. He had to leave His family, the disciples, in order to accomplish what His Father had called Him to do.

In my walk with the Lord I've been very clear on the fact that there is always a cost involved. We say that salvation is for free. But Jesus did pay the price – it cost our Master His life. For those of us who love Him with a passion, there is a cost. It may be that you've been ostracized by your friends because of your new stand of holiness for Jesus. It may be that you have to leave your family, as in my case, in order to preach the gospel.

The one thing I am sure of, though, is that nothing we do for God is wasted. This is the most fruitful part of my entire life that I'm living at the moment. I thank Him for choosing me to do it for Him.

The latter rain

Haggai 2:9

The glory of this latter house shall be greater than of the former, saith the Lord of hosts: and in this place will I give peace, saith the Lord of hosts.

This is one of the most exciting Scriptures I've read in a long time. The Lord is talking about building His house. A house? What He is referring to is not a concrete building; it's you and me! It is people's lives. The Lord says that the glory of the latter house shall be greater than that of the former. This means that the Lord's miracles are going to be more powerful in these last days than the ones He performed in the early days. Don't forget that He took 2.5 million Israelites out of Egypt and through the desert. He fed and clothed them for forty years. The Lord promises that the latter rain will be greater than the former.

I received a text message from one of the famous Springbok legends, Balie Swart, who was part of the 1995 World Cup rugby squad when South Africa won the William Webb Ellis Cup. At the time of his message, he was in France where the Springbok squad was getting ready to play in the quarter-finals. Obviously there was a tremendous amount of pressure on them as the whole world was eagerly waiting to see who the 2007 rugby world champions were going to be.

Balie Swart, a committed Christian, mentioned that he had conducted a Bible study session for the Springboks. They watched the DVD footage of the Mighty Men Conference that we had on the farm earlier in the year where we saw 7,400 men commit themselves to Christ (the latter rain). After having watched the fourth episode, five of the current players committed their lives to Christ.

My dear friend, God is on the move. Indeed, the latter rain is going to be much greater than the former. We are believing for nothing less than that and we believe that we are already experiencing a Holy Ghost revival in our blessed South Africa.

This revival that I'm referring to is spreading far beyond the borders of South Africa. Even as I'm writing now, they are preparing for a huge men's conference to take place in the western part of Australia, where between 3,000 and 5,000 men will come together for an encounter with God.

Men are hungry for God. The Lord is coming very soon. In fact – and you've heard me say this before – Jesus is not coming soon, He's on His way! The Lord says that He's shaking the heavens, the earth, the sea and the dry land (verse 6).

People return to God when the "shaking" takes place. It happened in my own life. It happens in every single person's life when we come to the realization that we cannot make it on our own. That's when the Lord is going to return in all His power and glory.

Actions speak louder than words

Titus 1:16

They profess that they know God…

You have read before in this book (for example 17 February) that at Shalom we say that faith has feet. Faith is not an object, like a cupboard or a chair, it's a doing word. It's a word that requires action, just like a verb such as "running" or "walking". As Christians, we need to start practising what we are preaching.

An anointed young rock singer, who has come to know the Lord in the last few years, is releasing a new album. He's a spiritual son of mine and yesterday I listened to one of his songs. It moved me deeply. He wrote me a letter saying that in these last days young people want to know what the Word of God stands for; what is right and what is wrong.

It seems that there may be too many grey areas in the Christian faith these days and the younger people are noticing this. People do not tolerate hypocrisy. What does the Word of God say about sex before marriage? It is very clear: it is not acceptable. Someone who sleeps with someone else before they are married is a fornicator. Very simple! That needs to be addressed, because according to the Word of God, fornicators are bound for hell.

Unfortunately, due to the sensitive nature of this truth, evangelists do not preach about it any more. This Scripture in Titus 1:16 says: "by their actions they deny him". In other words, what we preach we must live, and what we live we must preach so that people will not be deceived in any way.

Somebody once shared his worst nightmare with me. He dreamed he was in hell. People were up to their waists in bubbling mud; some even up to their shoulders. They were scared and drowning. In his dream he saw a man wading around, picking up people's heads by their hair, and looking at their faces. He was obviously searching for someone. In his dream he asked the man, "What are you doing?" He replied, "I'm looking for the preacher who put me in this place!"

It is a big responsibility to be a Christian. Anybody who professes to love Jesus is automatically an ambassador for God and therefore has to preach and live the undiluted Word of God. That takes tremendous faith and discipline.

Kingdom living

John 18:36

My kingdom is not of this world…

When Pontius Pilate asked Jesus whether He was the King of the Jews, the answer that Jesus gave him was, "My kingdom is not of this world." My dear friend, we are in the world but we must never be part of the world. You and I are sojourners passing through a foreign land. We are here only for a short while. Then we're going home to be with our beloved Saviour, Jesus Christ, in heaven forever.

If this kingdom is not ours, why is it that some of us are putting so much effort into this kingdom and none into the place where we are going to reside forever? Some of us are working so hard to maintain our earthly homes, careers, and lives that you'd think we're going to be here forever. I believe we're going to see the Lord returning very soon. I believe He's going to come on the clouds and that He'll be riding a white charger. He's coming to take us home to be with Him in heaven. Until then, though, we need to be sure that we're working for the kingdom to come.

I love this earth and I'm a naturalist, a farmer, but it's a fact, folks. If God is preparing a mansion for us in Paradise, then this place we're living in is just temporary. Today, I would exhort you to put your trust, your hope, your future and your savings into the kingdom that is yet to come.

You will only be able to take people to heaven with you. Not that fine horse you love riding so much, or that beautiful motorcar, that wonderful home, or the beach cottage. Not that farm or your business, only people. Be sure that your family is saved and that you value your relationships. Home is not an easy place to be a Christian. That's where we've got to work and put our effort, strength and our resources.

I've handed over my farms to my sons and therefore I don't have a farm any more. I live on their farm and I refuse to pay rent because I have a lot of Scottish blood in me! Seriously though, we need to invest in the kingdom that is coming. Jesus said, "This is not My kingdom." The kingdom He was speaking of is another kingdom, and we need to speak more of that kingdom as well.

Faithful God

Zechariah 1:5

Your fathers, where are they? and the prophets, do they live forever?

The Lord is asking us the question, "Where are all these people that were with you before?" They are gone. Nothing remains forever, except the Word of God and His faithfulness. Prophets come and prophets go. Even our loved ones are only with us for a season before they go home.

The Lord says that His Words will last forever. He says, "Heaven and earth will pass away but My Word will never pass away." The Lord puts His Word above His name. I want to declare to you today: you can trust God's Word. There aren't many things that you can trust in this world today. Sometimes, it feels as if you can't even trust yourself really, can you? You can trust the Word of God. If God has given you a promise and you say, "But Angus that promise hasn't come to fruition yet", be patient. It will come. If God has promised you, He will deliver.

He has never let me down yet. I love to go to meetings and challenge people: "Has anybody here been forsaken or let down by God? If so, please raise your hand." There's never a person who can do that. Everything God promises to do He does. We need to ensure that we don't let Him down either. We need to trust Him. Even when the prophets, your parents or even your fathers in faith are no longer with you, Jesus says, "I will be with you always."

John 15:13 says, "Greater love hath no man than this, that a man lay down his life for his friends." There's no one, save the King, who has ever died for you. He hasn't forsaken us, departed or gone away. He's right there with you. He loves you and He needs you, because He created you. He needs to have a fellowship with you.

Spend time with Him today. If you're feeling that someone has let you down or betrayed you, look to Jesus. He has never done that, and He never will!

Jealous for us

Zechariah 1:14(b)

I am jealous for Jerusalem and for Zion with a great jealousy.

When I first heard that the Lord is jealous for us, I said: "No, no. He's God. He doesn't have any inadequacies. He doesn't have any negative traits. He's God. He's pure and He's love." There is such a thing as good jealousy though. I'm jealous for my wife. I don't want anybody else looking at her, as she is my wife.

Jesus died for you and me and He's jealous for us. He paid a tremendous price for you and for me. Remember to give Him your absolute best today because He loves you so much. Because He's jealous for you, He will protect you and He will defend you. You say, "Where is He? I'm going through a bad time." He is right there next to you. Call on Him, speak to Him, walk with Him, and He'll guide you through that fire.

One thing the Lord does not tolerate is when you try to serve two masters; when you become unfaithful to Him; when you become like a prostitute and have no affiliation with Him; when you are standing with one foot in the world and one in the kingdom. Either you are for Him, or you are against Him (Matthew 12:30). He is definitely for you.

We need to nail our colours to the mast and give Him first priority in our lives. We need to honour Him because He is a good God. Not for what you can get out of Him, but just because He is who He is. My dear friend, He loves you so much and He wants to enjoy more fellowship with you. Please spend more time with Him, and less with the things of the world: your business; your work; the things that will actually mean nothing to you one day.

The way to stop someone from being jealous is to make sure that you give them your undivided attention, to make sure that you are loyal towards them and to make sure that you don't look in any other direction but to them alone. Ask any couple that is still madly in love, one of the worst things you can do is to not listen to your partner while sitting in a restaurant and instead to look at all the other people walking past. That makes them jealous. You have to give your loved one your undivided attention.

The same thing applies to Jesus, because God made us in His own image. When you spend time with people, make sure that those people feel that they are important, but that Jesus is the most important person in your life!

Peacemaker

Matthew 5:9

Blessed are the peacemakers: for they shall be called the children of God.

The Lord said, "Blessed are the peacemakers", not the peace lovers. Sometimes, in order to be a peacemaker, you actually have to be a confronter. You have to call sin by its name. You have to challenge somebody in order for real peace to be established.

Stephen was the first martyr in the New Testament. He died for his faith. The Pharisees, the church people, regarded him as a troublemaker, whilst he was actually doing the exact opposite. He was introducing the Prince of Peace to a godless generation. As a result he died for his faith.

This is the kind of peace that the Lord wants you and me to proclaim today. He wants us to stand up and be counted. It's not easy. He wants us to be prepared to be unpopular if necessary, because the peace that we are offering this world is not of this world. Jesus says in John 14:27, "My peace I give unto you: not as the world giveth, give I unto you. Let not your heart be troubled, neither let it be afraid." That is the peace that we are offering the world.

But the world doesn't necessarily want it because it comes at a price. It means that we have to lay down our lives, deny ourselves, take up our crosses and follow after Him. That may cause contention, war, and possibly bloodshed. Nevertheless, Jesus says, "Blessed are the peacemakers." You and I have a big responsibility today. We have to go into a world that is full of violence, destruction, and hatred, and act as peacemakers. We have to go and raise the banner of our Saviour, the One whose name is Prince of Peace, and tell the people that in order to have peace we must resolve matters with our God first and then with each other.

May God bless you today as you step out in faith as a peacemaker for Jesus Christ!

Sealed lips

John 19:9(b)

But Jesus gave him no answer.

My biggest problem in life is that I talk too much and listen too little. I have a wife who thinks before she speaks and this results in her making far fewer mistakes than I do.

Pontius Pilate was trying to get Jesus to answer, to speak up for Himself, but the Bible says that Jesus gave him no answer. Pontius Pilate asked, "Who are You?" He didn't answer.

My dear friend, you don't always have to give an answer. Sometimes, silence is the best answer of all. If someone is provoking you at work, at school, or on the sports field, just being quiet will sometimes have a greater impact than trying to retaliate.

They say that sarcasm is the lowest form of wit. That is something that we Christians must not use. When you are sarcastic, it is always at the expense of somebody else. Even so-called friendly jokes can cause sadness and unnecessary conflict among friends. Today, let us be like Jesus. When we speak, let it be a word of encouragement or a word that has a powerful meaning.

They say that a barking dog does not bite. It's the dog that lies under the tree and doesn't bark that you need to be wary of. If you keep on threatening people, they eventually stop taking any notice of you. I have noticed that with undisciplined children. If parents threaten to discipline their children, but never actually do anything, their threats will fall on deaf ears.

Sometimes you don't have to say a word to lay down your authority. My eldest son has two little girls. They have impeccable manners. He disciplined them well when they were younger. Now all he has to do is to look at them without even saying a word and they know exactly what they may or may not do. This gives his wife tremendous peace, especially when she's out with her friends. She's not running around the place, trying to bring the children under control. They do exactly what Mum says, because if they don't she tells Dad and they will be disciplined at home.

Proverbs 10:19 says that "In the multitude of words sin is not lacking. But he who restrains his lips is wise." Proverbs 17:28 says that sometimes by not saying anything people presume you to be wise, even if you're not. Yet, if you open your mouth and blurt out words without thinking, you may be taken for a fool.

Today, before we speak, let us count our words and then, like Jesus, let every one of them be spoken in love and with authority.

The apple of God's eye

Zechariah 2:8(b)

… for he that toucheth you toucheth the apple of his eye.

Are you feeling vulnerable today? Are you feeling defenceless or weak in any way? Are you feeling alone? I've got good news for you. Jesus says that you are the apple of His eye.

Remember, our God is a jealous God. He will have no other gods before Him. He will not allow anyone to touch the apple of His eye. He says in the book of Zechariah, "For he that toucheth you toucheth the apple of His eye." My dear friend, you might be feeling lonely or vulnerable right now. You might feel rejected and without any friends or family today. Maybe you are feeling fearful because of the violence around you, but God reminds you that you are the apple of His eye and that He will protect you every day of your life. He will hold your hand through the challenges that you may be facing today.

We always talk about a God of love, but He is also a God of wrath. He will not tolerate His children, the apples of His eye, being subjected to the evil one. He is our defence. He is not only our defence counsel; but also our defender.

Jesus Himself says, "Don't be afraid of him who can kill the body, but rather fear Him who can kill the body and the soul and send it to hell." That is the Lord Himself. If the Lord is for us, there is no need for us to fear, because what can man do to us?

To be the apple of His eye means that He delights in you today, my dear friend. He loves you and therefore created you in His own image. He loves everything about you. He loves you completely.

Today spend time with Him who calls you the apple of His eye.

Not using an army

Zechariah 4:6(a)

Not by might…

The Lord prefers to use the not-so-important people of this world to achieve His victories. He does this intentionally because He does not want to share His glory with man. He does this so that people are convinced that it was God who achieved the victory and not the person.

Let's take the example of David and Goliath. Saul was a great warrior. He was head and shoulders taller than any other man in Israel. Yet, in the battle against Goliath, he was totally outclassed and refused to go to battle against Goliath, and so did all of the other great warriors of Israel. God then went and used a small thirteen-year-old shepherd boy with a sling in his pocket to fight against Goliath.

Gideon's army was reduced from 32,500 men to 300. With those 300 men, Gideon gained a tremendous victory.

Jesus chose twelve men with no particular reputation. One of them betrayed Him and two of them denied Him. They were simple men with no education but the people knew that they were hand-picked by Jesus. He used those men to turn the world upside down and it's never been the same since.

Today God is calling you as well. He wants to use you. He says, "It's not by might… but by My Spirit," that He's going to change the world. Be available today, my dear friend. Do whatever it is that you do well and God will promote you.

Often, people come to me and say they want to become preachers; build children's homes; do great deeds for God. My advice to them is to start at the beginning. Go back and do whatever you are good at and God will promote you, just as He did with little David. God called on David while he was still a shepherd looking after his father's sheep. The time was right. God called him, anointed him, and appointed him. The Lord wants to do exactly the same thing with you and me.

Without force

Zechariah 4:6(b)

... nor by power...

One thing I praise God for is that our Saviour is a gentleman. He will never force you to do anything that you don't want to. He says in Revelation 3:20, "Behold I stand at the door and knock." A man told me many years ago, "Do you realize that this door only has a handle on the inside? The Lord intentionally positioned it like that so that He cannot get to you and to me unless we open the door." The Lord has all the power in the universe at His disposal, yet He chose to use a small baby in a manger, in a small town called Bethlehem, not only to be His spokesperson but His Redeemer for this tired world of ours as well.

I love God very much. He always uses the weak, the uneducated, the defenceless and the powerless to do His bidding in this world of ours. If you go back in history and look at some of the mightiest men of God, you'll find that they were mostly physically weak, uneducated men but they had a tremendous love for God.

William Carey was a cobbler who came from England, but he opened up the whole of India to the gospel. Hudson Taylor was not even a qualified doctor when he went to China. By faith he sent a thousand families across to China to be with him. He opened up China to the Word and the biggest revival in the world is taking place there right now. David Livingstone (1813–73) was a self-educated boy who worked in the cotton mills in Blantyre in Scotland. He educated himself by propping up a book in front of him when he was working a sixteen-hour day, spinning cotton. A man who in himself was weak but in God's eyes he was a giant. He opened up Africa to the gospel and brought to light the ongoing horrors of the slave trade.

I can name several more examples. God didn't use the power that He brought down from heaven. James and John were so tired of the rebelliousness of the Pharisees that they cried out to God, "Bring down fire from heaven and consume these people!" In the Garden of Gethsemane Peter wanted to exert power to defend the Lord against the chief priests' soldiers when they came to take Him away – but the Lord used other means.

It's the power of prayer that moves the hand of God. If you've tried everything you can today to alleviate that problem at work, or at home, or on the farm, and you don't know which way to turn, just turn to God in prayer. You'll be surprised at what little effort it takes to turn the situation in your favour.

The Spirit of God

Zechariah 4:6(c)

... but by my Spirit, saith the Lord of hosts.

In John 16:7, Jesus told His disciples that it was necessary for Him to leave so that He could send another, a Comforter, to be with us forever. Often at church services the Holy Spirit is not mentioned once. Yet He's the only One who has the anointing and power to set us free, to heal our diseases and our inequities.

I really want to exhort you this morning, before you go to work, to converse with the Spirit of God. He is the One who will go out with you and stay with you all day and all night long. You can speak to Him at any time and He'll give you godly counsel and direction for your life. He will show you the man or woman to marry, when to close down the business, or when to start one. He will show you who to beware of and who your friends are. Indeed, all He asks is that you be in touch with Him and spend time with Him every day.

I have read of many mighty men and women of God who were powerless to do anything in their own strength until they were baptized with the Holy Spirit. Then only were they reborn. One such person was Smith Wigglesworth. He was a very angry man. He was the man who used to organize the chairs for the meetings on a Sunday. His wife Polly was the preacher. The moment Smith Wigglesworth got baptized in the Holy Spirit, the power of God was evident in his life. Polly never preached again. She never got the opportunity because Smith Wigglesworth was the anointed speaker.

Even when we pray for the sick and we trust in God for signs and wonders, it has to be done through the Spirit of God.

Don't offend the Holy Spirit today. Spend lots of time conversing with Him and listen to Him speaking in your heart. He will give you the direction and wisdom that you never had. And don't forget to give glory to God once things have turned around for the better!

No favourites

Acts 10:34

… of a truth I perceive that God is no respecter of persons…

My wife, Jill, and I used to have the same argument over and over again. I used to say that God has favourites. As examples, I used to name King David, Abraham, and Joshua. But the older I get, the more I realize that my wife was quite right when she said that God has no favourites. God uses the "whosoevers". In fact, it says clearly in Romans 10:13, "For whosoever shall call upon the name of the Lord shall be saved." That's it in a nutshell; the "whosoevers".

So there are no favourites with God. Yes, He loved Peter, James and John and maybe spent more time with them than He did with the other twelve but He had no favourites. If you have a desire to serve God with all your heart, spend time with Him and He will honour that.

When I was a young boy I had a tremendous desire to preach the gospel of Jesus Christ. I believe that God gave me the desire because He saw that I was delighting myself in Him (Psalm 37:4). I had a very low self-esteem; no self-confidence. I wasn't popular at school; I was underweight and therefore not sought after by the girls. I didn't excel at sport. Yet I cried out to God and sought God with all my heart.

It was when I made a full commitment to Christ at the age of thirty-two that the Lord opened doors for me. Every single year, even as I'm writing this book, the blessings are getting greater. I can honestly testify that He has no favourites. He will use you, even today, if you open your heart to Him and say, "Lord, please use me. I'm available." Be prepared to do whatever He asks you to do. He is the One who will do the promotion later on.

Very often at a preaching engagement or a campaign, unemployed people come to me and ask for work. I ask them one question: "Will you be prepared to do whatever job God gives you?" They always say yes, and I say, "Well, then do it, and do it to the best of your ability. Someone will spot you and give you a promotion."

God has no favourites. He loves you with all of His heart, mind, soul and strength. What He wants is for you to do the same and serve others as He has served you.

Healed

Isaiah 53:5(b)

… and with his stripes we are healed.

I've been reading a book on prayer by a very well-known Christian author. I realized that most people do not believe in God for divine healing any longer. They try to rationalize divine healing, to explain it on the hand of many other factors. For example, they conducted a survey in which they found that Christian people have a greater chance of being healed than unbelievers, because their minds are at ease, their bodies are able to recover more quickly, and because there's peace in their hearts. It is also stated that they have a vision and that they have a desire to be healed. They eat well and look after their health and therefore their bodies have a natural ability to heal quicker than those who are not Christians. At the end of the day, the Bible states very clearly that by the stripes that Jesus received before He was crucified, we are healed.

While writing this book, I am listening to an old favourite gospel song: "There is power in the blood". I want to emphasize today that the "effectual fervent prayer of a righteous man availeth much" (James 5:16).

If you are unwell today, I want you to place your hand on that area which is causing you pain, or where your body is struggling to recover, and pray the prayer of faith:

> By the grace of the Lord Jesus Christ and by the blood that He shed on the Cross of Calvary, my sins have been forgiven and I have been healed.

Claim your healing today. I've seen and experienced it with my own eyes. God is my Healer and no one will tell me differently. I want to caution you not to try and explain or dilute the Word of God under any circumstances. Jesus is the same yesterday, today and forever (Hebrews 13:8). He healed the sick when He walked on the earth. He can heal you today and He can heal you tomorrow. We need to put our faith into practice by trusting and thanking Him.

A grain of mustard seed

Matthew 17:20

If ye have faith as a grain of mustard seed, ye shall say unto this mountain, Remove hence to yonder place; and it shall remove; and nothing shall be impossible unto you.

Joseph Hall (1574–1656) said, "One grain of faith is more precious than a pound of knowledge." So often we are taught the Word of God, taught to memorize Scripture, to memorize all the books of the Bible from Genesis through to Revelation. We become very knowledgeable about the Word of God. In fact, we become historians.

The Bible says that the letter killeth, but the spirit giveth life. Here is a man who says that one grain of faith is more precious than a pound of knowledge. The Lord Jesus Christ Himself says that if we have faith, be it as small as a mustard seed, just one seed, we can tell that mountain to move and it shall move – nothing shall be impossible to us (Matthew 17:20).

I've found in my walk with the Lord that the more we trust God, the more He reveals Himself to us. The more faithful we become to His commands, the more He trusts and directs us to step out of the boat and to walk on the water.

Peter is a very good example of a man who trusted God. Even in the middle of his walk of faith he panicked when he saw the huge waves around him – and as soon as he took his eyes off the Lord Jesus Christ, the source of his faith, he started to sink. Maybe you're doing exactly that this morning? But the moment that Peter called out to God, the Lord Jesus was there to take hold of his hand and to pick him up out of the water.

The same applies to you and me today. If we make a decision to trust the Lord in every aspect of our lives, whether it be financial or regarding our health or a relationship, He is faithful in restoring that which the locust and the canker worm have tried to destroy.

Once again, how do we get faith? Faith comes by hearing and hearing by the Word of God (Matthew 10:17). That's all; nothing else. I would encourage you today to get alongside people who have faith in Jesus Christ. Spend time with them, because you become like the people you spend time with. Steer away from those people who have a negative attitude towards life or the government, towards family, or their work situation. Get alongside those who are trusting the Lord, who are believing for the impossible, who are choosing to take one day at a time, who are cloud watchers – in other words, waiting for the Lord Jesus Christ to come back (and it could be at any time) – and who are enjoying life to the fullest.

That abundant life that the Lord promises us in John 10:10 is available to you today by faith. Put your problems, your fears, and your anxieties behind you and take a step of faith today. See the difference that God will make in your life.

Live by faith

Galatians 3:11

But that no man is justified by the law in the sight of God, it is evident: for, The just shall live by faith.

When Martin Luther came across this amazing truth, it set him completely free. He said, "Let us conclude that faith alone justifies and that faith alone fulfils the law." Like many of us, he was struggling.

It could be that some of us are trying to "earn" salvation by upholding the law. The law condemns but the Spirit, through faith, sets us free. It was that revelation that liberated this man. He was a Roman Catholic monk, attempting to live a life of holiness. He was trying to do all the right things: to behave himself; to keep calm; to not be greedy; and to not get caught up in lustful and materialistic things. The harder he tried, the more he failed. He would wear horsehair shirts to aggravate his skin to try and bring his flesh into submission to his will, and he failed. He would beat and starve himself. In the end he lost all hope. Then he came across this Scripture that the just shall live by faith.

You see, my dear friend, it's all about Jesus. It has got nothing to do with us. It's by grace that we've been saved, through faith, and not because of ourselves: it was a gift from God (Ephesians 2:8). What a mighty miracle it is. What a revelation.

Does that mean that we can sin as we please? Not at all! It does mean that we have to love the Lord Jesus Christ and walk the walk of faith, and God will take away all the sin in our lives and give us the freedom and liberty to soar like an eagle.

Go today, knowing that your name is written in the Lamb's Book of Life, not because you're a good person, but because you are a believer. And may the peace of God be with you.

Who has swindled you?

Galatians 3:1

O foolish Galatians, who hath bewitched you…?

This verse is very special to me. Here the Lord is saying that we all started well in the Spirit but we are trying now to become perfect in the flesh. When we are "new" Christians, it feels as if we are wearing rose-tinted glasses because life is just so beautiful. We're in love with Jesus because He has set us free and has given us a second chance.

Then, slowly but surely, we become self-righteous. We start to live by the law, by the flesh and not by faith. We become judgmental towards others, holier than thou and, in fact, like Pharisees. That life that we lived before we came to know Christ pales into insignificance. We start to look down on others and to preach down to others. That's a dangerous place to be at.

The Lord says, "You started so well in the Spirit and now you're trying to be made perfect in the flesh." Let us repent of this today, and remember the grace (undeserved loving kindness) by which God saved you and me.

We must never forget that. Let us exercise that same grace towards others who are struggling and who are trying to follow the right path. The love of Christ that we have today is because we have been reminded by God that it's by grace alone that we have been saved. We deserve to go to hell but, because of the love of God, we've been set free. To start off in the Spirit and end up becoming self-righteous is not acceptable to God. Let us repent today and say, "Lord, forgive us. Forgive us for judging others. Thank you for reminding us where we came from."

The Lord speaks about taking the plank out of your own eye before you try and take the splinter out of your brother's eye. You've heard the saying: "People who live in glass houses shouldn't throw stones". It's only because of what Christ has done for you and me on the Cross of Calvary that we have freedom.

Let us finish the race in the Spirit, as we started it the day we met God. How do we do that? By spending time reading the Word of God, in prayer, and by spending time with other Christians and reminding ourselves where we come from.

Expectation

Galatians 3:6

Abraham believed God, and it was accounted to him for righteousness.

C. S. Lewis (1898–1963) was a great Christian writer and he said that true faith is always accompanied by expectation.

I've found in my own life that the more I walk by faith, the more eager I am to find out what God is planning to do with my life. Faith is very contagious. James says, "Show me your faith without your works, and I will show you my faith by my works" (James 2:18, NKJV).

Since I've started to trust the Lord more and more, my life is becoming hopeful and exciting, because I now believe that through God I can accomplish things that five years ago I wouldn't have thought possible. In 2008, we were again expecting to host what we believed to be the biggest men's conference in the history of our nation. This time we were expecting in excess of between 25,000 and 30,000 men for a full weekend. We booked the biggest tent in the world. We did not charge any conference fee because we believed that God had told us to do that. In the end, we hosted 60,000 men!

Our expectation for this conference was absolutely mammoth. In fact, my dear friend, I'll go as far as to say to you that if God wasn't with us, we would be in serious trouble! But having said that, I feel more secure than ever before, because Angus Buchan is no longer in the driver's seat. The Lord Jesus Christ is. I said, "Lord, I can't wait to see what You are going to achieve with this event. You told me to do it and I know it is going to be a success."

I feel just like Abraham must have felt when he left that beautiful farm in Ur of the Chaldees to go to an unknown destination to start his life all over again. He went by faith. That's why God loved him so much.

Abraham was the only man in the Bible that I know of that God called His friend: "My friend, Abraham." He was called God's friend not because he was a good man, but because he believed and had a tremendous expectancy of God. And as we know, God gave him his heart's desire: a son, Isaac. Abraham became the father of many nations – and is indeed our father if we believe in Jesus Christ as the Son of God.

A hunger for God

2 Kings 2:9

... let a double portion of thy spirit be upon me.

Elisha refused to let Elijah out of his sight. Elijah didn't have time for this persistent young man as he was too busy. Elisha had such a hunger for God and wanted to be used by Him.

I want to ask you today, how hungry are you for God? You say there was a time when you were on fire for the Lord but, because of all the concerns of this world, you feel that your love for God has somewhat cooled. There's no time for that, my dear friend, if you want to be used by God. You have to have a hunger for God, just like Elisha had. Even the prophets, the mighty warriors of God, told Elisha to leave the prophet Elijah alone, but he refused.

I've just received a telephone call from a very disheartened friend of mine. He told his minister about a miracle that had taken place in his family in the past week and asked her to please encourage the congregation by sharing this with them, but the minister accidentally forgot. I encouraged him and reminded him that God has not forgotten and that maybe God felt that he should be the one to tell the congregation about the miracle himself.

So often we get disillusioned by those who do not seem to be completely committed to their work. Elisha was not one of them. Even when forty prophets told him to leave the man of God alone, he said, "No. I'm persisting. I want his mantle." He did persist and eventually he received the mantle because, when God took Elijah up into heaven (Elijah never died – God sent a chariot of fire to fetch him), he left his mantle with Elisha. You see, the other forty prophets weren't there at the time. The man who was hungry for God was, and he received the reward. He was greedy for the things of God and not satisfied to receive only a portion.

What about you? Are you happy with where you are with God at the moment? Are you asking and pleading with God to better your relationship with Him, to increase the power that He has available for you so that you can lay your hands upon the sick, heal them and lead people to Jesus Christ?

When God took Elijah up into heaven, Elisha was left with the mantle of God. Immediately, he rolled up the mantle (a cloak) and smote the water of the River Jordan with it. He cried out, "Where is the Lord God of Elijah?" When you are living a life that is righteous before God, you can ask God, even challenge Him in a godly manner, and He will respond. When Elisha asked, "Where is the God of Elijah?" the water parted and Elisha walked through with dry feet.

It is recorded in Scripture that Elisha performed exactly double the number of miracles that Elijah performed. Why? Because he had a hunger for God! Do you have a hunger for God today? If you do, God is going to meet you. Don't give up, because you might be on the brink of one of the greatest miracles of your life.

Have a blessed day.

Love in action

1 Corinthians 13:1

Though I speak with the tongues of men and of angels, and have not charity, I am become as sounding brass or a tinkling cymbal.

The Lord tells us that it doesn't matter how holy we are to the world: if we've been baptized with the Holy Spirit, if we can speak in tongues or if we are ministering to the poor. He says that if we do not have love, we are nothing more than a sounding brass or a tinkling cymbal.

I remember reading that Mahatma Gandhi once said that he would have had no problem following this man, Jesus of Nazareth. In fact he loved to sing the hymn "When I Survey the Wondrous Cross" on his way to the Hindu temple to worship foreign gods. "But," he said, "I cannot reconcile myself with His followers." Obviously he did not see love in us. Today, let us be aware that one of the most important commodities that people need to see in you and me is the love of Christ.

C. T. Studd (1860–1931) was a great English cricketer. He went out into the mission field and spread the gospel with all of his heart. He gave up everything he had, gave away his fortune and died in the Congo, preaching the gospel. He said, "The suspicions subtract. Faith adds. But love multiplies. It blesses twice; he who gives it and he who gets it."

That is a profound statement. If you're feeling unloved today, go and find someone who is lonely and without friends and just love them. You'll find that all of a sudden you'll be loved. Jesus Himself said, "Greater love hath no man than this, than a man lay down his life for his friends." Jesus laid down His life for you and me. The least we can do is to love our fellow man. In doing so, our loneliness will evaporate.

Matthew Henry, a wonderful Christian man of God, said, "Love is the very essence and life of the Christian religion." Without love we can't live. Juan Carlos Ortiz said that love is the oxygen of the kingdom.

Mother Teresa was known all over the world. Her ministry became one of the most powerful and well-known ministries that modern Christianity has ever seen. God gave her a simple instruction: to love the unlovely. She would literally take dying people out of the gutter, wash and clean them, and put them into a clean bed to die with some measure of dignity.

That's all she did. Her ministry touched the world.

As we go about our tasks today, let us be a sweet fragrance of love in a world where there is much hatred, much fear and too much mistrust.

Today, let us by faith choose to love the unlovely and to serve those that others avoid. The world is looking to you and me to love unconditionally. Go out today and be an agent for Jesus Christ.

Good manners

1 Corinthians 13:5

Doth not behave itself unseemly, seeketh not her own, is not easily provoked, thinketh no evil;

The Christian religion is again in the spotlight worldwide. Books such as *The Da Vinci Code*, and *The Gospel According to Judas* (amongst others) are trying to bring the sovereignty and holiness of God into disrepute.

My dear friend, today as you go about your daily chores, let your manners be of an excellent standard. In 1 Corinthians 13, which is all about love, it says that we must be of good behaviour and well mannered. It is so refreshing to see a young man helping an old lady across the street. That "sermon", preached in practice, is greater than any message preached in a church, with no action to follow.

As Christians, we have to address a number of issues in our own lives: not to be selfish; to prefer your brother or sister to yourself; not to be easily provoked – to name but a few examples. I admit to the fact that I have a short fuse and it's something that I've been working on, together with the Holy Spirit, to rectify. When you become a Christian you will be provoked and often accused of being a false Christian. You've got to ask the Lord to help you to remain calm and keep your temper intact.

And lastly, we must bar all evil thoughts. Start to think of only the good in people and you'll find that they will respond in a similar manner. If you think people are no good they'll turn out to be no good; especially your own family, your children, and your spouse. Always think the best of them, speak highly of them, encourage them and you'll find that they will change and start to become the people you perceive them to be in Christ.

I remember the story of a newborn Christian, a tough chap who worked as a guard on the railways. He was showing the driver of the train how to shunt (reverse) the train to hitch up a carriage at the back and got his hand trapped between the shackles as the carriage locked into the train. Eventually, they managed to free his hand and he fell to the ground. His hand was just a bloody mess. He moaned and groaned and then remembered that he was being observed by a lot of his former drinking buddies. They called the ambulance, but before they could take him to hospital he knelt on the ground in front of all his friends and repented to God. He asked Jesus to forgive him for his unsuitable manners as a Christian. Then he allowed them to take him to the hospital. That one act spoke louder than a multitude of sermons.

Let your actions speak louder than your words today.

Don't be afraid of evildoers

Psalm 37:1

Fret not thyself because of evildoers…

In this psalm, the Lord reminds us that we are not to be afraid of those workers of iniquity, because they will soon be cut down like the grass, and wither like the green herb. Often, we envy people in the world who seem to have it so much easier than us. They just seem to get on with life, even if it includes stealing, cheating, telling lies, and doing things that are ungodly, and yet they seem to get away with it. If we look at some of the world leaders performing outrageous atrocities, no one seems to lay a hand on them. Nobody even seems to care.

I am reminded of the tragedies north of our border, in countries like Sudan, where there are millions of starving refugees who are being murdered every day and no one is doing anything about it. The perpetrators seem to be getting away with it. I see businessmen in the marketplace and governments that are openly and defiantly going against the principles of God and they seem to be prospering.

The Lord advises us to not even be concerned about those people and definitely not to aspire to be like them. In the future, they will no longer exist. In fact, Jesus goes one step further and says that we must pray for those who persecute us and do evil against us because, unless they repent, they have a bleak future awaiting them.

Render unto Caesar what is Caesar's. Therefore, pay your income tax. Pray for your government no matter what the circumstances, so that God can be free to work on your behalf. The tragedy strikes when we compromise our stand for God, whether financially or on a moral issue – even if it's in the short term – by saying, "Lord, I'll rectify this problem. I just want to get out of this deep pit I'm in." But unfortunately the devil doesn't play like that. When you get caught up in his web, he doesn't let you go.

There's a Scripture that says, "Be sure your sin will find you out." Unfortunately, that so called shortcut, that quick-fix solution, never works.

Do things the right way, which means do things God's way. For example, if you owe someone money, let them know if you don't have the money to pay them but say that you'll pay them as soon as you can. Never revert to falsifying your accounting books. Don't think you'll get away with the illicit affair you're having and that your wife or husband will never find you out. They will.

Today, take this advice. Don't envy the ways of the world. Don't envy people who seem to be successful because they are taking shortcuts, because the Lord says to us that they will be cut down like the grass, and they will wither as the green herb.

Seek first the kingdom of God and His righteousness and all the rest will be added unto you. Do things the right way and keep yourself pure until the day you get married. Keep an honest set of books and your business will prosper. Do things God's way and He will make you victorious and He will bless you. Most of all, you will sleep well at night!

The fear of the Lord

Job 28:28

Behold, the fear of the Lord, that is wisdom; and to depart from evil is understanding.

All over the world people are searching for truth and wisdom. Joe Niemand, one of South Africa's top rock artists, found the Lord Jesus Christ a few years ago and is now writing Christian music. The title track on one of his latest CDs is called "Jericho" and is all about seeking the truth and trying to find out what is right and what is wrong. In this song he sings about young people who don't seem to know the difference between right and wrong. They are striving to gain wisdom and direction on how to live and how to conduct themselves.

Once again, we see from our Scripture today that wisdom is found when a person fears God. Not fear in the sense of being afraid, but fear in the sense of reverence. It's actually dangerous not to fear anything. I am reminded of a little boy who was totally fearless and it worried me a lot. He would walk up to an unfamiliar dog and put his face up against the dog's face. Obviously, the dog would bite him. He would put his hand into a burning fire. I felt fearful for this young boy because he had no fear whatsoever.

I notice the same foolishness in the conduct of young people today. When they have no fear of God, it implies that they don't care about what is going to happen to them when they die. They think that they're going to live forever. I feel anxious for these young people.

Try to stay away from evil. I really want to encourage you today to be a black and white person. There can be no grey areas in the kingdom of God. It's either right or it's wrong. As soon as you start to compromise, you stand to lose perception and the Holy Spirit can no longer help you.

One thing that I've come to understand in the last thirty years of preaching, especially with young people, is that they want to hear the truth. They might not like it but they want to hear it. Then they can make their own decisions. When I was called to preach the gospel, the Lord challenged me with Ezekiel 3:17–19: "Son of man, I have made you a watchman for the house of Israel" (NKJV). We have an obligation to people, especially our young people, to tell them the truth in love, so that they can then make their own decision.

When we fear God and we check before making a decision whether it will offend God, we become wise people. People come from far and wide to seek our counsel. It's not because we are clever; it is that the fear of God makes us wise. If you want to be a wise man or woman, start to obey the Word of God and you will see that life becomes much easier for you.

We see God

1 John 1:1

That which was from the beginning, which we have heard, which we have seen with our eyes, which we have looked upon, and our hands have handled, of the Word of life…

Farmers have a tremendous privilege. When we open our eyes in the morning we can hear Jesus talking through the singing of the birds. When we walk outside and smell the fresh air, we smell the fragrance of Jesus. When we go to plough our fields and turn the soil over for a new season, there's a scent, an aroma, which comes straight from heaven. When we see a cow giving birth to a calf, and the calf stands on its own legs for the first time, we see the handiwork of our Saviour. When we reap our harvest and run our fingers through the grain as it pours from the elevator of the harvesting machine into the trailers, we can touch and feel the love of God and know that many hungry mouths will be fed because of Him.

My dear friend, there are none so blind as those who don't want to see, but I tell you that Jesus Christ is as alive today as He was when He walked on the earth. The signs are all around us. When the full moon comes up at night we can see the majesty of His creation. He is God and He loves you more than all of this because He died for you.

G. K. Chesterton (1874–1936), a famous English writer, poet, and champion of the Christian faith, wrote:

There was a man who dwelt in the East centuries ago
And now I cannot look at a sheep or a sparrow,
A lily or a cornfield, a raven or a sunset,
A vineyard or a mountain, without thinking of him.

As you go about your work today, open your spiritual eyes and see the glory of Jesus. So the next time you see a little toddler eating ice-cream with half of it running down their fingers and onto their clothes, and they give you a big, innocent smile, know that Jesus is alive and working in your soul!

Jesus cleanses us

1 John 1:9

If we confess our sins, he is faithful and just to forgive us our sins, and to cleanse us from all unrighteousness.

Apart from the well-known Scripture in John 3:16 which says, "For God so loved the world..." the first Scripture I learned as a new Christian was 1 John 1:9. It was indeed a Scripture that set me free. When you give your life to Jesus, the first thing that happens is that you fall in love with Him. Everything becomes so beautiful, clean, and pure. Then the Holy Spirit starts to convict you – and the devil starts to accuse you – of areas in your life that are not right. This is the time when you need to remember this Scripture.

I see this Scripture as a giant pair of bolt cutters; similar to a pair of pliers with long handles and sharp, sharp teeth. A good bolt cutter can cut a chain in half. This Scripture is cutting away all the accusations from the devil, because he is the accuser of the brethren, the father of all lies. All those things that happened in the past have been covered by the blood of Jesus. Those sins were forgiven when you gave your life to the Lord.

Today, you can have a wonderful day knowing that there is no more condemnation for those who are in Christ Jesus (Romans 8:1). You are a brand new being in Christ. So, even as the devil brings accusations against you and the Holy Spirit brings conviction into your heart, confess your sins, because Jesus is faithful. He is just. What does that mean? It means that because He died on the Cross of Calvary, He is qualified to forgive you for every single sin you have ever committed, and He's the only One who is qualified to do so.

Go therefore and sin no more. The Lord says, "Turn around, walk away from that sin and never return to it, because you are forgiven and you are free indeed." Do not allow the devil to rob you of your new life today because of his lies. Just confess to all that is unpleasing to God, deal with it, and push on. If the Lord sets you free, you shall indeed be free forever.

I heard a beautiful narrative the other day. While reading a book, an archbishop was visited by a young girl. She said she had a word for him from the Lord. He said, "OK", but paid her no more attention. She repeatedly came back to him and said, "I have a word for you from the Lord."

Eventually, to keep her quiet, he said, "Right, well, let me tell you what I'll do. I confessed a sin this morning; a sin that I committed yesterday. You go and ask the Lord to tell you what that sin was. Come and tell me once He has told you, and then I'll hear what you have to say."

The little girl went off and came back the next day.

He asked, "Well, did you pray to the Lord?"

She said, "Yes."

"And did you ask the Lord what sin I committed and confessed?"

"Yes," the little girl said.

"Well, what was it?"

She said, "God said He couldn't remember."

In conclusion, my dear friend, remember: when God forgives He forgets. That's one of the reasons I love Him so much.

Gratitude

Luke 24:52

And they worshipped him, and returned to Jerusalem with great joy…

Many years ago I was in a church in Midrand, Johannesburg. A big neon sign decorated the front wall of the church. It said in bright lights, "Missionary work: gratitude for Calvary." These words made me realize yet again the greatness of what Jesus Christ has done for you and me.

That's what the disciples realized when they stood and worshipped Jesus after He had been raised from the dead and before He went to be with His Father. As He led them out to the hill of Bethany, He lifted up His hands, blessed them and, while He was blessing them, He was parted from them and carried up into heaven. The disciples worshipped Him and returned to Jerusalem with great happiness and joy.

That is why we set out to many parts of the world and preach the gospel; why we undertake hardships and choose to live a life that sometimes includes pain and suffering. It's because of what the Master has sacrificed for us. My life has a purpose now and is fuller than it has ever been. I have the joy of the Lord, which is my strength. I have a future in heaven. I have a family that is serving God. The least I can do is to go out and preach the Word of God.

One of my heroes is Dr Albert Schweitzer (1875–1965). He started an amazing hospital in a place called Lambarene, in the heart of the African jungle. He made a decision to serve God. He said, "There came to me as I awoke the thought that I must not accept this happiness as a matter of course but must give something in return for it. You see, I had to do something for Christ."

Salvation is free. Here was a man who was so overwhelmed by the wonderful miracle of Jesus Christ who saved him from eternal damnation, that he was compelled to share this newfound joy and love with as many other people as he could.

I remember the famous quote from Jim Elliott, the young missionary who was martyred for his faith in the Amazon jungle by the Auca Indians. He said, "It is no fool who gives what he cannot keep in order to gain what he cannot lose." I believe that sums it up. Albert Schweitzer gave what he could not keep – his life – in order to gain what he could not lose – eternal life.

Today, be sure that you are not wasting your valuable time doing something that is of no benefit to man or beast.

What's impossible for man is possible for God

Luke 1:37

For with God nothing shall be impossible.

When you got up today, did you say to yourself, "Well, today I don't know what to do. I've tried everything and nothing seems to be going right in my life"?

George Müller, that mighty man that God used to move mountains, and who in his lifetime sheltered 121,000 orphans, operated purely by faith. When he was asked what the secret of his success and his victorious Christian life was, he said, "There was a day when I died to George Müller, his opinions, his preferences, tastes and will; died to the world, its approval or censure; died to the approval or blame even of my brethren and friends; and since then I have studied only to show myself approved unto God."

Therein, my dear friend, lies the secrets of doing work for God which is impossible for man but quite possible for Him. George Müller studied only to show himself approved unto God. If you have to consider everyone else's opinion and follow each whim and fancy of mankind, you will rarely achieve anything worthwhile for God. When I'm preaching I say to people that I'm not interested in their opinion and they shouldn't be interested in mine. All we are concerned about is God's opinion of the matter. Today die to self. Don't be concerned about others' opinions about you. Start living for Jesus Christ and you will see how faith can significantly change your life. God always honours faithfulness.

It doesn't matter what situation you are faced with today. There might be a mountain so big that you feel that you will never be able to get to the other side. Ask God's opinion on the matter: whether you should continue with your business, or whether you should close it down; whether you should emigrate, or whether you should stay; whether you should marry, or whether you should stay single. God will show you through His Word. Stand firm on that decision and He will honour it.

God bless you as you walk by faith today.

Blessed are the believers

Luke 1:45

And blessed is she that believed...

Here was a young girl, approximately fifteen years old, who was visited by the archangel Gabriel and told that she was going to carry God in her womb for nine months. What an incredible statement!

I am looking at a very precious painting of mine, painted by a dear friend, Elga Rabe. It is a painting portraying the nativity scene. It shows a young girl who has just given birth to a baby and is absolutely exhausted. I'm sure she is still bleeding from the birth. She is looking in absolute disbelief at the most beautiful baby, our Saviour, Jesus Christ lying in a manger (a feeding trough). Sitting on his haunches to one side is a very respectable-looking young businessman from Nazareth, a carpenter by trade, whose name is Joseph. He is also staring in absolute amazement at the baby in the manger who was born from the womb of his wife-to-be, whom he had never touched, or had any physical encounter with at all. This is a painting of the holy nativity that I will cherish for the rest of my life.

My dear friend, God honoured a young handmaiden of faith. She believed what the angel Gabriel told her. She was more blessed than any other woman who has ever lived on the face of this earth.

God always honours faithfulness. Today choose to believe the promises of God over your life and you will experience life in abundance.

The fickleness of man

Luke 18:39

And they which went before rebuked him, that he should hold his peace: but he cried so much the more, Thou Son of David, have mercy on me.

This is a beautiful story about Bartimaeus, the blind man who sat at the side of the road begging and crying. Maybe you and I are feeling like Bartimaeus today: as if we are sitting at the side of the road, at the end of our tether? We don't know which way to turn and we are crying out to God to have mercy on us. Maybe someone scolded you today, telling you to keep quiet. However, maybe you have determined in your heart this morning that, by faith, you are going to cry out to God until He answers you and comes through for you in your situation.

The Bible tells us that Jesus is the same yesterday, today and forever (Hebrews 13:8). Bartimaeus took no notice of the people around him. He was so desperate to get his sight back through the healing hand of God. The Bible states that he cried out, "Thou Son of David, have mercy on me!"

Jesus stood still, turned around and said, "Who is that? What is it that you want Me to do for you?" My dear friend, God expects us to call out to Him by faith today and to make our needs known to Him. Not our wants, but our needs. He knows everything as He is God, but He wants to hear from you.

Bartimaeus said, "Lord, please, that I might get my sight back." Jesus answered Bartimaeus, "Your faith has saved you," and immediately he got his sight back and followed Jesus, glorifying God. Everybody who saw this gave praise unto God.

The most important part of this story for me is that Bartimaeus refused to listen to other people. His was only focusing on God. Forget about the fickleness of men, as today they are with you, but tomorrow they're gone. Love them and understand them, but put your trust and faith in Jesus Christ and He will see you through.

Your faith

Mark 5:34

Daughter, thy faith hath made thee whole...

God recently revealed to me the importance of trusting Him to increase our faith and to believe His promises for us.

Some evangelists can be quite ruthless. Obviously, these are not men of God, because men of God are gentle and sensitive to people's needs. Apparently, at a recent prayer meeting, when, for example, a person in a wheelchair was prayed for and the person did not respond, he was rebuked, castigated, and told, "You don't have the faith." Words like these can absolutely devastate a person who goes to meetings like these, trusting God for a miracle. That is something I will never, ever understand or condone.

However, there is the other side of the coin, where Jesus repeatedly said, "Your faith has made you well." As we read yesterday, He said that to Bartimaeus. Bartimaeus was persistent, irrespective of what people said. He understood what it meant not to trust the fickleness of man. Jesus came walking down the road, and he began to cry out, "Son of David, have mercy on a sinner like me!" The crowd told him to keep quiet, yet Jesus stopped, turned and said, "Who is that calling My name?" The people's attitude changed immediately. They picked him up and said, "Come, the Lord is calling to you."

My dear friend, stand on the promise that God has given to you. Be careful of the fickleness of man. It doesn't matter what people say, it's what God says that counts in the end.

In today's Scripture, the woman with the blood problem said, "If I can just touch the hem of His garment, I'll be healed." She did and she was healed immediately. Jesus spun around and asked, "Who touched Me?" The disciples laughed and said, "Lord, there are people pressing in from all sides." "No," Jesus said, "virtue has gone out of My body." Very humbly and very embarrassed, the woman said, "It was me, Lord," and Jesus replied, "Go in peace. Your faith has made you whole" (verse 34).

A similar situation presented itself with the leper who came back to give thanks. Ten of them were healed but only one came back, praising God. Jesus said to him, "Go in peace. Your faith has made you well" (Luke 17:19).

Today, extend your faith. Allow the Lord Jesus Christ to work in your life. Don't allow any hindrance or any shred of disbelief to enter your thoughts or your vocabulary. Remember, faith comes by hearing and hearing by reading the Word of God. Spend lots of time reading Jesus' Word and your faith will be increased.

Jesus was amazed

Mark 6:6

And he marvelled because of their unbelief.

My dear friend, the Lord is challenging me once again to be heedful of my faith becoming familiar. The people in Nazareth knew Jesus. They said amongst themselves, "Is this not the carpenter, the son of Mary, the brother of James, and Joses, and of Judah, and of Simon? And are not his sisters here with us?" And they were offended at Him (Mark 6:3). That's when Jesus made the well-known statement that a prophet is not without honour, except in his own country, and among his own kin, and in his own house (verse 4).

I can honestly give testimony to that as I've experienced it myself. I've been overseas and to other parts of South Africa, where I'm not very well known in a personal capacity. We laid our hands upon the sick, prayed the prayer of faith and God healed them. When working closer to home, where people know who we are, we find that their levels of faith are not quite the same. Unfortunately, there are only a few healings and miracles that take place amongst our own local folk. Don't allow the devil to steal from you and deprive you of a blessing from Jesus because of a spirit of unbelief.

This can be the result of familiarity. The definition in the dictionary of familiarity is "undue intimacy". When there's no respect for God, you are cutting off the power of God to operate in your life. The same applies to being a servant of God. If you don't acknowledge yourself as being a servant of God, the anointing that He has becomes invalid in your own life, because you don't believe. Just allow the evidence that you see around you and in your own life to convict you that Jesus Christ is a miracle-working God; that He is able to heal, to deliver, and to set free.

The longer I walk with the Lord the more I find myself saying: "Lord, I can't believe what has happened." I'm supposed to be a man of faith and yet I find myself saying this all the time. During this past year especially, I have seen tangible evidence of the Lord working through mighty signs, wonders, and miracles. Yet I have to concentrate on the Word of God continually, because when I look around me there's still so much sadness, distress, sickness, fear, violence, and anger. It's only when I fix my eyes on Jesus, the Author and Finisher of my faith (Hebrews 12:2), that I am able to continue to trust the Lord for the miracles in my life.

I need to encourage you to be careful, first of all, of the company you keep; secondly, of the media you surround yourself with; and thirdly, of the conversations you have with others, because they could tarnish and taint your character and personality. Faith is contagious. If you want faith, be around men and women who are operating in the realm of faith. Read their books and be encouraged by their lifestyles.

I continually spend time reading the life stories of great men of God like George Müller, who started the children's home in Bristol; like Hudson Taylor, who brought Christianity to China; like William Carey, who took the Word of God to India; and David Livingstone, who brought the Word of God to Africa. These men, all of them without exception, were men of great faith. They walked where angels feared to tread. Why? Because they believed in the promises of God!

G. Campbell Morgan said, "Seeing is not believing; seeing is seeing. Believing is being confident without seeing." That's what we've got to start doing today. Let us not be like Thomas, who said, "I'll believe when I can see." God revealed Himself to Thomas and said, "Blessed are those who come after you, who have not seen and yet believe."

Giants for God

2 Corinthians 12:9

... my strength is made perfect in weakness.

The Lord has a habit of taking the weak, the insecure, those who can't make it alone and turning them into His giants. One such giant was Dwight Lyman Moody (1837–99). He weighed 275 pounds and sported an enormous beard. He was a farm boy who had an incredible, insatiable love for God. That man started off as a shoe salesman. They said that if he hadn't become an evangelist he would have become a multibillionaire. He was so full of energy, fire, and anointing from God. He said, "Real true faith is man's weakness leaning on God's strength."

That's exactly what he did. He made use of his talents for Jesus. The story goes that he spoke at the University of Cambridge, one of the bastions of all the knowledge, strength, and power of the British empire, which in those days ruled the world. As they said, the sun never set on the British empire.

Being a country boy and not very eloquent in English, he was rather nervous when he had to address approximately a thousand young aspiring students who were future leaders, not only of the British nation, but of the world. These men would come dressed in their suits and bowler hats and sit down in the hall, which had a wooden floor, with their umbrellas in front of them. If the speaker wasn't good enough, they would all start to bang the wooden floor with their umbrellas until the speaker left the podium.

The farm boy from America who was anointed by God – a very weak man in himself but extremely powerful in Jesus Christ – got onto the platform and started to preach. He preached from his heart and as a result, the "Cambridge Seven" (seven men from the university cricket team) went to the Third World and preached the gospel in China and all over the world.

C. T. Studd, the very famous evangelist who was the most sought-after bachelor in Britain in those days, was one of those who left with them. He was a gentleman of note. He played cricket in summer and rode horses in winter. He left everything behind; he gave away his fortune and went and preached the gospel, first in India, then China and ended up in the Congo, where he eventually died. The WEC (Worldwide Evangelization Crusade) ministry was started by this same man.

This all came about through a weak man who trusted God for his strength. The Lord used D. L. Moody to speak to 100 million people in his lifetime – with no television, no radio, or any advertising. During his campaigns in Britain, people used to follow him from city to city.

On one occasion he was preaching to the students. After he had finished, a high-ranking lady of English nobility came up to him and said, "Mr Moody, that was the most atrocious English I have ever heard in my entire life." The man of God, not to be outdone, turned around and said, "Well, Ma'am, I'm using what English I've got for Jesus. Tell me, what are you doing with your English?" At the end of the day that's the bottom line: real, true faith is man's weakness leaning on God's strength.

Don't sell yourself short today when you go out into the world. If God is with you, there's no one that will stand against you (Romans 8:31).

The faithfulness of God

1 Thessalonians 5:24

Faithful is he…

A.W. Tozer said, "Faith rests upon the character of God, not upon the demonstration of laboratory or logic." Faith is all about the character of Jesus Christ.

My dear friend, this book is dedicated to speaking about faith in God, not faith in faith. As Tozer has put it so beautifully, it's not about how many signs and wonders are performed, or how logical it is. It's about a person. His name is Jesus Christ and He is a miracle worker. I have experienced Him in my own life, in many different ways, but the most intimate way is through my personal relationship with Him. He is indeed, without any doubt, my best friend. Without Him I will not make it.

You can take away all the signs, the wonders, and all the miracles in the Bible, even all the great events that have taken place – for example, the Red Sea parting and allowing 2.5 million Israelites to walk through, and then closing and drowning that most powerful of armies that was chasing after them. Or feeding 2.5 million people for forty years in the desert, their clothes and their sandals staying intact, providing water to drink and protection against wild animals. Or seeing the Lord protect that nation through centuries when they should have been obliterated when 6 million Jews were annihilated in concentration camps in Germany alone. And yet, the children of God are still alive and well, and the State of Israel is still intact.

Those are just some of the miracles. As a farmer I see God working in miraculous ways through nature on the farm that we live on. But those are not the things that convince me of my faith. My faith is structured around the Faithful One, the person of Jesus Christ, the personality and character of my God. It is He alone who keeps my faith alive. If no further miracle, sign, or wonder ever took place, my faith would still be strong because of my personal friendship with the Man from Galilee.

Today, don't be foolish like those in the Bible who said to Jesus, "Show us one more miracle, then we will really believe that You are God." He got angry and said, "You'll see no more miracles from Me!"

Faith comes by spending a lot of time with the Faithful One, Jesus Christ. Take everything to Jesus in prayer: your business; your work situation; your school; your marriage; whatever issue you may be battling with at the moment. Sit down quietly with Him before you go to work today and tell Him what your problems are, then leave the problems with Him and move on. You will be amazed at what God can do.

Jesus is never "out of season". He never sleeps, He never gets tired, He never gets grumpy. He will never say, "Oh, it's you again!" He is always waiting to hear from you. He is the One who will sort out your problem, no matter what it is, because He is for you and not against you. That is why Job could say, "Though He slay me, yet will I still trust Him" (Job 13:15, NKJV). He knew very well that God would never slay him. Jesus would die for him.

It doesn't matter what people say to you about the Lord. It doesn't matter if they say, "Well, when we see it we'll believe it." What is important is to get to know the character and the person of Jesus Christ. Then all of these other things will be added unto you (Matthew 6:33). As you focus on the Son of God, your life will become a life of sunshine, even though you're walking in darkness.

Make a decision today just to believe God unconditionally and your life will change forever. St Augustine, who lived so many years ago, said, "If you do not believe, you will not understand." Don't be one of those doubting Thomases who say, "I'll believe it when I see it."

Believe what the Word of God says, as I do. I believe that the Word is "Jesus in print"; 1 John 5:7 convinces me of that: "there are three that bear witness in heaven: the Father, the Word and the Holy Spirit" (NKJV). May God bless you richly today as you go forth, trusting the character of Jesus Christ!

Profitability

Mark 8:36

For what shall it profit a man, if he shall gain the whole world, and lose his own soul?

I remember listening to a tape recording many, many years ago, of an old Scottish preacher talking about visiting a farmer who had a big stone mill driven by a water wheel on his farm. It was grinding corn day and night. He told the farmer that he needed to get his life in order; that he had to put Jesus first and come to church. The farmer kept saying to the preacher, "I'm too busy working right now."

Eventually he got very sick and was dying. He made them put his bed right next to the mill so that he could hear the grinding of the mill. The pastor came to see him and tried to tell him about eternal life and eternal damnation. He was telling him, "Please Sir, reconsider your future." The sick old man who was dying said, "I can't hear you. I can't hear you; the mill is grinding the corn. It's making too much noise." As he was dying, he was still trying to make money and yet, within hours, he was going to die and meet his Maker face to face. How does that benefit a man?

Before you go out to the workplace today, sit down and reconsider how you are spending your time and on what you are focusing your effort. Are you like that foolish miller who still couldn't understand that he was going to a lost eternity and the mill was staying behind? The Bible says that where a man's heart is, that's where his treasure is. If your heart is in making money and gathering material objects, those things become your treasures.

My dear friend, I can promise you that there's only one thing that will leave this world with you when you die, and that's your soul; nothing else. Everything else will remain. I really believe that we need to get our priorities in order this morning. We should put God first and our families second; then God will enable us to make even more money to sow into the kingdom and help the poor and the needy. When we die, we will be able to take souls with us to heaven.

Remember the story about the foolish farmer who had a bumper crop? He sat down and said to himself, "I'm going to build a big barn and fill it with this huge harvest. I'm going to settle down, eat, drink and be merry." And the Lord said to him, "You foolish man, do you not realize that this very night your soul shall be required of you?"

There's nothing wrong with making money, being prosperous and successful. That's what God wants us to be. But we need to understand the importance of having our priorities in order, so that the Lord can bless us and our families.

All things

Philippians 4:13

I can do all things through Christ which strengtheneth me.

This is the Scripture which the Fijian world champion seven-a-side rugby team have on their jerseys when they run onto the field. It leaves no question as to why they are such a major force on the rugby pitch.

Just a week ago I watched them play against South Africa. Although the South African Springboks are considered to be the best team in the world, at one point I thought we might lose this particular match. These God-fearing Fijian men with a passion for Christ rose to the occasion. When they're on the rugby field they play hard rugby. I really feel in my heart that when people stand up for the Lord and they raise the standard, God supports them in a very special way.

There's another man who was convicted by this Scripture. His name was Oliver Cromwell. He was an English revolutionary military leader and statesman. In the year 1623, after thinking, "The world needs a man, a good man, a great man, a strong man," he seemed to hear a voice saying, "Thou art that man."

Cromwell later became leader of the Puritan commonwealth government. He says, "I came to the thirteenth verse of the fourth chapter of Philippians, where Paul said, 'I can do all things through Christ which strengtheneth me.' The faith began to work in my heart, to find comfort and support, and I said to myself: 'He that was Paul's Christ, is also my Christ.' And so I drew water out of the wells of salvation."

My dear friends, as we start this day, let's think about these timeless Scriptures. They hold the same power today as they did when Oliver Cromwell ruled Britain. This power has placed the tiny little country of Fiji right near the top of international rugby fame.

This Scripture can do the same for you and me if we believe with our whole heart today that we can do all things through Christ, who strengthens us. Seek out what God's will is for you. Then put this beautiful Scripture into practice and see what God can do in your life.

He is our Supplier

Philippians 4:19

But my God shall supply all your need according to his riches in glory by Christ Jesus.

Who or what are you trusting today? Are you trusting your ability to create business? Or maybe your physical stature because you're a good sportsman? Is your trust seated in your intelligence because you obtained a degree? Or do you trust in Jesus Christ, because He has promised you that He will supply in all of your need?

My dear friend, there's one important factor that we must take into consideration when we claim this Scripture. He didn't say He will supply in all of our want. He said He will supply in all of our need. There is a very big difference between want and need and this is often what confuses us. A want can sometimes be greed. Today, think about what it is that you are asking of God, then trust Him with everything that you have and He will bring it to pass.

I am reminded of the beautiful Scripture found in Psalm 37:25, which says, "I have been young, and now am old; Yet I have never seen the righteous forsaken, Nor his descendents begging for bread" (NKJV). The Lord takes care of His own. I've seen it happen in my own life. I've experienced it during the years of absolute, unrelenting drought, when I still managed to reap a crop that sustained my family, my extended family, and all those who were relying on my farm to provide them with food.

He will not let you down. He's never let me down yet. I often ask in meetings, "Is there anybody here who can say that God has ever allowed them to go hungry?" No one ever puts a hand up. He said that He will supply all of your need, and He means it.

Trust in God

Psalm 20:7

Some trust in chariots, and some in horses: But we will remember the name of the Lord our God.

I'm often reminded of the violent times which we live in with people dying way too often. If it's not in Iraq and Iran, or Syria or Afghanistan, or in South America where drug runners and gangsters rule, it's terrorist attacks in Europe, and even in my own beloved South Africa life seems to be so cheap at present. Many people are living in a traumatized society. In today's Scripture, David says he will trust in the name of the Lord his God. He will put everything that is of value to him in God's hands.

Martin Luther said, "I have held many things in my hands and lost them all; but whatever I placed in God's hands, that I still possess." As we face the new day, let us put our effort, strength, and riches in things which man cannot steal, take or destroy. Let us put our effort into spending time with God and our fellow man. Let us spend our time sowing that which has eternal value, and not focusing on temporary materialistic things.

As you drive that brand new motor vehicle out of the showroom and around the block, it has already lost value. Yes, I realize the need for transport, but it must not become something that you measure yourself against. Ask yourself, do you really need a house the size of the one that you are building?

We need to take stock today. Even as the great reformer Martin Luther said, everything he tried or had in his hands, he lost. The only thing that remained was what he had placed in God's hands. I can honestly say that I have experienced that as well.

At the end of the day, for me, the only things that last and are worthwhile in this life are things of eternal value, such as our salvation (Number 1); such as our relationships with our loved ones (Number 2); such as helping others find Christ (Number 3); and like sowing into the life of a homeless child, a defenceless mother, or an old widow (Number 4).

Store up riches for yourself in heaven that rust and moth cannot destroy and you will find that your life will suddenly become worth living.

When men say all manner of evil

Luke 6:23

Rejoice ye in that day, and leap for joy…

Jesus says, "Jump for joy when people say evil things about you for My name's sake." It doesn't mean that we should jump for joy when people say evil things about us that are justified. It means when people say evil things about us because we stand up for righteousness and for the truth.

Like never before in our world, God is looking for men and women of stature; those who will call sin by its name; those who will not be afraid to say what is right and what is wrong. That could cost them dearly, as it did the saints of old. I was recently reading about John Huss (1369–1415). He was a rector at the University of Prague and preached against the immorality of the church. He also preached against indulgences; a practice whereby people would pay the priest to try and escape the consequences of their sins and honestly believed that they were forgiven. He was summoned by the emperor to appear before the Council, who demanded that he recant all the things that he had been preaching, but he refused.

He was subsequently burnt at the stake. He said, "God is my witness that the great purpose of my preaching and writing was to convert men from sin. In the truth of that gospel, which I hitherto have written, taught and preached, I now joyfully die." A man who was prepared to die for what he believed in… .

It is hard to find a person of that calibre today. Let's pray that you and I are of that calibre, so that when somebody stands up at work and says something profane about our Lord and Saviour, we will have the courage to say, "Excuse me, that's my Saviour you're talking about." Or, "That's my Lord's name that you are taking in vain."

When you are told that all roads lead to heaven, you must be brave enough to say, "According to the Word of God in John 14:6, Jesus says that He alone is the Way, the Truth, and the Life, and no one goes to the Father but by Him." That takes immense courage. More than ever, young people around the world are showing the need to hear the unadulterated truth. It's the truth that will set them free (John 17:17).

Pray today, before you go out, that God will give you the courage to stand up for your faith when people challenge you about Christianity.

Diligence plus obedience

Zechariah 6:15(b)

And this will come to pass, if ye will diligently obey the voice of the Lord your God.

If we are going to expect the Lord Jesus Christ to honour our prayers and our vision, we have to become diligent in our faith. According to the Collins dictionary, to be diligent means to be careful and to persevere when carrying out tasks and duties. God wants us to be diligent and careful in carrying out our tasks and duties. God requires us to be diligent in what He has called us to do: to obey His voice and to do exactly what He says, without bending the rules.

You cannot serve two masters. Jesus says in Matthew 12:30, "He who is not with Me is against Me, and he who does not gather with Me scatters abroad." If we can uphold these conditions the Lord is free to work in our lives and to bring to fruition the vision and the plan that He has for each one of us. Whether it be a business venture, a sporting goal, or a command from God, you have to pursue the plan God has for you diligently.

Be obedient and don't bend the rules. There are no shortcuts to heaven. Pay your dues and be honourable in your actions towards your workers. When playing sport, do it honourably by being a good sportsman. Do everything in obedience to the Word of God, and God will do the rest.

Personal relationship

Ephesians 2:13

But now in Christ Jesus ye who sometimes were far off are made nigh by the blood of Christ.

Before I met Jesus I was looking at myself from the outside in. I used to envy the churchgoers, yet I didn't realize that the church was there for me, a sinner, as well. I used to have a strong desire to be in the presence of God. It was only when I became a born again Christian and acknowledged what Jesus Christ had done for me that I realized that I was able to enter the Holy of Holies because His blood was spilt for my sins. What a day that was! Never again do I want to go back to standing on the outside.

Intimacy with the Lord is the most important thing to me. The only way that I can be sure that it remains intact is through my relationship with Him. The onus to uphold our relationship does not rest upon me, but on Him. That's what's so beautiful. It's like the special grip used in a fireman's lift. The fireman takes hold of your forearm and you take hold of his forearm. He holds you with a strong grip and pulls you out of the fire. If you release your grip, if you can't hold on any more, he is still holding on to you because of his firm grip on your arm. The only thing that can separate me from God is the sin that I allow into my life. He will never stop loving me.

My prayer for each one of us as we go out into the world today, is that we won't allow our relationship, our closeness, our nearness, to be damaged in any way because of sin in our lives. My dear friend, Father God is such a holy God that He could not even look upon His own beloved Son hanging on the Cross because of the sin of the world that Jesus had taken upon Himself.

Today as you walk, walk in righteousness and holiness. Walk by faith in the Son of God, who loves you and gave His life for you. In that way the intimacy can only grow. When He's walking close to you and you to Him, you have nothing to fear.

More than we can imagine

Ephesians 3:20

Now unto him that is able to do exceedingly abundantly above all that we ask or think, according to the power that worketh in us…

This morning as I got up I thought of all the awesome things that God has done in my life. To be quite honest with you, it really blows me away. I'm not walking by sight alone any more, but by pure faith. If I were to walk by sight I would get into a state of fear and panic. I know that I could never accomplish the things that God has prepared for me this coming year if I had to rely on my own strength.

Over thirty years ago a man came to visit our family. Piet Uys was a mighty man of God. He came to our home and sat in our lounge; an absolute stranger. We put him up for the night. He brought his guitar with him and started to sing. Then he prophesied. He said, "If God were to show you now the things that He's going to use you for in the future, you'd never be able to contain them."

How true that has turned out to be! All the glory goes to Jesus Christ. That was over thirty years ago. When we look ahead to next year, we know that it's only through the Lord that we will be able to do what He wants us to do. It's the power of the Holy Spirit, of Jesus Christ, who works in us, that's going to make it possible.

My dear friend, the same applies to you. Lift up your eyes this morning. Start to walk by faith and not by sight (2 Corinthians 5:7). Lift the bar much higher. The capacity that is within you is so great that it can change the world forever. The Lord is saying to you this day, "Allow My power to work through you and you will accomplish that which you think is impossible."

Whether it be sickness in your body that needs healing, or a situation at work that you think no one can rectify – God can do it! He's more than able to. That's what He promises you today in this Scripture. Do I hear you say that the damage to your marriage is irrevocable? I can tell you that nothing is too hard for God. Do you want to accomplish something specific at school or university? Jesus Christ says that it is more than possible for those who believe.

Today, before you go out, pray and ask God to fill you with His power, His glory and His faith. Then go out and do it. Give Him the honour that He deserves.

Remember William Carey, the cobbler from England, who said, "Attempt great things for God and expect great things from God." He was the country boy who thought God was going to use him as a great evangelist. He hardly led anyone to Christ, but the Lord used him in an area where he had absolutely no concept of what God was going to do. He translated the Bible from English into Sanskrit, Hindustani, and Burmese. He became the chief interpreter at the high courts in Delhi for the British government. He was a man who started a huge printing press and distributed the gospel all across India. He changed India for Jesus. He was one man who knew that God could do exceedingly abundantly above all that we ask or think!

Even in darkness He remains with us

Genesis 39:21

But the Lord was with Joseph…

Today you might be going through a fiery trial and you might be saying, "Lord, I can't go on any more." The good news is that you can. After Joseph had been betrayed by his brothers and sold as a slave, he was thrown into jail. He then found favour with Potiphar, one of Pharaoh's captains. Potiphar's wife took a liking to Joseph and tried to have an affair with him. Joseph did not agree to this and she was offended. She told her husband that Joseph had tried to take advantage of her and therefore Joseph was thrown into jail. The Bible says that the Lord was with Joseph.

Madame Guyon was a godly woman in France; a mighty woman of God, a woman of holiness. She was also falsely accused and put in the Bastille, where she spent many years. She said, "I have learned to love the darkness of sorrow, for it is there that I see the brightness of God's face."

It doesn't matter what you're going through at this moment, but be sure that God is going through it with you. He will not leave you nor forsake you. He has promised you that (Hebrews 13:5). It's through the hardships in life that God teaches us many lessons. If I look back upon my life, it was during the times of my deepest pain and suffering that Jesus was closest to me.

Today, have courage, my friend. Even though it may seem as if everything is against you, God will never forsake you. He will walk with you and get you to the other side. You'll be able to rejoice and share with others the goodness and faithfulness of God.

Using what you've got

Exodus 4:2

... What is that in thine hand?

On 17 November 1989, when I had a clear call from our Lord to go out into the world to book town halls, city halls, stadiums, and tents – as well as sports fields – and preach the gospel to the lost, I said, "Lord, I don't have anything to go with." I was complaining, just like Moses.

I knew a little red-haired boy with a freckled face by the name of Thomas. Thomas had lost his daddy in a terrible accident at work before his tenth birthday. He used to come and sit on my lap at the services and I used to hug him and try to give him what his daddy couldn't any more.

One evening he came up to me during an evening church service. He was clasping a fistful of coins, exactly two rand and ninety-two cents. (I actually framed the money.) I asked, "Tom, what is this for, Son?" He said, "Uncle Angus, this is for the campaign."

God told me that He would provide for all of my needs according to His riches in glory. Since then I've had the privilege of speaking to kings and prime ministers, speaking in great stadiums all over the world, in huge tents and enormous city halls and town halls. It all began with the Lord sending a little boy to me to give me his pocket money for the campaign.

Moses was arguing with God, saying, "Lord, how are Pharaoh and the people of Egypt going to believe that You've sent me to tell them to let Your people go? I cannot speak eloquently. I am slow of speech and slow of tongue." He kept making excuses.

The Lord asked, "What is that in your hand?" He said, "Lord, it's a rod." The Lord said, "Cast it on the ground," and it turned into a snake. The Lord said, "Put forth your hand and take it by its tail." He caught it by its tail and it turned back into a rod. With that, he went and confronted the mightiest man on earth – a man the Egyptians perceived to be God Himself – and told him to let the people of Israel go. Eventually the people of Egypt were freed.

This morning God wants to say to you, "What do you have in your hand?" Use it! Stop finding excuses or complaining about how you've been short changed in life. Use what you have for Jesus and He will add to it and make it abundant.

The opposite of fear

2 Timothy 1:7(a)

For God has not given us the spirit of fear… (NKJV)

My country, South Africa, is one of the most beautiful countries in the world. Unfortunately, there is a tremendous spirit of fear amongst all races, all cultural groups, and all age groups. The only weapon that we can use against fear is faith. Not faith in faith, but faith in Jesus Christ.

The apostles themselves said, "Lord, increase our faith" (Luke 17:5). That is the only way that we can go into combat and fight against depressing times. It is faith that moves the hand of God. The Lord Jesus was so deeply touched by the Roman centurion when he said, "Lord, You don't even have to come to my house. Just say the word and my servant will be healed." Jesus said that He had never seen such faith in all of Israel.

Mary, the mother of Jesus, the most blessed woman who has ever walked the face of the earth, was a woman of faith. When she believed what the angel Gabriel had told her, God began to work in her life.

Don't listen to the lies of man. Don't even listen to the opinion of man, because man is very fickle. Today, if you're a hero, everybody wants to be your friend. Tomorrow, if you've failed, you're a villain and nobody has time for you. I've learned that the hard way many times before. It is God who honours faith.

I remember years ago when people were talking about the weather phenomenon El Niño. The newspapers were writing headline articles about it. The Zulu radio stations were telling the people not to plant maize because there was going to be no rain. I was at a campaign at King's Park Rugby Stadium and I said, "Forget about El Niño! I'm going back and I'm trusting God. I'm going to plant." I didn't share man's opinion. I listened to what God was saying to me. By raw faith I did it. I planted potatoes. The result was a bumper crop. We gave all the glory and honour to Jesus Christ.

The opposite of fear is faith. Today, if you are gripped by fear because your business is not doing well, because someone is sick in your family, because the future looks grim to you, turn your eyes to Jesus Christ. Remember that old song, "Turn your eyes upon Jesus. Look full in His wonderful face, and the things of earth will grow strangely dim… " That's exactly what we need to do today.

Turn your back on fear. Start to walk by faith and the Lord will change your whole mindset. There will be a paradigm shift in your spirit and you will start walking with your shoulders straight and your head lifted high, like a man who has been saved and redeemed and who has a future that is not determined by worldly circumstances.

God bless you today as you walk by faith and not by fear.

Vision

Proverbs 29:18

Where there is no vision, the people perish…

I have just returned from a conference in Pretoria. I was privileged to meet René Changuion, a man with tremendous vision. He himself admitted that he had been a motorcycle hooligan. In 1980 in Krugersdorp, South Africa, God gave him and nine others a vision to win his biking buddies over for Christ.

The seemingly wasted years of being a motorcycle hooligan were in fact the preparation for the ministry to motorcyclists. The primary function of CMA (Christian Motorcyclists Association) is to win motorcyclists for Christ. Jesus said, "Follow Me and I will make you fishers of men." The CMA has a passion for the Lord. They reach into areas that the average person could never reach. They wear their leathers and their boots and ride on their huge motorcycles with their brightly coloured helmets. On the back of their jackets they have the Cross of Jesus Christ. They are winning many souls for the Lord.

What is your vision today? You might say, "I'm just a farmer. What can I do?" Oh, my dear friend, you can speak to fellow farmers. You might say, "All I am is a clerk in a bank." Your vision can be for your fellow clerks to be saved. If you feel that your vision is growing cold, ignite it again this morning. Today, ask the Lord Jesus Christ to put a new fire in your heart and in your soul.

If you don't have a vision you won't finish the race…. Indeed, the Lord says that you'll perish. The New King James Bible says, "Where there is no revelation, the people cast off restraint." It is a lack of vision that keeps you from being a disciplined person. What gets me out of bed in the morning is my vision. What keeps me fit, physically and mentally, is the vision that God has given me to see the lost saved in my beloved South Africa and, indeed, the world. If that vision should perish, I would surely die.

Here at home, at Shalom Ministries, we say, "If your vision doesn't scare you, it's not big enough. You must attempt something that is so big that, if it's not from God, it's doomed to fail." Why is that? Because when it succeeds no one will say that it was you who did that. They will say, "Surely that was God, because that mere mortal could never have accomplished something like that!" Before you go out to face the day today, get on your knees beside your bed, or wherever you are reading this book, and ask God for forgiveness if your vision has died. Ask Him to rekindle and light up the vision which He gave you many years ago.

If you're a person who doesn't have a vision, if you're just going along with the crowd, break away. Let God give you a specific vision and run with it. It might seem small to you, but God will expand on your vision as He sees your faithfulness.

The undiluted Word of God

Proverbs 30:5

Every word of God is pure…

One tremendous advantage that we as believers have over the unbelievers, is that we have the truth at our disposal; 1 John 5:7 says that "there are three that bear witness in heaven: the Father, the Word and the Holy Spirit" (NKJV). The Word is Jesus Christ in print and it can be depended upon.

There's a stern warning from the Lord that is written in the book of Revelation. Through John, the Lord said that if one word was to be added to this Book, or one word taken away, "every plague in this Book will come upon you" (Revelation 22:18–19). It worries me sometimes when I hear young men say that they have had a new revelation from God. That might be OK; it might be a kind of revelation, but there is nothing new under the sun. In Proverbs 30:6, the writer says, "Add thou not unto his words, lest he reprove thee, and thou be found a liar." Don't add anything to the Word of God; don't take anything away from the Word.

The biggest threat to the Christian world today is not posed by Islam, Hinduism, or the New Age movement. Our faith is threatened by compromise. It is compromised when people start to modify the Word of God and begin to condone things that Jesus Christ never condoned, such as abortion, homosexuality, and divorce. God forgives us when we sin – that's why I can write this book. I am a sinner saved by grace (undeserved loving kindness). However, I may not preach something that is not in this Book. I may not say something that God didn't say, because if I do He will reprove me, and He is the only One I fear. I don't fear man. I fear God. I don't want to end up being a liar.

When we try to interpret things in the Bible without considering them in context or add things to it, the Bible loses its power. It's important to keep God's Word pure. It can then be depended upon. If you live according to the Word of God, He will bless you and guide you and show you the way forward.

Apply the Word literally to your life today: apply it to your business, your family, and your health and see how God will bring about change. God bless you as you go out today with the pure Word of God in your heart.

Trust God

Proverbs 3:5

Trust in the Lord with all thine heart; and lean not unto thine own understanding…

There is no more time left for us to make a plan. Farmers are great at making plans – the problem is that their plans hardly ever work. As of today, do not rely only on your own understanding; don't do things just because your forefathers did them or because they sound like a good idea, but start to rely on God's understanding and trust the Lord. Proverbs 3:6 says that if you acknowledge Him in all your ways, He will direct your paths. That is the truth.

If you acknowledge Jesus Christ as your Lord and Saviour wherever you go today, He will direct your path. If you are not ashamed of the gospel, Jesus Christ will go alongside you on the road. If you are one of those fair weather Christians who runs this way and that way, trusting God only when it suits you, don't expect support from your Saviour.

Today, promise to rededicate your farm or your business, your family, and your life to Jesus and just have faith. Start to trust the Word of God. Do what the Lord tells you to do and your life will never be the same again. Yes, you'll go through fiery trials. Show me one saint in the Bible who didn't. God will see to it that you come out on the other side, gloriously victorious.

Acknowledge Him in every facet of your life. Even now as I'm writing this book, early in the morning, it's quiet outside my prayer room. Our whole staff has gone up to the chapel to pray and to give God all the glory and the honour. Every Friday all the farm workers have one hour off to pray, and my son-in-law, who's running the farm at the moment, is leading them in prayer and thanksgiving.

People always say we're lucky because things go well on the farm. It's got nothing to do with luck. It has everything to do with acknowledging Jesus Christ.

A soft answer

Proverbs 15:1

A soft answer turneth away wrath: but grievous words *stir* up anger.

I've always been a man with a short fuse, especially before I came to know the Lord Jesus Christ as my Saviour. In fact, in Zululand, where we are farming in South Africa, the Zulu people have a tradition. They give a white man a different name. Generally, these names are very descriptive and are given to a person because of a certain characteristic. My name is "The Italian". The Italians were responsible for building the hydroelectric scheme in KwaZulu-Natal many years ago.

I want to put it on record that I am very fond of Italians. They are an affectionate nation, very impulsive, excitable, and as I have experienced, very warm and kind-hearted people. However, they tend to be short-tempered as well. When I arrived here I couldn't speak a word of Zulu, so I would use my hands and, obviously, the tone of my voice to try and get my point across. So they gave me the name "The Italian".

I trust and believe that since I've met Jesus Christ my temper has been curbed. I still get excited, but now for the right reasons! I realize that we often speak before we think and this causes misunderstandings and unhappiness.

Today, when you go about your business, be considerate. Think before you speak, especially to your loved ones. Start to speak in a soft, gentle manner and God will do the rest. God will avert a potential argument by merely a soft answer. It could even save your life if you answered the way Jesus would.

Maybe you need to think about that bracelet that many people wear on their arms that reads WWJD (What would Jesus do?). Before you answer a somewhat uncalled for accusation, think how Jesus would have answered it and then do so in a similar way. You'll find that people will be put to shame, especially those who make false accusations against you. They will be embarrassed by the way they speak to you and will probably come to apologize.

Go out today as God's ambassador and be reminded that whatever you say or do is going to affect the name of our Lord because people know who you are. Go in faith and call those things that aren't as if they were.

Tell people about the King. Tell people in a soft and gentle manner that Jesus loves them, because when we speak Jesus' language to people, they will respond with love and gentleness.

Before you go out today, speak to God about people before you speak to people about God, and it will make a tremendous difference in your life.

Divine healing

Zechariah 4:6

... but by my Spirit, saith the Lord of hosts.

While I was spending time with the Lord early this morning, He showed me again in this beautiful chapter in Zechariah the importance of praying for the sick in the correct manner. To pray for healing is part of the tools of the trade of the evangelist. Whenever I have a meeting I always, without fail, make a point of praying for the sick, because it's part of the work which the Lord Jesus Christ has given the evangelist to do. You'll see that Paul prayed for the sick, Peter and John prayed for the sick, and so did Philip.

Maybe you know of a person who is sick today. You are wondering if only the evangelists can pray for the sick. Of course not! Any believer has the authority and the power given to them by the Holy Spirit to pray for the sick. An interesting point though: Zechariah asked the Lord what the two olive trees that were planted on either side of the candlestick symbolized (Zechariah 4:12). He said that those were the anointed ones that stood by the Lord. Out of those branches came two golden pipes that drained the golden oil from the trees.

In James 5:14, the Lord says, "Is any sick among you? let him call for the elders of the church, and let them pray over him, anointing him with oil in the name of the Lord." The oil is the symbol of the Holy Spirit.

It is so important to do things the right way. However, it's not always possible to do that, because there might be a situation where you want to pray for someone but you don't have any oil.

Or, as sometimes happens when I'm praying in a stadium for the sick, there are so many people that I cannot get to each one of them, so we have to pray the prayer of FAITH. Not just pray, but pray the prayer of faith. That's where the difference lies.

Mark 6:12 says that the disciples went out two by two and preached the gospel that people should repent. The Bible says, "...and they anointed with oil many that were sick, and healed them" (verse 13).

We thank the Lord again today that it's not by might, nor by power, but by His Spirit that sick people are healed and miracles are performed. But it's done in a specific sequence. God says that we have to pray that prayer of faith. It's not the prayer of, "Que sera, sera" (whatever will be, will be). It's a case of, "Lord, please show me what I must pray for this person."

If the Lord says to you that He's going to take that person home, then don't pray for them to be healed. But if you feel in your spirit that the Lord is saying, "I want to raise this man up, but I'm looking for a man, a woman, of faith who can pray that prayer," then pray it. Take the bottle of oil with you. Remember that there's no power in the oil. The power is in the prayer of faith. The oil, however, is the symbol of the Holy Spirit.

Anoint the sick with oil. Why? Because Jesus said so, and God will raise them up.

Staggered not

Romans 4:20

He staggered not at the promise of God through unbelief; but was strong in faith, giving glory to God…

One of the men I admire greatly is a man of God by the name of George Müller, who was Prussian born.

With fifty cents in his pocket and much faith in God, he started a children's home in Bristol, England, where he gave shelter to more than 121,000 orphans in his lifetime. He lived until he was ninety-three years old. He went around the world preaching the gospel. He travelled 200,000 miles preaching in many countries, speaking in several different languages and addressing as many as 4,500–5,000 people at a time.

At the time of his death he was leading a congregation of 2,000 people. He was an incredible man who never faltered in his faith. He said, "The only way to acquire strong faith is to endure great trials. I have acquired my faith by standing firm amid severe trials."

My dear friend, if you are struggling today and wondering why God has forsaken you, why He has left you, or why you're going through such fiery trials, be encouraged. God is strengthening your faith for you to partake in a bigger plan He has for you!

Don't despise small things

Zechariah 4:10

For who hath despised the day of small things?

You might be feeling very small in the eyes of your peers this morning but take heart, my dear friend. If Jesus Christ is your Lord and Saviour you have nothing to fear.

As I'm writing this book the Rugby World Cup for 2007 is drawing to a close. This weekend the semi-finals will be played. If anything, people will remember this World Cup for the fact that the small minnows, as the small teams are known, knocked out the favourites, the big names, that came to the World Cup.

Fiji is a country that loves the Lord Jesus Christ with a passion. I believe the whole country is smaller than the Kruger National Park in South Africa. Yet they gave the South African team a run for their money. At one stage we thought they were going to beat us. Tonga, another small country with less than half a million inhabitants, played an outstanding match and even beat some of the teams that were earmarked as favourites to win the World Cup. In fact, apart from South Africa, there's not one other favourite left in the semi-finals. The Lord says, "Don't despise the day of small things."

You might have just started a new business and today you are feeling de-motivated and tired. Put your trust in the Lord. Keep your eyes fixed on Jesus. Don't listen to the negative comments of other people. God will raise you up. Every one of us has to start somewhere. Do you think that when Billy Graham preached his first sermon to six prisoners – one picking his teeth; another sleeping; another looking out of the window – that he thought he was destined to arguably become the greatest evangelist of his time? Of course not!

When Henry Ford designed his first motorcar, the Model T Ford, do you think he had any idea of what the motor industry was going to mean to mankind? It changed the destiny of the world. Just to give you an example: Did you know that the ostrich industry worldwide was affected by that motorcar designed by Henry Ford? Ladies stopped putting ostrich feathers in their hats after the motorcar came onto the scene because they couldn't fit those huge hats and plumes into the motorcar. The ostrich industry crashed because one man built a motorcar that everybody initially laughed at.

A small boy minding his father's sheep on the hill had no idea that he was destined to become the greatest king that Israel has ever had apart from Jesus Christ, the Son of God. Don't despise small things!

I love the Lord so much because He has a habit of choosing the "small things" to confuse the "big things" in this world. The reason He does that is because He doesn't want to share His glory with any man. He knows that when He uses you in that small capacity, when He takes the two fish and five barley loaves, multiplies them, and feeds a multitude, no man will take the glory for that. The glory can only belong to God.

Go out today and don't despise small beginnings. We all have to start somewhere. God will take everything that you give Him and multiply it, because He's in the multiplying business.

An ambassador for Jesus Christ

2 Chronicles 16:9(a)

… the eyes of the Lord run to and fro throughout the whole earth…

This morning the Lord is calling you, my dear friend. He is looking for the ones with loyal hearts and a willingness to be used by Him. Are you one of those who are saying today, "Lord, I wish You could use me." The Lord says, "I'm calling you."

From the age of sixteen I had a desire to serve God. The devil, and also the flesh and sin, deprived me of that until I was thirty-two years old. I wasted all that time. The only regret I have on this earth is that it took me so long to come through for the Lord 100 per cent.

Time passes at a tremendous rate. Don't waste time. You might say that you have no ability. God has the ability. You might say that you are not a speaker. Well, that's what Moses said as well. You might say that you have a limited education. The disciples had no education. It's the power of the Holy Spirit operating in you by faith that will raise you up to become an ambassador for Jesus Christ. You can start today. Start in your workplace, in your school, on the sports field, in your house. Don't say that you can't. You can.

God says that His eyes are roaming the whole earth. That's exactly how God uses me. I was reading a book on all the mighty men and women of God who have gone before us, and saw that just about ninety per cent of them had no special talents or abilities, but they had hearts that wanted to be used by God. God took what they had and used it.

He wants to be strong for you because He needs you as His ambassador. You say, "I'm a sinner." Every man has sinned. There's no man in this world who has not sinned. Romans 3:23 says, "for all have sinned and fall short of the glory of God" (NKJV). God says, "Repent." Stop doing it. Turn away from it. Walk away and God will use you.

Have a wonderful day today, mighty man or woman of God!

God with us

Isaiah 7:14

… and shall call his name Immanuel.

When you woke up this morning, were you feeling lonely? Were you feeling as if you were at the end of your tether? Were you feeling that you've been rejected by loved ones? Maybe you don't have a job, maybe your business isn't doing too well? I have good news for you this morning: God is dwelling with you and me.

The name Immanuel literally means "God with us". Jesus has promised you and me that He will never leave nor forsake us (Hebrews 13:5). Therefore you have nothing to fear today. If God is with you, all things will come right, but you need to acknowledge Him and give Him a place in your life, in your decision-making and in every other aspect of your life – be it good or bad.

Remember: don't go somewhere today if you know that Jesus would be embarrassed to go there. Wherever you go, ask yourself the question: Would the Lord feel at ease in this place? If the answer is no, then don't go there. If the answer is yes, do enter and be a part of what's happening in that place.

Remember your manners today, because God is with you. Remember to restrain your lips and watch your temper. You are being watched, not only by man, but by all the angels in heaven, because God is with you today. Wherever He goes, the angels follow.

Be a good ambassador today and don't be lonely. Speak to Him as you are driving in your car. He is listening to you.

You can pray in your very heart without even opening your mouth; in your office, on the farm, on the sports field, and in the classroom. He is indeed a Friend who will stick with you, even closer than a brother.

Have a blessed day and know that our God of heaven is with you every step of the way.

He performs all things for me

Psalm 57:2

I will cry unto God most high; unto God that performeth all things for me.

I've just received a message from a very, very dear brother of mine who sent me this Scripture. It is so appropriate because this coming Sunday, which is in three days' time, I'm going to be speaking at a healing meeting. The meeting is designed specifically for people to bring the sick, the lame, the blind, and the deaf so God can heal them. I'll be preaching a message and after that I'll be laying my hands upon the sick, anointing them with oil and praying for miracles in their lives. This Scripture is so encouraging because I am crying unto God and saying, "Lord, once again, perform all things for me."

If you're in a situation similar to mine, whereby you know that in your own carnal strength you cannot complete the task that is set before you, you can cry unto God today and ask Him to undertake the task for you. He will, my dear friend, I know. I know that Sunday is going to be an overwhelming day and that people will never forget it as long as they live, because Jesus is going to be there. He is going to be there and He is going to use my mouth, my lips and my hands. We are going to see miracles similar to those written about in the book of Acts. I would encourage you today, as you are waiting for your opportunity to preach the gospel, to get ready and be prepared.

Sometimes walking on water is truly the safest place to be because the boat is sinking anyway. The Lord has a habit of coming through for us every single time when we have no one and nothing else to turn to but Him. For me and my wife, faith has now become a lifestyle. Remember, it is the substance of things hoped for, the evidence of things not yet seen (Hebrews 11:1); that's what faith is.

Walking God's way

Jeremiah 10:2

Learn not the way of the heathen, and be not dismayed at the signs of heaven; for the heathen are dismayed at them.

It's extremely strange to me how the people of this world turn their backs on God. They don't want to know about the church or Christianity for many different reasons. Some of their reasons, unfortunately, are legitimate. However, when there's a problem they seem to turn to the Christian.

I've experienced this many times in my own life. They will not go to a person who is a compromiser; a person who hunts with the hounds and runs with the hares or a person who sits in a pub and listens to filthy stories. When it comes to the crunch, the unbeliever will never go to someone like that.

They'll seek out the godly person, the person who's transparent in his stance for God. If there's a terrible drought, these people will not go to compromisers and ask them to pray to God for rain. They'll come to the so called "over-the-top chaps" and ask us to ask God to send rain to the dry, dusty land. That's what they call us but we are just normal Christians!

When someone is having a marital problem they'll come and ask the believer. When there are incomprehensible things going on in the world, they'll come and ask the believer what it means, because God speaks to His own. I'm talking about earthquakes, tidal waves, epidemics of disease and destruction. They know – even though they might not, for whatever reason, want to become Christians at that time – what is right. Every person knows in their heart what is right and what is wrong.

Today when you go out, be aware of the fact that even though some people might not like you, it's very important that they respect you and what you stand for. Be prepared for them to come and see you, to speak to you, to ask for direction and information on what it means to be born again. We're coming to the climax of the ages and people are starting to realize that things are coming to a head. Now, like never before, it is harvest time. I'm not just talking about harvesting God's crop in stadiums, halls, and big tents. I'm talking about a one-on-one harvest, at the workbench and in the marketplace.

The heathen, the unbeliever, is asking serious questions about what is happening. You need to know and be able to tell him exactly what God is showing you. What is God showing you? He's showing you that life is but a vapour and that eternal life is yet to come. He's showing you that this life is only a twinkling of an eye; it's just the preparation time for eternal life. You need to tell them, in love, what it means to go to hell, to be separated from God forever. They need to know what it means to go to heaven, to be at peace.

Of course, if that's not happening in your own life, you cannot tell somebody else. I have a diary in which I write everything God speaks to me about. It's just an ordinary, agricultural diary. At the bottom of the page for today there's a saying, an African proverb: "A woman who is not successful in her own marriage has no advice to give younger generations". That's basically the bottom line. If we don't have that peace, that assurance, in our own lives, how can we give it to the world?

Spend a lot of time with God today and be prepared; have a sermon in your top pocket. When people ask you questions give them the answers. The answers are in the Bible. The answer is in your heart through the power of the Holy Spirit.

Women

John 19:25

Now there stood by the cross of Jesus his mother, and his mother's sister, Mary the wife of Cleophas, and Mary Magdalene.

William Booth, the famous evangelist who started the Salvation Army, was very much a man's man. He ran that army like any other kind of army. According to the figures, it was the biggest army in the world and, in fact, I think it still is. He would often be quoted as saying that his best soldiers were women.

I really want to thank God for the womenfolk today. My mother was such a remarkable lady. She was sick all her life; physically a very weak person but spiritually and mentally extremely strong, very loving and considerate. Indeed she was the heart of our home, as is my wife Jill.

There is a very true saying: "Behind every great man there is a woman". When Jesus was crucified on the Cross, all the disciples, barring John, fled and left Him hanging on the Cross. But not the women! In the early hours of the morning, after the body of Christ was buried in the tomb, the first person there was a woman. Her name was Mary Magdalene.

The woman is the heart of the home. The man might be the head of the home but the woman is the heart. I am travelling extensively at the moment and am visiting many different places, from palaces to little cottages. It's the woman who determines the ambience of the home. If you go into a home and the woman there is totally at peace, in love with Jesus Christ, there's a warmth and a fragrance in that home which cannot be denied. On the other hand, if you go into a home where the woman is not a believer and is very materialistic and worldly, you'll find that it doesn't matter if it's an absolute palace with the newest furniture and possessions, it is cold, and something is amiss.

I would like to encourage womenfolk this morning to continue to fulfil their role as the heart of the home, as the prayer warrior for their husbands, as the mothers for their children. I don't know how many mighty men of God I have read about, starting with John Wesley, will tell you that it was their mothers who made the difference in their lives. John Wesley's mother had numerous children; I think around nineteen. In the middle of the day she'd stop whatever she was doing, pull her apron over her head, and sit there. That was her time for prayer. All the children knew: "Don't trouble Mother. She's talking to Jesus."

We thank God for the Marys who were at the foot of the Cross when the Master needed it most.

One genuine miracle equals a thousand sermons

Romans 15:19

Through mighty signs and wonders, by the power of the Spirit of God…

Here we see Paul, the greatest preacher of all times (in my opinion), apart from the Master Himself, saying that it was through signs and wonders and by the power of the Holy Spirit that he preached the gospel to the Gentiles.

I can really give testimony to that. I remember trying to preach the gospel to the heathen in far off places, in the darkest corners of Africa, where the gospel had yet to be spoken in its entirety. I sometimes preached for an hour with no effect, only to be told in my heart by the Holy Spirit to "stop preaching, the people are not listening to you". I then started praying for the sick and saw how God began to work as people who had not walked in years without the assistance of crutches threw their crutches away and ran up and down the platform, healed!

It can be intimidating going into drought-stricken areas where farmers are absolutely desperate for rain and preaching the full gospel without any apologies. It is so humbling, however, when not being concerned about people's personal preferences, ideas or interpretations, but only about preaching the gospel in its fullness by the power of the Holy Spirit to see the rain pelting down after the meetings. Then there can be no argument about who the Son of God is.

When we preach the gospel in its simplicity, undiluted with no frills, then God arrives and mighty signs and wonders follow the preaching of His Word and many, many souls come to Christ. Let us be bold today as we tell people unashamedly that Jesus is the way. If the Holy Spirit lays it upon your heart to pray for somebody who is sick, pray for them.

Today, be sensitive. Don't embarrass people but pray for them nevertheless. God will honour those prayers. He did it for Paul and He'll do it for you and me.

Dying to live

Galatians 2:20

I am crucified with Christ: nevertheless I live; yet not I, but Christ liveth in me…

We are expecting to host a men's conference on my sons' farm. We are anticipating men in excess of 20,000 to camp on the farm and 10,000 will be commuting every day; a crowd consisting of about 30,000 men in all. We will be preparing 90,000 meals for the three days and we have hired the biggest tent in the whole world. It is the size of three rugby fields, side by side. It is going to be a mind-blowing occasion. The Lord has laid on my heart that the theme of this conference is going to be "Dying to Live". (In the end, 60,000 men came to the conference!)

"Unless a grain of wheat falls to the ground and dies, it remains alone" (NKJV) is what John 12:24 tells us. "But if it dies it will bear much fruit." As a farmer, I know that. The men outside are preparing the machines to plant the new crops because the spring rains have just arrived. The seed, if left on top of the ground, will not germinate and nothing will grow. It will still be alive but nothing will happen. When you put the seed under the ground and it starts to die, that's when the new life starts and the new plant is born. It multiplies itself 300–400 times.

So it is with you and me. Jesus wants us to die to self so that we can live for others. It's by dying that we live. That's why the Bible says it's more blessed to give than to receive. Today, as you go about your daily tasks, don't think so much about what you are going to accumulate for yourself. Rather think about how much you're going to give to others.

One of the richest men in the world was Robert Le Tourneau (1888–1969). He sold his business to the giant earth-moving people, the Caterpillar Company. He used to tithe ninety per cent of his income and keep ten per cent. He was a multi, multibillionaire. He used to say, "When you put your hand in your pocket don't ask, 'How much of my money am I going to give to God today?' but rather ask yourself, 'How much of God's money am I going to keep to myself today?' "

When your priorities are in order, then it is easy to live a life of prosperity in the truest sense of the word. It's when we refuse to die to self and become selfish that we start to struggle.

There's a beautiful little poem from Mrs Cowman's book, *Streams in the Desert*, which reads:

Measure your life by loss and not by gain,
Not by the
wine drunk but by the wine poured forth.
For love's
strength is found in love's sacrifice,
And he who suffers most has most to give.

I've yet to meet a man who has something to offer, who has not been through some kind of hardship, ordeal or testing. It seems that hardship, more than anything else, causes a person to mature. You can go to university, study, spend hours reading the Bible, but unless you walk the talk, you have little to offer. That's why I love sitting next to old farmers and old fishermen, men who have been around the block. They have stories to tell and they are so rich, so full of goodness, that they remind me of a plate of wholesome, homemade soup. That kind of goodness is only brought about after you have encountered your share of life's hardships. It's through dying that we live. It's through giving that we receive.

Today, go in peace and know that as you start to die, Christ will start to live in you. You will have the most fulfilled life that anybody can wish for!

Harvest time

Zechariah 8:22

... many people and strong nations shall come to seek the Lord of hosts.

Like never before, we are experiencing people seeking the truth and seeking peace. Jesus is the Prince of Peace. Jesus is the truth. I look back over the past thirty years or so that I've been preaching the gospel and I can honestly say that people are a lot more receptive to God's Word – the whole truth – and they want it undiluted.

I remember about ten years ago trying to organize a men's breakfast, inviting men to come and hear the Word of God. We did some extensive advertising and invited one of the top sportsmen of South Africa to act as speaker. A total of fourteen men arrived for the breakfast, four of which were from our own team. This was so disheartening since we were expecting a large crowd!

Earlier this year we erected a tent and catered for 5,000 men with much fear and trepidation. No fewer than 7,400 men arrived from all over the country. The Lord says that many people and strong nations shall come and seek the Lord of hosts. I want to remind you that people want to know what life is all about. All you have to do today, my dear friend, is to keep telling them what Jesus means to you. That is evangelism in a nutshell.

We have been invited to go and preach the gospel in Perth, Western Australia, at another men's conference. They informed me that they are expecting between 3,000 and 5,000 men. This kind of meeting was unheard of before.

This weekend I am leaving for the town of Potchefstroom, in the west of our country, to lead a meeting at the stadium there. I have been warned that if more than 22,000 people should arrive at the stadium, the gates will be closed due to a fire risk. Well, we are trusting the Lord that the fire of the Holy Spirit will descend upon us!

I really believe with all my heart that we are now approaching the last days. The Lord Jesus Christ is casting the net and gathering the lost in their multitudes. He doesn't want to see one person lost. Open your heart today. Open your spiritual eyes and ears today and you will find someone who needs to hear where to find the truth and where to find the peace.

Increase our faith

Luke 17:5

And the apostles said unto the Lord, Increase our faith.

We are currently living in a time in the history of this world during which people are feeling the need to grasp onto faith. I have never been exposed to such a large number of people who are suffering from depression, stress, anxiety, and fear, simply because they are not putting their trust in the right place.

There are so many people trying to disprove the Bible in these last days. As an example, take a look at the book and film *The Da Vinci Code*, which is riddled with contradictory suggestions – such as that the bones of Jesus have been found together with the casket he was buried in. Such absolute nonsense, wasting valuable time and effort when there is a God!

You don't have to be a farmer or a naturalist to open your eyes and look out of the window to see the evidence of God all around you. The beautiful sunrise, the birds flying across the sky going to a far off land, the new growth. We've just had our first spring rains and as I was jogging yesterday it was such a miracle to see the grass starting to push through. No big bang theory or Darwin's theory can ever explain anything like that. God is life. My dear friend, don't waste your precious time today trying to work out whether there is a God or not. Just believe it. Even the disciples said to the Lord, "Please Lord, help our unbelief."

The great American evangelist D. L. Moody said, "Real, true faith is man's weakness leaning on God's strength." Today you might be feeling weak in yourself. You might be feeling vulnerable because things are not going well with you. But God never changes. He is the same yesterday, today, and forever. By faith, get dressed today and step out into the world. Live to the full. Concentrate on the character of God, because that's how your faith will grow.

My hope is built on nothing less
Than Jesus' blood and righteousness;
I dare not trust the sweetest frame,
But wholly lean on Jesus' name.
On Christ the solid Rock I stand;
All other ground is sinking sand.

Edward Mote

What a beautiful hymn! Today, go out and enjoy life. Walk in the promises of God and do not rely on your own intellect or the theories of others, because it is a waste of time as we are serving a living God.

Judge not

Matthew 7:1

Judge not, that ye be not judged.

In this day and age with so much hardship, pain, and temptation, we need to be very careful not to be judgmental of others. In today's reading Jesus goes on to say, "Why are you concerned about the splinter in your brother's eye when you have a beam in your own eye? Take the beam out of your own eye first, and then you'll see more clearly to take the splinter out of your brother's eye."

My dear friend, this book is dedicated to speaking about faith in God, but we cannot walk in faith if we cannot see clearly. Henry Wadsworth Longfellow, who lived from 1807 to 1882, said, "I will leave the erring soul of my fellow man to Him." What we need to do for our fellow men and women is to pray for them and to believe by faith for miracles to happen in their lives.

Longfellow said,

> The little I have seen of the world… teaches me to look upon the errors of others in sorrow, not in anger. When I take the history of one poor heart that has sinned and suffered, and think of the struggles and the temptations it has passed through – the brief pulsations of joy – the feverish inquietude of hope and fear… the pressure of want, the desertion of friends… I… would fain leave the erring soul of my fellow-man with Him from whose hands it came.

As we see our fellow man suffering so much in these last days, confronted with all kinds of obstacles, let us pray for those who have fallen from grace, that God, who created them, will also save them.

Expectation

Psalm 62:5

My soul, wait thou only upon God; for my expectation is from him.

What is your expectation of God? It is like asking how long a piece of string is. How big is God? He is so big that our finite minds cannot even conceive or dream how big He is. He loves you and me and has our best interests at heart, always.

As I am writing this book right now, I'm waiting for a sign from God to continue to do one of the most exciting things that I've ever attempted in my life. I can't even reveal it to you at the moment, because I don't know if it's going to materialize. My favourite saying is, "Lord, I don't believe that You can do this." And I'm supposed to be a man of faith! Yet He just blesses me so incredibly.

I want to encourage you this morning to lift the bar of your expectations, because God wants to bless you. He wants to use you. You say, "But Angus, I'm a man of few words" or, "I'm a woman with little education"; "I'm a sinner who's made big mistakes." I want to tell you that if you repent this morning and by faith you write down your expectations on a piece of paper, God will give you the desires of your heart. You see, if you spend time with God, then you will ask according to the will of God and He always answers.

Don't let your expectation be of man, or about man. Let it be of God and about God. He'll open doors that you might have thought were impossible to open. He will make a way for you in a place where there seemed to be no way. He will restore that which the canker worm and the rust and moth have tried to destroy, because He is God. The Bible says, "Greater love hath no man than this, that a man lay down his life for his friends" (John 15:13), and Jesus Christ loves you so much that He was prepared to die for you.

Bring that expectation, that dream that you have, before the throne of God and allow Him to open and close doors.

It's OK sometimes to throw out a fleece before the Lord. That means, when you need a sign from God you can ask the Lord, just like Gideon did (Judges 6:37). He said, "Lord, I'm going to put out a fleece. Tomorrow morning, if the ground is dry, I want the fleece to be wet with dew." He put out the fleece and that's exactly what happened.

But he still didn't trust God, so he asked again, "This time I want You to please do the reverse; the fleece must be dry and the ground must be wet with dew." The Lord did that as well to prove to Gideon that He had heard his plea.

So it's OK sometimes, not always, to put a fleece before the Lord and say,

"Lord, I'm going to continue by faith to do this and I thank You that You'll give me a sign whether this is of You or not." Then go ahead and do it.

Remember, and we've said it many times before, that if Christ is for you, there's no one who can stand against you (Romans 8:31).

Three hundred men

Judges 7:7

And the Lord said unto Gideon, By the three hundred men that lapped I will save you.

Can you imagine getting troops together to fight a mammoth battle? There are thousands and thousands of the enemy standingbefore you.

There were 32,000 Israeli troops. The Lord said to Gideon, "You have too many soldiers. Bring them down to the water and reduce their numbers by submitting them to a simple task. Tell the men to drink water: put those who drink with their tongue, as a dog does, on one side." The number that drank by putting their hands to their mouths was about 300. The rest of the men bowed down on their knees and drank the water. The Lord said, "Take the 300 that drank the water from their hands."

You might feel today that you are faced by too many enemies, that the task at hand is too great and the mountain too high. God specializes in using the poor, the weak, the young, and the unqualified to fight His battles, simply because He does not want to share His glory with any man. If Gideon had won the battle with 32,000 soldiers, he could have said that he and his men had won. Because it was a mere 300 men against thousands of the enemy, everyone knew that only God could have achieved such a victory.

In your situation today you might feel that the odds are completely against you. You might be quite right, but my prayer for you is that you will have eyes to see the multitudes of angels that the Lord has put around you to protect you and to help you.

Remember the prophet Elisha and his servant Gehazi? Gehazi came out of their little hut, only to see that the enemy had them completely surrounded. He ran back in absolute fear and panic and said to the man of God, "We're hopelessly outnumbered!" Elisha said to his servant Gehazi, "Fear not: for they that be with us are more than they that be with them." The man of God asked the Lord to open his servant's eyes so that he could see the army of God, which outnumbered the enemy by far. When he saw it, his heart was at peace.

My prayer for you today is that God would open your spiritual eyes to see that they (meaning God's angels) are with us, outnumbering our enemies in this world.

The remnant

Zechariah 8:12(b)

… and I will cause the remnant of this people to possess all these things.

God has given His people a beautiful promise. He says that He will prosper all the seed of the remnant. The remnant are those people who are still standing; the people who are left after the others have deserted the Lord, denied the Lord, or followed other gods – the faithful ones. He says, "The vine shall give her fruit, the ground shall give her increase and the heavens shall give their dew" (the rain). God is reminding me again today that He is for His people. He is not against us. The Lord is not one who wants to punish His children.

Yes indeed, we are living in perilous times. It almost feels as if there's no more law and order; as if pestilence, disease, droughts, inflation, and economic chaos are ruling the day. Yet, in spite of all these things, God has promised us that His people, His remnant, will prosper. Know one thing today, that if God is for you there is no one that will stand against you. He says, "and they shall be my people, and I will be their God, in truth and in righteousness" (verse 8).

My dear friend, if we make sure that our own personal lives are in order with God, all we have to do today is to go out in faith and plant the seed, fertilize it well, and God will add the increase. I've been farming now for more than forty years and God has never let me down.

I've found that at the times when I've walked away from God, things have gone wrong because I've walked out from under His umbrella of protection. I remember once seeing an advertisement of one for the big insurance companies on television. They had a big yellow umbrella, providing safety and cover for those who remained under its shelter. When they moved out from under the protection of the umbrella, they got battered. I really believe that it's the same with the Lord. If we are walking in righteousness and obedience, He cannot help but bless His people, because that's what He's promised us.

Matthew 6:33 says, "Seek first the kingdom of God." Today, take time out to make sure there's nothing in your life, nothing in your business, that would bring dishonour to God or that is ungodly. If there is, root it out, just like you'd pull out a weed in your maize field, and deal with it so that God can bless your crop.

One thing that I have learned in my life is that God is a holy God. He cannot bless disobedience or sin. Deal with the problem, settle it, and by faith (the substance of things hoped for) go ahead with your business and you'll see the difference.

Gone fishing

John 21:3

Simon Peter saith unto them, I go a fishing.

Have you ever felt despondent about your life? Have you ever felt that maybe God has let you down, that the Lord is not on your side; that He's forsaken you? Maybe you're feeling that way today? Maybe things haven't turned out the way you expected them to?

That is exactly how Simon Peter felt. He had really and honestly thought the Lord Jesus Christ, his Saviour, his friend, was going to clean out the oppressive armies of Rome, set the Jews free, and be what He had promised to be – the Redeemer. Up until then, He hadn't redeemed anything. In fact, He had died on the Cross. Peter turned back to the only thing he knew, fishing, because he was a fisherman by trade.

Maybe you're reading this book today and doing exactly that? Maybe there was a time when you were on fire for Christ but because of dishonesty in the ministry, or an awkward situation, or because you have been disappointed by a member of your family, you've gone back to fishing. The good news today is that Peter's story doesn't end there. The Bible says that Jesus came. He arrived on the shores of Lake Galilee at Peter's Landing (that's what the place is known as today). I've been to Lake Galilee. I stood on the shore just where Jesus would have stood when He shouted out, "Boys, have you caught anything?" They had caught nothing.

Maybe at the moment your business is doing absolutely nothing since you decided to turn your back on God? Jesus said, "Cast the net on the right side of the ship, and ye shall find" (verse 6). It was only then that John recognized that it was the Lord. It might have been a misty morning because the fishermen didn't recognize Jesus. The Bible says that Peter heard His voice and threw on his fisherman's cloak. He cast himself into the sea and started swimming towards the Lord.

The amazing thing is that the Lord had already made a fire and had prepared a meal of fish and bread for them. Isn't He a wonderful God? He takes care of even our smallest needs. Then, of course, He challenged them. He spoke to Peter three times, "Feed my sheep." "Feed my lambs." "Feed my sheep." In other words, go back and do what you were doing when I was amongst you.

God would say to you today: "Don't turn your back on Me. I have done no harm to you." Finish the work that you were called to do, because time is limited.

Mind your own business

John 21:22

Jesus saith unto him, If I will that he tarry till I come, what is that to thee? follow thou me.

Peter was concerned because he knew that the disciples were going to die martyrs' deaths. He knew that John always stayed close to the Lord and he said, "Lord, what about John? Where does he fit in? What's going to happen to him? What does he have to do?" The Lord rebuked Peter and said, "Why does it concern you? You must only be concerned about following Me."

I think that's so important today. So many of us are not taking care of our own lives because we are too busy trying to be the Lord's policemen. We criticize people because they seem to preach about money all the time, we criticize others because they're getting divorced and remarried, we criticize other people of God because of their chosen lifestyles. The Lord says to us today, "Mind your own business. Don't worry about these people. I will deal with them in due course." My dear friend, God is a holy God. He will not tolerate sin in any degree.

I have heard of various ministries that have actually lost their way because they were envious, jealous, and preoccupied with another man's life, business, farm, or family. The Lord says, "Don't be concerned about others." You say, "But Angus, these people are blaspheming, they're not going to church, they're not serving God, yet God seems to be blessing them. Their farms and their businesses are thriving."

Well, what does the Lord say? He says, "Don't worry about that man. I will deal with him in due course." Remember the story of the rich farmer who said, "I'm going to build another barn because I have such a huge harvest. I'm going to store it all in there and then I'm going to sit down, eat, drink, and be merry." But the Lord said to him, "You foolish man, do you not realize that your life will be required of you this very night?"

It's not for you and me to judge. Even as the Lord said to Peter, "Don't be concerned about John. I will deal with John in My own way. You just follow after Me," the Lord would say to you today, "Don't be concerned about others."

It's only by the grace of God that you are saved, my dear friend. You are a sinner. The Bible says in Romans 3:23, "for all have sinned and fall short of the glory of God" (NKJV). Just be concerned about your own salvation and pray for that person who has taken advantage of the poor and needy.

The highest service

2 Timothy 4:2

Preach the word…

In these last days it is absolutely vital that we speak the Word of God straight from the heart. Young people, it seems, are in need of finding the truth. Jesus says the truth shall set you free.

I've been reading Roberts Liardon's book, *God's Generals*, a book about God's mighty men. He writes about the life of John Wycliffe, who translated the Bible from Latin into the common man's language of English in the fourteenth century. John Wycliffe said:

> The highest service to which man may attain on earth is to preach the law of God. This duty falls particularly to priests, in order that they may produce children of God. And for this cause Jesus Christ left other works, and occupied Himself mostly in preaching, and thus did the apostles, and on this account God loved them. We believe there is a better way; to avoid such that please and, instead, to trust God and to tell surely His law and especially His Gospel. And, since these words are God's words, they should be taken as believed, and God's words will give men new life more than other words that are for pleasure.

This man lived in 1330. Nothing has changed to this day. People compromise God's Word, water down God's Word, paraphrase God's Word and give it a different meaning. Even John Wycliffe knew nearly 700 years ago that when God's undiluted Word is preached, man gets new life.

You might say, "But Angus, I'm not a preacher, I'm a farmer, a businessman or business woman, a sportsman or sportswoman." Remember what Francis of Assisi said: "Preach the gospel at all costs and, only if you really have to, use words." Preaching is a lifestyle. It is not what you say but who you are. You should be an epistle. Wherever we walk, people should see Jesus in us. However, having said that, it is so very important to actually speak the Word of God with your mouth. It is, as Wycliffe said, "the power of the divine seed which overpowers strong men in arms, softens hard hearts and renews and changes people into divine men".

Of course we need to remind ourselves at all times that unless it is preached in the power of the Holy Spirit, it becomes another history lesson and is worthless. It's when the Holy Spirit is in a person that the power of God comes upon people and changes them forever as he opens his mouth wide and preaches God's Word.

I would really encourage you to keep to the Word of God in your life, because at the end of the day that's the only thing that people remember and it's the only thing that changes lives. It's the only thing that counts.

God bless you today as you go out as a living epistle. You can change anything you like but never, ever try to change the Word of God. Speak it as it is written and the results will be seen in people's lives forever. You might say that you have had no formal training and you're not a preacher. My dear friend, neither have I. But if you've been to the school of life, if you've been to the Cross of Calvary, if you know that Jesus has died for you, that He's been raised again, that He's in heaven and that He's waiting for you, that you are forgiven and that He's coming again, you're qualified! Just preach the Word.

Contentment

Hebrews 13:5

… and be content with such things as ye have.

Contentment is, I think, the one virtue that everyone is looking for in these last days. Peace of mind, to be at rest and to be at peace. Andrew Murray, a great South African pastor, teacher, and writer of many books, was a man God used to bring the greatest revival to South Africa that it has seen to date. (But we believe the biggest is yet to come; in fact it will be here very soon!) He spoke about "the deep sea of calmness". He said:

> Humility is perfect quietness of heart. It is to have no trouble. It is never to be fretted, or irritated, or sore, or disappointed. It is to expect nothing, to wonder at nothing that is done to me. It is to be at rest when nobody praises me and when I am blamed or despised. It is to have a blessed home in the Lord, where I can go and shut the door and kneel to my Father in secret and am at peace as in the deep sea of calmness, when all around and above is trouble.

It is that contentment which we are after. We've just been blessed with our fourth grandchild, my five-month-old grandson. Sometimes his mum, my youngest daughter Jilly, asks us to take care of him while she heads off to the shop. He's such a good, peaceful, contented little baby because he comes from a secure home. When his mother gets back, he recognizes her voice and a huge smile lights up his little face when he sees her. She picks him up and they cuddle. I see absolute contentment. I really believe that's what the Lord Jesus Christ is wanting from you and me. It must distress our heavenly Father, our Parent, so much when He sees His children fretting and running around, trying to find peace and a reason for living.

Today, spend time with God before you go to work, and then let the contentment of Jesus be with you. If you read on, you'll see that at the end of that verse He says, "For I will never leave you, I will never forsake you."

All of you

Matthew 12:30

He that is not with me is against me…

William Booth, that great man of God who formed the Salvation Army, was asked by Wilbur Chapman the secret to his success. He replied:

> I'll tell you the secret of my success. God has all there is of me. There have been men with greater brains than I, men with greater opportunities. But from the day that I got the poor of London in my heart and caught a vision of what Jesus Christ could do with them, I made up my mind that God should have all of William Booth there was. If anything has been achieved, it is because God has had all the adoration of my heart, all the power of my will and all the influence of my life.

So, my dear friend, if you want to be effective for Jesus Christ today, He requires all of you. The Scripture verse for today says that if you're not for Him you're against Him; if you do not gather with Him you actually scatter abroad.

This mighty man of God's secret was that he made a conscious decision to give Jesus everything he had. One year he wrote the word "Others" and sent it out as his Christmas greeting to all the Salvation Army workers around the world. He helped all who needed him, regardless of colour, creed, station, or condition of life. William Booth was for Jesus Christ and for Him alone, and as a result he formed and started the biggest army the world has ever seen to date – the army of God.

Today, try not to serve two masters. Serve only Jesus, and you will find that things will improve more than you could ever have hoped for.

Jesus is watching over us

Acts 7:56

Behold I see the heavens opened, and the Son of man standing on the right hand of God.

This is the account of St Stephen. Just when they were about to stone him to death, he looked up and saw Jesus standing at the right hand of God, watching over him.

I've just read a story about a mighty man of God, John Paton, a Scottish missionary. He left home in 1858 and found himself among cannibals on the New Hebrides, his life being in grave danger. He says, "They encircled us in a deadly ring and one kept urging another to strike the first blow. My heart rose up to the Lord Jesus; I saw Him watching everything from above. My peace came back to me like a wave from God. I realized that my life was immortal till my Master's work with me was done."

You might feel today that you are all alone, that you're up against a giant. John Paton said,

> Without the abiding consciousness of the presence and power of my Lord and Saviour, nothing in the world would have preserved me from losing my reason and perishing miserably. But His Words, "Lo I'm with you always, even unto the end," became to me so real that it would not have startled me to behold Him, as Stephen did, gazing down upon the scene. It is the sober truth that I had my nearest and most intimate glimpses of the presence of my Lord in those dread moments when musket [rifle], club and spear were being levelled at my life.

Often in our direst moments the Lord is closest to us and more real than at any other time. Such was the case with this man of God as well. So today, as you go about your chores, remember that you're not alone. There is One who is watching over you, who promised you in Hebrews 13:5, "I will never leave you nor forsake you" (NKJV).

1 December

Trust in God

Philippians 4:19

But my God shall supply all your need according to his riches in glory by Christ Jesus.

Are you putting your trust in your own ability? Are you putting your trust in material riches, or are you putting your trust in God? James Hudson Taylor was a missionary of amazing faith. He said:

> I used to ask God to help me. Then I asked if I may help Him. I ended up by asking Him to do His work through me. I will give you the motto of my life – Mark 11:22, "Have faith in God." You can reckon on God's faithfulness. My life has been so unpredictable. Sometimes I could trust and sometimes I could not, but in the instances when I could not trust, I reckoned that God would be faithful.
>
> The sweetest part, if one may speak of one part being sweeter than another, is the rest which full identification with Christ brings. I am no longer anxious about anything as I realize the Lord is able to carry out His will and His will is my will. It does not matter where He places me, or how – I leave that up to Him. If He places me in an easy situation He will give me His grace and for the most difficult situations, His grace is sufficient.

James Hudson Taylor was a man who went out to China as a young adult. He lived with the Chinese – he refused to live in the compound with all the other missionaries. He wore traditional Chinese clothes and wore a pigtail for which he was severely criticized. He set up a little dispensary and started to minister to the Chinese.

He initiated the China Inland Mission. The biggest revival in the world is taking place in mainland China today. You see, Hudson Taylor looked to the Lord to supply all his needs. He sowed good seed – the Word of God.

After the Boxer Rebellion, when all the Westerners were chased out of China and many were massacred, he was in dire straits. He was sick and recovering in Switzerland at the time. This was also the time when his friend George Müller wrote to him and said, "Rest in the faithfulness of the Faithful One."

Even if your faith is not as strong as it should be today, don't be afraid. Remember the Lord has promised you that He will be faithful to you and that He will provide all that you should need according to His riches in glory.

Finding your peace

1 Timothy 6:6

But godliness with contentment is great gain.

Hannah Whitall Smith was a well-known Christian author who was used by God in a powerful way. She wrote the classic book *The Christian's Secret of a Happy Life*. As she was growing older she wrote a little article in which she said:

> I'm nearly seventy-one years old. I always thought I would love to grow old and I find that it is even more delightful than I thought. It is so delicious to be done with things and to feel no need any longer to concern myself much about earthly affairs. I seem to be on the verge of a most delightful journey to a place of unknown joys and pleasures, and things here seem of so little importance compared to things there, that they have lost most of their interest for me.
>
> I cannot describe the sort of "done with the world" feeling that I have. It is not that I feel as if I were going to die at all, but simply that the world seems to mean nothing but a passageway to the real life beyond; and passageways are very unimportant places. It is of very little account what sort of things they contain, or how they are furnished. One just hurries through them to get to the place beyond.
>
> My wants seem to be gradually narrowing down. My personal wants, I mean, and I often think I could be quite content in the poorhouse! I don't know whether this is piety, or old age, or a little of each mixed together, but honestly the world and our life in it does seem of too little account to be worth making the least fuss over when one has such a magnificent prospect close at hand ahead of one; and I'm tremendously content to let one activity after another go, and to wait quietly and happily for the opening of the door at the end of the passageway that will let me in to my real abiding place. So you may think of me as happy and contented, surrounded with unnumbered blessings and delighted to be seventy-one years old.

This is from an old lady who accomplished most things in life, who'd been used by God but was quite content, at the end of her life, just to be waiting for the Lord to open the door at the end of the passage so that she could go home. My dear friend, don't hold on to your earthly possessions too tightly because the best part is yet to come.

The "whosoevers"

Romans 10:13

For whosoever shall call upon the name of the Lord shall be saved.

My dear friend, as you wait on God today, remember that He is such a gracious and loving God, He says, "whosoever… shall be saved." Whosoever means whosoever!

Maybe you're feeling very guilty today? Maybe yesterday was a bad day and you may have done things that you're not proud of? Maybe you said things that you wish you hadn't. Those ill-considered words become like the feathers of a torn feather pillow: once the feathers get caught in the wind you can never catch them and put them all back. You have to plead for the blood of Jesus and ask Him for His forgiveness.

The "whosoevers" are people like you and me – sinners saved by the grace of God. God says, "Go and sin no more, your sins are forgiven." It's not something we can just continue to do in a blasé manner.

Jesus is the Saviour of sinners, of the "whosoevers". It doesn't matter what you've done in the past, repent of your sins today. Start again and don't look back. "No man, having put his hand to the plough, and looking back, is fit for the kingdom of God" (Luke 9:62).

Jesus is calling you. If you call upon the name of the Lord you shall be saved. So, start again this morning. Don't carry your sins into the new day. Leave that 50-kg bag of cement behind at the foot of the Cross and start again.

Have a glorious day. Remember, if Christ is for you there is absolutely no one who can ever stand against you.

The more we read the Bible, the more we get faith

Romans 10:17

So then faith cometh by hearing, and hearing by the word of God.

People often ask me to pray for them so that they can have more faith. My response is, "I won't pray to God to give you more faith. I'll pray to God to give you such a hunger for His Word that you'll start to read it every day. As you read it, so your faith will grow."

Dwight Lyman Moody was one of the all-time great evangelists. At the age of twenty-three he started a Sunday school with 15,000 individuals. He knew every boy and girl by name. He visited them in their homes and knew most of their personal situations.

He made several great evangelistic tours of the British Isles and America. During his lifetime he is said to have covered millions of miles on preaching tours and to have spoken to over 100 million people. And that was in the days before television, radio and even telephones.

He said:

> I suppose that if all the times I have prayed for faith were put together, it would amount to months. I used to say, "What we want is faith. If we only have faith we can turn Chicago upside down, or the right side up." I hoped that someday faith would come down and strike me like lightning. But faith did not come.
>
> One day I read in the tenth chapter of Romans, "Faith cometh by hearing, and hearing by the Word of God." I closed my Bible and prayed for faith. I then opened my Bible and began to really study God's Word and my faith has been growing ever since.

So today, if you are in need of more faith, spend more time with God's Word. That's exactly what I am doing every day.

All things work together

Romans 8:28

And we know that all things work together for good to them that love God, to them who are the called according to his purpose.

Recently I was reading the book *Glimpses of God Through the Ages* by Esther Carls Dodgen, in which there is a beautiful testimony by Charles H. Spurgeon on how he got saved. An extract of his work follows:

> I sometimes think I might have been in darkness and despair until now had it not been for the goodness of God in sending a snowstorm one Sunday morning, while I was going to a certain place of worship. When I could go no further, I turned down a side street and came to a little primitive Methodist chapel. In that chapel there may have been a dozen or even fifteen people. The minister did not come that morning; he was snowed up, I suppose. At last, a very thin-looking man, a shoemaker or a tailor, or something of that sort, went up into the pulpit to preach. Now it is well that preachers should be instructed but this man was really stupid. He was obliged to stick to his text, for the simple reason that he had very little else to say. The text was, "Look unto me and be ye saved, all the ends of the earth" (Isaiah 45:22).
>
> He did not even pronounce the words rightly but that did not matter. There was, I thought, a glimpse of hope for me in that text. When he had gone to about that length and managed to spin out ten minutes or so, he was at the end of his tether. Then he looked at me and said, "Young man, look to Jesus Christ. Look! Look! You have nothin' to do but to look and live."
>
> I saw at once the way of salvation. I had been waiting to do fifty things, but when I heard that word "look", what a charming word it seemed to me. Oh, I looked until I almost had looked my eyes away. There and then, the cloud was gone, the darkness had rolled away, and that moment I saw the sun; and I could have risen that instant and sung with the most enthusiastic of them, of the precious blood of Christ and the simple faith which looks alone to Him. Oh, that someone had told me this before!

What a beautiful testimony of how things work together. Can you imagine if there had been no snowstorm? He would have gone to his usual church and would probably never, ever have given his life to Christ.

This man, Charles Haddon Spurgeon, who lived for fifty-eight years, was a most amazing child of God. At the age of nineteen he preached on a hillside to 27,000 people. At the age of twenty he was pastor of the great Metropolitan Tabernacle in London, which could seat a congregation of 10,000 people.

He published 2,000 sermons. His collection of sermons stands as the largest set of books by a single author in the history of the church, and he wrote 135 books, which is more than any other Christian author of his time. He founded orphanages, a Bible society, and a college for pastors. Yet, according to his very words, it took a very thin-looking shoemaker or tailor, who wasn't very clever, to command him to look to Jesus.

My dear friend, look to Jesus today. He has the answer to every one of your needs and He can give you a future that is as exciting and as meaningful as it was for Charles Haddon Spurgeon. He never even went to Bible college, yet God used him so powerfully because he gave his life to Christ at that little primitive Methodist church in a side lane.

All things work together for the good of those who love the Lord. Have a wonderful and exciting day.

Roll up your sleeves

John 21:17(b)

Jesus saith unto him, Feed my sheep.

As you read *A Mustard Seed,* how are things in your life? Peter and the disciples were totally disillusioned with life. They returned to their trade. If you remember, Peter was the one who had denied the Lord three times at the crucifixion. Three times Jesus asked, "Do you love Me?" By the third time, Peter was quite aggrieved and responded, "Lord, You know all things, and You know that I love You." Jesus said, "Feed My sheep."

Maybe as you're reading this you have become disillusioned with the calling of your life? God is calling you back again this morning and saying, "Feed My sheep. Finish the task that I called you to do all those years ago."

You might not be a preacher or a church member. You might be a farmer, a housewife, or a student, or unemployed, but that doesn't exempt you from feeding God's sheep. He wants you to feed His sheep. Feed them with what you say. Feed them with the love of Christ. Be Jesus to this dying world. Bind up the wounds of those who have been hurt. Encourage those who have been cast down. Talk life into those who are suffering from depression. Talk about peace to those who are in turmoil. Forgive those who have hurt you. Love the unloved. Get into the gutter with those who are lost and have given up hope. Restore them with the love of Christ. Feed His sheep.

The good shepherd always makes sure that his sheep have eaten before he eats. Maybe this morning some of us need to ask forgiveness for maybe being a bit too selfish. Remember, we've said in this book before, if your faith costs you nothing, it's worth nothing. Faith has feet. It's a doing word.

The Bible says that all creation is waiting with expectation for the manifestation of the sons of God (Romans 8:19). That's you and me. We have the answers. The political parties don't. They are trying their very best and so are the secular organizations. We thank God for every one of them, but the Lord is saying, "Feed My sheep."

Today we need to reach out to those who have left the body of Christ, those who have become disillusioned with Christianity because they've been unintentionally hurt by people in the church. We need to give them the hope of Christ. He has given us the means, the food, the bread of life and we need to feed them.

Jesus is saying to you for a third time today, "Go out and feed My sheep."

The harvest field

Matthew 9:38

Pray ye therefore the Lord of the harvest, that he will send forth labourers into his harvest.

Last night I returned from Potchefstroom, a city about two hours south of Johannesburg, South Africa. By faith, the men of God in the city booked the biggest stadium (a rugby stadium) in the city. We arrived there on Saturday.

The devil tried everything that he could to prevent us from reaching our destination. We drove from our farm to the nearest city to catch a plane only to find that the plane had been delayed for three-and-a-half hours. Eventually we got to Johannesburg and had a two-hour drive to the stadium. When we got to the stadium, the praise and worship team were already in full flow; in fact they were nearing the end of their input for the night. God gave me five minutes to get onto that stage and start preaching. What an afternoon! I'll never forget it for as long as I live.

My dear friends, I want to say to you that the harvest is white. That's what Jesus said. He said, "Pray to the Lord of the harvest that He might send the workers." We made an altar call, calling people forward to give their lives to Jesus for the first time ever. No one was bowing their heads. I can only describe it as a river of souls coming forward into the kingdom. We had a second prayer of recommitment for those who were initially unsure. A sea of faces came to the front.

I realized again the reason why we sacrifice certain things for God. For me, the biggest sacrifice is to leave my wife on a regular basis. My children are all grown up now, which leaves my wife on her own. She is the heart of the home and prefers to stay there and pray for us. I love her very much.

When I saw those people coming forward though, **that** is what makes the sacrifices worthwhile. There were broken souls, people weeping, people being set free, people laughing for joy because God had forgiven them, husbands and wives coming together, boys and girls hanging onto their daddies, because Daddy had just made a decision to stop walking his own way and to start walking God's way.

I want to say to you today that you don't have to be a great speaker. I'm not. You don't have to be very well educated. I'm not. You just have to have a heart for lost souls. Remember, evangelism is one hungry beggar showing another hungry beggar where to find bread. That's what happened this weekend. As a result there are many, many new souls in the kingdom. You see, the Word of God is what convicts people. It's not fancy stories. It's not your personality. It's His Word. If you deliver His Word, He does the rest.

God with us

Zechariah 8:23(b)

We will go with you: for we have heard that God is with you.

What an exciting statement! The Lord says that in the last days ten men from other countries and other language groups will take hold of the garments of one who knows Jesus, saying, "We will go with you, for we have heard that God is with you." What a beautiful promise.

People know that time is running out. People have tried to find peace in many different ways and they are getting disillusioned. They have tried entertainment, sport, different kinds of drugs, alcohol, immorality – and they have not found peace. People are panicking because they know that the time is short. They are looking for the truth, for the peace of God that surpasses all understanding. When they find a man, a woman, a young boy or girl, and recognize Jesus in that person's life they take hold of the person and do not let go.

Be understanding and patient. Some of us are tired and weary because people are continually pursuing us, but it's not really us they're interested in. It's the Lord in us. It's "Christ in you, the hope of glory" (Colossians 1:27).

If nobody is interested in what you've got to say, you need to take a hard look at yourself. Maybe Jesus isn't in your life and maybe these people don't want what you have because you appear to be unhappy. Maybe you are negative with no joy in your life. I really mean this, my dear friend. I say it with the greatest respect and love. Have a good, hard look at yourself.

If Jesus Christ is shining through you, ten men will take hold of your garments and will not let you go. The same thing applies to the churches. Young people will go where there is food, where there is fire and where there is joy and life. The Lord is changing everything and moving it all along. The church has been moving along right from its inception and He is doing it again.

Don't be so concerned about the name of the church that you are attending. Be more concerned about what is happening inside the church and the group of people who are moving with God. The cloud is moving and we need to move with the cloud. I know some mainstream denominations that are more on fire for Jesus Christ than many of the modern churches. I know some young, dynamic churches that are so excited for Jesus Christ that when you walk into the church you can feel the presence of the Lord.

We need to be praying for the sick. We need to challenge people to come to Jesus. We need to give people an opportunity to make a commitment to Christ. My dear friend, don't lead a person right up to that relationship with the Lord and then stop there without introducing them to the Lord. Pray with them. Pray with them in the workshop; pray with them at school; pray with them on the sports field; pray with them on the farm; pray with them in the mines. Pray with them. Lead them to Christ. They're desperate. They're asking for your help. They want to know, "What must I do to be born again?"

That's why Nicodemus came to Jesus by night. He was so ashamed. He didn't want anyone else to see him. Be sensitive to the time when you speak to people about our beloved Christ. Don't speak about our precious Lord and Saviour to someone who is under the influence of alcohol. It's dishonouring to God and it's wasteful. Rather wait until they are sober and then go and pray with them and speak with them, and they'll come through for God, just like I did and just like you did.

It is so encouraging. We don't have to be concerned about our marketing strategy. We don't have to be concerned about our advertising techniques. All we have to do is ensure that God is living in our hearts, and they will come to us. Then we must be ready to lead them all the way to the end.

Boast not

Galatians 6:14

But God forbid that I should glory, save in the cross of our Lord Jesus Christ...

Paul says in this Scripture that he does not boast about anything whatsoever, save in the Cross of the Lord Jesus Christ, by whom the world is crucified to him and him to the world. Humility is a great virtue. Sometimes we get so excited for Jesus that we become boastful. We start forgetting who we were before we were saved. When a man is a sinner and he comes through for Christ, he is so grateful for having been set free that he will never boast. He is so thankful that his name is written in the Lamb's Book of Life, that the last thing he wants to do is to boast.

The tragedy is that after we've known the Lord for some time we tend to forget what God has set us free from. Remember the parable that the Lord told us of the master who forgave his servant because he couldn't pay a small debt. Then, when the servant was owed a minute amount of money by a colleague, he would not release him but instead took him to the magistrate and had him thrown in jail.

We need to be very careful today that we don't become self-righteous, because if the truth would be known, we are all sinners saved by grace. Let all the glory go to Jesus Christ. If there's anything good in us at all, let it be credited to His name.

When we die, this world does not have a hold on us any more. It is really not important any more what other people think of us. What's important is what people think about Jesus Christ. That's where the liberty is. Then we can become like an eagle and soar to high places.

Be careful not to boast about something that actually has nothing to do with you, but has everything to do with Jesus. The troubles and the responsibilities of this world, and what people think about us, should not affect us at all if we are crucified and have completely surrendered ourselves to Christ.

If we boast today we need to boast of only one thing: that our names are written in the Lamb's Book of Life, not because we are good people, but because we believe.

Lifted up

John 12:32

And I, if I be lifted up from the earth, will draw all men unto me.

We have one objective, one purpose in this life as believers and that is to lift up the name of Jesus Christ. After we've been through all our programmes, our three-point sermons, our different ideas and plans to draw people to Christ, our breakfasts, our conferences, ladies' meetings, men's weekends away, youth activities – at the end of the day the only way that we will be able to draw people to Jesus Christ is if we exalt Him.

It's sad to hear someone deliver a polished message that hardly mentions the Master's name; maybe it is tagged on at the end of the sermon. That will not win a soul for Christ. That will not bring somebody home. That will not deliver a person from a life of alcoholism or drug addiction; only the exalted name of Jesus Christ will do that. We need to get back to basics, back to our grass roots. We need to tell people that Jesus Christ is the way, the truth and the life and that no one will come to the Father but by Him (John 14:6).

You might say that you're not very well educated, you've never been to Bible college and you're not qualified to lead a man to Christ. You don't have to. Christ Himself will lead the sinner to Him if you lift up His name. You see, Jesus is peace. Jesus is love. Jesus is hope. Jesus is forgiveness. As long as you continue to exalt His name, all these characteristics will be demonstrated to that person who is completely lost and seeking a new life.

That's why Jesus says in Matthew 11:28, "Come unto me, all ye that labour and are heavy laden, and I will give you rest." He continues, "Take my yoke upon you, and learn of me; for I am meek and lowly of heart: and ye shall find rest unto your souls. For my yoke is easy, and my burden is light" (verses 29–30).

Go out today and give that message to the "whosoevers" and watch what the Lord will do. That person at work you have been so weighed down by; that person who is so sad; that person who's struggling with the loss in their family; that person who is financially crippled; who today is physically ill. Just go and tell them about Jesus. Lift up the name of Jesus to them and He will draw them to Him.

Caring

John 19:26–27

Woman, behold thy son! Then saith he to the disciple, Behold thy mother!

What an example the Lord Jesus Christ is to each one of us. I don't think that there is a more painful way to die than to be crucified. They tell me that eventually you suffocate because you have to pull yourself up on those spikes that have been driven through your hands and your feet, in order to breathe. Eventually, when you're too weak to do that, you slump and cannot breathe and eventually you die.

Jesus was going through hell, literally, on that Cross, yet He could still look down and see His mother and the apostle John, and say, "Mother, this is going to be your son" and "My brother, this is going to be your mother. Take care of her." The Bible says that from that very hour the disciple took her into his own home.

That is the total opposite of what takes place in this world. In this world it is every person for themselves. You do what you can and don't worry about anybody else. God have mercy on us.

John 12:24 says, "Unless a grain of wheat falls to the ground and dies, it remains alone; but if it dies, it produces much grain" (NKJV). My biggest enemy is Angus Buchan, not the devil. When selfishness, self-preservation, and self-centredness step into the arena, I'm in trouble.

When I deny myself, take up my cross and follow Jesus, then only do things start to change in my life.

How selfish are you, my dear friend? Jesus was totally selfless and that's why His Father used Him so powerfully.

Today, forget about yourself and start thinking about others. You will see that your problems will suddenly diminish. Kathryn Kuhlman, a great evangelist and faith healer, was quoted as saying, "If you are feeling sick, go and find someone else that's sicker than you. Pray for them and you won't feel so sick." When you focus on the needs of others, your problems won't look half as big as the problems of others.

Jesus deprived Himself right to the very end. He even put His affairs in order before He went home to be with His Father. Before He could die, He made sure that His earthly mother was taken care of; that His very dear and special disciple had a mother who would take care of him. What unbelievable love that is! That's what the world needs from you and me today. It's very easy to praise God and to acknowledge Him as Lord and Saviour when everything is going well in your life. It takes a full-on Christian to still be able to exalt the name of Jesus when things are not going well, when they're in pain and enduring suffering. That's what the people in the world want to see. How is he going to handle it this time? Of course, we know the end result. If you put Jesus first, you'll have no problems doing so.

Charles Dickens's famous story *A Christmas Carol* tells how Ebenezer Scrooge went to sleep and dreamed that he had died. He was a very sour, grasping man. Then he realized just how selfish he'd been. When he woke up, he realized that it had only been a horrible nightmare and that he had a second chance. He changed his life completely: took better care of his employees; looked after his children, the needy, and the hungry. Suddenly, instead of being an ugly, selfish, bitter old man, he became the life and soul of the party, because he started to live for others.

Whatever you do today, do it for the benefit of others rather than for yourself, and God will take care of every single need that you have.

Dying to self

Galatians 2:20

I am crucified with Christ…

Truly the hardest thing to do is to die to self, is it not? People will always say to you, "No, no, I've given my life to Jesus, the old man is dead. It's the new man that lives." That's so true and we find confirmation of that in 2 Corinthians 5:17. But it's amazing how the old man rises up from time to time, is it not? It's like a sleeping dog. They say if you kick a dead dog it will not respond but I can assure you if you kick a dog that is alive and only sleeping, it will wake up and bite you!

So often we feel that we are doing well. The old us is dead; we've been crucified with Christ, "It's no longer I who live but Christ who lives in me." The life we now live in the flesh we live by faith in the Son of God, who loves us and gave His life for us. Yet, when somebody says something very personal, the hackles rise and straight away we try to defend ourselves.

My dear friend, today let us put the flesh down. It's not really important what people think about us. What's important is what people think about Jesus. Our biggest enemy, and I've said this many, many times before, is not the devil, but it's actually ourselves.

My biggest enemy is Angus Buchan. When Angus Buchan dies, then Jesus can live through him. When I'm concerned about what people think about me, I become defensive. I become fearful and insecure, because I know what a useless wretch I am. When I die to self, I can get onto the platform and speak to thousands and thousands of people and be totally free and liberated because I'm not concerned about what people think about me any more. I'm not alive, I'm dead. It's Christ who lives in me.

That's the liberty, the freedom, the boldness that we get when we surrender our lives to Christ. That's when we can take on that Mount Everest in our lives and feel no fear at all about getting to the top, because Christ is going to do it through us.

Loving our children

Ephesians 6:4

And, ye fathers, provoke not your children to wrath: but bring them up in the nurture and admonition of the Lord.

These words are printed on a bookmark that I got from the Ethelbert Children's Home in Malvern, KwaZulu-Natal, South Africa.

If a child lives with criticism,
he learns to condemn;
If a child lives with hostility,
he learns to fight;
If a child lives with ridicule,
he learns to be shy;
If a child lives with shame,
he learns to feel guilty;
If a child lives with tolerance,
he learns to be patient;
If a child lives with encouragement,
he learns with confidence;
If a child lives with praise,
he learns to appreciate;
If a child lives with fairness,
he learns justice;
If a child lives with security,
he learns to have faith;
If a child lives with approval,
he learns to like himself;
If a child lives with acceptance and friendship,
he learns to love; So he learns to find love in the world.

Children will not do as we tell them. They will do exactly what we do. I have five children and four grandchildren of my own and am hoping for many more. I learned as a young farmer that my children do exactly what I do. If I shout, they shout. If I'm gentle with animals, they are gentle with animals. If I work rough with my machinery, they work rough with their machinery. If I treat their mother with love and compassion, they will treat their wives, their husbands, in exactly the same way. If I treat my staff on the farm with equality and respect, they will do exactly the same.

The things that I do that are not good, they will also do. For example, if I take my family to church on a Sunday morning, drop them off at the front door, go and buy a newspaper at the tearoom and then sit under a tree and read the paper until the service is finished, they will do exactly the same thing.

Today let us make a covenant with God that we will start to live by example and not by word only.

In seeking we find

James 4:8

Draw nigh to God, and he will draw nigh to you.

May I ask you a question today? How much time do you spend with God each day? The time you spend with the Lord will determine how sincere you are about drawing near to Him. You spend a lot of time with a person that you love very much. That's a fact of life.

Do you remember the time when you first met your loved one, your husband, your wife, maybe your fiancée? Maybe even, as you are reading this, you're going out with someone that you're intending to marry? You just can't spend enough time with them, can you? What happens? The more time you spend with them, the more you get to know them and the more they get to know you. It's a beautiful snowball effect.

So it should be with the Lord Jesus Christ. The more time you spend with Him, the closer He draws to you. The fact of the matter is that He's always there but we are often too busy with the mundane things of life to listen and hear the voice speaking to our hearts.

Jesus says, "If you draw near to Me, I will draw near to you." I picked up this little reading, which I think is so special, and maybe this gives us an idea of what we need to be doing:

> Can you imagine this happening to you while you are sitting having your quiet time with the Lord? He says, "Good morning, this is God. Today I'll be handling all your problems. Please remember that I will not need your help. If the devil happens to deliver a situation to you that you cannot handle, DO NOT attempt to resolve it. Kindly put it in the SFJTD (Something for Jesus to Do) box. It will be addressed in MY time, not yours.
>
> "Once the matter is placed into the box, do not hold on to it or attempt to remove it. Holding on or the removal thereof will delay the resolution of your problem.
>
> "If it is a situation that you think you are capable of handling, please consult Me in prayer to be sure that it is the proper resolution. Because I do not sleep, nor slumber, there is no need for you to lose any sleep. Rest, My child! If you need to contact Me, I am only a prayer away."

The ultimate price

John 3:16

For God so loved the world…

I read this illustration of what our heavenly Father did for you and me by giving us His only begotten Son:

One day you pick up the paper and read about a small village in India that has a bad case of flu and four people have died. You take little notice and carry on reading through the sports section. The following day you switch on your radio on your way to work and the news is on. The crisis in India has gotten worse and there are now thirty villages affected and hundreds of people have died. After work you head home and put your feet up in the lounge and switch on the television to watch CNN and to catch up with the day's news, only to find out that the flu has now spread throughout India and into Pakistan. They now have given the flu a name – it's called the Killer Flu.

In the morning you awake to find out that the Killer Flu has crossed the subcontinent and has now killed millions. The French President closes all the borders to isolate the country. It's too late. There are two hikers dying of the Killer Flu in a Paris hospital. The flu now spreads incredibly quickly through Europe, killing millions of people. It catches Britain off guard, and rips through the country at an incredible rate.

The USA calls all the people together to say that they have found a cure but they need pure blood, untouched by the virus. They ask that all people come to the community halls to donate blood. You take your family down to your local hall and wait for further instructions. Later on, a man in a white coat comes out and starts to prick everybody's finger. You are all told to wait for an answer.

After an hour or so, there's a great noise coming from inside the hall. People come running out, screaming, "We have found a cure; we have found a cure." Everyone starts to cry. People are praying and they are thanking the Lord. The man in the white coat calms everybody down and shouts out a name. Your son tugs at your shirt. "Daddy, that's my name, isn't it?" You can't believe it. You slowly start pushing your way through the crowd until you reach the man in the white coat. "That was my son's name that you called out just now." The man excitedly takes your hand and leads your family through to a small room with a steel table in it. He hurriedly lifts your four-year-old son onto the table and he says, "We have to start as soon as possible."

"What do you mean?" you ask.

"We have to draw blood." You look at him in fear.

"What does all that mean?"

"You'll have to fill in a consent form," he says. "We need his blood, ALL OF IT."

You stare numbly at him, trying to understand what he has just said.

His voice continues, "There are millions of people dying. Your child will save the world." You reach down and you sign the paper. Your little boy is scared. "Daddy, please don't leave me, I'm scared. Mommy, please don't go. Daddy, please don't forsake me." You are led out of the room by the men in white coats. All you can hear is your little boy's voice, "Daddy, please don't leave me. Don't forsake me."

Author unknown

The time factor

Matthew 10:7

And as you go, preach, saying, "The kingdom of heaven is at hand." (NKJV)

My wife said to me the other day that she is very disillusioned when she doesn't hear the message of urgency preached. There was a time when just about every sermon preached had an urgency factor. It doesn't seem to be there any more, even though Jesus said, "Tell the people that the kingdom of God is at hand."

Folks, many of us are waiting for the Lord to return. The truth of the matter is that many of us might meet the Lord Jesus Christ personally, face to face, before the end of the world comes.

At our men's conference in 2007 we saw 7,400 men come together. On the Friday night a man named William O'Brien arrived from Pinetown, a city about one-and-a-half hour's drive from the farm. My son-in-law saw him sitting in the field that afternoon with his Bible on his lap looking out onto our maize fields, totally at peace. He had brought his little pickup truck and had his camping gear in the back.

That night, the first night of the conference, when preaching the gospel of Jesus Christ I felt a calling from the Lord to make an altar call to challenge people to come to Christ. I did it. Remember, obedience is better than sacrifice. I thank God for that, because many times I don't make the altar call on the first night. That night at twelve o'clock the Lord came and called William O'Brien home. He died. The men called me and I didn't even feel led to pray for his resurrection, for his life, because I believe that God had called him home.

It was a terrible shock and I thought that his death would put a damper on the conference. There were 7,400 men who had arrived from all over the country to attend it. On the contrary, however, it did the opposite. It brought about an urgency that we'd never experienced before. I was able to stand up on the Saturday morning to say that one of our brothers had gone home to be with Christ the previous night.

I can say that he was a brother and I can say that he has gone home, because he prayed the sinner's prayer. The bottom line is that people need to know that if we confess our faith in Jesus Christ with our mouths and believe in our hearts that He's been raised from the dead, we shall be saved (Romans 10:9). It's not good deeds; it's not even your lifestyle. It's a relationship with God. Like the thief on the cross who said, "Remember me, Lord, when you get to Paradise", and Jesus said, "You'll be with Me today in Paradise."

The refiner's fire

Revelation 6:17

For the great day of his wrath is come; and who shall be able to stand?

The day of the Lord is approaching very fast. I think all of us know that. Our God is coming to fetch us. He is a holy God, a righteous God. He is a God who cannot look upon sin. We saw that when Jesus, His own Son, died on the Cross at Calvary. He had taken our sin upon Himself and His heavenly Father could not even look upon Him. That's why Jesus called out, "My God, My God, why have You forsaken Me?" He is a righteous and a holy God.

The Lord talks about us being purified like silver and purged like gold by going through the refiner's fire. Maybe you're feeling like that at the moment? Maybe things just don't seem to be going right. Just rest in the Lord, my dear friend. He is working in us and through us to purify us, so that we can become like Christ.

I've not yet met a worthy man who has not been through a fiery trial. I can only use myself as an example. I was a young, arrogant upstart, a self-made man from a Scottish background, and I don't think you can get a prouder man than that. I suppose you could say that my theme song was "I did it my way". Well, my way didn't seem to be the right way. It's only been through fiery trials – and these trials are not over by any means – that God has been busy refining me.

There's nothing more rewarding than to be taught by a man who's been through much fire and testing. You will find that he does not speak too quickly, his words are few but every single one of them is powerful. When he opens his mouth it's the Lord Jesus Christ who speaks through him. He's not a man who points fingers at others. He is a forgiving, loving, compassionate, understanding, and patient man. Why? Because he has been through the refining fire himself.

Today, if you feel that the going is tough and you can't understand why, be patient! You will reap your harvest in due season if you do not lose heart (Galatians 6:9). The Lord is busy shaping you and me. At the time it's very painful but when you look back in years to come, you'll thank God for this time of hardship.

Go out today and know that the Lord has promised you that He will never leave you, nor forsake you. He is allowing you to go through a fiery trial because He wants good to come of it. It doesn't matter what it seems like at the moment – don't question God. God's plans are to perfect you so that you might be that spotless bride that He's coming back for on that great day of the Second Coming.

Let us start to realize that we're not going to be on this earth for ever. Let us start to realize that it doesn't matter whether you're eighteen or eighty – you can meet with the Lord this very day. Be sure, before you leave your home today, that your life is in order with the Lord, that you have no blame, no anger in your heart, that you've prayed the sinner's prayer and asked Jesus to be your Lord and Saviour.

Sticks and stones

Revelation 14:5

And in their mouth was found no guile...

There is a saying: "Sticks and stones will break my bones but words will never harm me". That is totally untrue. When you get beaten with sticks and stones, your body can recover but when people speak negatively about you and criticize you, they can break you down to such a degree that only the Lord Himself can heal you.

Today we need to be careful about how we use our words. Some Christians are so negative that the devil himself has no more work to do. Everything is doom, gloom, and heavy with negativity. They bring no glory to God. In fact – although they are not conscious of it – they become agents of the devil. Be careful how you talk, my dear friend. Maybe we need to repent today before we go out; repent of the things that we've spoken over our loved ones, over the family, over our business, over our nation, over people, over God's creation. We need to be so careful of what we say.

Men and women of faith always speak life and truth. The opposite of faith is fear. Fear comes over us when we speak about things which have a negative connotation attached to them. For example, if you say to your children, "You little devils, I wish I'd never given birth to you. What are you doing?" you are actually speaking a curse over their lives. Those are negative words. Those are words that Jesus Christ does not want to hear coming out of your or my mouth.

My headmaster told my mother to take me out of school when I was a young boy, because I'd never amount to anything in school. I often say, tongue-in-cheek, "I'd like to meet him one day and ask him how many books he has written and how many things he's done for God."

The impact of those negative words needs to be lessened. Maybe today, before you go out and about, you need to repent before God. If any negative words have been spoken over your family, denounce them in Jesus' name. Any word that's been spoken over you, saying that you'll never make it, needs to be broken.

A man came with his son to one of our conferences. God did a sovereign work of reconciliation between fathers and sons during that conference. The meeting was supposed to have lasted an hour. It lasted five-and-a-half hours. This man stood up on the platform and asked his son, who was sitting in the crowd, to please forgive him for not acknowledging him, for not loving him unconditionally and for not being proud of him. The young adult, eighteen years old, came running up and embraced his father in front of 600 men.

That young man could barely make the second rugby team. I've since heard that he is now a candidate for a provincial rugby side. He's made the first team in his school, he's made his district's team, and now he is potentially a candidate for professional rugby. Why? Because his dad spoke life over him!

The Bible says that Jesus walked into town and saw Nathanael standing underneath a tree. He said, "Nathanael… in whom is no guile!" (John 1:47). You see, Jesus knew Nathanael before Philip even introduced him. He said, "I saw you standing underneath that fig tree." Nathanael was absolutely amazed. Jesus said, "You will see even greater things than this."

The Lord knows every one of us. He knows our thoughts. He knows what we're going to say even before we say it. Let us start speaking life today. Let us become like Nathanael, a man in whose mouth was found no guile. Jesus chose Nathanael to be one of His disciples because he was a good man.

Today, I want to say this in conclusion: if you have nothing good to say about a person, rather say nothing than speak negative words. Ask God to show you something good in that person and God will give you compassion and mercy for that person.

Begin to speak life, not only over other people, but over yourself as well. David often did that: "My soul, why are you so cast down?" Start speaking about the good attributes that God has given you. He's given you so many gifts. Acknowledge them and use them today.

Remember John G. Lake's words: "When you get up in the morning, look in the mirror. Speak to the person in the mirror and say, 'God lives in you. Wherever you go today, God's going with you.'" Then go out and take on the world.

Have a wonderful day!

Time spent with God

Luke 21:37–38

And in the day time he was teaching in the temple; and at night he went out, and abode in the mount that is called the mount of Olives. And all the people came early in the morning to him in the temple, for to hear him.

The Lord says, "First the mountain, then the ministry. Time is very short. As you have honoured Me with your lips, honour Me now with your ministry. Move on to that place of active participation in My will.

Anticipation, meditation, and participation: there is a place for each of these as you move from one to the other and then back through the cycle again. Follow the life of Jesus in the Gospels and you will see the pattern repeated time after time. Never get bogged down at any one of these stages, always move on to the next one. I will teach you, but you must not hold back.

Out in the field and back to the mountain of prayer and communion. Solitude first and then service; and vice versa. Neither is complete in itself. Each is enriched by the other. In solitude I minister to you, and in service I minister through you to others. Both are essential to your growth, and others are robbed of a blessing if you hoard the riches of God and you fail to share them with other people."

I remember reading a book by Francis Frangipane in which he said that congregations are tired of listening to tired preachers. So profound and so true! If you are a person who shares the Word of God with anybody else – and every believer falls into that category, nobody is exempt – you need to be spending time with the Lord in order to be able to minister.

The word "minister" means to serve others. So try today, if possible, to extend your time on the mountain, your quiet time with the Lord, and you'll be so much richer for it. You will be able to go into a world that is absolutely starving for spiritual food, for hope, peace and truth.

God bless you as you go out today as Jesus' personal ambassador.

Be careful who comes to your door

John 15:13

Greater love hath no man than this.

Jesus says that you shall know His children by their love. Sometimes the hardest place to be a Christian is in your very own family. Every one of us is very good at putting on a mask when we go out to church, or to a sporting occasion, or if we go out socially, but at home we let the mask come off. We need to be very sensitive and careful how we treat our children and our loved ones.

I want to share with you a very sad story, but one that I believe to be true, although the author is unknown. It's a story about a soldier who was finally coming home having fought in Vietnam. He called his parents from San Francisco. "Mom and Dad, I'm coming home but I have a favour to ask. I have a friend I'd like to bring with me." His parents replied that they would love to meet the friend.

"There's something you should know," the young soldier continued. "He was hurt pretty badly in the war. He stepped on a landmine and he's lost an arm and a leg. He has nowhere else to go and I want him to come and live with us."

"I'm sorry to hear that, son. Maybe we can help him find somewhere to live."

"No, Mom and Dad, I want him to live with us."

"Son," said the father, "you don't know what you're asking. Someone with such a handicap would be a terrible burden on us. We have our own lives to live and we can't let something like this interfere with our lives. I think you should just come home and forget about this guy. He'll find a way to live on his own."

At that point the son hung up the phone. The parents heard nothing more from him. A few days later, however, they received a call from the San Francisco police. Their son had died after falling from a building, they were told. The police believed it was suicide.

The grief-stricken parents flew to San Francisco and were taken to the city morgue to identify the body of their son. They recognized him, but to their horror they also discovered something else that they didn't know. Their son had only one arm and one leg.

We need each other

Psalm 133:1

Behold, how good and how pleasant it is For brethren to dwell together in unity!

I found this story in a conservation pamphlet that was handed to us by the University of Natal, South Africa. It's called *Lessons from Geese*.

As each goose flaps its wings, it creates an uplift for the bird following. By flying in a V formation, the whole flock adds seventy-one per cent more flying range than if each bird flew alone.

Lesson: People who share a common direction and sense of community can get where they are going much quicker and easier, because they are traveling on the thrust of one another.

When a goose falls out of formation, it suddenly feels the drag and resistance of trying to fly alone and quickly gets back into formation to take advantage of the lift in power of the birds immediately in front.

Lesson: If we have as much sense as a goose, we will join in formation with those who are headed where we want to go.

When the lead goose gets tired, it rotates back into the formation and another goose flies at the point position.

Lesson: It pays to take turns doing the hard tasks and sharing leadership; with people, as with geese, interdependent with one another.

The geese in formation honk from behind to encourage those up front to keep up their speed.

Lesson: We need to make sure our honking from behind is encouraging, not something less helpful.

When a goose gets sick, or wounded, or shot down, two geese drop out of formation and follow their fellow member down to help provide protection. They stay with this member of the flock until he or she is able to fly again and then they launch out on their own with another formation, or try to catch up with their own flock.

Lesson: If we have as much sense as the geese, we'll stand by one another. God even uses nature to teach us very important lessons. Especially in the kingdom of God, there is no such thing as a lone ranger. John Wesley said that if you take a coal out of the fire and put it by itself, it goes out. Let us walk in unity. Psalm 133:3 tells us, "For there the Lord commanded the blessing, even life forevermore," when we do so.

What makes a dad?

Ephesians 6:2

Honour thy father and mother; (which is the first commandment) with promise.

God took the strength of a mountain,
The majesty of a tree,
The warmth of a summer sun,
The calm of a quiet sea,
The generous soul of nature,
The comforting arm of night,
The wisdom of the ages,
The power of the eagle's flight,
The joy of the morning spring,
The faith of a mustard seed,
The patience of eternity,
The depth of a family need,
Then God combined these qualities,
And when there was nothing more to add,
He knew His masterpiece was complete,
And so He called it
DAD!

Author unknown

Dads, this is what our children are expecting us to be. Mums, this is how you should consider your husband and the father of your children to be.

We have an awesome responsibility to live our faith at home and to build our family from there. From our family to our community; from our community to our district; from our district to our province; and from our province, yes indeed, to our nation!

God bless you today as you become a good dad; a good mum; a good family member.

Exercising patience towards others

Romans 5:3

And not only so, but we glory in tribulations also: knowing that tribulation worketh patience…

I have just read a beautiful example of how we should exercise patience towards others. We don't really know what other people are going through. So often we're in a rush to do something and we forget that people are going through many trials and much tribulation. I'm going to share this prayer by an unknown author with you:

> Heavenly Father, help us remember that the jerk who cut us off in traffic last night is a single mother who worked nine hours that day and is rushing home to cook dinner, help with the homework, do the laundry, and spend a few precious moments with her children.
>
> Help us to remember that the pierced, tattooed, disinterested young man who can't give the correct change is a worried nineteen year old college student, balancing his apprehension over final exams with his fear of not getting his student funds for the next semester.
>
> Remind us, Lord, that the scary looking bum begging for money in the same spot every day (who really ought to get a job) is a slave to mental illness, or addictions that we can only imagine in our worst nightmares.
>
> Help us to remember that the old couple walking annoyingly slowly through the store aisles and blocking our shopping progress are savouring this moment, knowing that, based on the biopsy report she got back last week, this will be the last year that they go shopping together.
>
> Heavenly Father, remind us each day that of all the gifts You give us, the greatest gift is love. It is not enough to share that love with those we hold dear. Open our hearts, not just to those who are close to us but to all humanity. Let us be slow to judge and quick to forgive, show patience, empathy and love.

Today, by faith, as we go out to face the world, let us be conscious of the fact that our fellow man is at this time being tested, sometimes very sorely! Let us ask the Holy Spirit to give us a great deal of compassion and patience.

It's between you and God

Matthew 5:8

Blessed are the pure in heart: for they shall see God.

People are often unreasonable, illogical and self-centred. Forgive them anyway.
If you are kind, people may accuse you of being selfish with ulterior motives.
Be kind anyway.
If you are successful, you will win some false friends and some true enemies. Succeed anyway.
If you are honest and frank, people may cheat you.
Be honest and frank anyway.
What you spent years building, someone could destroy overnight.
Build anyway.
If you find serenity and happiness, they may be jealous.
Be happy anyway.
The good you do today, people will often forget tomorrow.
Do good anyway.
Give the world the best you have, and it may never be enough.
Give the world the best you've got anyway.
You see, in the final analysis, it is between you and God. It was never between you and them anyway.

Mother Teresa

Miracle of miracles

Matthew 1:23

Behold, a virgin shall be with child, and shall bring forth a son, and they shall call his name Emmanuel, which being interpreted is, God with us.

I greet you on this glorious Christmas morning. I want to tell you about the greatest miracle that has ever taken place since before the beginning of the earth. God came down from heaven. He made Himself small enough to become a seed in the womb of a young virgin girl. He remained in her womb for nine months. When she gave birth, He was born in the humblest of shelters that one could imagine – a simple stable carved out of the side of a hill.

They had no cot for Him. They had no clothes, so they wrapped Him in swaddling linen and put Him in a manger. I'm a farmer; a manger is a feed trough for animals. His first visitors when He arrived on earth were simple animals – a donkey, some sheep and a few other animals. A young carpenter sat there looking wide-eyed with absolute disbelief in his eyes when he saw this young girl he was betrothed to be married to, a virgin who had never known a man, had given birth to the most beautiful baby that has ever been born.

The wise men arrived, coming from another part of the world, having been sent by God and following a star to come and pay homage to the King of kings and the Lord of lords. Shepherds watching their sheep on a nearby hillside saw the light over the stable and came to enquire and witnessed the greatest miracle of all. My dear friend, if you don't believe in miracles, you cannot be a Christian, because the Christian faith is a miracle. The miracle worker came to earth in a miraculous way.

The wonderful news is that He's coming back in a miraculous way to take us who believe in Him to be with Him in heaven forever. My prayer for you this Christmas is that God will take all the questions from your heart, all intellectual arguments out of your mind and just fill you with His faith so that you can believe and start the new year with childlike faith. May God bless you richly!

Watchmen are leaders

Ezekiel 3:17

Son of man, I have made thee a watchman unto the house of Israel:

A good watchman is not just someone who blows a trumpet. He is someone who leads by example. He is one who is disciplined and wakes up early in the morning. He is alert, can detect the enemy when they are coming, and can also lead others out of darkness and into the light of God. I have a beautiful piece of writing that I want to share with you, which I quote from John L. Mason's little book, *An Enemy called Average.*

A leader is always full of praise,
learns to use the phrases "thank you" and "please" on his way to the top.
Is always growing.
Is possessed with his dreams.
Launches forth before success is certain.
Is not afraid of confrontation.
Talks about his own mistakes before talking about someone else's.
Is a person of honesty and integrity.
Has a good name.
Makes others better.
Is quick to praise and encourage the smallest amount of improvement.
Is genuinely interested in others.
Looks for opportunities to find someone doing something right.
Takes others up with him.
Responds to his own failures and acknowledges them before others have to discover and reveal them.
Never allows murmuring – from himself or others.
Is specific in what he expects.
Holds accountable those who work with him.
Does what is right rather than what is popular.
Is a servant.

In conclusion, an old Arab proverb says: "An army of sheep led by a lion would defeat an army of lions led by a sheep."

Freely

Matthew 10:8

Heal the sick, cleanse the lepers, raise the dead, cast out devils: freely ye have received, freely give.

My dear old mother has gone to be with the Lord. She was a beautiful Christian lady. I had the privilege of praying the sinner's prayer with her. She used to pray for me a lot before God took her home, especially when I was preaching. She was a sickly woman most of her life. It was good to be nursed by her when I was sick when I was younger, because she had so much compassion and understanding of what I was going through.

The worst person to nurse anyone who is sick is someone who has never been sick before. They tend to get impatient, they tell you to pull yourself together and to believe the Word of God and pray, instead of doing the very opposite, which is just to love you.

Jesus said to the disciples, "Heal the sick." The sad thing is that many preach the gospel these days but they do not pray for the sick. Some men and women of God – who call themselves shepherds, God's preachers – don't even believe in healing today. That's a tragedy because this Bible that I'm reading is the same Bible they are reading. It never changes but it's ever new. I have seen the sick healed and I have seen demons being cast out.

Once, at a healing meeting we had on our farm, many sick people came from all over South Africa to be touched by God. Over forty people were baptized after the service. Out of their own will they went, fully clothed, into the waters of baptism in an old reservoir, because that was the only place we had. It was done spontaneously. God – healing the sick; casting out demons; raising the dead.

At Shalom we say, "One genuine miracle equals a thousand sermons." We've seen that happen so often. I've seen it happen in Central Africa. I was preaching my heart out and there was no response. There were Muslims all around, not necessarily coming to hear the gospel but to suppress what we were trying to do.

God told me (He speaks to me in my heart) to stop preaching, and He said, "See the man with the crutches in the front row? Pray for him and I'll heal him." I got down from the platform and told the people that God was going to heal this man. They all knew the man concerned. I didn't. The place instantly went quiet. The 5,000 people who had been causing a lot of disturbance only minutes before were now silent. I prayed the prayer of faith. God loosened the stiff leg that had a pin through it and which I didn't even know about. The man was running up and down shouting, "I'm healed! I'm healed!" I took his crutches away from him.

After that, all I had to do was make an altar call. Jesus did the rest.

I urge you today to pray for the sick, to believe in miracles, and not to be afraid of the demon world. The demons are subject to the Spirit of God. Just make sure, though, that you have a relationship with God. Paul had a good relationship with God – not like the sons of Sceva, who thought they would do it just because Jesus and Paul did it. The demons nearly killed them (Acts 19:16).

I would like you to understand one thing today: God has given you a new life for free. Go in turn and do it to your brother in Christ.

Don't quit

Philippians 3:14

I press toward the mark for the prize of the high calling of God in Christ Jesus.

The famous cyclist, Lance Armstrong, who won the Tour de France seven times, said, "Pain lasts for a day but to quit lasts forever." Don't quit.

In the Christian walk we are running the race of our lives. I've had the privilege of trying to finish the Comrades Marathon – arguably one of the world's greatest foot races, run over 89 km between Durban and Pietermaritzburg – and I came short by 15 kilometres. I ran 74 kilometres but I didn't quit. I dehydrated and passed out. One of our old prayer warriors, Aunty Moyra Mathieson, said, "Jesus turned the lights out." But I didn't quit.

I want to encourage you today, Christian. Don't quit. Whatever happens, don't quit. You don't know how close you are to the finish line. Jesus could be coming back today or tomorrow.

There's a little reading I'd like to share with you. It's called *Don't Quit*:

Is that what you want to do? Quit?
Anybody can do that. It takes no talent. It takes no guts.
It's exactly what your adversaries hope you will do.
Get your facts straight.
Know what you're talking about.
And keep going.

In the 1948 presidential election in the USA, the nation's leading political reporters all reported that Harry Truman would lose. He won.

Sir Winston Churchill said, "Never give in; never, never!" He stuck his chin out and wouldn't quit. Try sticking out your chin. Don't give up, ever.

And the wonderful thing that we have, my dear friend, is our faith that will stay with us till the end of the race. People who don't know Jesus Christ give up very easily. But with us, it's like an energy drink that we drink all day long! It's called faith and it comes through hearing. And hearing comes through the Word of God (Romans 10:17). That faith will enable you to never, ever quit.

Don't provoke God

Numbers 14:11

And the Lord said unto Moses, How long will this people provoke me? and how long will it be ere they believe me, for all the signs which I have shewed among them?

I want to share with you a beautiful reading written by that great Baptist preacher Charles H. Spurgeon, and sent to me by one of my intercessors. He says:

> Strive with all diligence to keep out that monster, unbelief. It so dishonours Christ that He will withdraw His visible presence if we insult Him by indulging in it. It is a true weed, the seeds of which we can never entirely extract from the soil, but we must aim at its root with zeal and perseverance. Among hateful things, it is the most to be abhorred. Its injurious nature is so venomous that he who exercises it, and he on whom it is exercised are both hurt thereby. In your case, oh believer, it is most wicked, for the mercies of the Lord in the past increase your guilt in doubting Him now. When you distrust the Lord Jesus, He may well cry out, "Behold I am crushed under you by a cart that crushes when loaded with grain." This is crowning His head with thorns of the sharpest kind.
>
> It is very cruel for a well beloved wife to mistrust a kind and faithful husband. The sin is needless, foolish and unwarranted. Jesus has never given the slightest ground for suspicion and it is hard to be doubted by those to whom our conduct is uniformly affectionate and true.
>
> Jesus is the Son of the Highest and has an unbounded wealth; it is shameful to doubt omnipotence and distrust all sufficiency. The cattle on a thousand hills will suffice for our most hungry feeding and the granaries of heaven are not likely to be emptied by our eating. If Christ were only a cistern, we might soon exhaust His fullness, but who can drown a fountain? Myriads of spirits have drawn their supplies from Him and not one of them has murmured at the scantiness of His resources.
>
> Away then with this lying traitor called unbelief, for his only errand is to cut the bonds of communion and make us mourn an absent Saviour. John Bunyan tells us that unbelief has as many lives as a cat. If so, let us kill one life now and continue the work until the whole nine are gone. Down with traitorous unbelief; my heart abhors it!

It is well with my soul

Psalm 31:1

In thee, O Lord, do I put my trust; let me never be ashamed: deliver me in thy righteousness.

Perhaps you are familiar with that well-known hymn "It is Well with My Soul"? The first verse reads:

When peace, like a river, attendeth my way;
When sorrows like sea billows roll;
Whatever my lot, Thou hast taught me to say:
It is well; it is well with my soul.

That beautiful hymn was written by Horatio Spafford. He was an extremely wealthy man, a godly man, who lived in Chicago. In 1871, when the great Chicago fire struck the city, the Spafford family worked tirelessly to help the victims of this inferno. Due to the stress and hard work, doctors advised his wife Anna to take a holiday. Horatio arranged for the family to cross to France on what was considered the safest and most luxurious ship of its time, the *Ville du Havre*.

Just before they were due to leave, Horatio discovered he could not make it due to business pressure. He said he would join his family later and sent his wife and four daughters ahead. On the voyage across the Atlantic Ocean, on a calm and starry night, the ship was rammed amid ships. Despite reassurances from the crew, the ship was split in two and it sank in fifteen minutes, taking the family below the ocean's waves.

Anna felt her infant daughter being ripped from her arms by the force of the sea as she too succumbed to the torrent of water washing over them. Anna was saved only by a miracle. A piece of wooden planking floated up from underneath her unconscious body and brought it to the surface. Only fifty-seven people were saved. Anna Spafford and the children's governess were among them. All four of the little girls were lost.

Upon arrival in Wales, Anna cabled Horatio, saying two words: "Saved alone." He quickly booked a passage on the next ship to meet his wife. As he travelled over the spot where the ship had sunk, the watery grave of his four daughters, he composed the hymn "It is Well with My Soul". The words expressed his continued faith in the face of disaster.

My dear friend, the fact that we are men and women of faith does not exempt us from suffering and times of trial and tribulation. This is one of the most famous hymns of all time, but this beautiful and encouraging hymn was written by a man in grave suffering.

They say that it is only when you crush a rose that you can really smell the fragrance; it is only when you crush an orange that you can taste the nectar. We are Christian men and women who walk by faith. We trust the Lord. We know that He will never let us down but we still have to walk the same road as everyone else. The difference is that we walk it in a different way. Some trust in chariots, and some in horses, but we will remember the name of the Lord our God (Psalm 20:7).

Today, irrespective of your circumstances, know one thing: God has promised you that He will never leave you, nor forsake you.

God's faithfulness

Lamentations 3:23

… great is thy faithfulness.

God's faithfulness is unconditional. He loves us, regardless. I heard such a beautiful story many years ago, which I want to share with you to try and give you an idea of how great God's faithfulness is.

It is the story of a man who was convicted of a crime and sent to jail for a long period of time. He was married at the time and had very young children. He had a beautiful young wife, who loved him desperately. He had made a terrible mistake and repented, but had to serve his sentence. He said to her before he went to jail, "Please, I don't want to write to you. I don't want our relationship to continue, because I'm going to be away for a long time. You are going to need someone to look after you. I want to release you, so that you can start a new life. Please don't write to me either." He wouldn't receive any of her letters.

He went to jail where he was a wonderful example of a man who was truly repentant and wanting to start a new life. After a few years he was up for parole and the prison warders reported on his behaviour to the head of the correctional services. They came to him one day and said, "Because of your good behaviour and your repentant heart, because of your Christian stand, we are going to release you much earlier than we anticipated. You will be free to go next week."

He couldn't believe what had happened. He was overjoyed. Then he remembered that he had told his wife a few years before, when he was sent to jail, to start a new life. He was very nervous to go back and see her, because if she had remarried and started a new life, he didn't want to interfere with it but he desperately wanted to see his children.

He wrote her a letter and said, "I am being released earlier on parole. I'll be coming on the train. Just out of town, where the railway line takes a bend, there's a huge oak tree. If you want me to come back home to you, I want you to tie a white ribbon in the tree. Then I'll know that you are still waiting for me." With that, he boarded the train and sat nervously in the compartment.

Some young teenagers – you know what teenagers are like – came and sat next to him and started speaking to him. They asked why he was looking so sad. The train stopped at a station where the children jumped off, ran around and jumped back on again. Once again, they sat with him and brought him some food. The train took off again.

Eventually he began to open his heart and told them the story. He said, "In about ten minutes' time this train's going to go around a bend. There's a big oak tree on the left-hand side. I don't have the courage to look out of the window. Can you please help me? Can you look out of the window to see if there is a white ribbon around the oak tree? It means I can go home, but if not, I'll just carry on with the train."

His heart was pumping as the train drew near to that bend. The young people had their heads out of the window, searching and looking. As they came around the bend he asked, "Can you see the oak tree?"

"Yes," they said, "we can see it on the left-hand side."

"What do you see?" he asked them. "Can you see a white ribbon?"

"No," they said, "we don't see a white ribbon." His heart sank.

They said, "We can see a white tablecloth and a woman's white dress. We can see a little boy's white trousers and a little girl's white dress."

With absolute joy in his heart, the man got off the train at the next stop and his family were waiting there to welcome him home!

My dear friend, that's how it is with you and me. Jesus loves us so much. It doesn't matter what you've done, or what you haven't done. His faithfulness is never ending and doesn't fail. All He wants you to do is to repent, apologize and start again. Remember today that the white ribbon in that tree is for you. Just apologize, acknowledge your sin, and carry on, because God's love will never, ever change towards you.